PAMELA'S DAUGHTERS

THE MACMILLAN COMPANY
NEW YORK · BOSTON · CHICAGO · DALLAS
ATLANTA · SAN FRANCISCO

MACMILLAN & CO., Limited
LONDON · BOMBAY · CALCUTTA
MELBOURNE

THE MACMILLAN COMPANY
OF CANADA, Limited
TORONTO

Hoppner, 1786

CAROLINE OF LICHTFIELD

"Fine by Defect and Delicately Weak"

PAMELA'S DAUGHTERS

By

ROBERT PALFREY UTTER

AND

GWENDOLYN BRIDGES NEEDHAM

NEW YORK

THE MACMILLAN COMPANY

1936

TO BEGIN WITH

(*or not, just as you please*)

THESE studies had their beginning in the winter of 1919–20 when
R. P. U. suggested to the editor of the *Woman's Home Companion,* then Mrs. Underwood, an article on "Fashions in Heroines."
She approved the idea, and he began the work. He has been at
it off and on from then to the date of this writing. For the first
seven years he carried it on sporadically in intervals, sometimes
wide-spaced, of other work. In the winter of 1927–28 he carried
the project to Europe, and there made notes of visual impressions
of the shifting silhouette in medieval and renaissance paintings.
On his return, G. B. N. joined the enterprise, and it went on
more steadily, but necessarily slowly because of the enormous
amount of material we must sift, select and organize.

We have tried to conceal the labor of the process, but the fact
must be obvious that if the work were presented exhaustively it
would be a pretty complete history of civilization. There have
been times when we felt that it would be easier to spend a lifetime or two on the work and make a volume of each chapter
than to try to condense it within the compass we had set ourselves.
But lifetimes are not easy to come by, and we held to our plan
of making for this time a sketch map indicating the main
features of the ground; then we, or whoever will, may survey
more in detail if and when we can. Meanwhile we ask our
critics to believe that we have no illusions as to the finality of
our work up to this point. We have made only a reconnaisance;
we hope and trust that when the final survey is made the details
will accord with the features we have laid down.

v

We believe, too, that we could defend every assertion we make, but we have done so as little as possible because we believe that the manners of defense are offensive. The mood of argumentation is not winning; footnotes and bibliographies are as forbidding as machine guns and barbed wire. We speak to all comers, and invite correspondence from specialists.

Of this burden of scholarly responsibility, R. P. U. stands ready to assume the heavier share. His was the inception and the main organization of the entire project, the final organization of each chapter, and the final writing for uniformity of literary style. G. B. N. initiated and carried through to the final writing Chapters II, VII, VIII, and IX, collected data on many special minor and major points, and gave wise counsel and co-operation throughout.

If there is any credit in the performance, we can only hope that there is enough to go round, for we must share with so many that it is with misgivings that we try to draw up the list; the work has been in hand so long that we have had time to forget obligations which when we incurred them seemed unforgettable. R. P. U. owes more than he can estimate to many classes of undergraduate students who have challenged, suggested and shaped ideas in the give and take of oral discussion. We owe much to some ten successive groups of graduate students in the University of California who have worked through this material with us, and contributed special investigations on one and another of its special topics. Professor Guy Montgomery has read the whole, and has helped with wise suggestions from his large store of special knowledge of the eighteenth century and with stimulating encouragement throughout. Mrs. Utter has given us notes and citations from many novels, English and French, has read our manuscript in all stages, has supplied suggestions and corrections, has helped us thrash out unformed ideas by discussion, and has been unsparing in sympathy, help and encouragement throughout the work. Professor Robert H. Lowie has been patient and generous in helping us in anthropological problems of our studies. We owe much to Miss Alice C. Roripaugh for investigations in the theory and practice of censorship, and in the behavior patterns of the rising generation. Miss M. Bôcher has read the whole manuscript and made many corrections and helpful suggestions. We are indebted to Miss Besse Ellen Backes for reading many novels and making skilful notes on them, to Miss Gail Wickwire for a study of the "no mother to guide her" heroines, to Miss Marion Shephard for research on the literature and fashions of the mid-nineteenth century, and to Miss Virginia Page and others who have collected and supplied information by way of facts, feelings and experiences of the generation born since 1900 into "the new multiverse."

We wish to express our gratitude to the publishers and authors for permission to quote selections from the following copyrighted material: *The Post Girl* by Edward Booth, *The Happy Highways* by Storm Jameson, and *The Road to the World* by Webb Waldron, all published by D. Appleton–Century Company, New York, N. Y.; *An Unmarried Father* by Floyd Dell, copyright 1927 by Doubleday, Doran and Company, Inc.; *The Premeditated Virgin* by Nalbro Bartley, Farrar & Rinehart, Inc.; "Women in Business," an article in the issue of August, 1935, of *Fortune* magazine; *Maggie Pepper* by Charles Klein, H. K. Fly Company; *Queen Victoria* by Lytton Strachey, *Bad Girl* by Viña Delmar, and a quatrain by T. S. Eliot, all published by Harcourt, Brace and Company, Inc.; *The Perennial Bachelor* by Anne Parrish, *A New England Nun* by Mary E. Wilkins Freeman, both published by Harper & Brothers; "Getting Along with Women," an article in the issue of October, 1935, *Harper's Magazine; The Education of Henry Adams* by Henry Adams, Houghton Mifflin Company; *A Deputy Was King* by G. B. Stern, Alfred A. Knopf, Inc.; *The Bonney Family* by Ruth Suckow, *Heavy Laden* by Philip Wylie, by special arrangement with Alfred A. Knopf, Inc.; "Help," an article in the issue of March 27, 1932, *Liberty* mag-

azine; *The.Way of All Women* by Dr. M. Esther Harding, Long-
mans, Green & Co.; *Mrs. Warren's Daughter* by Sir Harry John-
ston, *Poetical Works* of Matthew Arnold, both published by The
Macmillan Company; *Pageant of Youth* by Irving Stone, Julian
Messner, Inc. (for Alfred H. King); *Give Your Heart to the
Hawks* by Robinson Jeffers, Random House, Inc.; *Economics of
Fashion* by Dr. Paul H. Nystrom, The Ronald Press Company;
Curse of Beauty and *Only a Working Girl* by Geraldine Fleming,
Estelle's Millionaire Lover by Julia Edwards, *Lotta the Cloak
Model* by Laura Jean Libbey, and *For Gold or Soul* by Lurana
Sheldon, all published by Street & Smith Publications, Inc.; *A
Working Girl's Honor* by Caroline Hart and *Pretty Madcap
Dorothy* by Laura Jean Libbey, published by Arthur Westbrook
Company; *What Can She Do?* by E. P. Roe, by special arrange-
ment with Dodd, Mead and Company; and *Miss Cayley's Ad-
ventures* by Grant Allen, published by Grant Richards, London,
and G. P. Putnam's Sons, United States.

R. P. U.

G. B. N.

Berkeley, California,
January, 1936.

On the night of February 17, 1936, a month after the manuscript
was sent to the publishers, Mr. Utter was killed by a falling tree
as he crossed the campus of the University of California. The
tasks of seeing the book through publication and of preparing
the appendix and the index were carried on by G. B. N. who
wishes to express her gratitude to Miss Alice C. Roripaugh for
her unstinted help.

G. B. N.

September, 1936

THE CHAPTERS

"Chapter on chapter did I count,
As a curious traveller counts Stonehenge."
Sibrand of Schafnaburg.
(According to Browning)

ix

Age of Reason. Emotion by rule. Fashions in feelings. Emotional insignia of class distinctions. Tears of piety and contrition. The Doctrine of Original Virtue. The cataract and the passion. "Such sweet sorrow." The woman of feeling. The child of nature. Precious sorrows and divine sensibilities.

Fainting and the figure of fashion. Pamela and Cleopatra are sisters under their stays. Fainting as an index of the heart. As an act of fashion. Literary fainting as old as literature. A poetic formula for the expression of extreme emotion. As a badge of aristocracy. Long-winded romances and short-winded heroines. The stays of fashion and the mold of form. Pressure on "the sides of nature." The uncorseted silhouette and the Gothic romance. The sister of death is the mainstay of melodrama.

The delicate air as the minimum requirement for promotion by marriage. Helplessness and "the insolence of conscious rank." The rococo silhouette. Delicate strength and fragile vigor. Burke's specifications. "Fine by defect and delicately weak." The delicate air as a biological preference. "Either eyebrow like a silken thread." The delicate air and the tradition of false modesty in art. Paris the first gentleman who preferred blondes. The traditional behavior-pattern of the blonde. She has the delicate air by nature. Brown and brisk mean mischief and witchcraft. Delicacy refined to the ultra spheral. Early Victorian patterns. Plain and ringlets.

Enter, the old maid. Virginity as a profession. Tabitha Bramble. The striped cat and the female cat. Aunt Tabby an importation from Paris. "Fair Vestal throned by the west." The Utopia of Gallantry no place for the old maid. Decline of convents and rise of commerce. The learned lady has no chance. Serious proposals to ladies. Antiquated virgins, chaperons and lady inquisitors. The complacent Tranquilla. The intelligent woman's dilemma. Women are human beings. Taking arms against a host of tyrannies. Forsaken but patient one. A New England Nun. Doing credit to the single state. The business girl. The Glorified Spinster. The Bachelor Maid.

ILLUSTRATIONS

PAMELA'S DAUGHTERS

CHAPTER I

PAMELA

I, from a state of low degree,
Was plac'd in this good family:
Too high a fate for humble me,
The helpless, hopeless Pamela.

For what indeed is happiness,
But conscious innocence and peace?
And that's a treasure I possess;
Thank Heaven that gave it Pamela.

(Volume I, Letter XXXI.)

IF every woman in life is a daughter of Eve, so is every heroine in fiction a daughter of Pamela. If Eve were alive today, we should rejoice to analyze her, soul, mind, and body, as a basis for a biological and psychological study of her daughters. Pamela is as much alive as ever she was, and she is ours to analyze as we will in the search for the origin of the diverse species of heroines of English fiction. She was born in 1740 at the age of fifteen from the pen of Samuel Richardson. At birth she was two volumes long, but she soon grew to four. Whether or not the volumes of her corporate form are to be called the first English novel need not concern us. At least they signal the entrance of the heroine, so for us the first book of Pamela shall be the book called Genesis. Her name is a household word, and her story is widely known, but few there are in the twentieth century who read it "in the original."

Pamela Andrews was a serving-maid, "fifteen last February," whose parents lived not far from the country estate of Lady B. whom Pamela served. She was eleven when she entered service, a pretty child, modest, sweet-tempered, submissive, intelligent. Her mistress became very fond of her, made her her waiting-maid, and helped her to some education; "my lady's goodness," said Pamela, "had put me to write and cast accounts and made me a little expert at my needle, and otherwise qualified me above my degree." The death of this kind and indulgent mistress is the subject of Pamela's first letter to her parents, the opening words of the long story. Almost in her dying breath, Lady B. recommended Pamela to the consideration of her son, the new master, a handsome youth, very much accustomed to having his own way in everything, and he at the first opportunity shows her very special kindness. "She is all grateful confusion upon it, and thinks him the best of gentlemen." Her parents, in reply to the letter in which Pamela tells them this, express much concern for her lady's death, but "their chief trouble is lest she should have *too* grateful a sense of her master's favor; so as to be brought to anything dishonest or wicked." She assures them of her resolution to prefer her virtue to life itself, and "apprehends no danger at present from her master's favor." She is confirmed in this opinion by her master's ready consent to Lady Davers, his sister, when she proposes to take Pamela away as her own waiting-maid. But he makes her blush when he gives her some stays and stockings of her late mistress; he refuses to let her go with Lady Davers, and she becomes a trifle uneasy. She is genuinely shocked when he comes out openly with his proposition—"I tell you I will make a gentlewoman of you if you will be obliging, and don't stand in your own light,"—and he kisses her "with frightful eagerness." She plans to leave, but is rather frightened and helpless; after all, she is hardly more than a child. After a little natural hesitation, she confides in Mrs. Jervis, the good housekeeper, who sympathizes, advises, and takes her in as a room-mate for protection. Mr. B. bullies and terrorizes them both. Pamela, as befits her age, is at one moment a child, the next a brave woman; the maturing effect of her hard experience is nicely shaded. Her master grows bolder; he "offers freedoms to her," and "tauntingly ridicules her resistance." He "tells her that she shall return to her former poverty and distress," to which her parents reply by telling her "how welcome her return will be to them, as she will come innocent and honest"; they "will receive her with more pleasure than they had at her birth." But Mr. B. has worked upon Mrs. Jervis, who "gives her opinion that he will never attempt her again; and that she may stay if she will ask it as a favor." Pamela is not so easily overcome; she continues her preparations to go, and reports that she "hopes to set out in a few days." Her master bullies and persuades, then "hides himself in a closet, and overhears a discourse against himself between Mrs. Jervis and her, as they are going to rest. Being alarmed at the rustling of his gown, she, almost undressed, goes towards the closet; and he rushing out, she flies to the bed to Mrs. Jervis, and falls into fits." This is too much for Mrs. Jervis, who gives notice. The master nonchalantly agrees to let them go together, saying that he is probably going to get married anyway, and has no further interest in Pamela. She, reassured, lingers to go with Mrs. Jervis a week later. He then goes to work a little less crudely, chatting on indifferent matters, rallying her on her seriousness; at length telling her that he loves her, flattering her, suggesting that he will make her parents happy. She relates "the different agitations of her mind on this occasion, yet at last resolves to insist upon going away." After some further negotiations he agrees that she is to go, "gives leave for his travelling chariot and Lincolnshire coachman to carry her, and gives her five guineas." The chariot takes her to her master's seat in Lincolnshire, where she is imprisoned in the care of an unscrupulous jailor, Mrs. Jewkes, who subjects her to constraints and hardships and abuses that drive her to the verge of suicide. She tries every possible stratagem to escape or to communicate with her family or friends. He plans to marry her off a little above her station and use her husband as a screen for his amour, and again to gain her by a mock marriage. He offers her dazzling terms to become his mistress. The height of his endeavor is an attempt at rape from which Pamela is saved only by her weakness, fainting, and alarmingly protracted unconsciousness. His behaviour is oddly erratic, changing abruptly from tenderness to cruelty, from insult to courtship. He seizes and reads all her diary and letters, learns as the reader has learned every shading of her thought and feeling. He orders her to leave, and provides a carriage, but on her way he intercepts her with letters entreating her to return of her own will. She sees his heart, and thereby knows her own; the reader has seen it before, and her master has seen it in her letters. She knows now that she may go back. She returns, not to struggle, but to tenderness and respect, and the marriage follows close upon her return. So runs the original story, the first part. The rest though much greater in bulk is negligible in importance; it is merely the story of Pamela's success in the social rank to which her marriage has promoted her.

Pamela became a vogue almost before the reviewers could notice it. It was unfashionable not to have read it, and ladies flourished their copies at one another in public places as they flaunted their fashions in clothes. Sermons were chaunted in praise of it. By the time the reviewers got into action, it was little to their profit, whatever their opinions, policies or prejudices, to go against the current. It is characteristic of the rising tide of middle-class morality of the time that critics, parsons and lay-readers all praised it for its aid to the cause of virtue.

This should have been, and doubtless was highly gratifying to Richardson. He is quite explicit; he intended *Pamela* to be a moral tale, scarcely less than a dramatized sermon. He tells us so in his preface, a decalogue of *ifs,* only one or two of which are directly to the purpose here, but the whole is worth quoting since it furnished prefatory platitudes to so many of Richardson's successors, and even sounds a quaint echo in Mr. Kipling's poem, the gospel of the Girl Scouts.

If to divert and entertain, and at the same time to instruct and improve, the minds of the youth of both sexes:

If to inculcate religion and morality in so easy and agreeable a manner, as shall render them equally delightful and profitable:

If to set forth, in the most exemplary lights, the parental, the filial, the social duties:

If to paint vice in its proper colours, to make it deservedly odious; and to set virtue in its own amiable light, to make it lovely:

If to draw characters with justness, and to support them distinctly:

If to raise distress from natural causes, and excite compassion from just ones:

If to teach the man of fortune how to use it; the man of passion how to subdue it; and the man of intrigue, how gracefully, and with honour to himself, to reclaim:

If to give practical examples, worthy to be followed in the most critical and affecting cases, by the virgin, the bride, and the wife:

If to effect all these good ends, without raising a single idea throughout the whole, that shall shock the exactest purity, even in the warmest of those instances where purity would be most apprehensive:

If these be laudable recommendations, the Editor of the following letters, which have their foundation in truth, ventures to assert, that all these ends are attained here; and writes with the more assurance of success, as an Editor may be allowed to judge with more impartiality than is often to be found in an author.

The ventured assertion was a bold one, but the chorus of praise would indicate that the book made it good. We hear individual voices to that effect. "Mr. Pope declared that it would do more good than many volumes of sermons. Mr. Lucas, the esteemed author of *The Search after Happiness,* a much graver character than Pope, and not personally acquainted with the author, calls it 'the best book ever published, and calculated to do the most good.'" Dr. Johnson, who declared that novels were "the entertainment of minds unfurnished with ideas," books addressed "chiefly to the young, the ignorant, and the idle," which should therefore exhibit "the best examples only," believed that Richardson "taught the passions to move at the command of virtue." There is evidence enough that *Pamela* was popular with the moralists.

There is no such direct evidence that it was popular with the rakes, but it might well have been so. At least one of the moralists feared so. Dr. Watts, to whom Richardson sent the volumes of *Pamela,* "instead of compliments, writes him word, that he understands the ladies complain that they cannot read them without blushing." Mrs. Barbauld, writing some sixty years later, speaks of "the indelicate scenes" in *Pamela* as "indeed indefensible." Most notable of these is that of the attempted rape toward the end of Volume I. "I," says Pamela, "with my underclothes in my hand, all undressed, passed by the poor sleeping wench," who was her master in the wench's clothes. The tableau, like others in the same scene, is an apt subject for one of the naughty French engravings of the time. Had Richardson been scrutinizing them? A few years later the French painter, Greuze, did with his brush what Richardson had done with the pen. He painted moral and sentimental subjects, a father reading the Bible to his family, a village betrothal, a girl with a lamb, a girl with a dead bird. He painted a picture of a little girl with a broken jug, looking rather tearfully apprehensive, clutching her upgathered pinafore which holds flowers. Sentimental eyes have always looked kindly on her,—a sweet child; give her sixpence to make her jug whole. Would a rake look at it twice? Surely, if his eye fell on the roseleaf of her young breast, which is nearly the center of the picture. He would recognize the title, *La Cruche Cassée;* he who had broken such jugs would know that proverbially they cannot be mended. He would see the moist eye, the relaxed mouth—the face of a child, yes, but the disordered dress slips off the shoulders just so far as to show that she is old enough. He would note the position of the clutching hands on the uplifted pinafore. If Greuze had set out to please the sensualist with a picture of an adolescent girl in the moment of sexual experience, he could hardly have done it differently. If Greuze is

Greuze   *La Cruche Cassée*

PAMELA

Sentimental Rustic Beauty

rightly called an "unctuous moralist . . . at once complacent and indignant," one of the tribe who "denounce vice eloquently while gloating over its details," it might well have been Richardson who pointed him the way. *Pamela* is the study of an adolescent girl kept for months on the verge of sexual experience. Incessantly, night and day, it is on her mind; she is allowed to think of nothing else. Every finest gradation of her thought and feeling is registered with minute fidelity. If the rakes of *The Tatler* and *The Spectator* who pursued adolescent girls missed *Pamela*, it must be because they were turned away by the forbidding morality of the preface.

Even so, Richardson may have been entirely sincere, a moralist in a free-spoken age, sincerely showing examples of profligacy as a warning in a time when the psychological effects of such exhibitions were not so carefully calculated as such things are supposed to be today. Later times are not free from the same reproach. Temperance propaganda of the last century drew vivid pictures of bacchanalian scenes some of which were more alluring in their gaiety than the accompanying gloomy homilies were forbidding. Modern newspapers exploit crime in a way which is said to have a bad effect on impressionable youth. Just this is said of Richardson by Charlotte Palmer, a novelist of fifty years later, speaking of *Clarissa*, "the mischief of that enticing book may be told in a few words:—Vice is drawn in colours, and in countenance so pleasing, that we cannot detest it as we ought to do."

Pamela, then, would please the moralist and the prude. It would be titillating to the rake and the Mohock. From it the timid boy might learn how to attack the serving-maid of his desire. The superannuated virgin would read with delight the story of virtue pursued by inexorable man, gracefully yielding at last with the white banner of virtue still flying. Servant-maids would read it possibly for the moral Richardson offered them, more likely as a Cinderella escape from their ashes to imaginary high life, or as advice how to rise to the highest ranks of society. It would be popular with those who have nothing better to talk about than servants, and with those who tattle incessantly of love. The publisher who can gratify all these may safely neglect others if others there be.

If Richardson pleased all these, he did what every novelist since has tried to do, many, nay, most of them by using one term or another of Richardson's formula, or some combination of the qualities of his heroine. To the twentieth century reader Pamela seems grovelingly submissive. This places her in the larger of the two classes of women of literature, the submissive and the imperious, those who obey and those who command, the Penelopes and the Clytemnestras, the Griseldas and the Cleopatras. The original Griselda who gives the proverbial name to the submissive type, we know chiefly through the Clerk's Tale of Chaucer's *Canterbury Tales,* and the tenth novel of the tenth day in Boccaccio's *Decameron,* where it is summarized as follows:

The Marquis of Saluzzo, having been prevailed upon by his subjects to marry, in order to please himself in the affair, made choice of a countryman's daughter, by whom he had two children, which he pretended to put to death. Afterwards, seeming as though he were weary of her, and had taken another, he had his own daughter brought home, as if he had espoused her, whilst his wife was sent away in a most distressed condition. At length, being convinced of her patience, he brought her home again, presented her children to her, who were now of considerable years, and ever afterwards loved and honored her as his lady.

Griselda is indeed the archetype of the submissive woman. Her attitude toward her husband is "thy will, not mine, be done." When he takes from her her second child, as she believes to be put to death, she says, "My lord, study only your own ease and happiness, without the least care for me; for nothing is agreeable to me but what is pleasing to yourself." No other woman in fiction equals this pattern of submissive endurance. Pamela does not equal it, but in so far as she seems to the modern reader grovelingly submissive, she places herself in the Griselda class. And in her class appear the majority of her successors, the heroines of the English novel, which is middle class from the start, and the middle class code and imagination exclude the Cleopatra type as beyond its pale and beyond its comprehension. Pamela has spirit and energy; it is only because she holds herself to a strictly defensive position within the lines of what she considers her duty that we call her submissive. As such she stands at the head of a line of heroines continuous from her day to ours.

Pamela's pedigree has another strain that takes us back to Griselda; she comes of the peasant or farmer class. She is one of a long line of farmer's daughters of romance and ballad who have interested young scions of nobility and bourgeoisie. The aristocratic or bourgeois lover almost invariably rationalizes his prejudice by perceiving in his chosen female of the lower species traits of almost human intelligence and beauty—or his author does it for him. Of Griselda we are told,

. . . the young bride showed apparently, that with her garments she had changed both her mind and behaviour. She had a most agreeable person, and was so amiable, and so good-natured withal, that she seemed rather a lord's daughter than a poor shepherd's; at which every one that knew her before was greatly surprised.

This is all very well in a tale which calls so little on our sense of fact as does this of Boccaccio's, but Richardson has a different task. His attempt, whether he knew it by name or not, was for realism, and the form of his story is such that if the heroine cannot make the reader feel her aristocratic graces and accomplishments, he will remain ignorant of them. The first hint of it is in the first letter, already quoted in the outline of the plot. Pamela gives us more details later, at a time when she expects to return to her parents and be a common farmer's daughter.

. . . I have been brought up wrong as matters stand. For, you know, my good lady, now in heaven, loved singing and dancing; and, as she would have it, I had a voice, she made me learn both; and often and often she has made me sing her an innocent song, and a good psalm too, and dance before her. And I must learn to flower and draw too, and to work fine work with my needle; why, all this too I have got pretty tolerably at my finger's end, as they say; and she used to praise me, and was a good judge of such matters. . . . So I shall make a fine figure with my singing and my dancing, when I come home to you! Nay, I shall be unfit even for a *May-day* holiday-time; for these minuets, rigadoons and French dances, that I have been practising, will make me but ill company for my milk-maid companions that are to be. To be sure I had better, as things stand, have learned to wash and scour, and brew and bake, and such like . . . So I, t'other day, tried, when Rachael's back was turned, if I could not scour a pewter plate she had begun. I see I could do't by degrees: It only blistered my hand in two places.

The whole list of her accomplishments covers exactly the items of a lady's education at the time, and for nearly a century thereafter. In beauty she is equally well equipped:

And Lady Brooks said, "See that shape! I never saw such a face and shape in my life; why, she must be better descended than you have told me!" which is a pretty exact equivalent of "she seemed rather a lord's daughter than a poor shepherd's." Lady Brooks's remark was made in Pamela's presence. Other details Richardson conveys to us through Pamela's reports with less of verisimilitude. She reports word for word a conversation of a page in length about her beauty and virtue which she makes no pretence to have heard with no more plausible introduction than

. . . it seems they said to my master, when the jokes flew about, Well, Mr. B——, we understand you have a servant-maid, who is the greatest beauty in the country; . . .

The most nearly complete description she gives of herself is in terms of her costume when she rather self-consciously dresses for the part of the farmer's daughter at the time when she confidently expects to return to her parents.

And so, when I had dined, upstairs I went, and locked myself into my little room. There I tricked myself up as well as I could in my new garb, and put on my round-eared ordinary cap; but with a green knot however, and my homespun gown and petticoat, and plain leather shoes; but yet they are what they call Spanish leather; and my ordinary hose, ordinary I mean to what I have been lately used to; though I shall think good yarn may do very well for every day when I come home. A plain muslin tucker I put on, and my black silk necklace, instead of the French necklace my lady gave me; and put the ear-rings out of my ears; and when I was quite equipped, I took my straw hat in my hand, with its two blue strings, and looked about me in the glass, as proud as anything— To say truth, I never liked myself so well in my life.

The image here is like one of Chardin's neatly turned-out country girls, but not quite so sincere, for it has also a dash of the lady in masquerade. The self-consciousness is no more than normal, such as any pretty girl would feel when looking in the mirror. It does not go so far as to permit her to give us details we might like to have, the color of her eyes and hair. Richardson might easily have slipped these details into Pamela's exact reports of conversations which she did not hear. Probably he omitted them as he did from Lovelace's detailed description of Clarissa because he realized the advantage of a description of the heroine detailed enough to seem individual but deceptively vague enough to allow each reader to supply the image of his own ideal. Pamela is a farmer's daughter fit to be a lady; small wonder if now and then she looks like a lady masquerading as a farmer's daughter.

Of intelligence, too, she has more than enough for the social position for which she is destined—more than would necessarily be expected of one born to social rank, but perhaps none too much for one who is to attain it. Her intelligence shows chiefly in her adroitness in defensive argument. This skill, of course, Richardson gives her for his purpose, but he does it successfully;

he makes it very completely a part of the character, and natural enough under the circumstances. She is at bay, fighting for what is dearer to her than life. Just as a physical fight for life brings forth degrees of strength and adroitness that seem before and afterwards beyond the man's power, so it is with Pamela's mental power and verbal skill. Under the circumstances it is not too much for a girl of sixteen. It is intelligence rather than knowledge or wisdom; it calls for no more knowledge or experience than a girl of her age and training might naturally have, and on that basis added years would be of no advantage to her. It does not appear that she exceeds either her master or his sister in intelligence. It is true that up to a time soon after her marriage—about the middle of Volume II—she has always the better of either in any argument, but that may be merely her advantage of position; she is on the side of obvious right and simple truth. If she were more intelligent, it would not necessarily be a perversion of probability. I am not aware that her master's age is specified. If she were from two to four years younger than he it would be natural for her mental age to be equal or superior to his. Mr. B. has never before had to use his wits; Pamela has always employed hers. If he had little wit and little learning he would be true to the type of the gentry of Richardson's time; we have Defoe's testimony for that. If lords and gentlemen thought that intelligence was a necessary qualification for promotion to their order, Richardson has well served them with a lesson in the very process of playing up to their prejudice.

In another respect, sensibility as indicated by the readiness of her tears, Pamela would less surely qualify for aristocracy. In the courtly romances before her time, sensibility, quickness of emotional response, is one of the signs that distinguish aristocracy from the stodgy peasant who is almost universally represented as "brother to the insensible clod." Of sensibility before Pamela's time and after it, tears are a ready index, according to the practice of those who try to portray it. In the courtly romances of the former age they are frequent enough; in the novel of sensibility immediately following *Pamela* they gush in torrents. Pamela weeps; indeed, she has good cause. But because she does not weep for nothing, she can hardly (no matter what modern readers may think of her) qualify as a heroine of sensibility. The situations which bring her tears are not imaginary but very real. By contrast with the torrential weepers that came after her she is almost stoical. None the less, Richardson manages to exhibit in her and in her story the traits of sensibility and sentimentality which become so wildly exaggerated in the later novel. Indeed, when we come toward the end of the story to Mr. B.'s "notice of a starting tear" with the words, "Let me kiss away this pearly fugitive," we may well feel that the later novel has little to add except quantity. A pearly fugitive is a mere drop in the bucket of liquid sorrow.

Fainting, the other conspicuous trait of helpless aristocracy in the romances, Pamela does not practice after she becomes a lady. She faints three or four times in the early part of the story when her master is most bold and direct in his attacks. The first time it happens, her master is unkind enough to suggest that it is a pretense, but Richardson makes it seem real enough; she falls flat on her face on the floor instead of sinking gracefully back on a sofa. On two later occasions her fainting is the result of his bold attempts at rape, and serves to thwart the attempts. Mr. B.'s increasing concern over her prolonged unconsciousness at these times shows the change in his feeling toward her. Her physical delicacy is her salvation; her weakness is her strength. On her part, it is not a mere ladylike accomplishment, but if her daughters inherited the trait, they made the most of it. And here as usual we may connect fainting with the fashion for the laced figure; it was a period of tight lacing, and when Pamela faints, Mrs. Jervis cuts her stay-laces.

Pamela's mental and moral delicacy has nearly the same history as her physical delicacy. In tracing it we may pass by her

stubborn defense of her chastity, for that is at first a question
of economics, and later of love, rather than of delicacy or prudery.
It does, to be sure, so far put her on her guard with her master
as to give her now and then the appearance of false modesty.
This shows in one of the early letters when he gives her some
of her late mistress's clothes. Among them are

. . . four pair of fine white cotton stockings, and three pair of fine
silk ones; and two pair of rich stays. I was quite astonished, and
unable to speak for a while; but yet I was ashamed to take the
stockings; for Mrs. Jervis was not there: If she had, it would have
been nothing. I believe I received them very awkwardly; for he smiled
at my awkwardness, and said, Don't blush, Pamela: Dost think I
don't know pretty maids should wear shoes and stockings?

I was so confounded at these words, you might have beat me down
with a feather. For you must think, there was no answer to be
made to this: So, like a fool, I was ready to cry; and went away
courtesying and blushing, I am sure, up to the ears; for, though
there was no harm in what he said, yet I did not know how to take
it.

This might seem false modesty, unnecessary alarm, but the reader
who knows that this is Mr. B.'s preliminary test must admit
that Pamela does well to be wary. Later, when matters have gone
much farther, she rebukes Mrs. Jewkes for speaking too explicitly
of her master's intentions toward her.

Said I, Mrs. Jewkes, don't talk nastily to me: . . . next to bad actions
are bad words; for they could not be spoken, if they were not in the
heart.—Come to bed, purity! said she. You are a nonesuch, I suppose.

This is the extent of her freedom of speech with her fellow
servants. Richardson represents the modesty of a bride with her
husband in a letter which she dates "Sunday, the fourth day of
my happiness:"

He was pleased to take notice of my dress; and spanning my waist
with his hands, said, What a sweet shape is here! It would make one
regret to lose it; and yet, my beloved Pamela, I shall think nothing
but that loss wanting to complete my happiness.—I put my bold

hand before his mouth, and said, Hush, hush! O fie, sir!—The freest thing you have ever yet said, since I have been yours!—He kissed my hand, and said, Such an innocent wish, my dearest, may be permitted me, because it is the end of the institution.—But say, Would such a case be unwelcome to my Pamela?—I will say, sir, said I, and hid my blushing face on my bosom, that your wishes, in everything, shall be mine; but, pray, sir, say no more. He kindly saluted me, and thanked me, and changed the subject.—I was not too free, I hope.

If this is prudery, it is at least more "free" than the typical Victorian bride who "whispers something" into her husband's ear, or perhaps her mother's. This modesty of Pamela's is the one respect in which Richardson takes no pains to prepare her for aristocracy. Later on, when Pamela's wished-for pregnancy becomes an apparent fact, Lady Davers "in her free quality way," takes notice of it in the presence of others:

. . . Let me observe you a little, my sweet-faced girl!—I hope I am right: I hope you will do credit to my brother, as he has done you credit.—Why do you let her lace so tight, Mr. B——?

I was unable to look up, as you may believe, miss. My face, all over scarlet, was hid in my bosom, and I looked *so silly!*—

Mr. B. comes to her rescue, and congratulations fly about, ending with Lady Davers' remark to her brother, "But you are a happy man, Mr. B., that your lady's bashfulness is the principal mark by which we can judge she is not of the quality." The suggestion here is plain enough that the "female delicacy" of the later novel comes from its middle-class practitioners.

In sensibility Pamela may fall short of the later fashion, but she is a sentimentalist at heart; her daughters have a hereditary right to the trait which they develop to such extremes. Pamela does not weep at the beauty of a landscape, but she can be sentimental about herself. At a time when Mr. B. chooses to let her think she is going back to her parents, she divides her clothes into three parcels, those her mistress gave her, those Mr. B. has given her

since, and those she has provided for herself. The second bundle
she rejects as the price of shame:

... So in conscience, in honour, in everything, I have nothing to
say to thee, thou *second wicked* bundle!
But, said I, come to my arms, my dear *third* parcel, the companion
of my poverty, and the witness of my honesty; and may I never
deserve the least rag that is contained in thee, when I forfeit a title
to that innocence that I hope will ever be the pride of my life! ...
and so I hugged my *third* bundle.

There are instances enough of this sort in which the sentimentality
is Pamela's, and as many again in which it is Richardson's.
Such is the occasion shortly before the marriage when Mr. B.
wishes to exhibit Pamela to some of his friends. He arranges the
scene carefully, with the guests in an "alcove":

This alcove fronts the longest gravel walk in the garden, so that
they saw me all the way I came for a good way: and my master told
me afterwards, with pleasure, all they said of me.
Will you forgive the little vain slut, your daughter, if I tell you
all, as he was pleased to tell me?

She is dressed in her "ordinary garb" deliberately posed as the
"pretty rustic." She accedes to the trial without much demur,
"I said I was ashamed; but I would obey him." So Richardson
holds the stage with her blushes and confusion the whole length
of the longest walk in the garden, and echoes it through pages
of Pamela's account of it to her parents. We have another carefully posed scene when, after the marriage, Pamela's father comes
to see her, thinking she has been "ruined." They place him
where Pamela will not see him as she enters, seat themselves where
they can see every shade of expression on his face, and then send
for Pamela. It is a subject for the painter Greuze, one he may
have taken a lesson from.
Greuze and Chardin furnish us with the best of illustrations to
Richardson. The sentimental rustic beauties of Greuze, the

pretty serving maids of Chardin, furnish excellent images for the scenes of *Pamela*. One such image Richardson gives us in the description already quoted of Pamela in the clothes she donned for her journey home. We see her again as she dresses the day before her marriage in

. . . fine linen, silk shoes, and fine white cotton stockings, a fine quilted coat, a French necklace, and a laced cambric handkerchief, and clean gloves; and, taking my fan in my hand, I, like a little proud hussy, looked in the glass, and thought myself a gentlewoman once more; but I forgot not to return due thanks, for being able to put on this dress with so much comfort.

These descriptions are all that show of Pamela to the outward eye; they show scarcely so much as the silhouette save to those who know the fashions of the time. Such as they are, these are the last glimpses we have. Twice after her marriage we have shimmers of white satin,—mere suggestions of elegance but nothing the eye can rest on. From beginning to end she reports constant praise of her beauty, but without details. Richardson wisely sets the general pattern of beauty and leaves us to fill in details according to personal preference.

Pamela is the story of an adolescent girl ripened to womanhood by experiences which stir the depths of her heart and soul. Before her marriage, the traits of adolescence are plain to read in her story. Her contemplation of suicide, if it is not tragic, is characteristic of her age. "They'll be sorry when they see me dead!" Can you remember gloating over the idea? And what was your mental age at the time? It is a part, perhaps, of the idea of martyrdom as an ideal, which belongs to the same mental age. Pamela would die a saint. This trait of adolescence holds through the centuries, at least from Shakespeare to Booth Tarkington, from Isabella in *Measure for Measure* to Willie Baxter in *Seventeen*. Isabella would gladly die on the scruple of her virginity. Willie Baxter poses in the attitude of Sidney Carton on the steps of the scaffold with, "It is a far, far better thing I do than I have ever done." Pamela's stubborn defense, too, has in it a trait of the child; none can be more stubborn than a child in defense of what he considers personal rights. And at what age do we begin to keep a diary with the sentimental thought of people reading it with awe and admiration after we are dead, or ourselves reading it with mingled smiles and tears at the age of eighty? Pamela has a childish sense of the value of her preserved emotions; and her faith is justified, for in them she lives today. Pamela is like a child who is at one moment an angel, at another a miser, a sentimentalist, an imp of satan, a thoroughly human being. Thus for nearly two hundred years she has been all things to all men: an innocent child, a case for the psychiatrist, a noble woman, a Shavian superman, the glory of her sex, a disgrace to womanhood, a saint, a pervert, a martyr, an entirely normal girl. In so far as she is human and normal, she is so because she has many traits and qualities, no one of which adequately represents her without the others. Her daughters, the heroines of later fiction, too often have to get along with one trait apiece—as if the heritage had to be divided among the heiresses. Hence come the type-form heroines who may be more or less safely classified according to the traits they inherit, and we have the Prude, the Weeper, the Fainter, "The Lass with the Delicate Air," the "fallen" heroine, and the poor working girl. One or two others there are who show relationship in collateral branches. Without defining here the exact degree of cousinship we may claim them as members of the family, include them in the sorority, and discuss them all as Pamela's daughters.

CHAPTER II

WHAT COULD THE POOR GIRL DO?

"I kept true to this notion, that a woman should never be kept for a mistress that had the money to make herself a wife."

Moll Flanders.

THE typical plot of the English novel has love for the starting-post and marriage for the finish-line. It is always an obstacle race —if the course were smooth there would be no story—and almost always the obstacles are economic. If kisses were dollars Strephon and Chloe could live "forever happy and forever young." If girlish charms were golden ducats Prince Charming might condescend. Pamela, standing at the genesis of the English novel as its Eve, bequeathed this curse to her innumerable progeny, and if we look into the life histories of two Liliths who preceded her, Moll Flanders and Roxana, common prostitute and king's mistress, we find they met the same problem each after her own way. Confronted with the problem of hammering a living out of an unyielding world with no more equipment than she is born with, what can the poor girl do?

What could Pamela do? If she had succeeded in passing barred doors and locked gates, she would have been a runaway servant with no means of honest livelihood because she would have had no recommendation from her last employer. Rightly was this recommendation called a "character," for without it she was ruined. Without a character she had no chance of further service. Without earning capacity she would have brought starvation with her if she had returned to her father. Without a dowry she had no chance of marriage. The choice was then dishonest livelihood or no livelihood, prostitution or death. Moll Flanders and Roxana, confronted with the same dilemma, did not choose death; Pamela was at times in a mood to court it. But despair did not prevail. Shrewdly or intuitively she saw that she had a dowry that was as good as cash in the right market. She used it cleverly while the game was playing; love came to her aid, and she won what was the only approved prize in the woman's market of her day, marriage.

The love plot with economic obstacles is the mainstay of the English novel. One may make bold to say (since no one will make the count) that it appears in a substantial majority of all the novels ever written in English. In the eighteenth century in England the women wrote most of the novels; the men wrote only the best ones. Naturally the women gave leading rôles to heroines, and wrote much from experience, and since most of the inferior novels are pot-boilers, we know that they wrestled with the world for a living, and had felt the economic difficulties as solid and bruising obstacles. Men too who were successful with heroines of their own times used this plot with imperishable effect in the nineteenth century, Thackeray, Trollope and Meredith, for example. But after Richardson it was the special property of the women novelists, and reached its apotheosis in the work of Jane Austen, who used no other. The novel, then, used this plot prevailingly from the very beginning. Not so the drama, which lived centuries without it, and never depended on it. To account wholly for the difference we should have to reckon many causes, but the most important is the difference in economic conditions between the times when the two forms had their beginnings.

The drama began in the Middle Ages. Capitalism, the great revolutionary, was beginning its work, and with the first germs of decay which it put into the feudal system, it began to have its effect on the status of women. As the lord of the castle learned more and more to take money in lieu of personal service from his vassals, his lady became less and less the serviceable chatelaine with the keys at her girdle, trainer of children, healer skilled in remedies and nursing. More and more she became the display figure on which her lord draped the signals of his economic conquests. With the capitalistic organization of industry, the same thing happened in the middle class. In the time of Elizabeth, the dramatist Dekker shows us the wife of a merchant who becomes Lord Mayor of London bustling among her husband's apprentices, serving them their beer and keeping them to their work. In the time of Anne we see women of this class withdrawn from all contact with trade, busily engaged in aping their social superiors. Among the working classes, men in the time of Elizabeth depended widely on their wives for help which they could not afford to hire. In the time of Anne, working-class women, like those of the middle class, gentry and nobility, had become economically dependent on their husbands. This change was brought about largely by the capitalistic organization of industry.

Under the domestic system of industry a wife was no less an economic asset to a man than a husband was to a woman. They bore practically equal shares in the economic burden of the family. They worked together as a unit, the wife not only performing the household tasks, but working with the man in whatever industry was his. Thus it was less often a question of whether a man could afford to marry than whether he could afford not to. But by the beginning of the eighteenth century the capitalistic organization of industry on an individual basis had advanced so far as to free men from much of their economic dependence on their wives, and woman's economic value was lessened. To the same effect was the decline of the guilds and the rise of governmental regulation in the matters which they had controlled. A woman might gain membership in a guild by marriage, and after the death of her husband she could retain membership in his guild or company with full trading privileges.

When industry was organized, she could not so much as learn his trade, for he carried it on at his master's place of business instead of in his own cottage. Working women, neither organized nor trained to meet new conditions, were pretty completely deprived of opportunity to share in the more profitable forms of production. In those families who could afford it, the woman was limited to the work of the home. In those who needed more wages than the man earned, the woman had to enter the labor-market as an individual, and become a wage-earner in one or another of the unprotected trades. Either way, she worked quite as hard as before and earned less.

At the same time that the organization of industry pushed women into the "domestic sphere," it began to invade it and lessen her work there. In former times, even if her work were purely domestic, she was a producer no less than a consumer, and very little a purchasing agent. But the beginning of centralized manufacturing was the beginning of the process that has since gone so far, the production in finished form of every necessity and every conceivable luxury. One by one woman's age-old occupations disappeared, household spinning and weaving, brewing and baking, preserving and mending—the process has gone on and on until she need not even cut into slices the daily bread that comes to her without a prayer. In rural districts, to be sure, where changes came slowly, she still had her uses, and continued long to be a producer as well as a distributor. But in the cities, and in general, she became a luxury rather than an asset.

These changes in the economic condition of woman worked in various ways their effects on her status. They gave the women of the aristocracy and the upper middle class more and more leisure time; they limited the work of women of the lower middle class pretty strictly to the "domestic sphere." These women became comfortably dependent on their husbands. The working woman was at this stage less comfortable because she had less money, but she was less dependent on her husband because her work in the home was a contribution to the upkeep of the family almost the equivalent of his. Her economic condition was worse than that of her socially superior sister because she was less opulent, while her economic status was better because she was less the parasite. The superiority of the women of leisure is social rather than economic.

As a social distinction, women (and men too, for that matter) have sought leisure from feudal times to our own, and few of them have known what to do with it when they got it. "Gentility consisted in doing nothing." In practically all his writings, Defoe illustrates this truth. In the autumn of 1662 Pepys was bickering with his wife about her "having a woman" to wait on her. "I do perceive," he remarks, "that it is want of worke that do make her and all other people think of ways of spending their time worse." He tried blunderingly to make occupation for her, and says later on,

I see that she is confirmed in it that all I do is by design, and that my very keeping of the house in dirt, and the doing this and anything else in the house, is but to find her employment to keep her within, and from minding of her pleasure, which though I am sorry to see she minds it, is true enough in a great degree.

Pepys was clever enough in some matters, but in his dealings with his wife he shows as little intelligence as he assumes in her. From his time on for a hundred years or more comments on the futile life of the woman of leisure range from the satiric to the pathetic, from comic to tragic. In 1712 Addison satirized it in the form of a journal of a society butterfly.

Wednesday. From eight until ten. Drank two dishes of chocolate in bed, and fell asleep after them.

From ten to eleven. Eat a slice of bread and butter, drank a dish of Bohea, read the Spectator.

From eleven to one. At my toilette, tried a new head. Gave orders for *Veny* to be combed and washed. *Mem.* I look best in blue.

From one until half an hour after two. Drove to the *'Change*. Cheapened a couple of fans.

Until four. At dinner. *Mem.* Mr. *Froth* passed by in his new liveries.

From four to six. Dressed, paid a visit to old Lady *Blithe* and her sister, having before heard they were gone out of town that day.

From six to eleven. At basset. *Mem.* Never set again upon the ace of diamonds.

About sixty years later, Dr. Gregory, physician and scientist of Edinburgh, writes in *A Father's Legacy* to his daughter:

The intention of your being taught needlework, knitting and such like, is not on account of the intrinsic value of all you can do with your hands, which is trifling, but . . . to enable you to fill up, in a tolerably agreeable way, some of the many solitary hours you must necessarily pass at home . . .

He flatters the economic value of the work of her hands; if he were candid he would rate it at absolute zero. Even so it is better than the pastimes of Clarinda of the journal in *The Spectator*, for she would lose five or six guineas an evening at basset. "Gentility consisted in doing nothing," or less than nothing.

A corner-stone of the society in which capitalism began to work its changes in the economic condition of women was the theory of the subjection of women to their husbands. The idea seems to have come into Europe from the Orient; it is more Hebrew than Roman or Germanic, and it built itself into European society along with Christianity and the Bible. Most writers who mention it in the Middle Ages and the Renaissance attribute it to St. Paul. "St. Paul teaches," said Erasmus of Rotterdam, "that wives ought to be subject to their own husbands with all reverence. And St. Peter proposes the example of Sarah to us, who called her husband Abraham Lord." A century and a half later the principle was taken fully for granted; in 1699 a Dorsetshire clergyman said in a wedding sermon, speaking of women:

God had also fully indicated her function when he deliberately created her for the Profit and Comfort of man. A good wife should be like a Mirrour which hath no image of its own, but receives its stamp from the face that looks into it.

She must not only obey his commands, but must bring

unto him the very Desires of the Heart to be regulated by him so far, that it should not be lawful for her to will or desire what she herself liked, but only what her husband should approve and allow.

Thus did society sanction this subjection by naming it the law of God, immutable, inviolable, unquestionable. Thus did the church fathers, their successors, and others who were interested try for centuries to make this "law" work by proclamation, re-iteration, and every other means within their power. Whether these means alone would have succeeded we shall never know. The propagators of the doctrine did not know that other forces were working with them. The economic changes of the rise of capitalism made woman in fact as well as in theory subject to man. Who could assert woman's equality when she was in complete economic subjection to her husband? Yet it might have been the stars in their courses fighting against her for all anyone knew of the actual causes of her enslavement until the Age of Anne. Then Defoe perceived that the doctrine of female inferiority and woman's economic helplessness went hand in hand, and suggested that men of his time took advantage of the situation; "they will not make them useful," he said, "that they may not value themselves upon it, and make themselves, as it were, the equals of their husbands."

Working-class women of course continued to work in agriculture, in the textile trades, as hucksters and pedlars, and increasingly in domestic service. Even so, workers in manufacturing establishments were accused of idleness and luxury in a period of high wages, and reduction of wages was proposed as a means of making them "sober, industrious and obedient."

Women in domestic service, we are told, have become so scarce (about 1725),

that an ordinary tradesman cannot well keep one, but his wife, who might be useful in his shop or business, must do the drudgery of household affairs; and all this because our servant-wenches are so puffed up with pride nowadays that they never think they go fine enough; it is a hard matter to know the mistress from the maid by their dress; nay often the maid shall be the finer of the two.

The writer, Defoe, complains no less of women of the tradesman class as aspiring to leisure:

In former times tradesmen's widows valued themselves upon the shop and trade, or the warehouse and trade that was left them; and, at least, if they did not carry on the trade in their own names, they could keep it up till they put it off to advantage; . . . But now the ladies are above it, and disdain it so much, that they choose rather to go without the prospect of a second marriage, in virtue of the trade, then stoop to the mechanic low step of carrying on the business.

and necessarily at the same time disdaining work:

The tradesman is foolishly vain of making his wife a gentlewoman, forsooth; he will have her sit above in the parlour, receive visits, drink tea, and entertain her neighbours, or take a coach and go abroad; but as to the business, she shall not stoop to touch it; he has apprentices and journeymen, and there is no need of it.

The same feeling applied to housework shows in a novel of Charlotte Palmer's toward the close of the century:

"Men of fortune like their wives to command respect, and not to be like as if they had been ladies maids, or housekeepers!—I cannot say I should like to see my daughters pickling and preserving, and putting their hands into a pan of flower [*sic*], and all that; let them keep their tambour, their music, their filligree, and their drawing; that's quite enough."

Embroidery, music and drawing, it was all they knew and all they needed to know. The empty head was cultivated as carefully as the idle hand. The notion of gentility consisting in idleness brought scholarship to a low ebb no less among men than among women, as conspicuous in the universities as in girls' boarding-schools. These, what there were of them, offered young gentlewomen (we may guess that most of them were merely aspirants to that title) curricula consisting of "the Needle, the French Tongue, Dancing, a little music on the harpsichord or spinet, Reading, Writing," and sometimes "the casting of accounts in a small way." Item by item these are the hall-marks of the gentlewoman that become visible through the Cinderella-guise of the fair Incognita in Fanny Burney's *The Wanderer.* The household is ravished overhearing her play on the harp and sing, and "nearly stupified" to discover who is performing, "for no one . . . had ever considered her but as a needy travelling adventurer." "And pray," they ask, "where might such a body as you learn these things?—And what use can such a body want them for?" Next they discover that she is expert in "the useful and appropriate female accomplishment of needlework." A few pages more and it appears that she can read aloud "with the nicest discrimination"; next that she can write, "and the beautiful clearness of the handwriting and the correctness of the punctuation and orthography, convinced him that her education had been as successfully cultivated for intellectual improvement, as for elegant accomplishment." Spelling and punctuation, the most elementary mechanical training, were, then, rated as intellectual accomplishment; high achievement for the female mind. The fact makes us look askance at Miss Burney's other heroines, Evelina and Cecilia, whom she represents as intelligent and endowed with graces of the mind; probably she did well not to go into details. The Wanderer has other accomplishments. As a refugee from France she may be expected to know French to perfection, but it is only as a gentlewoman that she shines in the "latest cotillion" just imported from the continent, of which the steps, the figure, the time, all were familiar to her; and she taught the young Selina, dropt hints to Elinor, endeavored to set Miss Bydel right, and gave a general, though unpremeditated lesson to every one, by the measured grace and lightness of her motions, which, little as her attire were adapted to such a purpose, were equally striking for elegance and modesty.

At last she is discovered idly sketching on the back of a letter the view from the window. It is a real sketch, not lines memorized from a drawing-master.

It was beautifully executed, and undoubtedly from nature. Harleigh, with mingled astonishment and admiration, clasped his hands, and energetically exclaimed, "Accomplished creature! who—and what are you?"

There is no better single illustration than these scenes afford of the question "What could the poor girl do?" as the theme of fiction, for the Wanderer is cast on the shore of England almost as Crusoe is cast on his island, deprived of every conceivable advantage outside her person and mind—indeed she has scarcely those, for she is temporarily deprived of her beauty by the exigency of her disguise and is almost distracted by what she has suffered. She has almost literally "nothing to wear," and she has no money. Thus she enters the game for a husband with her virginity for a stake, and her native skill to play it. Her education, indeed, gives her the entree to the gaming table, but nothing directly remunerative. Like *The Wanderer,* novel after novel testifies that there was no thought of training girls for any gainful occupation; their destiny was marriage, and naught but training in idleness pointed them toward it. Cynthia in Sarah Fielding's *David Simple,* of whom we shall see more in later chapters, complained about the middle of the century that her mother always snatched away any book, saying,

"Miss must not inquire too far into things, it would turn her Brain; she had better mind her Needle-work, and such things as were useful for Women; reading and poring on Books, would never get me a husband."

Determined to gain a livelihood "by industry rather than by marriage," Ellen Percy in Mary Brunton's *Discipline* (1814) realizes the uselessness of the so-called education of girls of her class.

What channel had the customs of society left open to the industry of woman? The only one which seemed within my reach was the tuition of youth; and I felt myself less dependent when I recollected my thorough knowledge of music and my acquaintance with other arts of idleness. When, indeed, I considered how small a part of the education of a rational and accountable being I was after all fitted to undertake, I shrunk from the awful responsibility of the charge.

On the basis of her bitter experience she learns to define education as "learning what is afterwards to be useful." Even Lady Mary Wortley Montagu, whose views were fairly realistic for her time, does not suggest education for remunerative work, though she puts forward something better than worthless needlework to fill in the long, solitary hours to come. She is writing (about 1763) to her daughter, Lady Bute, about the education of her granddaughter, who, she thinks, may not be married.

As you had no defect either in mind or person to hinder, and much in your circumstances to attract, the highest offers, it seemed your business to learn how to live in the world, as it is hers to know how to be easy out of it . . . every woman endeavors to breed her daughter a fine lady, qualifying her for a station in which she will never appear, and at the same time incapacitating her for that retirement to which she is destined. No entertainment is so cheap as reading, nor any pleasure so lasting. She will not want new fashions, nor regret the loss of expensive diversions, or variety of company, if she can be amused with an author in her closet. . . .

At the same time I recommend books, I neither exclude work nor drawing. I think it is as scandalous for a woman not to know how to use a needle, as for a man not to know how to use a sword . . .

The second caution to be given her (and which is most absolutely necessary) is to conceal whatever learning she attains, with as much solicitude as she would hide crookedness or lameness; the parade of it can only serve to draw on her the envy, and consequently the most inveterate hatred, of all he and she fools, which will certainly be at least three parts in four of all her acquaintance. The use of knowledge in our sex, besides the amusement of solitude, is to moderate the passions, and learn to be contented with a small expense, which are the certain effects of a studious life; and it may be preferable even to that fame which men have engrossed to themselves, and will not suffer us to share.

The ultimate end of your education was to make you a good wife (and I have the comfort to hear that you are one): hers ought to be, to make her happy in a virgin state.

There is at least one intimation that a little business education might be of service, even to a gentlewoman, and married at that. In Maria Edgeworth's *Belinda* (1801), Lady Delacour's husband has wasted her fortune; her uncle tells her that with all her wit she is a dupe; " 'tis a shame for a woman of your sense to be such a fool, and to know nothing of business; and if you knew nothing yourself, could not you send for me?" "I was too ignorant to know—that I knew nothing," was her answer.

Marriage no less than education withered under the economic blight, and marriages in all walks of life became openly contracts of barter and sale. Mercenary marriages were, of course, nothing new. The feudal concept of marriage as a contract of material convenience whose constraints excluded love had largely prevailed in spite of the efforts of the church to confine love to, or bring it into, the bounds of marriage. Intermarriages between the bourgeoisie and the upper classes as sales of social rank for money were well known in the thirteenth century, and have been equally frequent ever since. Defoe discussed them at length in 1725 by way of showing their effect on the "Compleat Gentleman." Steele in 1710 notes that mercenary marriages had then recently become a regular procedure in the middle class: "Honest Coupler, the Conveyancer," he says, finds that among the "generality of parents . . . the marriage settlements that are now used have grown fashionable even within his memory." Defoe notes it among the tradesmen: "a man's knowledge of his trade and business ought to be set against a sum of money on the female part." Steele, dramatizing the situation in *The Tender Husband,* is satirical, but probably not far from actuality:

> SIR HARRY: Ay, but Brother, you rate her too high, the War has fetched down the Price of Women: The whole Nation is overrun with Petticoats; our Daughters lie upon our Hands, Brother Tipkin; Girls are Drugs, Sir, mere Drugs.
>
> TIPKIN: Look y', Sir Harry— Let Girls be what they will—a thousand Pound a Year, is a thousand Pound a Year; and a Thousand Pound a Year is neither Girl nor Boy.

A mere drug, sir; that is what the rise of capitalism made of woman; flattered, courted, honored, in an age before "chivalry has fallen into the ash-can," but with no function in life but that of sex—"all dolled up but no place to go." In spite of all we can learn of her business enterprise, it is hardly an exaggeration to say that marriage and prostitution were the only ways that were wide open to her. Defoe was a shrewd economist almost before the science had a name; his Moll Flanders had no illusions. "I kept true to this notion," she says, "that a woman should never be kept for a mistress that had money to make herself a wife." Moll stated the fact bluntly, but fact it was. A woman's sex function was her dowry if she had no cash; the market was frankly open, and she might take it to the Exchange, which was marriage, or play it on the Curb, which was prostitution. What price chastity?

The answer is plain to read in the annals of the time. Chastity was priceless because it was the only thing God had given to woman which commanded a price. "Consider," said Dr. Johnson, "of what importance to society the chastity of woman is. Upon that all the property in the world depends." Priceless indeed—"all the property in the world"—these be high stakes, and "frailty, thy name is woman!" What if she loses? Then, says Dr. Johnson, all is indeed lost; "they who forfeit it should not have any possibility of being restored to good character; nor should the children by an illicit connection attain the full right of lawful children." Boswell sees in this "that acute discrimination, that solid judgement, and that knowledge of human nature, for which he was upon all occasions remarkable." We who sit farther from him than did Boswell see more of both acuteness and solidity in the judgment of Defoe. Between Richardson and Scott one could scarcely find a novel in which the determining factor of the heroine's fate, whether she rises to marriage or stoops to folly, is not money and property; to point out instances would be to check over the entire list. When they reflect the facts, they reflect them truly; when they try to analyze them they flounder blindly—all except the clear-sighted Moll Flanders.

With girls a drug on the market, Dr. Johnson would seem to have set the price too high. A shrewder observer of the market might have read it as did Prince Hal in his time of "civil buffeting": "we shall buy maidenheads as they buy hobnails, by the hundreds." In the novels it is safe to say that there is not a single lapse from virtue or a fall into prostitution that is not brought about directly or indirectly by economic pressure. Records of life are to the same effect. In all gainful occupations no less than in the marriage market girls were "drugs, Sir, mere drugs," and in larger numbers than ever before they were driven to prostitution for a livelihood. Even there the competition was keener than ever, for the lure of the city was being felt in the country, drawing eager, inexperienced girls to the supposed delights of London. Employment agencies were open feeders of the brothels, and sooner or later, surely when their money was exhausted and there was no employment without credentials, they were herded into the only career open to them.

From these conditions, too, there arose another figure as often tragic as comic. The unmarried woman of marriageable age or more, in former times the honorable, at least harmless "spinster of this parish," becomes in life and in fiction that "odious creature, the old maid." As "Aunt Tabitha" she has a later chapter to herself; it is enough to say here that no way of life was honorable, was approved, was even tolerable for a woman but marriage. If she had not money enough to furnish a dowry for an advantageous marriage, she was lucky if it were enough to maintain her in an independent state of "genteel poverty." If not, the best she could hope for would be well-nigh intolerable dependence; to be a helpless burden on the hands of family or friends. Dowries must be ample, too, for men were scarce; the Civil War, the wars with Holland, the fighting in Scotland and Ireland, wars with France and wars in America had reduced the numbers of men at the very time when other conditions had reduced the price of women, and so the price of marriage went up. The nunneries were closed; there was no refuge in the cloister. The pattern of the Virgin Queen had long since passed from the throne and from the minds of men. Not all the preaching that the church could devote to the beauty of virginity could make the mature virgin in real life anything but a by-word and a scoffing.

"What channel had the customs of society left open to the industry of woman?" asks Mrs. Brunton's Ellen Percy. The question rises to a wail on the lips of Miss Burney's Juliet Granville (mentioned above as "the Wanderer" and "the fair Incognita"):

"How few," she cried, "how circumscribed, are the attainments of women! and how much fewer and more circumscribed still are those which may, in their consequences, be useful as well as ornamental, to the higher or educated class! those through which, in the reverses of fortune, a FEMALE may reap benefit without abasement! those which, while preserving her from pecuniary distress, will not aggravate the hardships or sorrows of her changed conditions, either by immediate humiliation, or by what, eventually, her connexions may consider as disgrace!"

"The higher or educated class!" What could Richardson's Clarissa Harlowe (1748) have done if she had escaped from the snares of Lovelace, cut off as she was from all hope of succor from her family? Her family was as we shall note later of the upper middle class, prosperous India merchants with country estates, but their tradition would not help her. Business was business, then as now, and a woman was only a woman. "Custom," says Defoe,

> Custom has made some trades not proper for the women to meddle in; such as linen and woollen-drapers, mercers, goldsmiths, all sorts of dealers by commission, and the like. Custom, I say, has made these trades so effectually to shut out the women, that what with custom and the women's generally thinking it below them, we never or rarely see any women in such shops or warehouses.

Here and in his comment on supercilious tradesmen's widows (p. 26) Defoe shows two of the obstacles. Few trades were customarily open to women; as a matter of fact there were only two, millinery and mantua-making. Into others, the only gate through which a woman could enter was matrimony. Despite the decreasing number, there were still enough women engaged in trade to make their inclusion necessary in all acts of Parliament dealing with bankruptcy. And it is the list of bankrupts published monthly in the *Gentleman's Magazine* that stands as one of the few sources of detailed information about women in business in the eighteenth century, furnishing better testimony to their courage and initiative than to their ability and success. In these lists for the period between 1731 and 1737 we find record of thirty-five women engaged in sixteen different trades. Eleven of these were engaged in the two trades recognized as proper for women, millinery and mantua-making. There were also five mercers, three distillers, two grocers, two weavers, two linen-drapers, a baker, a tallow-chandler, an upholsterer, a brewer, a clothier, a coffee-woman, a vintner, an innholder, a hosier, and, oddly, a dealer in lime. Without knowing anything about it, we guess that except for the milliners and mantua-makers these women were widows, that they would not have been in trade if they had not married into it. There is, however, one who is not so easily accounted for, one who was in partnership with a man whose name does not identify him as husband, son, or brother: "John Pack and Mary Field, of Gracechurch Street, London, Merchants." There are a dozen possible explanations, all guess-work and equally worthless; one of them is that Mary Field found another gate than matrimony through which to enter the field of business.

There were women in business in London, even in professions, whose success gave them distinction enough to make their deaths worth noting in the *Gentleman's Magazine*. There we learn of the "Mistress of the Great Lace Shop in Old Bond Street," who left a fortune of 19,000 pounds; the keeper of "the great China Warehouse in Exeter Change"; keeper of "the great India Warehouse in Leadenhall Street," who left ten thousand pounds, a fortune less in distinction than the fact that "Her Majesty, when Princess used to sup there on Masquerade Nights." Two instances at least give us a hint of what the poor girl could do with initiative and energy. Joan Dant, on the death of her husband, a weaver, became a pedlar, carrying an assortment of mercery, hosiery, and haberdashery on her back from house to house in London. When she had saved sufficient capital, she engaged in the wholesale trade, and at her death in 1715 was worth 9,000 pounds. Clarissa Harlowe, Ellen Percy, Juliet Granville, females of delicate sensibility, could of course have done no such thing. One pictures them going from door to door with their packs, trailed by amorous baronets and earls! Dorothy Petty would set them a better example.

The said *Dorothy* (who is the Daughter of a Divine of the Church of *England,* now deceas'd) did set up an *Insurance Office* on *Births, Mariages* and *Services,* in order thereby to serve the Publik, and get an honest Livelyhood for herself. . . . The said *Dorothy* had such

Success in her Undertaking, that more Claims were paid, and more Stamps us'd for Policies and Certificates in her Office than in all other the like Offices in *London* besides; which good Fortune was chiefly owing to the Fairness and Justice of her Proceedings in the said Business: for all the Money paid into the Office was entered in one Book, and all the Money paid out upon Claims was set down in another Book, and all People had Liberty to peruse both, so that there could not possibly be the least Fraud in the Management thereof.

But such an achievement calls for a fund of initiative, energy and self-confidence far beyond the command of the delicate languishers of the novels of sensibility.

Juliet Granville achieved an evening's success in an amateur theatrical performance, and her enemies circulated rumors that she belonged on the stage. The profession was practically the only one freely open to women; success in it won instantly recognition, honors and rewards equal to those which went to the men who succeeded. But Juliet was not up to it—just as well for her that her author would not mar her delicacy, was reserving her for the higher sphere of empty-headed gentility for which her intelligence, measured by spelling and punctuation, fitted her. Her incredible mismanagement of everything in which she acted for herself testifies that she was not a Bracegirdle, a Barry, an Oldfield. Mrs. Bracegirdle retired in 1707 and lived for forty years in comfort on her savings. Mrs. Barry reached her pinnacle a little earlier, and Mrs. Oldfield a little later; doubtless both reaped similar harvests if they were thrifty enough to store them. But Puritan and Cavalier had done the work between them; a woman could not touch the stage and not be defiled, in reputation if not in fact. It was no place for a genteel heroine.

To write for the stage was quite as bad. So far as we know, Mrs. Aphra Behn was the first woman to earn independence by writing. She wriggled into fame so adroitly that her trail is hard to follow; we are learning that her autobiographical data were written to sell, not for later historians to take seriously. But it is plain to see that in carrying out her resolution to earn her living by "the quill which was then hardly more respectable than the witches' broom-stick," she wrote with indefatigable industry, gained widespread recognition for both plays and novels, and that her path was beset with difficulties. If it is true that her success was due to the fact that she could write like a man, it is no less true that her chief obstacle was her sex—one passage from a preface testifies to both. She is speaking of *The Dutch Lover:*

Indeed that day 'twas Acted first, there comes me into the Pit, a long, lither, phlegmatick, white, ill-favour'd, wretched Fop, an Officer in Masquerade newly transported with a Scarf & Feather out of France, a sorry Animal that has nought else to shield it from the uttermost contempt of all mankind, but that respect which we afford to Rats and Toads, which though we do not well allow to live, yet when considered as a part of God's creation, we make honourable mention of them. A thing, Reader—but no more of such a smelt: This thing, I tell ye, opening that which serves it for a mouth, out issued such a noise as this to those that sate about it, that they were to expect a woful Play, God damn him, for 'twas a woman's.

Other women of the craft were Mary de la Rivière Manley, Susannah Centlivre, Laetitia Pilkington, and Eliza Haywood. Intrepidly they pioneered where Mrs. Behn had scouted. In an age of vitriolic political writing, Mrs. Manley competed creditably with the best of the men, and won applause from the most vitriolic of them all, Dean Swift himself. Her best sellers were in the field of titillating scandal. She had a heart of oak and the skin of a rhinoceros; no vituperation or reprisal could stop her. In another world the Wife of Bath clasps her joyously to an ample bosom as the true and longed-for vindicator of her sex:

> *By god, if wommen hadde writen stories,*
> *As clerkes han with-inne hir oratories,*
> *They wolde han writen of men more wikednesse,*
> *Than all the mark of Adam may redresse.*

Clarissa Harlowe was indeed a voluminous and a clever writer, but her heart was not of oak; it throbbed with sensibility, and her skin was aristocratically delicate. She might have hidden in an ivory tower to write sentimental novels, but she could hardly have faced a publisher with them. Not hers was the literary world of the Wife of Bath and the wife of Manley.

Clarissa, if she had had her living to earn, would doubtless have turned first as do all her sisters in fiction to the teaching of children. Ellen Percy in undertaking the task bewailed the lack of education. What she needed, if we are to believe the novelists, was the art of a sycophant; we know from other testimony (if we may believe our historians) that the higher learning had no earning power for a women. Elizabeth Elstob was truly a scholar; she numbered Anglo-Saxon among the eight languages besides her own of which she was mistress. Now after two centuries we remember her for her scholarship; in her time she taught little children.

Medicine and nursing were not gainful occupations for women in the eighteenth century. Both had long been within her range as part of her "domestic sphere"; nursing was so still, and therefore was not remunerative. Sir Charles Grandison gives us a short view of this situation as Richardson saw it in 1753. Sir Charles is advising his uncle to turn away the woman who has been serving him as both nurse and mistress, and to marry, because neither men-servants nor a hired female nurse would be tolerable. "Male nurses are unnatural creatures!" says Sir Charles. "(There is not such a character that can be respectable.) Women's sphere is the house, and their shining-place the sick-chamber, in which they can exert all their amiable, and, shall I say, lenient qualities? Marry, my lord, by all means." If this passage is, as it seems to be, the origin of the familiar line "woman's place is in the home," it is noteworthy, not only to find so familiar a line in a book which nobody reads, but to find it linked with the notion of the exclusion of men from a profession which set women on the threshold of another, medicine, which at the time Richardson wrote was considered as "unnatural" for them as was nursing for men. Medicine was even then emerging into the realm of science, and women were barred at the door; no medical school would admit them. Even in midwifery, long woman's inviolable mystery, they began to feel the lack of scientific training, though the general practitioner who took obstetrical work was more often than not contemptuously called the "man-midwife" in the fiction of the time. To the women midwives the danger of masculine competition, and the lack of training in themselves, became apparent, and they tried in vain to meet it. As early as 1687, Mrs. Elizabeth Cellier proposed to the King a scheme for a royal hospital and training course for midwives, but it came to nothing.

In quackery women reaped large rewards, but no heroine could have done it without exchanging her soul of delicacy for a spirit of three-ply brass. Katherine Daffy trumpeted the virtues of "Daffy's Famous Elixir Salutis," an opiate for troublesome children. She was a small operator as compared with Joanna Stephens who performed the unparalleled feat of making her "Medicine for the Stone" a national affair by act of Parliament. She began by the "testimonial racket," and sensational publicity stunts, such as ordering the body of one of her deceased patients opened to prove that he died of "erysiplatous" and not of the stone. Finally, to provide for her old age, she proposed "to make her Medicines for the Stone publick on Consideration of the sum of 5,000 pounds to be raised by Contribution, and lodg'd with Mr. Drummond, Banker." Within six months 1250 pounds had been contributed, generous as an expression of faith, but not enough money, so Parliament came forward with the passage of "An Act for providing a Reward (5,000 pounds) to Joanna Stephens, upon a proper Discovery to be made by her, for the use of the Publick of the Medicines prepar'd by her for the Cure of the Stone." To this the King gave his assent, 14 June, 1739. It was a masterpiece of alchemy, to change her brass into gold by act of Parliament.

Mrs. Mapp, the celebrated bonesetter of Epsom, rose higher in fame, and fell lower into poverty. In the summer of 1736 she performed such cures at Epsom that the town offered her a bonus of a hundred guineas to practice there a year. The *Gentleman's Magazine* published an article about her that sounds too much like an advertisement: "She has cured Persons who have been above 20 Years disabled and has given incredible relief in the most difficult Cases." And if a heroine is in want of a husband, here is an example for her; "The money she got procured her a husband; but he did not stay with her above a Fortnight; and then went off with 100 guineas." Indeed her personality might well prove more winning to the public than to a lover:

A Lady passing Kent-street in her Chariot towards the Borough, dressed in a Robe de Chambre, the People gave out she was a certain Woman of Quality from an Electorate in Germany, whereupon a great Mob followed, and bestowed on her many bitter Reproaches, till Madam perceiving some Mistake, look'd out and accosted them in this familiar Manner, *D—n your Bloods, don't you know me! I am Mrs. Mapp the Bone-setter.* Upon which they suddenly chang'd their Revilings into loud Huzzas.

Her dauntless spirit and reputed cures won her more good-humored notoriety than respect; she was represented on the stage and sung in a ballad, but a year and a half after her first appearance at Epsom she died "so poor that the Parish were forced to bury her." The example might set Moll Flanders to thinking; it would set Clarissa to shuddering.

The examples of Joan Dant and Dorothy Petty, however, might give Pamela and Clarissa food for serious thought. These two business women met masculine difficulties realistically, instead of conjuring up "Female Difficulties" and fainting at the sight of them.

How mighty . . . are the DIFFICULTIES with which a FEMALE has to struggle! Her honour always in danger of being assailed, her delicacy of being offended, her strength of being exhausted, and her virtue of being calumniated! Yet even DIFFICULTIES such as these are not insurmountable, where mental courage, operating through patience, prudence, and principle, supply physical force, combat disappointment, and keep the untamed spirits superior to failure, and ever alive to hope.

These are the closing lines of Fanny Burney's *The Wanderer,* the subtitle of which is FEMALE DIFFICULTIES. The mental courage by which the heroine surmounts them is a feeble type of passive resistance, flight, and sheer luck. There is no physical force, and if the spirit is untamed, it is because it was never wild. "Her honour always in danger of being assailed,"—go and tell it to Joan Dant! "Her delicacy of being offended,"—try that on Dorothy Petty; she was a parson's daughter. Female honor and female delicacy—"the Gobble-uns'll git yu if yu don't watch out." —There is the whole built-up theory of female helplessness in the face of FEMALE DIFFICULTIES on which the commercial success of Joan and Dorothy cast an "oblique light." Ironically enough it was as we have seen commercial success that built it up, the rise of capitalism that floated women up into the leisure and the helpless class where many of them wanted to be, and others must be except the few with intelligence, initiative and energy, plus, perhaps, a realistic view of life and not too many inhibitions. The fate against which women in life, and in fiction struggled in the eighteenth century was to them truly "unrelated causes," a shaping destiny of economic forces working through conventions of society on human character. The Helpless Female was shaped by the forces that were shaping civilization. Just as inevitably as selection and environment mold biological characteristics, so the forces we have been tracing molded the legacy of Pamela to her daughters and granddaughters, the sentimental heroines of the eighteenth century, and the Victorian ones of the nineteenth. Certain physical, mental and moral traits become artificially female, others, more or less antithetical, are male. Delicacy, sensibility, chastity, these three (and the greatest of these is chastity), such are the canonical virtues of Pamela's daughters for a century and a half after Pamela. We shall trace somewhat of their history and their effects in later chapters; here we note them as the constituents of the soft tissue of the helpless female—she has no back-bone. Delicacy, physical, mental and moral, becomes so essentially female that it develops into feebleness in all three categories. Mental delicacy points to spelling and punctuation as intellectual achievement and dictates the concealment of any higher powers if they exist. Moral delicacy prevents a girl from receiving money if she has so far transgressed as to earn it. With this powerful equipment of feebleness she must defend her priceless chastity. If the villain tries to violate it, she must not violate her delicacy by slapping his face; if the villain pursues her, she must not show either speed or endurance in her flight. Delicacy holds her helpless; chastity must be defended. It is an unfailing dilemma, good for five volumes of sorrows in the hands of any delicate authoress.

For delicate the authoress always is; what can she do, poor girl, any more than her heroine? If she were a Mrs. Behn, she would write spicy plays. If she were a Mrs. Bracegirdle, she would act them. If she were a Joan Dant or a Dorothy Petty, she would not be writing sentimental novels for a living. In her tower she looks in her glass and weaves her web; the glass shows FEMALE DIFFICULTIES besetting every path outside. What can the poor girl do?

CHAPTER III

THE IMPORTANCE OF BEING A PRUDE

Trip upon trenchers and dance upon dishes,
My mother has sent me to gather some balm.
She bade me go lightly and come again quickly,
For fear that the young men should do me some harm.

To the twentieth century reader, nothing is more characteristic
of the novel of the former age—any of its former ages, from that
of Anne through that of Victoria—than the tendency of the
heroine to go lightly for fear that the young men should do her
some harm. Of this sort of heroine, Pamela is the prototype in
so far as she is memorable mainly for her heroic effort to prevent
a particular young man from doing her a specific harm. In this
attitude she stands as the literary ancestress of a generation of
prudes. But in the beginning she is not a prude, however important she may have found it later to become one. She shows
as a servant among servants, and as a lady among ladies, and
Richardson shades her development nicely from the one station
in life to the other. As a servant, she has enough freedom of
speech and action with her fellows to make her realistically
one of them, and enough effect of her superior education to give
her the exact degree of distinction from them that Richardson
wanted her to have. She is a shade above them in restraint of
speech, but she has no false modesty about undressing with them.
She has just so much more of "delicacy" that they call her
"purity" when she shows it, and suggest affectation in her conduct—"You are a nonesuch, I suppose." What she needs beyond
that, she assumes as she goes along through the middle class
to the borders of gentility, but she uses it easily; it does not

43

hamper her motions nor block her path. But it cramps her daughters at every turn. Like corsets, high heels, and long trains, it hampers the freedom of every move. In most of the novels after *Pamela,* the fear of "indelicacy" rises as an obstacle second in importance only to economic difficulties. The reasons for this are various and widely scattered, but they fit together to form a curious chapter in social history.

Lexicographers find their earliest citations of the words *indelicate* and *indelicacy* in the works of Sir Richard Steele and Samuel Richardson. They could not possibly have had more appropriate godfathers. Have they disappeared from our vocabularies? Between the early eighteenth and early twentieth centuries, they have denoted and connoted a wide variety of infractions of the code of propriety. Pope's Belinda (not Maria Edgeworth's) might have used them for anything that would "stain her honour or her new brocade." They applied most usually to minor improprieties in matters which indirectly or remotely suggested sex, but often applied to other improprieties, very much as in major lapses the word *honor* would cover either sort of offense. Hear, for example, the wail of Juliet, the fair Incognita of Fanny Burney's *The Wanderer* (1814):

". . . how insufficient," she exclaimed, "is a FEMALE to herself! How utterly dependent upon situation—connexions—circumstance! how nameless, how forever fresh-springing are her DIFFICULTIES, when she would owe her existence to her own exertions! Her conduct is criticised, not scrutinized; her character is censured, not examined; her labours are unhonoured, and her qualifications are but lures to ill-will! Calumny hovers over her head, and slander follows her footsteps!"

The occasion for this complaint is the fact that she has too much "delicacy" to try to collect money that is due her for giving music lessons to young ladies. Even when she does get the money, she doesn't like it; her delicacy is as much offended in having it as in lacking it:

However respectable reason and justice render pecuniary emolument, where honorably earned, there is something indefinable which stands between spirit and delicacy, that makes the first reception of money in detail, by those not brought up to gain it, embarrassing and painful.

Here the delicacy is the offense to assumed aristocracy of dealing with money in the bourgeois fashion, "in detail." It is an offense to "honor." Both words, *delicacy* and *honor* would apply to another situation of Juliet's. She has to forego an important trip to France because she learns that her admirer has already taken passage on the very ship on which she must sail. Here the inhibition is remotely connected with sex. We might call any of the three "false modesty," and would be sure to differentiate the last as *prudery*. As a working definition, let us take *prudery* to mean, false delicacy, false modesty, false feeling, hypocrisy, pretense of feeling, any word, phrase, action or attitude dictated by convention or fashion rather than real feeling, about sex, nudity, various parts of the body and their functions, and about words denoting or ever so remotely suggesting any of these. This last type we may set off as *verbal prudery*. Prudery is the attempt to abolish all difficulties and all uncomfortable situations by pretending that they don't exist. For purposes of this discussion, let us call Juliet's embarrassment about money "false delicacy," and her refusal to sail on the same ship with her admirer, prudery.

Prudery is the pretense of perfect virtue. When delicacy was synonymous with virtue, prudery was the imitation of delicacy. When delicacy was the fashion, one wore it whether it fitted or not, and it became necessary to distinguish between mere delicacy, and "real," "true," or "natural" delicacy. When practitioners of free manners boasted delicacy, they called those of the stricter code prudes. The precisians, then, must needs call attention to trade-marks and formulae, and advertise the fact that no imitation is just as good, but lacks the peculiar virtues of the original. This is admirably illustrated in the novels of Mrs. Anne Hughes, *Caroline,* 1787, and *Henry and Isabella,* 1788. The heroine of *Henry and Isabella,* who is known as Juliana until the wicked nurse confesses, "though possessed of the truest refinement of heart and sentiment, had little of that false delicacy which represents sincerity as a breach of refinement." A Peer who is struck by her beauty inquires about her from a rival belle who seeks to discourage him by detraction:

No doubt she has a great many lovers, (said the Peer:) not one that I know of (answered his informer;) she's so extremely prudish, that she frights them all away. Then she is fonder of books than men, (said his Lordship, smiling.) She has seen nothing of the world, (replied Miss Mordant) and her notions, and sentiments upon many occasions are as whimsical and oldfashioned, as if she had lived before the flood: and among others I have heard her say, that she thinks it very wrong, and inconsistent with the character of a woman of true delicacy and honour, to have more than one professed admirer at a time. Oh, most Gothic indeed, (cried Lord Belford) where could she acquire such uncommon ideas?

Caroline, too, was well brought up by her clerical father, whose "former knowledge of the world enabled him to distinguish dignity from pretence, and levity from wit. He well knew what propriety required from the female character," so we may take his little homily at its face value:

It is not surprising, my love, (said he,) that you should be deceived by the mask with which politeness endeavours to cover the face of licentiousness. A well-bred woman will always in her public conduct imitate the manners of a virtuous one: for, nothing is in its own nature so vulgar as vice. But there is no companion more dangerous, to an innocent and unsuspecting mind . . . For when the barrier of delicacy is broken down, which may justly be said to divide the boundaries of virtue and vice, what bad consequences may not be feared?

This exhibits the very hypocrisy in conventional morality and behavior which since Victoria has been scorned as Victorian, and provides a figure of speech in the definition of delicacy, a barrier between virtue and vice, which displays its utility as an obstacle in fiction. Throughout the novel, Caroline's sincere virtue is not mentioned as delicacy without the qualifying adjective. Her dignity on an occasion was "not the effect of affectation, but of real delicacy." When toward the end of Volume III Sir William Beaumont offers his hand, his heart, and his princely fortune, "her whole behaviour was such as, without the shadow of infringement upon the strictest delicacy, informed him of her esteem and approbation. He . . . was treated with openness and delicate sincerity . . ." Delicacy, we perceive, is like "eggs," "fresh eggs," and "strictly fresh eggs." The distinction applies even to Caroline's meals, "nothing could be more truly delicate than her repast." Money matters are on much the same footing. After her father's death, an old friend of his arranges her affairs. "He then, with the utmost delicacy, inquired if she had any commands with him in the character of her banker." This comes midway in the age of delicacy in the novel (which was also the age of sensibility). It was midway in the long reign of George III, "Farmer George," whose court stood for coarse manners which the press coarsely caricatured. It was a bourgeois monarch, a bourgeois court, a ruling class whose wealth and power had turned them from puritanism to a coarse indulgence that suggests caricature of aristocratic manners. The situation typified by the Launcelot-Guinevere intrigue of high romance had come down in life. In the comedy of the Restoration the shop-keeper and his wife played Arthur and Guinevere to the Launcelot of a Harry Wildair. The trial of Queen Caroline brings it dangerously near the police court. Meanwhile, on its high standard, the white flag of "real delicacy" fluttered bravely in the novel!

The history of modesty is significant social history. The modesty of English women, true, false, and non-existent, has a significant history in the English novel for the last two hundred years. It extends from Pamela who blushed over a pair of stockings when her master gave them to her, through a long line of those who turned green and yellow rather than tell their love, to Mona Milton, a model of 1920, who pounded on the hero's locked door screaming, "Make me a woman!" The fact that these two extremes, almost incredible circumspection and almost incredible frankness, come at the chronological extremes of the history of the English novel, does not mean that the scale is evenly graded between them, nor yet that the novel is a faithful indicator of every fluctuation throughout the period. It is, however, if we can read it for what it is worth, an interesting indicator of acknowledged or advocated standards.

Of all Pamela's daughters, the one most molded by prudery is the god-daughter of Victoria. The coefficient of Victorian prudery is the coefficient of Victorian fiction in the mind of the modern reader. Twentieth-century scorn of nineteenth-century manners rests on the charge of insincerity. Mention the attempt to abolish difficulties, particularly the problems of sex, by pretending that they do not exist, and your hearer of later times will name it Victorianism. He has in mind a pattern of the Victorian heroine that to him is as absurd as a fashion plate of the former age. If you elicit his impressions and piece them together you can make a mosaic portrait of the type. In the beginning, before her lover comes, she is unawakened, virginal as virginity itself. She is at one and the same time as sexless as a china doll and as feminine as a practised coquette. Her innocence is really abysmal ignorance, but the effect of it is the same as that of the completest sophistication and circumspection. She is perpetually on guard against evils of which she cannot know anything, alertly sensitive to acts, words, implications which could not conceivably have any significance to her; their danger she is supposed to recognize by instinct. She is irreparably damaged if anyone sees an inch of her skin beyond the orthodox limits of exposure. She is of the tribe of St. Pierre's Virginie (1788) who perishes in a shipwreck rather than strip to swim ashore. There is no evidence that she is anything but a head and a pair of hands attached at appropriate places to a costume. If under the costume there are any bodily organs but a heart, we never hear of their functioning. When food passes her lips, it passes into oblivion. After a shipwreck, she can survive for weeks, the only woman in an open boat with a crew of sailors, suffering everything except the suppression of her excretory necessities or the suppression of her modesty to relieve them. She is armored in clothes and chastity. Of the chastity we hear much; of the clothes, none are mentioned but those we see, save in times of swooning a whisper of her stays. When her lover comes, she is still virginal, but in such a state of mind and feeling that in an instant and at a word she can change from fancy free to pure unalterable passion. Her word of betrothal is as irrevocable as a marriage vow. Her love is deep and ineradicable, but it is all of the spirit and nothing of the body, for she has no body. In her ball dress she may show us that her "bosom is faultlessly moulded," but the rest is silence. We infer that she might nourish children, but know no possibility of her conceiving or bearing them. That she might have any sexual feeling is unthinkable. That even in married life she has any sexual experience is not hinted. It is true that between the last two chapters of volume three she has managed to produce three or four fine children, but no one could guess how she did it, for it takes place discreetly off-stage, and bears no more relation to life than do similar episodes in the lives of other saints.

Obviously enough, this is not the portrait of a real woman, and it cannot be drawn from the pages of novelists whose women are real. Many figures of Dickens might have posed for it in one attitude or another, but practically none in Thackeray, though careless readers might nominate Amelia Sedley. It is not found in any approach to entirety in the works of Trollope, Mrs. Gaskell, or George Eliot. One by one the items are there, but to pluck them out of the living figures and put them together would not make so much as an authentic corpse. To Hardy and Meredith this figure is almost unknown. An artist who speaks widely to all time speaks but narrowly to his own. The novelist who reflects in most detail the fashion of today is out of fashion tomorrow. This outmoded heroine, then, we find in her entirety only in the faded pages of such novelists as Dinah Maria Mulock, Mary E. Braddon, Grace Aguilar, George Alfred Lawrence, and a host of others of lesser note. We call her Victorian because we find her in nineteenth century novels and not in novels of the eighteenth century or of the twentieth century. We do not find her in eighteenth century novels because we do not read them, or read only the ones that do not exhibit her. In so far as Richardson, Fielding, Smollett and Sterne speak to us today, it is because their characters are human beings rather than fashion-plates. But in the ephemeral novel we can find this "Victorian" heroine begotten and conceived with the novel itself, and of full stature before Victoria was born.

Nothing illustrates this fact better than the history in the novel of the first principle of prudery, that where innocence is ignorance 'tis criminal to be wise, or what you don't know won't hurt you. When this was the guiding principle, the best armor for the protection of maiden purity was supposed to be a stout pair of stays and complete ignorance of the nature of chastity and all its enemies. Virginity seemed no less of the mind than of the body. Its delicacy was such that if a girl so much as knew she had it, it was tarnished, and if she knew more, it was gone. Many there are who think so still for reasons that have not changed in two centuries. Other reasons there are which have changed— or have they only changed their costumes? In the time of Pamela, the principle of ignorance seems the outgrowth of a society in which the girl is thought of as a small body of virtue completely surrounded by wickedness, and the type situation is that of the middle- or working-class girl besieged by aristocratic rakes. Here and there is a male who is not sexually predatory, but there are not enough to go round for all the novels, much less for all the girls. The best the girl has to hope for, the art she is trained to practise, is to stand them off as best she can in general until she can marry one in particular. Such was Pamela's situation. She defended it with her "virtue" which had its "reward" in successful marriage. For half a century or more her ethics were unchallenged; then, about 1800, Mrs. Barbauld suggested that Pamela's standards were not set high enough. "It is difficult," she says, "to imagine how a young woman of so much purity of mind should feel her affections engaged to a man during a series of the grossest attempts upon her virtue." The plain fact is that Pamela did love the man whether she "ought" to have done so or not, and artlessly saw no reason why she should not marry him when the time came—and no one who reads the book attentively can doubt that she would have done so quite as readily had he been a footman or a beggar.

If Pamela had read *The Tatler,* she might have found a counsel of perfection, for the standard had been raised nearly a hundred years before Mrs. Barbauld, namely, on June 25th, 1709, in the 33d *Tatler,* in a narrative supplied by "Mrs. Jenny Distaff, half-sister to Mr. Bickerstaff." It is the story of a subtle attempt of an aristocratic rake foiled by the direct appeal of simple innocence. The counsel comes in the last paragraph:

This Nobleman has since frequently made his addresses to me with honour; but I have as often refused them; as well knowing that familiarity and marriage will make him, on some ill-natured occasion, call all I said in the arbour a theatrical action. Besides that, I glory in contemning a man, who had thoughts to my dishonour. If this method were the imitation of the whole Sex, innocence would be the only dress of beauty; and all affectation by any other arts to please the eyes of men would be banished to the stews for ever. The conquest of passion gives ten times more happiness than we can reap from the gratification of it; and she, that has got over such a one as mine, will stand among Beaux and Pretty Fellows, with as much safety as in a summer's day among grasshoppers and butterflies.

But Pamela did not read the back numbers of *The Tatler,* and remained in ignorance of her misdemeanor. She did not feel called upon to remain unmarried in order to set the rakes in their place and set an example to affronted chastity.

The first heroine who emerges (there may be others hidden in the dust of time) with a reason for refusing the rake is Lucy Wellers, who has the title rôle in an anonymous novel ("by a lady") of 1754. It is one of the tribe of serving-maid novels which is said to have followed *Pamela,* but it has this important variation on the theme, that when the gentlemanly rake who has attempted Lucy's virtue finds her irresistible and offers her marriage, she refuses him on a shrewd calculation of factors not altogether ethical:

The baronet's proposition was a tempting one to a young person situated as she was; and seemed to offer a state of affluence, far beyond her most sanguine expectations. She was for some time engaged in the advantages accruing from such a match. Here was a large fortune, a title, and what the world esteems a fine gentleman, courting her acceptance on terms which virtue did not forbid. Yet, did not all these allurements prevent her from reflecting upon the ignominious treatment she had received from the proposer. She considered, that the affections of a heart so accustomed to deceit and so enslaved by violent passions, could never be expected to fix on any one object for a long time; and consequently did not merit such a return as she should be inclined to make to the man whose name she should wear.

She imagined he might be willing in the present gust of his passion, to make her his wife; but, as his whole conduct on this occasion, had proved that her person alone had excited that passion; (which reflection to a young lady of her delicacy, afforded no favourable idea of it) she reflected of how short a duration that affection must be which was built on so precarious a foundation . . . if he should grow cool, which was to be expected . . . he might impute her resistance

Heath's "Book of Beauty," 1844   *Miss Sandys*

THE LASS WITH THE DELICATE AIR

"The sylphid elegance of spheral beauty"

formerly to mercenary motives, and call it a stratagem to draw him into a marriage.

This thought was insupportable to her; and her understanding suggested that in that case, she must lead a life of misery, for which no fortune, however affluent, could compensate. She then called to mind . . . Mr. Godfrey; and . . . thought there was a much fairer prospect of happiness with a man of his morals and character, though his circumstances were so far inferior to those of the baronet. And . . . she led a very easy life where she was, and had an assurance . . . of a provision during her life, . . . that she thought with economy might support her with peace of mind, which she preferred to a splendid outside, and a heart full of misery.

It is worth noting, too, that when she refuses the baronet, she tells him that if he had offered marriage in the first place, she would have accepted, for at that time she thought well of him. As it was, the considerations which led to her refusal were more hedonistic than ethical; she might have had baronet, title and fortune "on terms which virtue did not forbid."

Ophelia Lenox, in Sarah Fielding's *The History of Ophelia* (1760), faces a similar problem without so much worldly wisdom as had Lucy Wellers to apply to its solution. Ophelia is a child of nature before Rousseau. She is of the same age as Rousseau's Julie (1760), but not a twin, for on the Welsh border of England, it would seem, "nature" is more puritanical than it is in Switzerland. Ophelia is a feminine companion piece to the author's David Simple of sixteen years before. Her aunt, who in her day has had bitter experience with the perfidy of man, has brought her up to her sixteenth or seventeenth year in complete retirement, complete "natural" virtue and sensibility, and complete ignorance of the ways of the world. Lord Dorchester, a sentimentalist who plays the part of the rake, captures her and carries her away from all this. For his own purposes he keeps her in ignorance of sex and all its influences on human behavior in the world of polite society, and introduces her gradually to society's other customs. The author sustains this situation beyond all limits of credibility until she has reviewed the fashionable world, greatly to its discredit, through the eyes of her child of nature, much as she did in *David Simple*. Then she awakens Ophelia to the cruel truth, whereupon Ophelia escapes and hides from Lord Dorchester, to whom she is deeply devoted, innocently thinking her attachment is deep friendship. Dorchester soon finds her in her hiding-place, and sincerely offers her marriage, which she refuses.

"That I love you," I replied, "I am much too well convinced by painful Experience; but you have so forfeited my Esteem, that I cannot comply with your Proposal. I could not be happy if I was married to you, consequently should not make you so. Your Passion for me is the same it was, . . . you would find your mistake too late, after we were both made Sacrifices to the Deception. I have lost all my Confidence in you . . ."

This argument is like Lucy Wellers' except that happiness seems to depend more directly on virtue.

I was fortified by the full Belief that I could not be happy with one so defective in his Principles, on the Goodness of which must depend the felicity of all those small Societies; as Esteem is a necessary Foundation for a lasting Love: I could not believe this Change in him arose from an Amendment of Heart, but from Despair of Success in his former Schemes, and was convinced it would therefore be Madness to unite myself, for Life, with one who had no better Motive; for no Suffering can equal that of being married to a Man of whom one has a bad Opinion.

Dorchester persuades a lady whose virtue is genuine enough, but more realistic than Ophelia's to intercede for him. Her argument sounds an early note of Victorianism.

. . . that I ought not to expect consummate Virtue among a degenerate People; that it was scarcely possible to find a Man who had any Scruples in Regard to his Behavior to Women. . . . Men of the best Characters . . . esteemed Matrimony as entirely a political Institution . . . She told me how much I ought to allow for the Force of Custom and Education; these had both tended to make him [Dorchester] look on Chastity as a very small Virtue, for that it was made the Subject of Ridicule in such Men as were possessed of it.

But natural virtue cannot be misled by worldly virtue.

I should be deficient in Sincerity, were I not to confess that Miss *Baden's* Persuasions a little staggered my Resolution. . . . But I soon became sensible that this was the Dictate of my Passion. Bad Examples and pernicious Habits, had, in a Degree, perverted Miss *Baden;* the Frequency of Vice had deadened her Sense of it; but I had no such Excuse; Custom had not confounded my Ideas of Right and Wrong, and therefore to have united myself with a Person whom I knew guilty of Vice, was, in a Degree, to become vicious; . . . and to put ourselves in a Situation that must hazard our Integrity, is a great Proof that it is not at that Time sufficiently strong.

Nevertheless, that is just what Ophelia does in the end. Dorchester appeals to the high-minded aunt, who reads him a long lecture on his sins (which, if any, have been committed off-stage, except for the kidnapping of Ophelia). This he bears so meekly that she is convinced that he is going to be good, so she hands over the immaculate Ophelia, with a recommendation to mercy.

Can you do less, my Lord, than reward *Ophelia's* Love and my Compassion, by preserving the Principles you now profess, and by keeping the strictest Guard over yourself, lest you should again deviate from the Path of Virtue? I know you are not absolutely a Rake, and therein I place my Hopes.

No, he is not absolutely a rake, and therein lies the lame and impotent conclusion of the tale. No doubt this weak surrender would have incurred Mrs. Barbauld's censure if she had deigned to notice it.

Again in 1760, Charlotte Lennox approaches the goal but does not arrive. Her Henrietta, in the novel of that name, is tormented by the unwelcome attentions of Lord B—— who offers to make her his mistress at a time when she, though the granddaughter of an earl, is lady's-maid to the merchant's daughter to whom Lord B—— is engaged. Of course she repulses him, and suffers the calumny and hardship usual in such cases. At length, when he thinks she will be an heiress after all (as any moron might perceive she would be when Mrs. Lennox had filled her three volumes), he makes her an offer of marriage. Even before this she and her confidante discuss the possibility:

"But surely, my dear," said Mrs. Willis, "your gratitude would be engaged, should Lord B——, in the present inequality of your circumstances, make you an offer of his hand."

"Not at all," replied Henrietta with some warmth: "no man has a right to the love or esteem of a woman on whom he 'has entertained dishonourable designs, and, failing in them, offers marriage at last. The lover, who marries his mistress only because he cannot gain her upon easier terms, has just as much generosity as the highwayman who leaves a traveller in possession of his money, because he is not able to take it from him."

"Well, well, my dear miss," said Mrs. Willis, smiling, "I can collect this at least from the nice distinctions you make, that your heart is absolutely free; you would not reason so well, were there any secret passion in the case."

Probably not. Ophelia was in love with the rake and married him; Henrietta is not in love with the rake and refuses him. Clearly we have not yet a test case, though Henrietta makes a generalization that comes near to a formulation of the principle which the later moralists emphasize.

It was in the year 1792 that the great principle blazed upon the waiting world—unless some watcher of the moral skies whose voice is still unheard saw it earlier. In 1792 Charlotte Palmer wrote of "the mischief of that enticing book *Clarissa*," the sentence quoted above on p. 7. It was in 1792 that Charlotte Smith (one grows giddy trying to sort the Charlottes, real and fictitious, of this decade) wrote of *Pamela* and *Clarissa* in *Desmond*:

In regard to novels, I cannot help remarking another strange inconsistency, which is, that the great name of Richardson (and great it certainly deserves to be), makes, by a kind of hereditary prescriptive deference, those scenes, those descriptions, pass uncensured in Pamela and Clarissa, which are infinitely more improper for the perusal of young women, than any that can be found in the novels of the present day; of which, indeed, it may be said, that, if they do no good, they do no harm; . . .

Thus the modest Charlottes fly their shafts at Richardson without scoring on Mrs. Barbauld's tally-sheet, for they find no fault with either heroine either for marrying or not marrying the rake. It is Mrs. Jane West, still in 1792, who lays down the law fully and explicitly. The principle really was not so new as it may have seemed. Mrs West might have got it from Jenny Distaff's letter in *The Tatler;* Steele may have slyly distilled it from the *Lysistrata* of Aristophanes; but it looks toward the generally accepted theory that a "nice" girl will not marry a man who is not as "nice" as herself, particularly if he has demonstrated his character by attempting her virtue. If Mrs. West is, as she seems to be, the first to declare this explicitly, she is the mother of the code for which Victoria stands sponsor, and it was born in 1792. Mrs. West's novel is *The Advantages of Education, or the History of Maria Williams.* The mother of the heroine is a model mother, a model of Mrs. West's own invention, made according to exact specifications for an exact purpose, which is to bring up a daughter whose upbringing shall prevent her from falling a victim to the gentleman-seducer. Mrs. Williams herself made the mistake of marrying the man who had tried to gain her without marriage, and she "educates" her daughter to avoid the mistake to which she owes her existence. Maria has discovered the perfidy of Sir Henry Neville. "Never," she exclaims,

"Never shall affluence and felicity court me to his nuptials. Nay, did he entreat my pardon, and in the most solemn manner attest his penitence, I would abjure and hate him!"
Mrs. Williams . . . applauded her resolution, and strengthened it by observing that marriage with a man whom we ceased to esteem, was a horrid act of solemn perjury.

"Guilt," said she, "is often so atrocious as to suppose that the innocence which it fails to subvert, ought to be its reward; but a woman possessed of moral principle—I should use a higher term— of religious hope, will be cautious how she risks sentiments to her- self so dear, by a permanent connexion with one who proves himself the enemy of virtue. If she can so far forgive her intended seducer as to marry him, the world may justly attribute her resistance to pride and cunning rather than to virgin purity; . . ."

This reminds us of Lucy Wellers in so far as the decision is made on the basis of the girl's individual happiness, but Mrs. West tries to put it on a higher plane by the pious rolling of the eyes toward heaven, the suggestion that it involves eternal happi- ness. Lucy Wellers feared that the man who desired only her person would soon tire of it; Mrs. Williams thinks that a girl of genuine virtue could not be happy with a man who has demon- strated that he had none. She puts it in the form of a generaliza- tion, a principle, and elevates it by the mention of religious hope. Mrs. West is a puritan—evidence that she is so appears in a later chapter—but she leaves the duty of propaganda to her successors, notably Mrs. Hofland and Miss Edgeworth.

Regina Maria Roche is more romantic and less puritanic. She seems to listen to the sirens rather than to the "stern Daughter of the Voice of God." The chaste Amanda, heroine of *The Children of the Abbey,* 1796, rejects with scorn Lord Mortimer's proposition to make her his mistress. Her scorn shows him his mistake, and he seeks opportunity for "explanation," but she considers the affront reason enough for rejecting his honorable advances for the period of six pages, after which she receives his apologies and reinstates him in her favor, and if they are not married for five hundred pages more, it is not this early affront that keeps them apart.

Five years later, virtue seems more forbidding, and a girl who would marry a rake must save her face by a Victorian appearance of ignorance. In Maria Edgeworth's *Belinda,* 1801, Belinda Port-

man and her fashionable mentor Lady Delacour, are convinced, as
is the reader also, that Belinda's leading suitor, Clarence Hervey,
is keeping a mistress. Lady Delacour gives her advice:

> Do not look so shocked, my dear . . . I congratulate you . . .
> that the thing is no worse—it is all in rule and in course—when a
> man marries, he sets up new equipages, and casts off old mistresses;
> or if you like to see the thing as a woman of sentiment rather than
> as a woman of the world, here is the prettiest opportunity for your
> lover's making a sacrifice . . . consider, as no one knows this naughty
> thing but ourselves, we are not called upon to bristle up our morality,
> and the most moral ladies in the world do not expect men to be as
> moral as themselves: so we may suit the measure of our external
> indignation to our real feelings. . . . I advise you to *d'aller votre
> train* with Clarence, without seeming to suspect him in the least;
> there is nothing like innocence in these cases, my dear: but I know
> . . . that you would sooner die the death of the sentimental—than
> follow my advice.

Later on, Lady Delacour asks Belinda about another lover who
is then in her favor, "Would you, if you discovered that Mr.
Vincent had a mistress, discard him forever from your thoughts?"
Belinda replies, "If I discovered that he had deceived and behaved
dishonourably to any woman, I certainly should banish him forever from my regard." Indeed, she does banish him for less than
that; she dismisses him when she discovers that he is addicted to
gambling.

Lady Delacour does not represent Miss Edgeworth's ethics,
but she does represent very accurately what the twentieth century
calls Victorian in the hypocrisy of the middle-class code. Its ideal
is represented by Belinda herself, and it is explicitly set forth as
a code of ethics by the sturdy moralists of such novels as *Integrity,
Self Control, Discipline, Decision, Fortitude, Self Denial.* In Mrs.
Brunton's *Self Control* (1811), the heroine, Laura Montreville,
is as deeply in love with the gentlemanly rake, Col. Hargrave, as
is Pamela or Clarissa, but she resists him as heroically as Pamela,
no less after than before he seeks her in marriage, and rebukes her

fashionable mentor (a necessary tool to the moralizing novelist) for urging her to accept him. She completely conquers her love, and resists Col. Hargrave to the day of his death. Emily Shelburne in Mrs. Hofland's *Integrity* (1824) refuses a highly eligible offer from a man who had designs on her while she was in the depths of poverty. The fact is made occasion for a complete exposition of the duty of a girl in Emily's position, or Pamela's, in the form of an argument of several pages between Lady Julia, Emily's fashionable mentor who, of course, urges the marriage, and her husband, Sir Joshua. Lady Julia sums up:

". . . though it is a wrong thing, a *very* wrong thing, for men to be guilty in the way they are, yet what can be done? We cannot shut our door on such people, without absolutely excluding all society . . . what can a woman do?"

"Julia! Julia!" cried Sir Joshua in great emotion, "do not allow these shallow reasons so to impose upon your understanding; you know perfectly well, that in the present situation of society, women can do everything. The selfish libertine who bends to no principle . . . would yet shrink from the frown of a woman of fashion, nor dare to intrude in the pure circle with which she may always surround herself. Much has been done of late years, by which, as a people, our vices are rendered less obtrusive; but much remains to do, and, in my opinion, women, who from their personal attractions, rank, and fortune, have become leaders in society, have an awful duty to perform . . . It is theirs . . . to distinguish between him who honours their sex (and the laws which protect its weakness), and *him* who, in injuring one, degrades you all.

Here we find expressed and implied the theory and practice of the Victorian code. You ought not to marry a man who has behaved dishonorably to yourself or any woman. But "the most moral ladies do not expect men to be as moral as themselves." They must, then, demand what they do not expect. The expectation is that at least nine hundred and ninety-nine men do "behave dishonorably." If you enforce the demand, your chance of marriage is incalculably slight, practically nil. You can't abjure marriage; therefore you preach the demand and practise the expectation. When "no one knows the naughty thing" no one is called on to "bristle up her morality." Proclaim virtue and shut your eyes to evil. Prudery is pretence of perfect virtue. The importance of being a prude is that it gains you a chance of marriage.

The striking fact is that this code is the one we call Victorian when we look back at it from the beginning of the twentieth century, whereas if we look at it from the beginning of the eighteenth century we seem to owe it to Sir Richard Steele. The so-called "Victorian compromise" was not, in truth, uncompromisingly Victorian. It was the offspring of William and Mary, ushered into the world by Sir Richard Steele, wet-nursed by Queen Victoria, and baptised by Gilbert K. Chesterton. The quarrel which it compromised was long and bitter. Not long before Steele's time it had been open war; a king had been beheaded, and a commoner had ruled the kingdom. That time there was no quarter and no compromise. There was less bloodshed a decade later when the King came back, but still no compromise. "The Cavalier Parliament," says the historian, "was less anxious than the King for a compromise. Scarcely had it met when it made a savage attack on the Puritans and their religion." The next turn, the Revolution of 1688, was bloodless. It brought to the throne the head of an ancient and princely house, but he came immediately from a nation of thrifty burghers. Anyone who had enough of the goodwill of both parties to come to the throne at that time without bloodshed was in himself a middle term, a compromise. William was a royal gentleman, but he did not pretend to hold a warrant from God to pursue his pleasure at the expense of the proletariat. On the contrary, he disapproved of such manners, and tried to put them down, not puritanically by the edge of the sword, but royally by proclamation and legally by act of Parliament. Here is the real beginning of the compromise which Mr. Chesterton names Victorian for its most illustrious practitioner.

It might well be named for Steele, its most illustrious propagator. He lived it and wrote it in all his life and all his work, for his conscience was as lively as his heart. As a young officer of the Guards, he loved the revelry of his aristocratic comrades, as they loved his vivacity and wit. "These frequent scenes of revelry and mirth were, however, on the part of Steele intermingled with the most galling reflections on his weakness and folly, on his perpetual waste of talents and of time." So says his pious biographer, Nathan Drake, and continues:

To render the hours of contrition and repentance more effectual for reformation, and to impress the truths of virtue and religion more strongly on his mind, he employed the intervals snatched from the orgies of voluptuousness in composing for his own private use, a valuable little manual, entitled *The Christian Hero.* The effort was, alas! unavailing; for, however laudable and well intended were the resolutions of his solitude, the succeeding day saw him minister to the mirth of vice, and protract the revels of debauchery; and he returned to his closet with a heart wrung with keener anguish, and a mind more deeply depressed by a sense of its own humiliation.

It would be instructive to continue the story in the words of the conscientious Dr. Drake, whose life of seventy years ended the year before Victoria, so aptly does he anticipate the good Queen and reflect her back upon the Age of Anne. Steele published *The Christian Hero* to show that an officer in the Guards need not necessarily be a profligate. To regain his reputation as a wit and a gentleman, he had to follow it immediately by a comedy of fashionable satire. Every line he wrote in *The Tatler* and *The Spectator* aims to put gentlemanly gaiety into the middle class, and middle-class sobriety and thrift into the aristocracy. Bevil Junior in *The Conscious Lovers* is the Christian Hero in person. Even when Steele comes out openly with the puritan pen-name of Nestor Ironside in *The Guardian,* the facts of his life reassure us. He could never be a cavalier for he could never leave repentance. He could never be a puritan for he could never learn thrift. He was the Victorian compromise. And if he looked down from the gold bar of Heaven on the dawn of the nineteenth century, he saw with complacence his airy suggestion built into the granite front of the Victorian code.

Prudery makes its public appearance in England with the political triumph of the middle class, and the word which names it comes at the same time, signalling the reaction against it of the opponents of middle-class manners. The word came from France, but the French lexicographers appear to be wrong in their account of it (Littré refers it to the Latin *prudens*), for it has more to do with pride than with prudence. For most of its history, the pride it denotes is that of the middle class, and as often as not it is false pride. The French word *prudhomme* did not last long in its first meaning of a *valiant warrior,* but was soon applied to the solid citizen of the capitalist class. *Prude femme* was formed to match it; what else could it mean but the middle-class wife whose virtues were as the feathers of the peacock? Naturally the feather she displayed most conspicuously, and assumed if she had it not, was modesty, and of course its conspicuous display is the best proof of its falsity. The English lexicographer, Murray, finds the word *prude* in its modern sense first in the works of Colley Cibber and Mrs. de la Rivière Manley, both of whom were opponents of the puritan. Almost as promptly, Steele took it up, and used it to his purpose. On the third of December, 1709, in the 102nd *Tatler,* he tells his readers that "Prude is a Courtly word for a female Hypocrite." He sees it as belonging to the court party, the opponents of puritanism. To Colley Cibber and Mrs. Manley, and no less to many of us today, anyone is a hyprocite who professes a stricter code of morals than their own. Puritans, then, were hypocrites; female puritans were therefore prudes. Steele belongs to both parties at once. In his first notice of the word, he says only what both sides would readily agree to. A month or two later he devotes a paper to the Prude and the Coquette, in which, standing in no man's land, he shoots impartially in both directions.

The Prude and the Coquette, as different as they appear in their behaviour, are in reality the same kind of women: The motive of action in both is the affectation of pleasing men. They are sisters of the same blood and constitution; only one chooses a grave, and the other a light dress. The Prude appears more virtuous, the Coquette more vicious, than she really is. The distant behaviour of the Prude tends to the same purpose as the advances of the Coquette; and you have as little reason to fall into despair from the severity of one, as to conceive hopes from the familiarity of the other. What leads you into a clear sense of their character is, that you may observe each of them has the distinction of Sex in all her thoughts, words, and actions.

Here the severe manners represent the puritan and the free manners represent the cavalier; the prude stands for the one and the coquette for the other; and Steele is characteristically trying to reconcile them on the basis of sincerity. The difference between them lies only in manners which he thinks they ought to discard. Elsewhere he is more severe in dealing with the rake, the male of the court species. His suggestion that women could purify society by denying themselves to all men known to be of rakish tendencies is a comical echo of the ribaldries of Aristophanes tuned to the key of a sermon, and has only a little lighter touch than the same suggestion made by the women moralists at the other end of the century, Mrs. Brunton and Mrs. Hofland. But Mrs. Brunton is a Scot, and Mrs. Hofland is under the shadow of Calvin; there is no compromise in their war on the rake. The compromise of the Glorious Revolution had effected a *modus vivendi,* but it had not settled all the details of social life. The men who longed for the court manners of the second Charles and the second James organized into such groups as the Mohocks and the Hell-Fire Club, or else worked individually (as the abundant literature on the lives of the rakes testifies), to re-establish the divine right of the gentleman to take his fun where he finds it, court influence to the contrary notwithstanding. This is the background of the English novel from William of Orange to William the Fourth, from Anne to Victoria, from Richardson to Scott. Richardson, in his earnest endeavor to guard girls against the attraction of the gentlemanly seducer, made the attractions clear. Fielding and Smollet have sympathy for the high- spirited stallion so long as he means well. Sterne, Prebendary though he was of York, had a very naughty twinkle in his eye. Of the women novelists, some want a man who is good, others want a man who is not so good that he hasn't learned to be a good lover. Can you learn to be a good lover without being for a time at least a bad man? Can you learn to swim by hanging your clothes on a hickory limb? Mrs. Frances Moore, Regina Maria Roche, Jane Porter, and others, think perhaps you can, and their endeavors to draw the rake bad enough to be titillating and good enough to marry, with "every bad habit a lady could wish," make fresh hilarities of their faded beauties. Uncompromisingly on the other side were the women moralists, Miss Edgeworth, Mrs. Brunton, Mrs. Hofland, Mrs. Opie, and their school. Indeed, taking the novel by and large, the small with the great, it very steadily represents middle-class opposition to free or aristocratic manners, and becomes almost Calvinistic in its severity about 1800. The establishment of Victoria on the throne tipped the scale in favor of the code of the women novelists, and confirmed it as ostensibly the code of society. In so far as it was impracticable, irreconcilable with the facts, it professed more than it practised and was hypocritical as a society pattern of conduct. Thackeray's keen sense for hypocrisy has no difficulty in perceiving it in Victorian delicacy: He has to inform his readers without making them blush that their worst suspicions about Becky and Lord Steyne are justified. Fielding in the eighteenth century and Aldous Huxley in the twentieth would have shown the two naked in their bed. Thackeray takes advantage of the fact that he cannot.

We must pass over a part of Mrs. Rebecca Crawley's biography with that lightness and delicacy which the world demands—the moral world, that has, perhaps, no particular objection to vice, but an insuperable objection to hearing vice called by its proper name. There are things we do and know perfectly well in Vanity Fair, though we never speak of them: . . . and a polite world will no more bear to read an authentic description of vice than a truly refined English or American female will permit the word breeches to be pronounced in her chaste hearing. And yet, Madam, both are walking the world before our faces every day, without much shocking us. If you were to blush every time they went by, what complexions you would have! It is only when their naughty names are called out that your modesty has any occasion to show alarm or sense of outrage, and it has been the wish of the present writer, all through this story, deferentially to submit to the fashion at present prevailing, and only to hint at the presence of wickedness in a light, easy, and agreeable manner, so that nobody's fine feelings may be offended. I defy anyone to say that our Becky, who has certainly some vices, has not been presented to the public in a perfectly genteel and inoffensive manner. In describing this syren, singing and smiling, coaxing and cajoling, the author, with modest pride, asks his readers all round, has he once forgotten the laws of politeness, and showed the monster's hideous tail above water? No! Those who like may peep down under the waves that are pretty transparent, and see it writhing and twirling, diabolically hideous and slimy, flapping amongst bones, or curling round corpses; but above the waterline, I ask, has not everything been proper, agreeable, and decorous, and has any the most squeamish immoralist in Vanity Fair a right to cry fie? When, however, the syren disappears and dives down below, down among the dead men, the water of course grows turbid over her, and it is labor lost to look into it ever so curiously. . . . And so, when Becky is out of the way, be sure that she is not particularly well employed, and that the less that is said about her doings is in fact the better.

Never from the twentieth century has flown a truer arrow or one with a keener barb than this "squeamish immoralist." It is questionable, too, whether at that time, ten years after Victoria came to the throne, squeamish immorality would have been named for the Queen. Had she by then set the example of delicacy, true or false? Greville writes in his diary, November 26, 1839:

The Queen wrote to all her family and announced her marriage to them. When she saw the Duchess of Gloucester in town, and told her she was to make her declaration the next day, the Duchess asked her if it was not a nervous thing to do. She said, "Yes; but I did a much more nervous thing a little while ago." "What was that?" "I proposed to Prince Albert."

What a queen has to do to get her man! And what "'Victorian" heroine would not burn, or be an old maid, before she would follow the example? Three months later, Greville lodges against her the charge of indelicacy!

Her honeymoon seems to be a very curious affair, more strange than delicate, and even her best friends are shocked and hurt at her not conforming more than she is doing to English customs and not continuing for a short space in that retirement, which modesty and native delicacy generally prescribe, and which few Englishwomen would be content to avoid, but she does not think any such restraint necessary. Married on Monday, she collected an immense party on Wednesday, and sent off in a hurry for Clarence Paget, to go down and assist at a ball or rather dance, which she chose to have at the Castle last night. This is a proceeding quite unparalleled, and Lady Palmerston said to me last night that she was much vexed that she had nobody about her who could venture to tell her that this was not becoming and would appear indelicate; but she has nobody who dares tell her, or she will not endure to hear such truth. Normandy said to me the same thing. It is a pity Melbourne, when she desired him to go there on Wednesday, did not tell her she had better not have him, nor anybody except perhaps her own family. He probably did not think about it. It was much remarked too that she and Prince Albert were up very early on Tuesday morning walking about, which is very contrary to her former habits. Strange that a bridal night should be so short, and I told Lady Palmerston that this was not the way to provide us with a Prince of Wales.

Perhaps the code might more appropriately be named for the Prince Consort.

September 6, 1841: Melbourne said he thought the Prince must be at the bottom of these (appointments and exclusions at the Court), that he was extremely strait-laced and a great stickler for morality, whereas she was rather the other way, and did not much care about niceties of moral choice . . .

September 7, 1841: . . . I had some talk with him about the applicants, when he [the Duke of Wellington] told me in confirmation of what Melbourne had said, that it was the Prince who insisted on spotless character (the Queen not caring a straw about it) . . .

The pattern of delicacy, then, may be no more characteristic of Victoria than it is peculiar to her time, but for her it is named.

For a hundred years from 1750 to 1850 it showed no appreciable change. It would be amusing to collect a nosegay of these flowers of English delicacy; one could gather them in sheaves from the pages of minor fiction. Some that were exhibited to their readers in all seriousness in their day would now seem like caricatures. More to our purpose are examples that we can take with some seriousness. Such is Adela Waltham, heroine of *Demos,* by George Gissing, 1886. She has been brought up under the innocence-is-ignorance theory. Without knowing what love is, she is in love with Hubert Eldon, a disinherited young gentleman who seems to have gone to the bad. Mrs. Waltham refuses him admission to the house, and tells her daughter:

"It was impossible for you to be in the same room with him. . . . I thought there might be no need to speak to you about things you ought never to hear mentioned. . . . The sad truth is that Mr. Eldon has utterly disgraced himself . . . He was living at Paris and other such places in the most shocking dissipation. Things are reported of him which I could not breathe to you; He is a bad young man."

All Adela knows about it is something she has read:

[To Adela] the final phrase was like a thunderstroke. In a certain profound work on the history of her country which she had been in the habit of studying, the author, discussing the character of Cromwell, achieved a most impressive climax in the words, "He was a bold, bad man." The adjective "bad" derived for Adela a dark energy from her recollection of that passage; it connoted every imaginable phase of moral degradation. "Dissipation" too; to her pure mind the word had a terrible sound; it sketched in lurid outlines hideous lurking places of vice and disease. "Paris and other such places." With the name of Paris she associated a feeling of reprobation; Paris was the headquarters of sin—at all events on earth. In Paris people went to the theatre on Sunday; that fact alone shed storm-light over the illustrious capital.

She knows, then, no more of sin than she can learn in Sunday-school.

. . . Drawing analogies from the story of her faith, she imaged Hubert as the angel who fell from extreme purity to a terrible lordship of perdition. Of his sins she had the dimmest conception; she was told that they were sins of impurity, and her understanding of such could scarcely have been expressed save in the general language of her prayers. Guarded jealously at every moment of her life, the world had made no blur on the fair tablet of her mind; her Eden had suffered no invasion.

Adela's mother steers her toward a *mariage de convenance:*

. . . She read over the marriage service frequently. There stood the promise—to love, to honour, and to obey. Honour and obedience she might render to him, but what of love? The question arose, what did love mean? . . . Adela could not believe that "to love" in the sense of the marriage service and "to be in love" as her heart understood it were one and the same thing. The Puritanism of her training led her to mistrust profoundly those impulses of mere nature . . . Yet it said "love." Perchance that was something which would come after marriage; the promise, observe, concerned the future . . .

"Mother, may I marry without feeling that—that I love him?"

The face was flushed now for a moment. Adela had never spoken that word to anyone . . .

By its date, this pattern is Victorian, but a hundred years earlier it would be just as acceptable under the name of delicacy—so, too,

it is called in its own time, for in Adela her lover sees "the exquisite delicacy apparent in all she did or said," and "a supreme
modesty which she alone could inspire."

In 1795, Matthew Gregory Lewis in *The Monk* made some
wicked comments on the sanctity of ignorance. Leonella speaking to Antonia of Ambrosio says:

". . . he is reported to be so strict an observer of chastity that he
knows not in what consists the difference of man and woman: the
common people, therefore, esteem him to be a saint."

"Does that make one a saint?" inquired Antonia. "Bless me, then
am I one."

"Holy St. Barbara!" exclaimed Leonella, "What a question! Fie,
child, fie! these are not fit subjects for a young woman to handle.
You should not seem to remember that there is such a thing as a
man in the world, and you ought to imagine everybody to be of the
same sex as yourself. I should like to see you give people to understand that you know that a man has no breasts, and no hips, and
no . . ."

Luckily for Antonia's ignorance, which her aunt's lecture would
soon have dispelled, an universal murmur through the church announced the preacher's arrival.

Later, Ambrosio finds Antonia reading the Bible in her bedroom, and sits down beside her. She makes no objection because
"she knew not that there was more impropriety in conversing
with him in one room than another." But when he learns what she
is reading, "How," said the friar to himself, "Antonia reads the
Bible, and is still so ignorant?" He makes inquiries and discovers that Antonia's

prudent mother, while she admired the beauties of the sacred writings, was convinced that, unrestricted, no reading more improper
could be permitted a young woman. Many of the narratives can
tend only to excite ideas the worst calculated for a female breast;
everything is called plainly and roundly by its name, and the annals
of a brothel would scarcely furnish a greater choice of indecent expressions . . . She had in consequence [resolved] . . . that it should

be copied out with her own hand, and all improper passages either altered or omitted . . . such was the Bible which Antonia was reading.

The time comes when Antonia's mother perceives that complete ignorance is not complete protection:

She now endeavored to make her daughter aware of the risk which she had run; but she was obliged to treat the subject with caution, lest, in removing the bandage of ignorance, the veil of innocence should be rent away. She therefore contented herself with warning Antonia to be upon her guard, and ordering her, should the abbot persist in his visits, never to receive them but in company.

But Antonia, not knowing what she had to fear, is still in danger—"Elvira had not sufficiently explained herself upon the nature of his designs, to make a girl so ignorant of the world as her daughter aware how dangerous was his acquaintance." Antonia then learns the facts from the usual vulgar source. Her old nurse, "explaining the monk's designs and their probable consequences in terms much clearer than Elvira's though not quite so delicate, had succeeded in alarming her young lady, and persuading her to treat him more distantly than she had hitherto done."

Whatever Lewis's intention, these passages are a clear enough exposition of the practice of the innocence-ignorance theory, and indication that it did not change for a century before the time of George Gissing. They cast, too, a satiric light on the teachings of the Roman Church. Wherever it stood or stands on the question of birth control, it is clear that Leonella, no less than the Wife of Bath, believed that its ideal of absolute virginity was hopelessly out of tune with the obvious facts of biology. The Church, they gathered, preached the sanctity of virginity. The Wife of Bath attributes to St. Paul the teaching that it is better for the human race to perish from the face of the earth than that it should be propagated by sexual intercourse. Perhaps Paul became a saint because "he was so strict an observer of chastity that he knew not in what consisted the difference of man and woman." Nuns were forbidden to look at their own bodies. A convent-bred girl of the twentieth century tells of being taught to wear her bathing suit in the bathtub. Some such feeling is spontaneous at times. A girl born in the last decade of the nineteenth century tells of it. "I remember," she says, "during early adolescence not looking at my own naked body, and avoiding seeing myself in the mirror. Some of this feeling was perhaps due to over-sensitiveness and a lack of emotional outlet." But in the main it was and is an attitude of mind cultivated either at the behest of the Church, or for its value in society and in the marriage market because of its connotation of virginity and youth. Today its connotation of youth would be extreme. If we believe what comes to us out of the laboratories, we must infer that the age of a child innocent of sex would be less than nothing. But in the dark ages before we were enlightened by Freud, there was more lee-way. "Now by my maidenhead at twelve years old!" exclaims Juliet's nurse, and we are justified in inferring no surety after that age. Chaucer tells us that the Wife of Bath had five au-thorised husbands, "husbands at church door," not to mention "other company in youth." Later she tells us that since she was twelve years old she had been married five times. Perhaps the "youth" of her "other company" was from twelve to four-teen.

Youth seems on the whole to have held steadier quotations on the marriage exchange than virginity. One need not go far into anthropology to learn that virginity has not in all times and in all places been so highly esteemed as ostensibly it is among "civilized" people since its esteem began to be held a measure of civilization. When a man got his bride by love or war, all was fair, and virginity was more likely to be studiously destroyed than studiously preserved. But when he got his bride by purchase, he, for some undetermined reason began to feel that he had not his money's worth except she were unused. The plain fact is that virginity gets its rating from capitalism, and rises with the rise of the capitalist class, perfumed in Christian times with the odor of sanctity from the Church. It was like the money which was its index of value; if you needed it you couldn't have too much of it, you couldn't make too sure of it, or make your possession of it too obvious. The complete, certain and obvious virginity is that of a girl in the pre-sexual stages of childhood. These are the facts which determined the pattern of childish virginity which we find in the novel.

Certainly it was good bait for the fishers of men, equally indispensable and equally alluring whatever the character of the man. If his heart and mind were like the Kingdom of Heaven, a girl who could be as a little child could the more easily enter in. As for the rakes, the older they grew in iniquity, the younger they liked 'em. An earlier page of these studies (p. 6) calls attention to this in the work of Richardson and in that of the French painter, Greuze. Other painters in other times have found beautiful models in adolescent girls, such as the "Printemps" of Puvis de Chavannes and the "Diane" of Ary Bitters, both in the Luxembourg. But without checking over statistics, one gathers from general impressions of galleries and museums that the taste was more prevalent in the eighteenth century than at other times. Houdon has many engaging studies of children, in which his marble "Baigneuse" in the Metropolitan Museum might almost be included if the age of the model is what it seems. Falconet has another—it is in the Louvre—of the same age or younger. His also are the three plump twelve-year-old "graces" in white marble standing (also in the Louvre) round the pillar of the urn-shaped clock. These examples are not enough to mark the taste as especially that of the time, but the *ars erotica* of France indicates it so very clearly. Boucher's models in his exhibited paintings are for the most part girls of sixteen. In the suppressed paintings the merest children show high sophistication in the art of love. In the *gravures galantes* the fact appears beyond question. In these engravings and mezzotints the impudent little courtesans who exhibit their most intimate charms to powdered and ruffled gallants have the same freshly rounded bodies and infantile faces as the little girls of Falconet. These prints seem to belong in the period from about 1700 to about 1775, the Regency and Louis XV, so far as one can judge from the coiffures of the nude figures and the clothes of the men. These impubic bodies and baby faces show that in the brothel there was a fashion of extreme youth. Some of these seem to belong to periods of the fashion for powdered hair, which would show the young face with white hair in the drawing-room and the baby face and budding body in the brothel. This contrast probably signifies a time of high sophistication and increasing furtiveness in the sexual life. The prints that exhibit it were, of course, displayed much more openly than would have been possible in the following century; profligacy would not hide its head as the Puritans tried to make it do, nor were Court manners at all what the Puritans wished they were. Still there is in these prints much peeping through keyholes and lurking behind bed-curtains which is in marked contrast to the directness and vigor of the erotic art of the Renaissance, or indeed of any earlier period. That there was the same taste in England in 1760 Johnstone's *Chrysal* testifies. The valet of an elderly rake, a general, is also his procurer. He suggests

"A very fine girl as your excellency could wish to see." "How old?" —"About sixteen."—"Psha, mellow pears! I loathe such trash."— . . . "If your excellency pleases but to wait a little, I have one in my eye, that will suit your taste exactly; a sweeter child is not in all England."—". . . but how old?"—"Just ten and finely grown."— "Right, the right age . . ."

But if childish innocence and ignorance was a lure for the rakes, it was no less necessary as a defense against them. Directly it might serve as in the story in *The Tatler* to soften a stony heart. Indirectly, negatively, it was a necessity, for, at least in theory, if a girl did not have it the rakes would swarm after her, seemingly in the belief that if she knew anything she would do anything. In Maria Edgeworth's *Patronage*, 1814, Caroline Percy discovers that her suitor, Mr. Buckhurst Falconer, whose offer of marriage she has just refused, has seduced a girl in the neighborhood. Caroline's younger sister, Rosamund, whose artless comments on life serve to bring out many a precept, wishes "that Caroline's last letter had not gone to Buckhurst, that she might have given her refusal on this special account, in the most severe and indignant terms which the English language could supply." Mrs. Percy dissents from this opinion on the ground that though it might have shown proper feeling for Caroline to be angry enough to write such a letter, it would not have been well to do it:

You may recollect more than one heroine of a novel, who discards a lover upon such a discovery as was made by you last night. It is a common novel incident, and, of course, from novels, every young lady, even, who might not have *felt* without a precedent, knows how she ought to express herself in such circumstances. But you will observe, my dear, that both in novels and in real life, young ladies generally like and encourage men of feeling in contradistinction to men of principle, and too often men of gallantry in preference to men of correct morals: in short, that such a character as that of Mr. Buckhurst Falconer is just the kind of person with whom many women would fall in love. By suffering this to be thought the taste of our sex, ladies encourage libertinism in general, more than they can possible discourage it by the loudest display of indignation against particular instances.—If, like your sister Caroline, young ladies would show that they really do not prefer such men, it would do essential service. And observe, my dear Rosamund, this can be done by every young woman with perfect delicacy: but I do not see how she can, with propriety and good effect, do more. It is a subject ladies cannot well discuss; a subject on which the manners and customs of the world are so much at variance with religion and morality, that entering upon the discussion would lead to greater difficulties than you are aware of. It is therefore best for our sex

to show their disapprobation of vice, and to prove their sense of
virtue and religion by their conduct, rather than to proclaim it to the
world in words. Had Caroline in her letter expressed her indignation
in the most severe terms that the English language could supply, she
would only have exposed herself to the ridicule of Mr. Buckhurst
Falconer's fashionable companions, as a prating, preaching prude,
without doing the least good to him, or to anyone living.

Here we have directions for applying the principle advocated in
passages already quoted from Miss Edgeworth and Mrs.
Brunton. Use with discretion, enforce by acts not words, a
principle which it is not proper for ladies to discuss for reasons
which little Rosamund is not aware of. Suffice it to say that words
on the subject would expose Caroline to the "ridicule" (a euphemism aimed at Rosamund?) of her suitor's fashionable fellow
rakes. They would call her a preaching prude.

Mrs. Percy condemned as indelicate the ways of mothers who
played the marriage market for what they could get from it.
If she had been one of them, she would doubtless have encouraged the unawakened virginal attitude in a daughter as a
real advantage to her manoeuvers. It is so to Adela's mother in
the passages cited from Gissing's *Demos*. Before Juliet has met
Romeo she is docile enough to her mother's suggestion that she
shall marry Paris; afterward she is all steel and fire against it.
Naturally, mothers who are seeking to make economically advantageous marriages for their daughters would encourage the
early-Juliet manner. If a girl knew the realities of marriage, the
thought of entering into them with a man whose person was not
acceptable to her would shatter her docility. The best way was to
keep her young and tell her nothing. Also it was the easiest way.
One is tempted to say that after mothers became prudish it was
hard for them to instruct their daughters in the realities of marriage. But it would seem that this difficulty either antedates
the beginnings of prudery or extends them beyond the dawn of
history, for where is the record of such instruction coming freely

and easily from the lips of the mother? Juliet in Act I is unawakened and virginal, and her nurse jeers at her for it. Later she is eager for Romeo to come to her bed. Had her Rabelaisian nurse enlightened her meanwhile, as did the nurse of Monk Lewis's heroine?

In still another way is the virginal-unawakened attitude a protection to a girl. If she does not know what love is, she does not know when she is in love; if she does not know she is in love, she is not subject to disappointment. The ideal way, so often depicted in American Sunday-school books for girls in the last century, is to remain fancy-free until the fairy prince actually offers you the kiss. An example is in *Burrcliff*, 1853, by J. T. Trowbridge:

We will also pass over the sweet surprise of that memorable time when Mr. Marclay, who had watched her long, and studied her with careful and tender eyes, told her that it was his hope and wish some day to make her his wife. He knew no other being in all the world, he said, whose love was necessary to complete his happiness; and he could imagine none better qualified to forward and adorn the sacred mission to which his life was devoted. Olive had never dreamed of this. She did not even know until that hour, that the feeling she herself had cherished for her teacher was deep, pure, holy love. She was like the heroine of the fairy tale, who, walking unconsciously on enchanted ground through the calm hours of a summer night, knew not the source of all the odorous delights that stole upon her sense, until the morning marched with golden pomp upon the scene, discovering in a dawn of glory the paradise of beauty into which her charmed feet had strayed.

Our friend Caroline Percy of *Patronage* is a cooler practitioner. Rosamund, her impulsive little sister, has noticed that Col. Hungerford "possesses every virtue, public and private, that can make him worthy of you—not a single fault . . . temper, manners, talents, character, fortune, family, fame, everything the heart of woman can desire," and to all intents she advises her sister to fall in love with this paragon. But Caroline is prudent:

"[I] have not been insensible to any of the delightful, any of the romantic circumstances of the *vision;* but I saw it was only a vision— and one that might lead me into waking, lasting misery."

"Misery! lasting! How?" said Rosamund.

". . . I cannot forget that the delicacy, honour, pride, prudence of our sex, forbid a woman to think of any man as a lover, till he gives her reason to believe that he feels love for her . . . If there be no harm, there might be much danger . . . better not to think of the subject at all, since we can do no good by thinking of it, and may do harm."

Rosamund argues very ably on the other side, and Caroline answers her still more ably, until, in two or three pages the whole theory and practice of the principle are displayed. Then, within two or three pages more, circumstance brings in the verdict for Caroline's side. Col. Hungerford declares for another lady, and the reader perceives that Caroline would have been in a very awkward position if she had followed Rosamund's advice, which was dictated by feeling and not by judgment. Equally explicit is the exposition in Jane Austen's *Pride and Prejudice*, written earlier than *Patronage*, perhaps, but published at almost the same time, only here the declaration is not so clearly that of the author as of her characters. Elizabeth Bennet and Charlotte Lucas observe the incipient stage of the love affair of Bingley and Jane. Jane, they perceived, "was yielding to the preference which she had begun to entertain for him from the first, and was in a way to be very much in love." Elizabeth is glad that Jane is not likely to betray her state to "the suspicions of the impertinent." Charlotte, who soon proves a shrewd player of the game, is not of the same mind. She says:

". . . If a woman conceals her affection [successfully] from the object of it, she may lose the opportunity of fixing him . . . We can all *begin* freely—a slight preference is natural enough; but there are very few of us who have heart enough to be really in love without encouragement. In nine cases out of ten, a woman had better shew *more* affection than she feels . . . Jane should make the most of every half hour in which she can command his attention. When she is secure of him, there will be leisure for falling in love as much as she chuses."

"Your plan is a good one," replied Elizabeth, "where nothing is in question but the desire of being well married; and if I were determined to get a rich husband, or any husband, I dare say I should adopt it . . ."

Elizabeth's reply is not a declaration of principle from the author, but, as events soon show, a word to the wise reader on the character and purpose of Charlotte Lucas, in whose mind "nothing is in question but the desire" of getting any husband. Neither is it necessarily a declaration from the author (though many readers would take it as such) when we find a similar principle on the lips of Elinor, who is so universally said to speak the part of the sense in *Sense and Sensibility.* She is speaking of Edward Ferrars' supposed "regard" for her when she says,

There are moments when the extent of it seems doubtful; and till his sentiments are fully known, you cannot wonder at my wishing to avoid any encouragement of my own partiality, by believing or calling it more than it is.

And from this point on the whole book develops the contrast between conduct on this principle, and its antithesis.

The argument between Rosamund and Caroline is between the head and the heart, between judgment and feeling, as the guide of life. It begins with Richardson, and runs straight down through the eighteenth century, with the novelists aligned in controversial array on the two sides of it. Richardson believed that the head should guide the heart; he was for passion under control; his object was to "teach the man of passion how to subdue it." Fielding did not believe in inhibitions; he despised Richardson's calculated utilitarian morality, and found it easy to forgive wrong done by a generous young man whose acts are dictated by warm feelings. Smollett is of much the same opinion. Next comes the vogue of Rousseau and of the emotional whimsicalities of Sterne, and Mackenzie sweeps the field with a flood of feeling. Against it the moralists hastened to erect their dikes. In the world of Mackenzie and his followers, the man of feeling is the hero, and the man of the world the villain. In the novels of Miss Edgeworth and the women moralists, the romantic Roussellian lady is the villainess. Miss Edgeworth's *Leonora* is an entire novel devoted to this theme; it is her "short view" of the dangers of romanticism as a code of life, love and ethics, an answer to the *Nouvelle Héloïse,* a warning against the serpent Julie in the garden of Britain. It is in essence an allegory, the Duchess speaking the part of Sense, Leonora, Natural Sensibility, Olivia, Wantonness under the guise of Fashionable Romanticism. All that Sense can say against feeling as a guide to conduct, the Duchess says ably. All that Natural Sensibility can say in favor of it, Leonora says intelligently; she represents "sensible sensibility." Miss Austen wrote *Sense and Sensibility* in 1797–8 and published it five years after *Leonora,* i.e., in 1811. In 1801, five years before *Leonora,* Miss Edgeworth exhibited in *Belinda* the figure of Harriet Freke, a lady of revolutionary principles, which to the author means unprincipled. Would any of her indelicacies get her any "publicity" in the twentieth century? She swaggers, plays the races, participates in more or less athletic sports, occasionally wears men's clothes, and fights a duel. Would her revolutionary ideas attract attention, or have we revolved round to them?

". . . All shame is false shame—we should be a great deal better without it. What say you, Miss Portman?—Silent, hey? Silence that speaks."

"Miss Portman's blushes," said Mr. Vincent, "speak *for* her."

"*Against* her," said Mrs. Freke: "women blush because they understand."

"And you would have them understand without blushing?" said Mr. Percival. "I grant you that nothing can be more different than innocence and ignorance. Female delicacy—"

"This is just the way you men spoil women," cried Mrs. Freke, "by talking to them of the *delicacy of their sex,* and such stuff. This *delicacy* enslaves the pretty delicate dears."

"No; it enslaves us," said Mr. Vincent.

"I hate slavery! Vive la liberté!" cried Mrs. Freke. "I'm a champion for the Rights of Women."

"I am an advocate for their happiness," said Mr. Percival, "and for their delicacy as I think it conduces to their happiness."

"I'm an enemy to their delicacy as I am sure it conduces to their misery.". . ."Your most delicate women are always the greatest hypocrites; and in my opinion, no hypocrite can or ought to be happy."

"But you have not proved the hypocrisy," said Belinda. "Delicacy is not, I hope, an indisputable proof of it? If you mean *false* delicacy—"

"To cut the matter short at once," cried Mrs. Freke, "why, when a woman likes a man, does she not go and tell him so honestly?"

Belinda, surprised by this question from a woman, was too much abashed instantly to answer.

"Because she's a hypocrite. That is and must be the answer."

"No," said Mr. Percival, "because if she be a woman of sense, she knows that by such a step she would disgust the object of her affection."

"Cunning!—cunning!—cunning!—the arms of the weakest."

"Prudence! prudence!—the arms of the strongest. Taking the best means to secure our own happiness without injuring that of others is the best proof of sense and strength of mind, whether in man or woman. Fortunately for society, the same conduct in ladies which best secures their happiness most increases ours."

Mrs. Freke . . . exclaimed, "You may say what you will, but the present system of society is radically wrong:—whatever is, is wrong . . . If you want to know what I would do to improve the world, I'll tell you: I'd have both sexes call things by their right names."

". . . should we find things much improved by tearing away what has been called the decent drapery of life?"

"Drapery . . .", cried Mrs. Freke, "whether wet or dry, is the most confoundedly indecent thing in the world."

One may read here a sort of inferiority complex of Miss Edgeworth's. She is all for outspoken honesty; in all her tales it always wins. Probably this point of female reticence which she could not concede worried her, and she makes here the best defense of it that she can. To make occasion for the defense of reticence, she puts the suggestion of outspoken honesty on the lips of the villain, for she has arbitrarily made Mrs. Freke responsible for plot and intrigue that nearly bring ruin upon the central characters. This is nothing more than an unconvincing assertion that villainy and revolutionary doctrine go hand in hand.

A still earlier brief for the head as against the heart is an attempt to counteract the doctrines of Rousseau by fiction in *The Memoirs of Emma Courtney,* by Mary Hays, 1796. The author declares in her preface that she means to represent Emma as a human being "loving virtue while enslaved by passion." Emma reads the *Nouvelle Héloïse,* and soon thereafter falls in love with Augustus Harley without having seen him, by means of a portrait and his mother's stories of his virtues. Acquaintance with him confirms her passion, which she declares to him in a letter she gives him as he starts on a journey. He does not reply. She follows him, tries to see him, and persecutes him with passionate letters. She offers to become his mistress, and gets scarcely so much as an acknowledgement of the offer. At last she discovers that he is a married man, having been secretly married before she met him. In despair and poverty she marries a persistent suitor. At length her husband discovers her love for Augustus, together with the fact that Augustus had loved her all the time he was repelling her advances. The discovery drives her husband into crime and suicide. From all this we infer that passion should be governed by reason. A later figure drawn to the same pattern as Harriet Freke is Madame D'Arblay's Elinor in *The Wanderer,* 1814. She tells one admirer that she hates him, sends word to another man that she loves him, incessantly harangues all hearers on the rights of women and other revolutionary doctrine. Rejected for want of delicacy by the man she loves, she flourishes a pistol and attempts suicide. If there were any of Pamela's daughters or Eve's who did not know that it was better to endure green and yellow melancholy than to be in love before she was sure of her man, or to let anyone know it if she were, it was not the fault of the well-meaning women novelists.

Steele, too, was early in the field with a lightly feathered shaft released in the 60th *Tatler* from Will's Coffee House, August 26 (1709). It dramatises the way with a lady's maid of one Strephon, who "had so little complaisance as to say a woman is never taken by her reason, but always by her passion."

Strephon is a perfect master in this kind of persuasion: His way is, to run over with a soft air a multitude of words, without meaning or connexion; but such as do each of them apart give a pleasing idea, though they have nothing to do with each other as he assembles them. After the common phrases of salutation, and making his entry into the room, I perceived he had taken the fair nymph's hand and kissing it said, Witness to my happiness ye groves! be still ye rivulets! oh! woods, caves, fountains, trees, dales, mountains, and streams! oh! fairest! could you love me? To which I overheard her answer with a very pretty lisp, Oh! *Strephon* you are a dangerous creature: Why do you talk these tender things to me? But you men of wit— Is it then possible, said the enamoured *Strephon,* that she regards my sorrows? Oh! pity, thou balmy cure to an heart overloaded. If rapture, solicitation, soft desire, and pleasing anxiety— but still I live in the most afflicting of all circumstances, doubt— cannot my charmer name the place and moment?

> There all those joys insatiably to prove,
> With which rich beauty feeds the glutton, Love.

Forgive me, Madam, it is not that my heart is weary of its chain, but— This incoherent stuff was answered by a tender sigh, Why do you put your wit to a weak woman?

Pamela, as appears clearly in the scene of the attempted rape, has no hesitation in undressing completely in the presence of other maid-servants, and has no objection on the score of modesty to sleeping with one or another of them. The Scotch moralists are stricter. Mrs. Brunton, in *Self Control,* 1811, suggests a higher standard of modesty than this for men:

Mr. Wentworth had himself been educated at a public school, and never recollected without shuddering, the hour when his youthful modesty first had shrunk from sharing his bed with a stranger.

Pamela would, of course, have been consumed with shame and fear if she had known that the "sleeping wench" beside her as she passed all undressed was her master. Not so in the time of King Arthur, nor yet in the time of Malory. "Sir Launcelot," Malory tells us, "took the fairest lady by the hand that ever he saw, and she was all naked as a needle." There was good reason for it, to be sure; the room was "as hot as a stew," and the lady had suffered it for five years by an enchantment which could be removed only when Launcelot took her by the hand, but later heroines would have preferred the pains, be they those of hell for eternity, to relief at the price. Of these the archetype is St. Pierre's Virginie, 1788. The passage already cited is worth quoting: In a scene of storm and shipwreck, those on shore see the figure of a girl appear on the stern gallery of the *Saint-Géran*.

It was Virginia . . . All the sailors had thrown themselves into the sea. There remained but one on the bridge, who was quite naked and muscled like a Hercules. He approached Virginia with respect: we saw him throw himself on his knees and try to take off her clothes; but she, pushing him away with dignity, turned her looks aside. One heard the cries of the spectators redoubled: "Save her, save her, do not leave her!" [A towering wave threatens the ship.] At this terrible sight, the sailor leaped into the sea alone; and Virginia, seeing death inevitable, put one hand on her skirt, the other on her heart, and, lifting on high her serene eyes, looked like an angel about to take its flight to heaven.

The steps between Malory and St. Pierre take us through the Renaissance, and show us something of the development of verbal prudery as well as literary standards of nudity. Chaucer used unhesitatingly when he had occasion the words for which *Lady Chatterley's Lover* was outlawed as soon as it appeared. The occasion was comedy; the words are on the lips of the Wife of

Bath and others in her rank of life with the exception of one
instance in Chaucer's description of the Parson, which to us is
poetry of high seriousness, but may not have been so to him. In
Troilus and Criseyde, which was certainly a matter of high
seriousness to him, we see Cressida as Troilus comes to her bedside, her round, high breasts and long, straight side, and the line
about the Parson in the prologue suggests that if Chaucer had
chosen to say more, he could have said it with dignity without
circumlocution. If so, he is probably the last of his time, for
his successors, without shunning nudity, show verbal prudery in
suggesting what they dare not name as he did. The *Faerie Queene*
has beautiful pictures with nude figures that remind us of paintings of the Renaissance but Spenser's words are veiled except for
one which has since become vulgar. One is a full length picture of
Serena when her savage captors had stripped her for the sacrifice.
Here Spenser uses a circumlocution where Chaucer might have
used the colloquial word. What is more, Spenser gives Serena
two stanzas of shame for her nakedness, whereas in Malory the
naked lady puts on her clothes in Sir Launcelot's presence without
a word of embarrassment or apology, and invites him to go with
her to the chapel to give thanks for her deliverance. In the
Arcadia of Sir Philip Sidney, contemporary with the *Faerie
Queene,* we have the picture of the Princess Philoclea bathing in
the river, in more detail than similar passages in Spenser, but to
the same effect, unless it be for an added sophistication. The
enumerator of the charms of Philoclea's bare body is her lover
so disguised that she thinks him a woman, and strips herself
freely in his presence. In both Spenser and Sidney we may note
that the word *belly* is in no disrepute, but may be used in serious
descriptions for effects of beauty.

The era of the Virgin Queen was not the age of prudery—
that age was named for Victoria, wife and mother with an ample
brood. What we find in Spenser and Sidney is characteristic of
Elizabethan literature. Marlowe translated Ovid in a spirit as

frank as his author's. Shakespeare's *Venus and Adonis* and *Rape of Lucrece* are to the inner eye like spacious halls decorated with frescoes of the Renaissance. In the gallery of women he has left us in his plays, there are those with every kind of modesty but false modesty. Desdemona, indeed, shrinks from the plain word which Othello has used.

Des. Am I that name, Iago?
Iago.   What name, fair lady?
Des. Such as she said my lord did say I was?
Emilia. He called her whore; a beggar in his drink,
         Could not have laid such terms upon his callet.

Her shudder, however, is not at the word, but at what has happened to her. Portia, wife of Brutus, is a model for matrons, but she does not hesitate to say that unless she is completely in his confidence, "Portia is Brutus' harlot, not his wife." No need to multiply examples to show that the women of Shakespeare's plays (and his men no less) are free from fear of petty violations of an arbitrary code of fashionable manners. Prudery is not characteristic of the drama until it begins to take its color from puritanism. The biblical drama is no more mealy-mouthed than the Bible itself. The Elizabethan drama is no more mealy-mouthed than was Elizabeth herself. The Restoration drama may be guilty of false profligacy, but never of false modesty. The profligacy of the Restoration comedy was false in so far as it was an exaggerated gesture of defiance and contempt toward puritanism, an exaggerated emphasis on the phase of aristocratic manners that was most enraging to aristocracy's opponents. It was false to the extent that it was not genuinely aristocratic. Historians tell us that the titled families of England that were rooted in Norman and Saxon times were practically eradicated by the Wars of the Roses. The aristocrats who opposed Cromwell's plebeians were comparatively new creations, not far removed from the common clay of the class against whom they fought;

"gentlemen born, aye, and have been any time these four hours." This is a condition that demands scrupulous attention to, and loud insistance on, its outward and visible signs. One must speak and act at all times, seasonable and unseasonable, with "aristocratic freedom."

Aristocratic freedom was to Jeremy Collier immorality and profaneness. He took a short view and a summary measure, directed a stiff spray of antiseptic against the offending mass of corruption, and the English stage has never been the same since. The court was on his side, but there was a strong opposition, and from the controversy the words *prude* and *prudery* and all that they stood for emerged. In the minds of the Puritans, the fear of nudity and the fear of God were one, forever amalgamated by the lesson of the Book called Genesis. But at first the moralists were not conspicuously squeamish. James Thomson was a Scot, but not too much a Calvinist to display in *Summer, 1727,* an engagingly prim little pastel of Musidora undressing and bathing under the unsuspected gaze of Damon, who loves her most respectfully. She "stripped her beauteous limbs . . . from the snowy leg, and slender foot, the inverted silk she drew; . . . the soft touch dissolved the virgin zone, and, through the parted robe, th' alternate breast, with youth wild-throbbing, on thy lawless gaze in full luxuriance rose [at this stage Gainsborough painted her] . . . from her naked limbs of glowing white, . . . in folds loose-floating fell the fainter lawn; and fair-exposed she stood." "Ye prudes in virtue, say, say, ye severest, what would you have done?" Well, Damon's gaze is "lawless" only because it is unauthorized. Torn between ecstasy and delicacy, he first gazes, then flees after tossing a written message to the bank of the stream:

> *"Bathe on, my fair,*
> *Yet unbeheld save by the sacred eye*
> *Of faithful love: I go to guard thy haunt,*
> *To keep from thy recess each vagrant foot,*
> *And each licentious eye."*

Musidora is first struck with "wild surprize" then with "mixed emotions hard to be described." "At length a tender calm hush'd by degrees the tumult of her soul," and she replied to Damon's message:

> *"Dear youth, sole judge of what these verses mean,*
> *By fortune too much favour'd, but by love,*
> *Alas! not favour'd less, be still as now*
> *Discreet: the time may come you need not fly."*

From all this we infer that Musidora's real name might have been Mary Morison or Jean Armour, that in spite of slender foot and fainter lawn she was a healthy, and healthy-minded, girl not afraid to be bodily in love with a trustworthy lover. St. Pierre's Virginie, one feels, might well choose to die rather than to undress, for if she undressed she would be less than nothing. Not so Musidora.

Not so Pamela, who is quite as real and solid with her clothes in her hand as with them on her back. Solid, too, are the charms of her sister (according to Fielding) Fanny Andrews:

Fanny was now in the nineteenth year of her age: she was tall and delicately shaped; but not one of those slender young women, who seem rather intended to hang up in the hall of an anatomist than for any other purpose. On the contrary, she was so plump, that she seemed bursting through her tight stays, especially in the part which confined her swelling breasts. Nor did her hips want the assistance of a hoop to extend them. The exact shape of her arms denoted the form of those limbs which she concealed; and though they were a little reddened by her labour, yet if her sleeve slipped above her elbow, or her handkerchief discovered any part of her neck, a whiteness appeared which the finest Italian paint would be unable to reach. Her hair was of a chestnut brown, and nature had been extremely lavish to her of it, which she had cut, and on Sundays used to curl down her neck in the modern fashion. Her forehead was high; her eyebrows arched, and rather full than otherwise; her eyes black and sparkling; her nose just inclining to the Roman; her lips red and moist, and her under lip, according to the opinion of the ladies, too pouting. Her teeth were white, but not exactly even. The small-pox had left only one mark on her chin, which was so large, it might have been mistaken for a dimple, had not her left cheek produced one so near a neighbor to it, that the former served only as a foil to the latter. Her complexion was fair, a little injured by the sun, but overspread with such a bloom, that the finest ladies would have exchanged all their white for it: add to these a countenance, in which, though she was extremely bashful, a sensibility appeared almost incredible; and a sweetness, whenever she smiled, beyond either imitation or description. To conclude all, she had a natural gentility, superior to the acquisition of art, and which surprised all who beheld her.

Richardson's word-portrait of Clarissa, Fielding's of Sophia, Smollett's of Narcissa and of Emilia (all quoted in Chapter VI) no matter how they dwell on costume, make us feel that these girls have well-rounded bodies under their clothes, and you feel, too, the men who write of them might well say as Chaucer said of his Emelye, when she bathes in water from a spring, "and yet it were a game to heren al." There is more to tell if they chose to tell it. Of this we are not so sure when we read descriptions of the heroines of the women novelists of the middle of the century and later. Ethelinda (1751) "was a perfect pattern of beauty, and her conduct was regulated by the nicest decency." Of the corporality of Lucy Wellers (1754) we learn only that "her face and shape were quite faultless, and there was so much innocence and sensibility in her countenance, as seemed to promise her mind equally possessed of them." In *The Rival Mother* (1755) the faces of Julia and Felicia are described in detail—a gray eye or so, but not to the purpose. Perhaps they had bodies; Julia "was tall and well shaped, and danced and walked admirably." Felicia "was not so tall as her sister, her waist was small, and her shape so well proportioned, that the smallest defect did not appear in it." It was nothing but a "shape," a frame for the dressmaker to work on, for we learn later that she had nothing below her neck by which a surgeon could determine her sex. He dresses a wound she receives while disguised as a young man, and informs the company "that the young stranger whose wound he had just dressed, was a woman in disguise. That he had discovered it by the delicacy of her features and complexion, and still more evidently by the most beautiful neck he ever saw." Earlier treatments of such discoveries are not so discreet.

In 1581, Barnaby Riche put forth a quarto volume of "verie pleasaunt discourses fit for a peaceable tyme: Gathered together for the onely delight of the courteous Gentlewomen, bothe of Englande and Irelande, for whose onely pleasure thei were collected together, and unto whom thei are directed and dedicated by Barnabe Riche, Gentleman." In it is the story of Silla, the prototype of Shakespeare's Viola, with whom she contrasts violently in every respect except in the general trend of her adventures. Silla, disguised as the page Silvio, is accused of being responsible for the pregnancy of the lady Julina, and in order to prove to Julina the impossibility of the charge (which is the act of her twin brother) must demonstrate her sex. She obtains an interview with Julina "in a place seurally by them selues," and here (remember that the masculine pronouns refer to Silvio who is really Silla)

. . . loosing his garments down to his stomacke, and shewed Julina his breastes and pretie teats, surmounting farre the whiteness of Snowe itself, saiying: Loe Madame, behold here the partie whom who [*sic*] have chalenged to be the father of your childe, see I am a woman the daughter of a noble Duke . . .

This is a fair sample of the story which Barnaby Riche offers to the delight of gentlewomen of the sixteenth century. Perhaps its blatant "sex-appeal" is no stronger than that of films offered to the delectation of courteous gentlewomen of the twentieth century. A hundred and forty years later, Mrs. Penelope Aubin (*The Adventures of the Count de Vinevil,* 1721) has the lovely Ardelisa in disguise in the service of a "lustful Turk." She deals with the situation directly but without display. "At these words he clasp'd her in his Arms, and rudely opening her Breast, discover'd that she was of the soft sex." A hundred years later Mrs. Catherine G. Ward deals with the situation neither stimulatingly nor directly, but prudishly. It is in *The Mysteries of St. Clair,* 1824, which might well claim the title of the worst of the Gothic romances. The heroine is disguised as a page in the service of Sir Walter de Ruthven, and, as a matter of course, faints at an emotional crisis near the end of the book.

There was no time, however, for further reflection on a circumstance so singular and mysterious, for the fainting boy required assistance and there was no one human being in the way to offer it to him but Sir Walter de Ruthven, and if there had been, he would not, in a case so doubtful, have permitted anyone to have approached him but himself; which the moment he did to unbutton his vest, in order for him to receive the balmy sweetness of the fresh air, a piercing shriek uttered by the fainting youth astonished and confounded him: and in low and whispering accents he demanded to know the cause of his astonishing emotion, when faintly the boy replied,— . . . I will deceive you no longer, brave Sir Walter de Ruthven, for Morgiana was not formed for deception: I am then even she . . .

"Morgiana was not formed for deception,"—the line has a comic suggestion of a hint that she had something below her neck by which Sir Walter might have discovered her sex. Of course, Mrs. Ward did not mean it so, and the passage as she meant it is absurd enough as an example of her delicacy in going lightly where the Elizabethan Barnaby Riche is heavily explicit. It was a euphemism that has lasted long. Fielding deftly reduces it to the depths of absurdity in the description of Amelia pronounced by her detractor, Mrs. James:

. . . Her neck likewise is too protuberant for the genteel size, especially as she laces herself; for no woman, in my opinion, can be genteel, who is not entirely flat before: . . .

Would Mrs. James have used the word *protuberant* if she had known how exactly it specified what she was trying to conceal in vagueness and false anatomy? Trollope's Lucy Robarts (*Framley Parsonage,* 1861) "had no neck at all worth speaking of,—no neck, I mean, that ever produced eloquence." This was in an age when the bosom was a sculptured unity and the breast was all one, but even in a later time of freer speech when the breasts are featured, molded, carefully twofold in dress and advertising, they seldom get the plural noun.

The heroine who is built according to the specifications of sexlessness in mind and body must love intensely, but totally without sexual desire. According to all patterns in fashion between, say, 1775 and 1890, love is woman's crowning glory, but sexual desire or feeling brands her as an outcast from society. It was not so before the Puritan Revolution. Juliet's superb expression of her eagerness for her bridegroom to come to her bed was not cut for stage presentation till the world had grown prudish. And it was not the men who introduced prudery into the novel. The fathers of the English novel who give their heroines healthy bodies give them also healthy minds, level heads, and an adequate knowledge of life. If Sophia Western does not know what marriage involves, it is not for want of plain speaking on her father's part. If Emilia Gauntlet does not know, it is not the fault of the amorous Peregrine Pickle. But the heroines of the women novelists theoretically do not know that love involves sexual relations, and are at the same time as skittish of any mention of love as they would be of blunt mention of the physical facts. So it is with Emmera, the "fair American," who plays the title rôle in a novel of 1767, when Sir Philip declares his passion:

—Oh! my dearest—only companion—why will you not return the truest—most ardent passion that ever warm'd a human breast?

Alas! Sir Philip, why will you use a language I cannot, must not hear?—Do not, for Heaven's sake, do not take advantage of my situation—be content to know, that I value you infinitely beyond the idea of all other men—you know not how much I esteem you—

Esteem me—Emmera—

Be not captious at a word: You know not with what—affection
—I—

Oh! Sinclair! what blushes and confusion! what painting of the modest soul!—

Fanny Burney's Evelina (1778) shies at the imminence of Lord Orville's proposal like the nervous filly that she is:

"Is it possible," said he gravely, "Miss Anville can doubt my sincerity?"

"I can't imagine," cried I, "what Mrs. Selwyn has done with these books."

"Would to Heaven," continued he, "I might flatter myself you would allow me to prove it!"

"I must run up stairs," cried I, greatly confused, "and ask what she has done with them."

This, too, in spite of the fact that Lord Orville is ideally constructed by a young girl author according to the best specifications of the answer to the maiden's prayer—one type of maiden's prayer. He is gentle, respectful, distantly adoring, a boudoir pastel in tones softened from the colors of the chivalric and the pastoral romances, the institutions of chivalry and the courts of love. It is carried to an extreme of absurdity in *Female Stability,* 1780, in which the fair Adeline succeeds in remaining a virgin and at the same time simmering in a fervid atmosphere of love through five sturdy volumes. Tearfully true to the memory of the lost Adolphus, who died before their appointed wedding, she refuses a noble duke (*bis*), an earl, two baronets, a captain in the Royal Navy—none of lesser rank dare offer, but all bow down. These are all high-tension lovers who cannot control their passion, but Adeline can control them. Her performance is like that of a daring horsewoman driving high-spirited stallions four- or six-in-hand who nearly get away with her every minute. They would eat each other alive were it not for her sweet influence. No one else could control them. The whole puts love and marriage on the basis of the dream of an adolescent girl who does not know or wishes to shun the physical facts. It is passion to the *nth* degree with no physical basis, no physical contact beyond the kissing of hands and a brotherly embrace from a violent lover who simply cannot be prevented from going so far, but never goes farther. The wild stallions come to heel like lap dogs, and provide all delights of love that are possible without disturbance to virginity, all the delicacy of spinsterhood with none of its reproaches. Doubtless the author and many readers considered it a miracle of delicate iridescence. Dean Swift if he had lived to read it would probably have thought it the kind of suppression of actualities that makes them nasty, the sort of thing against which he aimed his *Strephon and Chloe.* One infers that he would have preferred Burton's discussion of "the Symptomes of Maids, Nuns and Widows Melancholy" to the novel whose title page declares that its pages will reveal "how the fond Nymph with Rapture burns." Such a novel we may be sure is written "by a Lady" for adolescent girls, designed to keep their emotions at the simmering point without exciting their bodies. In these novels the nymph may burn for *the* man whom the novelist has designed for her chaste use, but never for *a* man. So it is, too, in the nineteenth century, the "nice" heroine may "go into a decline" from disappointment in love, or, if the shock is severe, lie for weeks at the point of death from "brain fever," but these are always the symptoms of a thwarted love affair, and not merely those "of Maids, Nuns and Widows." Not until the twentieth century can a woman novelist without forfeiting the reader's sympathy for the heroine show her in such an attitude as this:

She yanked down her middy blouse until it showed the hollow between her large white breasts. She felt a weakness go over her, and a terrible straining longing. All the sturdy strength seemed to go out of her limbs in a thrill of strange, blissful agony.

In these periods of prudery, too, there seems to be a puritanical consciousness not shown in other periods of literature of the sexual significance of the kiss. Kisses are lightly given and taken in Elizabethan times, as greetings of no portent between men and women comparatively little known to one another. But the women novelists of the late eighteenth century and early nineteenth century will no more allow an unauthorized man to take a kiss from the lips of the heroine than to commit rape on her body. If such a thing seems to happen we may be sure that the man who seems the ravisher is to be whitewashed and disinfected to make a proper husband—so it is, for example, in Regina Maria Roche's *Children of the Abbey,* one of the earliest instances establishing the canon that if a man kisses the heroine on the lips the reader may know then and thereafter that the author has picked that man for the heroine's husband. One wonders how much they knew. If they had had in mind the whole of the Hindu art of love, codified from the first kiss to the last stage of the last act, and believed that the first kiss led inevitably to the last act, they could hardly have been more scrupulous in their avoidance of the kiss. And in their care to avoid one evil they steer upon another. Many a girl at the introspective stage of life has been near suicide because some variation in the rhythm of her life has made her fear that she was pregnant from a man's kiss. Does this agony come from reading in her novels of three steps in an order so regular as to seem inevitable, a kiss, a wedding, a baby?

Prudery has many colors of which each has a hundred shades. Every possible color and shade registers in the English novel, each has its effect on the coloration of the whole, and each has its social significance. But through all its manifestations the basis of prudery is constant. Steele pointed it out when the phenomenon was finding its name in English, and he who said so nearly the first word on the subject may be allowed the last; it is that the prude "has the distinction of sex in all her thoughts, words, and actions."

CHAPTER IV

LIQUID SORROW

She stopped and wiped her gentle eyes, that swam with liquid sorrow.
CHARLOTTE PALMER, *Female Stability*, 1780.

Tears, idle tears, I know not what they mean.
TENNYSON, *The Princess.*

THE history of liquid sorrow, the life cycle of the weeping heroine, is a chapter of fashion in the History of Gloom. That history is as long as the records of the human race, but to make a chapter on the vogue of the tearful heroine in the English novel, we need not go farther back than Pamela, except for forays and excursions. Not that Pamela is much of a weeper. Modern readers are apt to call her one, but show them a real specimen of the type and they admit readily that Pamela cannot qualify; or persuade them to check over the times and occasions of her tears, and they find that she weeps no more than any girl would. Anything more of weeping than she does might defeat Richardson's purpose, which is to teach control of the passions, or to teach us not to have passions. Indeed, we do not find the type in all its glory in novels of permanent value because they are works of art, and the true weeper inhabits only works of fashion.

Pamela's tears are mere drops, but liquid sorrow begins to trickle even in her time. Four years after *Pamela,* in 1744, came *David Simple,* by Sarah Fielding, Henry Fielding's sister. Its episodic plot features no single heroine, but its successive ladies are pretty uniformly called upon to register sensibility by tears.

Here she fell into such a violent Passion of Crying, it was some time before she could speak.

He found her dissolved in Tears, and in such an Agony, that she was hardly able to speak to him.

. . . at last, for want of Words to vent her Rage, she *burst into Tears*. [Italics are the author's.]

Her Countenance was become wan with Affliction, and Tears stood in her Eyes, which she seemed unwilling to let fall, lest she should add to the Sorrow of the Man she sat by, and which, however, she was not able to restrain. . . . The young Woman, in a low Voice, interrupted with Sobs and Tears, begged the Landlady to have Patience; . . . *David's* Tears flowed as fast as hers, . . .

DAVID therefore related to her *Cynthia's* Story; the Distresses of which moved *Camilla* in such a manner, she could not refrain from weeping.

VALENTINE was struck dumb with this Generosity. Tenderness and Gratitude for such uncommon Benevolence, was to be answered in no other way, but by flowing Tears.

The men, we note, are quite as prone to tears as the women. Note, too, that as yet they call for no apology, unless it be a sort of exposition of the code for "manly tears":

. . . poor *David* could hear no more, not being able to stifle his Sighs and Tears, at the Idea of such a Scene; for he did not think it beneath a Man to cry from Tenderness, tho' he would have thought it much too effeminate to be moved to Tears by any Accident that concerned himself only.

The trickle of tears in *David Simple* increases to a continuous flow the following year (1745) in an anonymous romance, *Leonora*:

. . . in vain she called Reason to her Assistance to hush her Sighs and dry the flowing Torrents of her unavailing Tears; but the departure of Loveless sunk her quite, and made her retire in the greatest Disorder to the Apartment appointed for her.

Farther on we have the phrase "drowned in sorrow," which is perhaps a variant on "sunk" in this passage. Manly tears flow here without apology. Two brothers happen to recall the death of the son of one and nephew of the other, dead some years since:

> In pronouncing these Words they reclined their Heads on each others Bosoms, all their manly Resolutions were subdu'd; Tears, the silent Attendants on Grief, stole down their Cheeks to interrupt their Speech; in vain the struggling Words labour'd to express the inward Anguish that oppress'd them.
> Hippolytus touch'd at the moving Scene, dropp'd a silent Tear.

We learn, too, that "the greatest disorder" of tears need not give the heroine the slightest concern for her appearance; it was Leonora's tearful countenance that fatally wounded the heart of Torrismond:

> Sure some envious Daemon, Foe to my Repose, first led me to behold her in all the Pomp and Majesty of Grief, when Tears that fill'd her lovely Eyes shew'd Pity in the Chrystal Drops.

Sarah Fielding translated the emotional values of *Pamela* into terms of liquid sorrow, and Richardson followed her lead in *Sir Charles Grandison,* which fairly gurgles with manly tears, and tinkles with those of the ladies. Then Sterne and Rousseau tapped copious reservoirs, and fiction becomes a quagmire; witness this from the *Sentimental Journey,* 1768:

> . . . as she uttered them, the tears trickled down her cheeks.
> I sat down close by her; and Maria let me wipe them away as they fell, with my handkerchief.—I then steeped it in my own—and then in her's—and then in mine—and then I wip'd her's again—and as I did it, I felt such undescribable emotions within me, as I am sure could not be accounted for from any combinations of matter and motion.
> I am positive I have a soul; nor can all the books with which materialists have pestered the world ever convince me to the contrary.

Here Sterne elevates sensibility to the rank of a religion; it is his retort to the materialists, his share of the divine, his assurance of

Pajou, 1790   *Psyché*

PRECIOUS SORROWS AND DIVINE SENSIBILITIES

eternity. Liquid sorrow is the visible sign of it; he finds the protomorphic drop in Heaven, the tear with which the Recording Angel blots out the entry of Uncle Toby's oath.

One glimpse we have of liquid sorrow in a transcript from life, recorded by a novelist whose work, up to then, was by no means tearful. Fanny Burney records it in her diary under date of Monday, June 14, 1779, the year after the publication of *Evelina*. Sophy Streatfield is said to have wept over a rebuff which Mr. Seward suffered from Dr. Johnson, and Sir Philip professes to be envious.

SIR PHILIP.—Well, I have heard so much of these tears, that I would give the universe to have a sight of them.

MRS. THRALE.—Well, she shall cry again if you like it.

S. S.—No, pray, Mrs. Thrale.

SIR PHILIP.—Oh, pray do! pray let me see a little of it.

MRS. THRALE.—Yes, do cry a little, Sophy (in a wheedling voice), pray do! Consider, now, you are going to-day, and it's very hard if you won't cry a little: indeed, S. S., you ought to cry.

Now for the wonder of wonders. When Mrs. Thrale, in a coaxing voice, suited to a nurse soothing a baby, had run on for some time,—while all the rest of us in laughter, joined in the request,—two crystal tears came into the soft eyes of the S. S., and rolled gently down her cheeks! Such a sight I never saw before, nor could I have believed. She offered not to conceal or dissipate them: on the contrary, she really contrived to have them seen by everybody. She looked, indeed, uncommonly handsome; for her pretty face was not . . . blubbered; it was smooth and elegant, and neither her features nor complexion were at all ruffled; nay, indeed, she was smiling all the time. . . .

Loud and rude bursts of laughter broke from us all at once . . . She seemed the whole time, totally insensible to the numerous strange and, indeed, impertinent speeches which were made, and to be very well satisfied that she was only manifesting a tenderness of disposition that increased the beauty of her countenance. At least I can put no other construction upon her conduct, which was, without exception, the strangest I ever saw.

Not even the fashionable novelist, then, expects to find outside the novel a heroine who manifests sensibility, remaining all

the while totally insensible, but complacently believing herself
to be of tender disposition, who is placid, beautiful, even smiling
as she weeps. In life this excites rude laughter and impertinent comment; in the novel it calls for induced currents of
tears.

In sentimental fiction, tears are by this time a bottomless
ocean raging with storms of passion, and as for the heroine,
"thar she blows, an' spouts, an' bellers, an' wallers!"—blows with
sighs, spouts with tears, bellows with grief, and wallows in sentiment. On it we ship with Charlotte Palmer in *Female Stability,*
1780, five volumes of unmitigated misery whence comes the
pearl of price which adorns the head of this chapter. We have
met the heroine, Adeline, who exhibits female stability by a cease-
less flow of tears for a dead lover and unwavering refusal of a
series of high-voltage suitors. The plot of this thanatopsis is contrived for the sole purpose of turning up tearful situations in
rapid succession:

"Why are you so cruel; tell me, Adeline, why are you so cruel?" . . .
His manly eyes were filled with tears . . . He . . . hastily retired
to hide his emotion. I wiped a tear from my eye and entered the
apartment. I found my friend sitting pensively by herself . . . She
burst into tears; I mingled mine with her's glad of this opportunity
to ease my oppressed heart.

. . . her charming eyes wet with the tears she had just shed, seemed
to emit a milder ray; and promised more complacency than usual:
her cheeks glowing with the warmth of sensibility, wore heightened
graces: in short, she shone like some celestial being. She looked
on me some time with an appearance of grief . . . She wiped her
eyes: I took her hand, a pearly tear fell on mine. "Am I the cause,
the hated cause, of these precious drops?". . . This was too much;
her generosity overcame me, and I was obliged to turn from her, my
emotions were so violent: I drew out my handkerchief, and leaned
against the wainscot. Oh, Medway! I am ashamed to acknowledge
it, but I felt the trickling tear steal down my cheek: Unconscious of
my weakness for a moment I suffered it to take its course . . . I
dared not trust myself to look at her; and still covered my face with

the handkerchief I held in my hands. Never did I feel such exquisite emotions as at that moment.

His shame here is soon shown to be false modesty; he expresses admiration for the appearance of another man in the same attitude, extending the idea that a weeper is beautiful in tears to include men:

Here he was overcome by his emotions; his voice faltered, and he was obliged to stop. I never saw Sir Edward look to the advantage he did at this moment; his whole countenance had a serious and earnest appearance, that bore strong testimony to the truth of what he said; an animated glow adorned his face, and gave an additional expression to his eyes, which added to the tenderness depicted on his countenance, made him the most engaging figure imaginable; his noble resignation, so explicit and generous, amazed and pleased me.

Sometimes the precious drops fall singly:

. . . the pearly drop which she had forbidden to flow escaped unperceived its crystal prison, and was stealing down her cheeks; it fell upon her hand; she wiped it off and smiled . . . "I am happy if my sad story has afforded you any satisfaction . . ."

But usually they are more abundant:

". . . Adieu, most beloved of women!" continued he, throwing his arms about me: "Permit me this one dear embrace at parting with you!". . . He stopped and wetted my cheeks with the drops of sensibility that fell from his eyes. I could not conceal my feelings, but expressed them in liquid torrents.

Thus they flow on and on, from page to page, from paroxysm to paroxysm, from volume to volume. At the end Adeline subsides into a middle-aged routine of weeping, a mere daily dozen at the tomb of the lost Augustus, which we may imagine keeps her happy for the rest of her life:

I followed her into the church-yard, which is not far from the upper end of the park, she stopped at the family vault; and, taking a key from her pocket, opened the door, and closed it after her; this strange sight had such an effect on my spirits, that, had I not leaned against a tree, I should certainly have fallen down; in about half an hour she came up again, locked the door, and put the key in her pocket; I observed she wiped her eyes frequently; and endeavored to suppress the emotions which preyed upon her peace.

Whence these tears? Why does the period known in the history of thought as the Age of Reason record itself in the history of the novel in terms of tearful hysteria that would disgrace a girl's boarding-school? Two answers are obvious. First, just because it was the Age of Reason. The age cannot be completely one of reason so long as emotion, which it cannot suppress or destroy, remains outside its control. Therefore it seeks to bring emotion under its control. Since it cannot eradicate emotion it must govern it by rules. There shall be no emotion save such as is decorous in the drawing-room. Polite life is an art; if reality or intensity of emotion makes the artist unmindful, he fails. Form, which is mainly rational, prescribes occasions for feeling, its degrees of intensity, and manners of expression. Emotion by rule is insincerity, and insincerity of emotion is of the essence of sentimentality. Second, because of the Puritan victory, the influence of which has dominated the English novel for about ninety per cent of its term of life. It has tinged most of the novels of the eighteenth and nineteenth centuries with "that type of sentimentalism which regards the useful, the stimulating and the moral elements in works of art as essential." This is the handicap which Christianity from its beginning imposed upon art, a heavy fog of moral purpose through which art must shine as best it can. English Puritanism turned art into propaganda, inculcating the code that utility made fashionable. A newly dominant party seeking to turn art to its purpose constrains it to insincerity and sentimentalism. The novelists of the formative period of the novel in England are almost unanimous in their declaration that the "purpose" of the novel is to improve the morals of its readers. The novel remains sentimental until its writers learn better what they are about. These considerations, however, do not tell the whole story; probably we cannot tell it until we know much more than we do about the wellsprings of irrationality in human behavior. It is easier to account in general for the presence of the phenomenon than in particular for the peculiarities of its manifestation at the time. It is easy to diagnose the tearful hysteria of the novel of sensibility as an acute phase of the history of gloom, a local and temporal manifestation of certain constants in human character.

One of these constants is literary and fashionable melancholy. In Anglo-Saxon literature its color was a sort of stoic pessimism, dark but not tearful—"It is better that a man avenge his friend than that he mourn much." In the Middle Ages its color is religious, and its imagery that of the Dance of Death. In the Renaissance its guise is Hamlet-like; it was not Horace Walpole, nor yet Shakespeare, who "invented" the Byronic hero; he "just growed." The figure is not new when Milton exhibited it in a robe of darkest grain at midnight hour in high lonely tower outwatching the Bear, singing:

> *Hail! thou Goddess, sage and holy!*
> *Hail! divinest Melancholy!*

It stalks through successive schools of "graveyard poetry" in the seventeenth, eighteenth and nineteenth centuries. It dominates the American scene from the *Bay Psalm Book* and the *New England Primer* through generations of thanatopses of all kinds, weeping willows, tombstones, urns, customary suits of solemn black; indeed, the whole nation up to where rolls the Oregon was one mighty sepulchre until Mark Twain taught it to give up its dead and take to laughter. The greater artists forge this fashionable melancholy into works of art according to their degree: *The Fall of the House of Usher, Childe Harold, Il Penseroso, Hamlet.* The lesser artists sentimentalize it or popularize it into works of fashion, built so largely of its temporal and local manifestations that when these have evaporated the residue is worthless. Tears and melancholy are as constant in their presence as skirts and trousers, and as variable in their fashions.

The constance and variability of fashions in emotions, no less than in clothes, has much of its basis in the fundamental fact that we tend to imitate the class to which we aspire. If the middle and working classes looking at the gentry and nobility think they see appearance of feeling, or appearance of suppression of feeling, they will seek the same appearance, whether they understand its significance or not. And just as surely as they seek superiority by assimilating their manners and appearance to those whom they deem superior, just so will the upper classes seek to avoid the resemblance, and emphasize their superiority, by new and more striking marks of differentiation. The aristocrat, looking down at the peasant, sees him as a mere brother to the insensible clod, and by way of contrast cultivates sensibility. He sees, too, that when the peasant does display any elementary emotions he is vulgarly noisy about it, monstrous guffaws of laughter or unseemly boo-hoos of grief. My lord, then, cultivates complete stoicism or polite restraint. Thus the whirligig of fashion whisks us round and round our circle of sensibility, polite restraint and stoicism.

The aspirant from a lower class would be safe most of the time in trying to appear "as melancholy as a gentleman." The "melancholy posture" implies suppression which implies feeling, and is opposite to the two points which are opposite each other, peasant insensibility and peasant noisiness of expression. The aspirant might see it, too, as the outward sign of another prerogative of the upper classes, education, which might induce either a more or less philosophical pessimism or religious melancholy, as in priests and bishops who rated as gentles and nobles. And the plebeian, even if he were not a social aspirant, might find a Christlike pattern for religious melancholy if he looked to the "man of sorrows, acquainted with grief."

Liquid sorrow has babbled through the runways of literature since its earliest stages, but tears show little social significance in European tales before feudalism. Early narrative literature deals mainly with royal or noble heroes; figures of lesser rank seldom appear save for comic parts. These heroes are like children in that they express only two emotions, pleasure and pain, the one by tears, the other by laughter, with no degrees on the scale between. Here is no emotional or behavioristic distinction between king and shepherd; the society represented is simply organized, pastoral or other, such that a shepherd who was a good slinger might smite a Goliath between the eyes and become a king. In the *Beowulf,* Hrothgar has some sixty lines of grief for the death of Aeschere; his prolixity elicits from Beowulf the terse comment that action towards revenge would be more worth while. There are more words than tears in the passage; so are there when Achilles unpacks his heart of its heaviness for the death of Patroclus. Such passages as these are the work of narrative poets or minstrels speaking to simple-minded men of action, poets scarcely better qualified than their hearers to discriminate or express subtle shades of individual feelings. Their business is to shadow forth their heroes on gigantic scale, deeds, emotions and all. They inflate a simple emotion to the required scale merely by stuffing it with words. When ballad and epic have grief to record on a smaller scale, they click it off with a formula. In the *Iliad* and the *Odyssey* strong men weep whenever anything goes wrong, probably because that is the only way the minstrel has of showing how they feel about it. In the ballads a few clichés cover all instances: "the tear blinded her ee," "Lady Margaret tore her yellow hair," "wringing her hands, tearing her hair his lady she was seen," "out cam his auld mither greeting fu' sair," and other such.

In the *cante-fable* of *Aucassin and Nicolette* there is an obvious attempt to set the gentleman high above and apart from the peasant. The marks of differentiation in appearance are grotesquely exaggerated in the description of the peasant whom Aucassin meets in the wood when he is seeking Nicolette and weeping because he does not find her. He tells the peasant that he is weeping because he has lost a white hound, the fairest in the world. The peasant then shows himself every inch a peasant, first by being too stupid to understand Aucassin's figure of speech, second by deriding Aucassin for weeping and by boasting of hardships and sorrows he himself has suffered without weeping. Aucassin is an early example of the Man of Feeling; the peasant perhaps the first appearance of the Man with the Hoe, brother to the ox, brutal of jaw, slant of brow, the light blown out within the brain. As an example of heroic exaggeration of the symptoms of gentlemanly sorrow, we may note what happened to Garnish of the Mount in Malory's "Book of Sir Balin le Savage": "And when Garnish beheld her so lying, for pure sorrow his mouth and nose brast out on bleeding . . . and then he made sorrow out of measure."

It is this romance tradition of aristocratic feeling which passes at long last into the novel. The romances of feudal times directly or indirectly set up a sort of code for the use and expression of the emotions of ladies and gentlemen. Ladies may weep on all occasions of vexation, pain and sorrow. Gentlemen may weep for the pains of love, in sympathy with others, especially as a mark of chivalric friendship, and in sorrow for the death of others. They seem to show stoicism in the endurance of physical pain, particularly in combat or battle, and in the endurance of the pangs of death. Feudalism wrote this code into romances that deal with chivalric material, and adapted classical material to its requirements in romances that drew on Greek and Roman sources. Familiarity with classical literature, especially the Greek, was so largely one of the prerogatives of the upper classes as to be one of the insignia of aristocracy, and literature adapting or imitating any of its material from the beginning of the Renaissance through the eighteenth century was sure to show the courtly-chivalric code of manners, morals and behavior on the part of characters who were supposed to have lived centuries before chivalry, as does Chaucer, for example, in *The Knight's Tale* and the *Troilus*. Thus the romances of the sixteenth and seventeenth centuries, whether they were pastoral, heroic or chivalric, exhibit the courtly code for the emotions. As feudalism declines and capitalism advances, chivalry becomes more and more the empty formalism of aristocracy, and the emptier it becomes the louder it resounds with hollow insistence. In *The Countess of Pembroke's Arcadia,* Sir Philip Sidney devotes a whole folio volume to the contrast between peasant and prince, just as he devoted a lifetime to personal display of knightly deportment.

From such narratives as the *Arcadia* there flowed a current of romance that mingled with the river of realism to form the modern novel. On the surface we see little appearance of romance in the formative period of the English novel; from Defoe through Smollett realism is your only wear, until Horace Walpole attempted as he said, "to blend the two kinds of romance, the ancient and the modern," and by the modern romance he meant the modern novel. But even in the first quarter of the century we may see romance following realism step for step if we know where to look for it. The first step in realism is Defoe's *Robinson Crusoe,* 1719. Almost side by side with it comes a much shorter novel which quite as clearly as *The Castle of Otranto,* though less explicitly, tries to blend the realism of Defoe with the romance of the former age. The title page demonstrates the fact: "The Strange Adventures of the Count *de Vinevil* and his Family. Being an account of what happen'd to them whilst they resided at *Constantinople.* And of Mademoiselle ARDELISA, his Daughter's being shipwreck'd on the Uninhabited Island *Delos,* in her return to *France,* with VIOLETTA, a *Venetian* Lady, the Captain of the Ship, a Priest, and five Sailors. The Manner of their living there, and strange Deliverance by the Arrival of a Ship commanded by VIOLETTA's Father. ARDELISA's Entertainment at *Venice,* and

safe Return to *France*. By Mrs. Aubin . . . London, . . .
M.DCC.XXI." If the influence of *Robinson Crusoe* is not clear
enough in this title page, one has only to turn to the preface,
where it is explicit: "As for the Truth of what this Narrative contains, since *Robinson Cruso* has been so well receiv'd, which is
more improbable, I know no reason why this should be thought
a Fiction." Once aboard the lugger we are likely to forget Defoe
and his realism of detail, for we find ourselves in company with
lords and ladies who show their fine feelings by tears and fainting, and pattern their behavior according to the Courts of Love.
The occasion of the voyage is, indeed, a commercial venture,
but commerce is no feature of the tale; instead wealth is always
conveniently (if fortuitously) at hand when anyone needs to get
married, and conveniently absent when anyone wants to lead
the simple life, all according to the tradition of the pastoral and
chivalric romances.

As with *Robinson Crusoe,* so with *Pamela;* romance followed
close on its heels. Most of the "servant-girl romances" which
are said to have sprung up in the sunshine of Richardson's success
have, for better or for worse, disappeared. One which has survived
is *The Life of Patty Saunders. Written by Herself* . . . 1752.
This pins itself to Richardson's coat-tails by starting its heroine
in the working class, and staging an abduction with a forced
journey in a carriage, *à la Pamela,* and to Defoe's by a shipwreck
or two and a desert island. The rest is compounded of fairy tale
and chivalric romance set forth in terms of the Restoration Comedy. The heroine's journey lands her in the castle of the wicked
knight or the ogre who keeps damsels in duress vile, but the
chapter heading translates him into a contemporary rake: "Biddy
describes the Master of the Castle, Laird C—r—k, and her condition. Shews his Rapes every Year. All his Women Servants cast
Whores of his Father's." It suggests a psychoanalysis of the
fairy tale by its rendition of dream fantasy in plain sexual terms.
Here perhaps more clearly than in *The Count of Vinevil* we can

see romance and realism mingled but not blended, but they are both fair examples of their numerous kind, and enable us to trace the obscure channels by which romance flows into the current of the novel before the time of Walpole, Mrs. Radcliffe, Monk Lewis, Beckford, and the other practitioners of Gothics and terrors. The channels of romance are conduits of liquid sorrow, but they are not the only ones.

In so far as romance is Cavalier literature, and realism Puritan, we might expect liquid sorrow to be more characteristic of realism than of romance, of sobriety rather than of gaiety. If liquid sorrow is strictly fashionable sensibility, it is not conspicuously exhibited except for condemnation or satire in realistic literature; if it includes tears of piety and contrition, Puritanism can show it abundantly enough. Defoe's novels are autobiographies of sailor and soldier, prostitute and pirate. Such as these must needs be thoroughly hard-boiled, and so Defoe cooks them for so long as is necessary to get them into trouble, then come tears and repentance. "I had great reason to consider it as a determination of Heaven," says Crusoe, "that in this desolate place, and in this desolate manner, I should end my life. The tears would run plentifully down my face when I made these reflections; . . ." In fact, if you re-read the book as a document of Puritanism, you begin to think that Defoe gives almost as many pages to Crusoe's soul as to his body, and that the establishment of his dominion over the island, "my reign or my captivity as you choose to call it," is merely the outward shadowing forth of what goes on in his mind and spirit. Shall the relation of his soul to his body be reign or captivity? As with the sailor, so with the prostitute and with the pirate. Moll Flanders is the sentimental prostitute, and Captain Singleton turns in the end to thrift and good works. Twentieth-century abridgements of *Robinson Crusoe* reject page after page of the story of Crusoe's lonely conversion as distasteful sentimentality; the twentieth century is more sentimental about gangsters than about God. Sentimentality is self-conscious sentiment, and sentiment looks self-conscious to us when we ourselves could not hold or express the sentiment without self-consciousness. There are passages in Defoe on the basis of which we may fairly accuse him, but in the main we may safely take him for a sincere moralist. Unless tears of puritan repentance are liquid sorrow, Defoe shows little of it.

If sentimentality is one with liquid sorrow, Richardson has it. Pamela is from the start as completely the religious sentimentalist as is Crusoe after his conversion, and Clarissa and Anna Howe are no less. By contrast with Crusoe, Pamela, working girl though she is, moves in the fashionable world. Since she is to be promoted to membership in it, Richardson has her in training from the start, and though she "knows her place," ladylike sensibility always fits her as closely as her piety. She weeps for good cause at various times when her master is badgering her. When she is Lady B. she weeps like a lady for gratitude, love, sympathy and vexation. But the sheer sentimentality of liquid sorrows shows more clearly in other figures. Pamela's parents are farmers, but not insensible clods; they weep very readily. Mrs. Jervis, the housekeeper, barely above the servant class, weeps for five pages while Pamela showers bounty upon her; the close of the scene is quite in the best manner of liquid sorrow:

> She could not speak: tears ran down her cheeks in plentiful currents: her modest hand put gently from her my offering hand, and her bosom heaved, and she sobbed with the painful tumult that seemed to struggle within her, and which, for some few moments, made her incapable of speaking.

But most sentimental of all are the tears of the unregenerate Sir Jacob Swynford and the hard-boiled Jackey:

> "Bless you!—O Christ!" said he, and stamped—"Who can choose but bless you?" And he kneeled down, and wrapped his arms about me.—"But curse me," that was his strange word, "if ever I was so touched before!". . . And the tears, as he spoke, ran down his rough

cheeks; which moved me a good deal: for to see a man with so hard a countenance weep, was a touching sight.

Mr. H——, putting his handkerchief to his eyes, his aunt said, "What's the matter, Jackey?"—"The matter!" answered he; "I don't know how the d——l it is— But here's strange doings, as ever I knew —For here, day after day, one's ready to cry, without knowing whether it be for joy or sorrow!—What a plague's the matter with me, I wonder!"—And out he went; the two ladies, whose charming eyes, too, glistened with pleasure, smiling at the effect the scene had on Mr. H——, and at what he said.

Here we have manly tears quite according to the chivalric code; they drip from nearly every page of *Sir Charles Grandison*. It might account for something, but not for everything, to suppose that Richardson knew little of the behavior of ladies and gentlemen beyond what he might have read in chivalric romances.

Most important of all in the consideration of the quality of Richardson's sentimentality is his sense of emotional values. His declared purpose in *Pamela* is "to teach the man of passion how to subdue it"; his effect was to teach the novelist of passion how to dramatize it. The real climax of the plot is Pamela's discovery that her heart was herself—"Thus foolishly dialogued I with my heart; and yet, all the time, this heart is Pamela." Richardson's art was supreme in his ability to extract the last drop of emotional essence from every situation in his story; witness the scene in which Pamela parades the longest walk in the garden under the battery of the eyes of a garden-house full of ladies and gentlemen, and more notably that in which Goodman Andrews comes to rescue Pamela if he can, and finds her virtue not lost but rewarded. These scenes are too long to quote, for the emotional essence is distilled thoroughly drop by drop for page after page. The process is even more slow and thorough in *Clarissa*. It is indubitably of the essence of Richardson's moral purpose. It is our feelings, he implies, that move us to actions right and wrong. The motion may come from a feeling so obscure as to be unperceived, unsuspected. Therefore no feeling is trivial enough to neglect. Each down to the minutest must be observed, scrutinized, analyzed quantitatively and qualitatively for its faintest traces of right and wrong. This self-consciousness in every conscious moment is essential in Richardson's purpose and method, and self-consciousness in all moments is inevitably sentimentality in most. The method is of great importance in the history of the novel. It is important in the history of Pamela's daughters because they inherit from her the trait of self-consciousness that so often spells sentimentality, and the sensibility that so often finds expression in terms of liquid sorrow.

If this microscopic emotional analysis has been of service to the novel, it is a rare instance of a serviceable gift from the enemy. Usually when the moralist forces a "purpose" on art, he debases the art by crude alloys of propaganda and sentimentality. Sentimentality is here very conspicuously, but its inexorable finality of analysis is almost scientifically rigorous, and the rigor is that of the introspection of puritanism. Before Richardson, Defoe has this method in some of his passages of puritanism, such for example as those in which Crusoe debates his scruples about killing cannibals. The method is part and parcel of American puritanism. It shows in the searchings of the heart to determine calling and election, and the searchings of the physical world for signs of the metaphysical, for indications of the will of God by which the community and the individual may be governed, to which each and all may submit the human will.

If we take at its face value Richardson's expression of purpose, to teach control of the passions, his division of sense from sensibility would seem to be the same as Jane Austen's. In *Sense and Sensibility,* Marianne Dashwood is pretty universally supposed to represent the heart, or feeling uncontrolled, and her sister Elinor to represent the head, or passion controlled by reason and the will. Jane Austen in so far as she justifies Elinor stands for reason in control and seems to take her place on Richardson's side. At first glance, then, we may see the line running straight from Richardson to Jane Austen, with the novelists and their heroines ranged decisively on the one side and the other.

If, however, we undertake to survey the line with transit and rod, we find the task not so simple as it looked in the reconnaissance. Richardson believes in reason in control, yes, but he upholds for our sober acceptance women, and men too, more absurdly emotional than any extremes of Marianne Dashwood. Jane Austen advocates sense, yes, but her Lucy Steele who is all head and no heart is obviously on the wrong side of the fence; she is not sense, but a sort of critique of pure reason. Obviously there must be emotions to control—Elinor has profound feelings—or there can be no "sense" in Jane Austen's signification of the term. Sense, then, means reason with just the right admixture of true feeling. Sensibility if you approve of it means the same thing; if you don't approve of it, it means silly or dangerous emotionalism, or heartless fashionable insincerity. It is like poetry; if you love it you give its name to everything you cherish, and praise and exalt it to the highest; if you dislike it you give its name to all that you detest, and kick it round the floor. Jane Austen gives its name to the dangerous emotionalism of Marianne and the fashionable hard insincerity of Lady Middleton. Sterne sets it on the throne of God, and calls his individual part of it his immortal soul.

We call Richardson the father of the novel of sensibility, but the term was scarcely in his vocabulary in its literary sense. We call Fielding his opponent, and think of him as withering Richardson's sensibility with robust blasts of sense. We may quite as accurately think of him as withering Richardson's prudential sense with blasts of robust human feeling. *Joseph Andrews* is, of course, a counterblast to *Pamela,* directed, however, not against excess in her tears but against policy in her tenacity of virtue. If sense means virtue based on policy, a utilitarian code of morals, and sensibility means right and ready feeling, or intuitive morals, Fielding would be for sensibility and in opposition to the father of the novel of sensibility. His sister's novel, *David Simple,* is, so far as this investigation has gone, the first out-and-out novel of sensibility, the first we know which exhibits the type hero of the genre, the type which Mackenzie later named the man of feeling. David has all the marks of the type. He is instantly ready with sympathy for the suffering and oppressed, and no less ready to express sympathy by tears. He has the cardinal virtue of gulli-bility; that is, he is so guileless himself as to be totally unsuspecting of guile in others, and you may, as Sterne wrote of his father, "cheat him ten times a day if nine is not sufficient for your purpose."

Did Sarah Fielding learn from her brother that gullibility was a virtue? In it he clothes his militant man of feeling, Parson Adams, as in a shining garment: "As he never had any intention to deceive, so he never suspected such a design in others . . . sim-plicity was his characteristic." In its earliest recorded meaning in English, simplicity was a virtue, for *simple* meant "free from duplicity, dissimulation, or guile," and expressed the Biblical virtue of the dove. In times in which standards are set by merchants and advertisers, Simple Simon is a "good" customer only when he has "purchasing power." To them, gullibility is a virtue in one sense; it is so in quite another to the novelist of sensibility who looks back to pre-capitalistic society as to a Golden Age. In their works we see gullibility as the shining halo which all wear who are to stand in contrast with the calculating, hard-hearted people who get rich. It is comparable with the Biblical virtue of poverty except in that it is usually associated with the aristocratic virtue of com-plete disdain of all getting or keeping of money, a virtue con-trasting with the puritan-bourgeois virtue of thrift. The man-of-feeling hero of the novel of sensibility is almost invariably robbed of his patrimony at the start by someone more calculating than himself (David's brother performed this service for him), and sets out to conquer a hard-boiled world with a soft heart in his breast and half a crown in his pocket. The half crown he gives to the first beggar he meets, and the heart to all comers. His adventures are contrived to bring him in contact with all the hard spots of the world, and in contrast with all the hard-hearted types of worldly society. *David Simple* exhibits all this and more. As we have seen, it flows freely with liquid sorrow, and its very title page uses the qualifying adjective, "in search of a *real* friend" which is so characteristic of later attempts to distinguish the real article from the spurious. It is a genuine novel of sensibility. Its author was Richardson's friend and admirer and Fielding's sister. Both Richardson and Fielding are on record with hearty praise of the book. It can hardly be Richardson's sensibility that Fielding attacked. *Tom Jones* is no more than *Joseph Andrews* in opposition to excess display of feeling. Tom may be red-blooded and two-fisted, but he weeps and faints as readily as does Sophia, and is as ready with sympathy and charity as any other man of feeling. He is done out of his patrimony by the scheme of a villainous relative, and tosses his last half crown to the first beggar he meets as he goes out into the world. What is, then, Fielding's quarrel with Richardson? Not the amount of feeling, but the amount of control. Fielding runs his hero through life like a bull through a china shop and calls on us to admire his strength and energy; not the nicety with which he misses a Dresden vase, but the fact that he comes out the front door at last, just where anyone else would have come out. To Fielding a bull who could go through a china shop without breaking anything would seem emasculate, fit for nothing but to drag the plough. The bull who wrecks the shop is a bull of mettle, even though he weep over the wreckage. The difference between Richardson and Fielding, then, is in degree rather than in kind. They might agree that feeling is the motive power to action. Richardson would drive cautiously through the traffic of life in low gear. Fielding would keep the throttle open and condone such accidents as seem inevitable to high power at full speed. Booth, the hero of Fielding's third novel, *Amelia,* is almost as completely the man of feeling as is David Simple. Incidentally it is amusing to note one minor item in which Fielding sentimentalizes Richardson. Pamela's first child is named Billy, but it is Fielding's *Amelia* which brings into the menagerie of sentimentalism the small boy named Billy as one of its most conspicuous exhibits.

A characteristic doctrine of sensibility is one which is so nearly the opposite of the idea of original sin that we may name it original virtue. It is the belief that man in an "original" or "natural" state is good until he is spoiled by contamination from society. Evil is a culture that can live only in the medium called society or civilization. It does not arise where man lives in a solitary or natural state, and if transported there is unlikely to flourish. Originally or naturally man does not have it, but somehow it is generated by men living together under certain conditions. This doctrine is commonly attributed to Rousseau, and most often called by his name, but it was current in England at least fifty years before Rousseau recoined it. He formulated it in his first work of any importance, his *Dissertation on the Sciences and the Arts,* 1750:

I hardly dare speak of those happy nations who do not even know the name of those vices which we are at such pains to suppress; of the savages of America whose simple and natural regulations Montaigne does not hesitate to prefer, not only to the laws of Plato, but even to the most perfect form of government which philosophy can imagine.

This doctrine makes its appearance in English fiction before the novel in the *Oroonoko* of Mrs. Aphra Behn, 1668, and was part and parcel of English sentimentalism right through to Wordsworth and beyond. Since no one could possibly hold it who had ever come in contact with men in any "primitive" state, or who knew anything of anthropology as a science, it has always been sufficiently remote from actuality to be good food for romance. It appears, then, at its height in novels that have perished of oversensibility and over-heightened romance.

Such is the anonymous *The Adventures of Emmera; or, The Fair American. Exemplifying the Peculiar Advantages of Society and Retirement*, 1767 (cited above in Chapter III), in which a paradise of sweet and simple savages is located somewhere between Philadelphia and Lake Ontario by a romancer who very obviously has never visited the region. It is the story of a sophisticated Englishman, Sir Philip Chetwin, who finds a child of nature and of English parents in a secluded valley in Pennsylvania where Philadelphia is the nearest port and it is only a slight journey to Lake Ontario but a very considerable one to Lake Erie. The good unspoiled savages are her friends and protectors; they will rush to her aid in swarms whenever she runs up a signal of distress. Chetwin adds himself to her list of friends, and lives an idyllic and blameless life with her in her earthly paradise. At length he takes her to England, where she shows revulsion at the sophistications and cruelties of society. Accordingly they load two or three ships with sophistications in the shape of tools and other appurtenances, and go back to complicate and contaminate aboriginal society in the wilds of Pennsylvania. One of the simplicities of the place is the ease with which letters travel to and from London. Chetwin tries to describe Emmera in a letter to his friend Forrester, but his emotions are almost too much for him; the dashes, presumably, represent sobs and gasps:

Nature! by heaven in her happiest moment, for once formed divine perfection. Think not I rave, but she is the divinity of these wild regions! By my soul, she's more than mortal! and I adore her.—
Really, Charles, I can write no more—you must expect no account—I am unable to give it—Entranced—All emotion!—wild as the winds—Methinks she sails through crystal lakes—or walks through emerald groves—now floating on the wings of kissing air, through dazzling worlds, receiving homage as she moves! The queen of beauty's empire stept for a moment from her distant throne to play the tyrant in this nether world! To fill our souls with hapless love, and by the magic of her enchanting eye to change us to gazing

maniacs, wildly wandering—sighing—loving—no—not despairing.
—There—there— . . . let my fancy but for one moment gaze at
that sweet image of more than human tenderness, and, alas, I am
again undone—my brain will turn the next.

Contrast this with his father's opinions:

It is the earnest wish of my soul, that I may conduct myself through
life with that steady and determined perseverance in the path of unprejudiced reason, which can alone render a man superior to the
fopperies of opinion and fashion. This necessary resolution is the
most philosophic guide on which the human mind can depend. . . .
I resided for some time in several parts of Europe, and formed an
extensive acquaintance with men whose names would flatter the
vanity of some men to repeat: In a word, I rendered myself as complete a master of European manners as I was able; and it was the
reflections I drew from that knowledge which induced me to seek
for more natural ideas and purer practice in a country just on the
verge of cultivation—for I laid it down as a maxim, that a country
must abound in the necessaries of life before the superfluities could
deluge it with luxury and vice.

Maniacal wild wanderings and steady perseverance in the path of
unprejudiced reason may seem as the poles apart, but both point
as unerringly toward Rousseau as do the natural ideas and pure
practices of the savages of America. To these distance lends
special enchantment, and contrast gives added charm, as Emmera views them from across the sea:

. . . Sir George, complimenting her in a flighty manner on her leaving such a wilderness of savages, the word gave her a disgust—
    I don't understand that expression, Sir: Pray what do you mean
by savages?
    Mean, Madam! 'Pon honour, I mean the very reverse of what
they ought to be, that were illumin'd by such beauty as your's—
You know what I mean—you can tell, Madam.
    I suppose you mean the Indians, Sir—but so far are they, in my
opinion, from being savages, that I assure you, Sir, they are neither
vain of their dress—nor conceited of their impertinence—nor had I
ever a compliment paid me by one of them at the expence of common
sense and sincerity.

Trivial as *The Adventures of Emmera* is in itself, it is worth noting where it exhibits signs of the times either earlier or more clearly than do the important works of its day. Two more straws we find in it which show which way the wind is blowing; two threads whose color we shall trace through other patterns. One is sensibility extending to ecstasy in the presence of the beauties of nature, ecstasy which calls for tears as the tide of liquid sorrow rises, and often serves, like the roseleaf under a dozen mattresses, as the test of the true princess. The other is humanitarian sensibility, the extension of sympathy to the sufferings of animals. The first appears in Chetwin. He writes to Forrester a rhapsody of description of an ideal landscape which docile nature in Pennsylvania has formed by strict observances of all the rules of Burke on the Sublime. Here he sees "all the enchanting negligence of the most picturesque fancy. The moment I threw my eyes over this delicious spot," he writes—no small feat, by the way, if we may take his word for the altitudes—"all my faculties were for the moment suspended, I could scarce draw my breath for gazing with such statue-like attention at the amazing beauties of this little spot." The sounding cataract, we perceive, haunted him like a passion twenty-three years before Wordsworth told us that it did the same for him, and that in the presence of "these beauteous forms . . . the breath of this corporeal frame and even the motion of our human blood [are] almost suspended." The other trait, sympathy with animals, shows best in Emmera. In England she sees a man beating a horse.

Emmera's humane heart was touch'd at the sight exceedingly—the tears ran down her cheeks, and she lifted up her hands at the barbarity of the fellow. [After this and other instances of cruelty, she says] Oh! Sir Philip, my blood runs cold to think of the intolerable wickedness in the world, and amongst people that think themselves refined in their understandings and polished in their ideas! These are the people that call the Americans savages! Virtuous and amiable people have quitted the neighbourhood of men to become the companions of brutes!

Sympathy with animals and advocacy of humane treatment of them is conspicuous in the history of sensibility from Shaftesbury to Wordsworth, but we see little indication of it in the novel until Sterne gives us Uncle Toby's famous apostrophe to the fly and the sentimental interview with the donkey in the gateway at Lyons. Between Chaucer's Prioress and Emmera there are few heroines who weep over the pains of dog or horse under the lash.

Was the author of *Emmera* ignorant of the fact that the authentic annals of Indian captivity reveal acts of cruelty and lust quite as fiendish as any that adorn the police blotters of civilization? Not so Mrs. Frances Moore Brooke, author of *Lady Julia Mandeville, Emily Montague,* and others. Mrs. Brooke was an ardent admirer of Rousseau—she swallowed the hook, but her experience in Canada opened her eyes to the line and the sinker. She can admire Rousseau without finding it necessary to canonize him, or sacrilegious to disagree with him. One of her characters in *Emily Montague* (1769), Col. Rivers, subscribes to the doctrine of original virtue: "I agree," he says, "that mankind are born virtuous and that it is education and example which make them otherwise." Another, William Fermor, disagrees with Rousseau:

Rousseau has taken great pains to prove that the most uncultivated nations are the most virtuous; I have all due respect for this philosopher, of whose writings I am an enthusiastic admirer; but I have a still greater respect for truth, which I believe in this instance is not on his side. . . . From all that I have heard and observed of these people, it appears to me an undoubted fact, that the most civilized Indian nations are the most virtuous; a fact which makes directly against Rousseau's ideal system . . . That the savages have virtues, candor must own; but only a love of paradox can make any man assert that they have more than polished nations.

She finds quite as much magnificence in the American scene as the author of *Emmera* could supply from his imagination or his manual of landscape gardening, but she does not pretend that man can live by natural magnificence alone. She describes the Falls of Montmorenci in winter with her eye on the object:

> As you gradually approach the bay you are struck with an awe, which increases every moment, as you come nearer, from the grandeur of a scene, which is one of the noblest works of nature; the beauty, the proportion, the solemnity, the wild magnificence of which, surpassing every possible effect of art, impress one strongly with the idea of its Divine Almighty Architect.
>
> The rock on the east side, which is the first in view as you approach, is a smooth and almost perpendicular precipice, of the same height as the fall; the top, which a little overhangs, is beautifully covered with pines, firs, and evergreens of various kinds, whose verdant lustre is rendered at this season more shining and lovely by the surrounding snow, as well as by that which is sprinkled irregularly on their branches, and glitters half melted in the sunbeams; a thousand smaller shrubs are scattered on the side of the ascent, and having their roots in almost imperceptible clefts of the rock, seem to those below to grow in air.

This is orthodox enough, but hark to the heresy!

> The scenery is to be sure divine, but one grows weary of mere scenery: the most enchanting prospect soon loses its power of pleasing, when the eye is accustomed to it: we gaze at first transported on the charms of nature, but, alas! it will not do; we sigh for society, the conversation of those dear to us; the more animated pleasures of the heart.

So much for the romantic souls who think they "could gaze forever enraptured." Enraptured Mrs. Brooke surely is, reverence and awe are hers, but she has no illusions about the eternal permanence of the passion. And you cannot doubt that she has experienced the American Atlantic seaboard in winter when you read:

> We have had a great deal of snow already, but it melts away; 'tis a lovely day, but a odd mixture of summer and winter: in some places you see half a foot of snow lying, in others the dust is even troublesome.

She is strong for sensibility; it is a virtue, and "virtue" (in Pamela's sense of the word) is not a virtue without it:

> What a charm, my dear Lucy, is there in sensibility! 'Tis the magnet which attracts all to itself: virtue may command esteem, understanding and talents admiration, beauty a transient desire; but 'tis sensibility alone which can inspire love.
> The same dear affections, the same tender sensibility, the most precious gift of Heaven inform our minds, and make us peculiarly capable of exquisite happiness or misery.

It may come from heaven, but it is not in her religion the sole occupant of the throne of God; it is possible to have too much of it and too little of anything else. In her earlier novel, *Lady Julia Mandeville*, 1762, not only the heroine, Lady Julia, but the hero, Henry, lose at once the ideal happiness that is within their grasp and their lives also by the over-excitability of commendable feelings. Lady Anne through too much sense, precaution, bids fair to miss her happiness, but learns sensibility in time from Lady Julia. Henry is a study of the man of feeling to the same effect as Romeo; if you have too much sensibility you are not likely to live long enough to acquire any sense. Lady Julia and Lady Anne are the woman of feeling and the woman of the world before Mackenzie displayed their masculine counterparts. Mrs. Brooke exhibited the romantic lady as a tragic figure for our sympathy before the starched moralists, Maria Edgeworth, Mrs. Brunton, Madame D'Arblay, made her into a source of contamination. Jane Austen redeemed her and brushed enough mud off her to make her presentable as Marianne Dashwood. Mrs. Brooke surveyed the ground of *Sense and Sensibility* eight years before Jane Austen was born. Jane Austen is a middle term between Mrs. Brooke and the Moralists; Mrs. Brooke is a middle term between the sentimentalists and their opponents. In terms of liquid sorrow, Miss Edgeworth and Mrs. Brunton are prohibitionists; Mrs. Brooke is for temperance. She stands for sensible sensibility.

The outcry against the woman of feeling, alias the romantic lady, was often, as we saw in the last chapter, a matter of prudery. In the history of sensibility she has two other phases according as the author approves or disapproves, is a philosophical or a practical moralist, an idealist or a utilitarian in morals. The idealist makes her an ideal child of nature, the other school uses her as a warning example.

Sarah Fielding is an idealist. To stand beside her early example of the man of feeling, *David Simple,* she presented later a woman of feeling in *The History of Ophelia.* David is "simple" because he is "natural." Ophelia is no less; she is natural in her feelings, in her education (if any), in her views of society, in her ideas about clothes—not that she goes without them, but society would say she might as well go bare as to dispense as she does with stays and so nearly with hoops. She has been brought up as far from the madding crowd as one can get in the Island of Britain until she is about sixteen, when she is released to go through the ranks of society (paraded for the purpose) like a watering-cart, washing its sins with her tears. The idea is much the same as that of *David Simple* but it had received much impetus from Rousseau since 1744. Thomas Day, the author of the once-famous *Sandford and Merton,* actually tried to put it in practice, and attempted to shape the development of a female child according to the strict rules of Émile into an artless state of nature to be his bride. Wordsworth in 1799 described her so accurately that the literary type has been named the "Lucy bride." She is "a violet by a mossy stone, half hidden from the eye"; of her Nature says:

> "*A lovelier flower*
> *On earth was never sown;*
> *This Child I to myself will take;*
> *She shall be mine, and I will make*
> *A Lady of my own."*

> "*Myself will to my darling be*
> *Both law and impulse: . . ."*

That was precisely Day's idea, but he made the mistake of trying to build his lady of flesh and blood. In real life the experiment failed, but on paper it worked perfectly and had continued success in the novel of sensibility. The question was what she was good for and who was good enough for her when she was finished. Ophelia's natural virtue like Pamela's of different origin serves to reform a rake.

A moralist of experience was Mrs. Mary Hays, whose *Memoirs of Emma Courtney,* 1796, is called "semi-autobiographical." She drank deep of liquid sorrow, and wrote to warn others against the enchanting draught. As usual, Rousseau is the Circe of the cup, the instant wellspring of liquid sorrow.

In the course of my researches, the Heloise of Rousseau fell into my hands—Ah! with what transport, with what enthusiasm, did I peruse this dangerous, enchanting work!—How shall I paint the sensations that were excited in my mind!—The pleasure I experienced approached the limits of pain—it was tumult—all the ardour of my character was excited. [Her uncle finds her weeping over it, and takes it away from her.] . . . but the impression made on my mind was never to be effaced—it was even productive of a long chain of consequences that will continue to operate till the day of my death.

The chain of consequences is too long to follow here; it riveted Emma for life, "a human being loving virtue while enslaved by passion," one whose "errors were the offspring of sensibility." She allows herself to fall in love with Augustus at sight of his portrait, fans the flame when he rescues her from danger, declares it to him without reserve. Naturally the result is three volumes of mystery, agony, rage and despair, through which Emma behaves with fortitude and constancy, arriving in the end at a sort of tranquillity, for we leave her with a competency, an adopted son of Augustus, and presumably chastened passions to comfort her later years. Such an end was not dark enough to serve Mrs. Hays's purpose, for many readers have mistaken it, and have supposed that the tranquil end justifies the earlier passions.

Mrs. Hays was not the first, nor by any means the last, to attribute all the woes of an uninhibited damsel to the reading of the *Nouvelle Héloïse,* but you may search long for another so modern in her psychology or so well versed in Rousseau. Are the "advantages of retirement" exploited in *Emmera* strictly orthodox? Not if Mrs. Hays represents her author justly on her title page, where, without citing chapter and verse, she attributes this to Rousseau:

The perceptions of persons in retirement are very different from those of people in the great world: Their passions, being differently modified, are differently expressed; their imaginations, constantly impressed by the same objects, are more violently affected. The same small number of images continually return, mix with every idea, and create those strange and false notions, so remarkable in people who spend their lives in solitude.

She seems to quote Rousseau to counteract ideas which passed current as Roussellian:

People in general, says Rousseau, do not sufficiently consider the influence which first attachments, between man and woman, have over the remainder of their lives: they do not perceive, that an impression so strong, and so lively, as that of love, is productive of a long chain of effects, which pass unobserved in a course of years, yet nevertheless, continue to operate till the day of their deaths.

This is almost word for word the effect of the *Nouvelle Héloïse* cited above; does Rousseau, then, warn us against himself? He would seem to be like Freud and other kinds of knowledge in that a little of him is a dangerous thing, and if you don't know much about him you can use him on either side of an argument. The philosophical Mr. Francis, seeking at one point in the story to calm Emma's wild heart, agrees with Rousseau that if we put our trust in nature and the simple virtues we are not likely to go far wrong, but he mistrusts sensibility:

Endeavor to continue your wants, and aspire only to a rational independence; by exercising your faculties, still the importunate sug-

gestions of your sensibility; preserve your sincerity, cherish the in-
genuous warmth unsophisticated feeling, but let discernment precede
confidence . . . suspect that your judgment is in danger of becoming
the dupe of your affections.

Mrs. Hays's definition of romance, "a vague term applied to everything we do not understand, or are unwilling to imitate," is nearly
as sharp as George Eliot's of the romantics, "gentlemen who have
no particular talent for the finite, but a general sense that the infinite is the right thing for them." None the less, sensibility is the
mark of a superior spirit:

> Rousseau was right when he asserted that, "Common men know
> nothing of violent sorrows, nor do great passions ever break out in
> weak minds. Energy of sentiment is the characteristic of a noble soul."

There are other ferments at work here than merely Rousseau;
Mrs. Hays quotes Mary Wollstonecraft, and Holcroft's *Anna St.
Ives*. These were giddily subversive, and called down much of
the wrath of the righteous, but Rousseau had to bear the brunt of
it. Novel after novel which brought the woman of feeling to disaster started her on her easy descent by a shove from the *Nouvelle
Héloïse*. It is hard for the twentieth century to understand the
strength of the feeling against it. Read it and feel if you can the
pleasure approaching the limits of pain, the tumult, the dangerous
enchantment. How can we reconstruct the state of society in which
it would have such effects? How can we understand the novel
of sensibility and the attitude toward Rousseau unless we do?
The *Nouvelle Héloïse* is as indubitably a work of art as are the
paintings of Lancret and Watteau. Like them it enchants us as
a scene of distant quietude, but not with tumult—as soon think
of getting drunk on a cup of jasmine tea. But to Emma Courtney
and her kind it was like triple distilled gin, and the propaganda
against it was like the temperance propaganda of a later time.
Maria Edgeworth's *Leonora*, cited in the last chapter, is the *Ten
Nights in a Bar-Room* of the movement, and in addition to this

entire novel devoted to the cause, she preaches it in nearly every one of the *Tales of Fashionable Life*. In *Leonora,* the reprehensible Olivia is saturated with Rousseau, metaphysics and German novels, specifically *The Sorrows of Werther,* ready to flare at the touch of a match, hopeless, good for nothing but to play the villain. So it is with Harriet Freke in *Belinda*. Elinor in Madame D'Arblay's *The Wanderer* is, if not a villain, a very horrible example. If the heroine is too far gone in Rousseau to be saved, we have tragedy, as in Mrs. Brooke's *Lady Julia Mandeville*. The fault is not in the stars but in the *Nouvelle Héloïse;* if Shakespeare had had a Rousseau, Juliet's disaster would have been properly motivated. If the heroine is not too deeply infected, she may be saved, as in Miss Edgeworth's *Leonora* and *Vivian*. If the heroine is perfect in character, immune to the virus of Rousseau, the victim will be a minor figure, a mere subhead in the sermon, as in Mrs. Brunton's *Self Control:*

Having no character of her own, Julia was always, as nearly as she was able, the heroine whom the last read novel inclined her to personate . . . in the midst of this fit, she, in an evil hour, opened a volume of the Novelle [*sic*] Eloise, which had before disturbed many wiser heads. The shifts were left unfinished, the sermons thrown aside, and Miss Julia returned with renewed *impetus* to the sentimental.

Fashions in intoxicants determine fashions in propaganda; the pack is in full cry whatever is running; in 1780 it was the *Nouvelle Héloïse,* a century later it was the demon rum, and fifty years after that it was bathtub gin. Rousseau idealized Julie of frail virtue; Goethe cast a glamorous light over youth's sentimental aspiration for a married woman. Among themselves the puritans whispered that Rousseau preached fornication and Goethe sanctioned adultery. Aloud they rumbled vague anathemas. In their novels they dramatized dire results. In the market they offered propaganda of fashion as works of art.

"Dear sensibility!" exclaimed Sterne, "source inexhaustible of all that's precious in our joys, or costly in our sorrows!" All dealers in the precious wares saw the advertising value of the words and blazoned them on title pages and at heads of chapters. In spite of the announcement that the source was inexhaustible, there was a boom in the market for gems of sensibility and precious drops, with strong featuring of the delight whether the setting was joy or sorrow. "Chearful sadness" and "delicious sorrow" had been conspicuous enough before Sterne, as for example in *The Fool of Quality* of Henry Brooke, 1766, the pages of which are spread thickly with epicurean enjoyment of grief:

Here Harry for a while held his handkerchief to his eyes, while his fond uncle dropped a silent tear of delight at beholding the amiable emotion of his beloved.

. . . while Mr. Fenton sat, and his Harry stood beside him both wrapped in their own delicious sensibilities.

He entered and seated himself in silence beside the Earl, he there wept near an hour without uttering a syllable . . . But their tears were the tears of sympathizing humanity, or rather tears of delight on observing the sweet sensibilities of their darling.

As Harry thought it his duty, so he thought it to be his delight, to weep and lament his Maria.

And even before Sterne sought to justify fashion by promoting it to religion, Brooke tried to rationalize it into a code of ethics:

"Tell me, my dear sir," said Harry, "are there different kinds of grief, or is it merely that grief affects us in different manners? When I wept for my dear father, my mother, and brother, my affliction was anguishing and altogether bitter, without any species of alleviating sensation to compensate my misery. But it was far otherwise with me to-night. When I grieved in the grief of your old and faithful domestics, I felt my heart breaking, but I was pleased that it should break; I felt that it was my happiness so to grieve, and I could wish a return of the same sweet sensations."

"The reason is this, my love: When you lamented your parents, you lamented yourself in your private and personal losses; your affliction was just, it was natural, it was laudable; but still it was confined; it participated but little of the emotion that is excited by the affliction of others; and the anguish was the keener by being nearly limited to your own bosom and your own concerns. But in the griefs of my old and loving servants this night, you became wholly expanded; you went out of yourself; you felt, without reflection, how delightful it is to go forth with your God, in his social, generous, noble, and divine sensibilities; and you delightfully felt, my Harry, that such a house of mourning is more joyous to your soul, than all the festivals that flesh and sense can open before you."

God, we may note, is nicely in the fashion of the time with his social sensibilities. He has, perhaps, changed his style since the days of Beowulf, when it was better that a man avenge his friend than that he mourn much. Now (in 1766) it seems better to mourn much than to do anything about it because mourning is a virtue, and if you alleviate sorrow you remove the cause of mourning, which is to cut off virtue at its source. Thus logically the lady was justified who provided the classic example of sentimentality by weeping over fictitious sorrows in the theatre while her coachman froze to death on the box outside.

This descent in vigor of the heroes from the *Beowulf* to *The Fool of Quality* is hardly more noteworthy than the falling off from the vigorous men of sensibility of Fielding, Parson Adams and Tom Jones, who are primarily men of action, to the lachrymose sentimentality of the men in *The Fool of Quality*. The intermediate steps are Sterne and Mackenzie. There is a similar difference between Pamela's sturdy will to resistance and Sophia Western's vigorous independent action and the pale tearfulness of the sentimental heroine of the end of the century. Mrs. Ann Radcliffe exhibits the sentimental heroine at full length. Of her character we may make a mosaic portrait out of phrases from her author: She is very frequently "overcome by a faintness, and retires to her chamber," usually unable to eat any supper before she goes. She resolves not to weep, but "her resolution yields to excess of grief." Her chief pleasure is to weep unobserved. Successive afflictions reduce her to the point of death, but she does not die; instead her afflictions "soften into melancholy." She has always a lute by her which she "touches with a fine melancholy expression which comes from the heart." She thinks of her lover "with a mingled sensation of esteem, tenderness and anxiety." She is never swept off her feet by the force of her love; her passion always causes her to faint before she can do anything rash. You often doubt the reality of her love because it is circumspect to the verge of sophistication. She has an ever-present sense of the proprieties, no less of the possibilities, of every situation—"Emily perceived that she could not reject an ordinary civility without expressing by her refusal the expectation of something more." At the sound of a footstep her first thought is to remember that she is unprotected. She "indulges in the mournful sweetness of bidding farewell to the beloved shades of her childhood," and a moment later her "imagination soars through the realms of space, and aspires to the First Great Cause which pervades and governs all being." Summoned for hasty flight, she packs her books first. She is seldom too agitated to compose verses on romantic or gloomy scenery or incidents. She is so delicate that a breath would extinguish her, yet she is dragged through inferno after inferno of horrors and lives to be the mother of stalwart heroes. One suspects that her delicate Gothic tracery is built on a heavy Romanesque foundation.

This figure seems impossibly absurd to twentieth-century readers, but Mrs. Radcliffe shows it at its best. Her heroines seem genuinely vertebrate in comparison with some of the moist unpleasant jellyfish spawned by her contemporaries and predecessors. The foundation that supports what endurance they have is built of stoicism and fortitude, which Mrs. Radcliffe supplies, not, it would seem, to make character human or interesting, but merely as inevitable to the plot. It is a necessary adaptation when the sentimental romance takes on effects of terror. There cannot be even imagined terrors without imagined rigors—not even Mrs. Radcliffe could terrorize a jellyfish; there must be a spine for the chills to run up and down. The hero of a romance of terror must be a man of feeling in order to be susceptible to terrors, and at the same time stoic enough to survive them. Thus Osbert, in *The Castles of Athlin and Dunbayne,* 1789, a Highlander with his foot on his native heath, behaves like a London lady when he happens to lose his way in the Highlands:

. . . he looked in vain for the objects which had directed him; and his heart, for the first time, felt the repulse of fear . . . He remained for some time in a silent dread not wholly unpleasing, but which was soon heightened to a degree of terror not to be endured . . .

He behaves like an American Indian when led out to execution:

He beheld the preparations for his execution, the instruments of death, the guards arranged in files, with an eye undaunted . . . He beheld every object with indifference . . .

But there must be tears, so the author invokes the thought of his mother:

. . . when the remembrance of his mother, overwhelmed with sorrow, rushed upon his mind, and quite unmanned him; the tears started in his eyes, and he sunk senseless on the ground.

This is strictly according to the code of high romance, and proves conclusively that he is a gentleman. To the same effect is the conduct of the heroine, whose sensibility to effects of nature differentiates her from peasant and villain, and at the same time gives her fortitude to endure passively, witness Ellena in *The Italian,* 1797:

To Ellena, whose mind was capable of being highly elevated, or sweetly soothed, by scenes of nature, the discovery of this little turret was an important circumstance. Hither she could come, and her soul, refreshed by the views it afforded, would acquire strength to bear her, and with equanimity, thro' the persecutions that might await her. Here, gazing upon the stupendous imagery around her, looking, as it were, beyond the awful veil which obscures the features of the Deity, and conceals Him from the eyes of his creatures, dwelling as with a present God in the midst of his sublime works; with a

mind thus elevated, how insignificant would appear to her the transactions and the suffering of this world! How poor the boasted power
of man, when the fall of a single cliff from these mountains would
with ease destroy thousands of his race assembled on the plains below! How would it avail them, that they were accoutred for battle,
armed with all the instruments of destruction that human invention
ever fashioned? Thus man, the giant who now held her in captivity,
would shrink to the diminutiveness of a fairy; and she would experience, that his force was unable to enchain her soul, or compel her
to fear him, while he was destitute of virtue.

Two later passages are carefully arranged in contrast to this to
show that the villain, Schedoni, and a peasant, Paulo, received
no such reinforcement of spirit from scenes of the sublime in
nature.

But while Mrs. Radcliffe was refining the sentimental romance
toward the sublime with the best of her effects of terror, her
contemporaries were driving it to the extreme of the ridiculous.
In the same year as *The Italian,* 1797, appeared a three-volume
romance whose title page proclaimed it, *"Munster Abbey,* A
Romance: interspersed with reflections on Virtue and Morality:
written by Sir Samuel Egerton Leigh. In Three Volumes."

> *Virtue, our present peace, our future prize.*
> *Man's unprecarious, natural estate,*
> *Improvable at will, in virtue lies!*
> *Its tenure sure; its income is divine."*

Following the preface (a gem too perfect to cut for this setting)
is a subscription list of thirty-three pages from the Duke of
Argyle to Sir William Young, Bart., M.P. Its heroine is Julia
Melville, "a young lady of extreme beauty and accomplishments," "amiable in the sight of all," decorated with "a serene
and lovely smile decked by a tender tear of sensibility which
trembled down her cheeks," or if you prefer, "the trembling
tear of tenderness,—which in its usual form tottered down her
cheek, evinced the soft emotion of her spotless mind." This tear

might be the only one she has, for she never parts with it; it may tremble or even totter, but it never gets anywhere; it is always just there. Perhaps she treasures it as the only evidence that she has a mind of any sort, spotless or other, for her actions do not "evince" any such thing. She becomes Mrs. Belford without obtaining her mother's consent, but after a few pages her mother forgives her and approaches Munster Abbey to visit her. "Bless me!" exclaimed Mrs. Melville with an air of astonishment, "with what injustice did I stile [*sic*] this noble mansion an inconsiderable cottage!"

At length arriving at the garden-gate, which, with equal precipitation, they entered, Mrs. Belford, who was seated on a bench by her husband, at the foot of a sheet of water which parted them from the house, suddenly beheld her mother.

Elated with joy at the unexpected visit, which hurried innumerable hopes and reflections over her tender mind in an instant, and forgetting all thought but that of flying swiftly to the embraces of a beloved parent, she rushed directly forward, pursuing as she fancied at the time, from the straightness of her course, the readiest road; and with her eyes fixed on Mrs. Melville, whose appearance had thrown aside the usual caution of her footsteps, she plunged into the centre of the pond. Oh, Heavens!—what a moment!—Belford attempted to fly to her assistance; but he had not proceeded many steps before horror overwhelmed him, and he fell senseless to the ground: Mrs. Melville and Julia, swooned in the same state of insensibility.

The servant, unacquainted with the art of swimming, and apprehensive of his own fate, should he venture into water of such considerable depth, hurried with all imaginable swiftness to the house for assistance. What an awful moment was this!—what was to be hoped!—all aid for a time suspended, and yet not an instant to be lost!—The mind prone to vice would have despaired: but the soul endowed with morality and confidence in the mercy of Him whom we are justified in believing is all merciful, can never cherish hopeless reflections. All help was still suspended—the struggling fair, unable any longer to contend for life, yielded to her fate with that composure, which the virtuous only can experience in the moments of departing life.—She cast her eyes towards Heaven, where her mind and soul surely were directed. In this moment of serious meditation, she was perfectly sensible of her danger, but the blessings of a pure conscience constituted her a stranger to every fear; and, when she had reason to believe her dissolution was near at hand, it was with pleasure she reflected that soon she would be relieved of her dying agonies.

At length, when on the verge of closing her eyes from the dim light of this world, to open them in a pure and perfect atmosphere, the kind and liberal hand of Providence waved its influence o'er the dismal scene, and cast away the gloom.

How was it contrived?—Next to a miracle were the means by which the amiable Mrs. Belford was restored to her distracted and disconsolate friends.

Faithful Munster, an old favorite Newfoundland dog of Belford's, named after the place, was the welcome instrument of deliverance.

Approaching the pond in the critical moment, and viewing his mistress helpless in the humid space, he sagaciously plunged into the pool, and, seizing the end of her sash which floated, drew her cautiously to the side of the bank, where he contrived to raise her head above the surface of the water, by quitting the sash, and with anxious care holding her hat in his teeth, until more assistance could be procured.

Thirty-three pages of ladies and gentlemen, twelve hundred and fifty or more of them, subscribed to this nonsense in 1797 because they thought it was written by a gentleman. They could tell that he was a gentleman because he called a pond a "humid space," because when one of his characters wanted to say of another, "if he had died I should have known it," the nearest he can come to it is,

. . . had the well constructed organs of life ceased to play within his callous bosom, and had his heart, which never fluttered with compassion, yielded its long exerted pulse to the chill embraces of death, I should, doubtless, through some channel, have been apprised of the event.

Absurdity aspiring to the sublime has reached its topmost pinnacle to defy the lightning,—and the lightning was gathering. The Comic Spirit incarnate sat in Steventon parsonage writing *Sense and Sensibility* and *Northanger Abbey*. Did Jane Austen read *Munster Abbey* along with *The Mysteries of Udolpho* and *Horrid Mysteries?*

Such are the channels of liquid sorrow; we may idle through them to laugh at the fantastic structures along their courses. We may also note that not all tears are so idle as they seem, and though at first we "know not what they mean," we may find meaning if we can endure. If we are to give liquid sorrow its due, we shall probably have to admit that it helped to turn more than one mill wheel in its turbulent flow.

The humanitarian movement probably owes more to the novel of sensibility than has ever been reckoned. If it had any such effect on its readers as its opponents feared, it must have gone far to develop in the public a "sentiment" in the sense in which the psychologists use the word—something like an acquired or developed tendency to feel. If it made them weep it made them go through the motions of feeling, so to speak, and the psychologists again, specifically Lange and James, tell us that "we feel sorry because we cry, afraid because we tremble, angry because we strike, and not that we cry, strike, or tremble because we are sorry, angry, or fearful as the case may be." Emmera, the Fair American, cried when she saw a man beat a horse; her readers cried because she cried, and because they cried they were sorry for the abused horse. Sentimental novels took their heroes and heroines into insane asylums and prisons to find tearful scenes. Readers who wept over these scenes acquired the tendency to deplore the abuse of prisoners and insane patients. If a backing of public feeling has been of any service to reformers of prisons and hospitals for the insane, we can hardly doubt that the novel of sensibility has served them well, as it must have served also in attempts to alleviate or abolish the evils of prostitution, slavery, child labor, and other such.

We may think of the literary history of the eighteenth century as a march from sense to sensibility or as a journey from sensibility to sense with equal propriety, for at the one end we find reason and passion, and at the other passion and reason. Has human thought made progress, or merely flitted from fashion to fashion? In the first quarter of the eighteenth century it was fashionable to believe that human nature was to be perfected by the divine gift of reason, and Swift was protesting that reason was not a gift but a capacity, and that the way to perfection was as thorny as ever. In the first quarter of the nineteenth century Jane Austen was the satirist, subjecting the pink vapors of sensibility to a cold blast of humor and common sense. At the same time Keats was writing to his friend Bailey:

I am certain of nothing but of the holiness of the heart's affections, and the truth of imagination. What the imagination seizes as Beauty must be Truth—whether it existed before or not,—for I have the same idea of all our passions as of Love: they are all, in their sublime, creative of essential Beauty . . . I have never yet been able to perceive how anything can be known for Truth by consecutive reasoning—and yet it must be.

Thus stood sense and passion in 1817, and so they stood in 1717. Is it a mere paper whirligig, or does something happen? The year 1818 that saw the publication of *Northanger Abbey* was the year also of Keats's *Endymion* and of Scott's *Rob Roy*. "Our passions," says Keats, "are all, in their sublime, creative of essential beauty." Sixty-two years earlier Burke had made his careful distinction between the sublime and the beautiful. He voiced the sense of the time that where there was any feeling that looked toward fear there was no beauty. The Alps, then, and the tragedies of Shakespeare, were sublime, but not beautiful. Rousseau discovered the Alps, and Horace Walpole discovered *Hamlet*. *Hamlet* is the literary father of *The Castle of Otranto* and grandfather of the Gothic romance. Mrs. Radcliffe carried these discoveries into every village in England. Liquid sorrow had prepared the channels through which they spread. It worked drop by drop in its first runnels, but at last it swept the way clear for literature to move from the mood of *vers de société* to the mood of tragedy, from low tragedy to high tragedy, from blood and thunder to true romance. It takes us to the lost synthesis of the sublime and the beautiful, to the renascence of Shakespeare. Its service is a restoration of forgotten beauty.

CHAPTER V

"CUT MY LACE, CHARMIAN"

> CLEOPATRA: *Cut my lace, Charmian, come;*
> *So Antony loves.*
>
> *Antony and Cleopatra*, I, 4.

CLEOPATRA was a queen; a lady, that is, and a thoroughbred, and if ever a woman did, she had at her finger tips all the controls by which to manage a man. Whatever she may not have worn in the days of her life, we know that on Shakespeare's stage she wore ruff and farthingale, and a gown the lines of which made of her body a triangle of which the long sides ran from the shoulders to a sharp point between the thighs. These were the lines of the stays the lace of which she calls on Charmian to cut to release her suffering sides lest she swoon. Clearly she has no intention of fainting; she has made the gesture already at the very beginning of this memorable interview with Antony:

> *Help me away, dear Charmian, I shall fall:*
> *It cannot be thus long, the sides of nature*
> *Will not sustain it.*

When she is really overcome in Act III, Scene 9, it is a different story:

CLEO. Ah! stand by.
EROS. The Queen, my lord, the Queen.

And Enobarbus tells us what to expect:

ANT. I must be gone.
ENO. Under a compelling occasion let women die. It were a pity

to cast them away for nothing; though between them and a great cause they should be esteemed nothing. Cleopatra, catching but the least noise of this, dies instantly; I have seen her die twenty times upon far poorer moment. I do think there is mettle in death which commits some loving act upon her, she hath such a celerity in dying.

It is a far cry from the Queen of Egypt to Pamela, the little serving maid of Lady B., but they are sisters under their stays. They are daughters of Eve, though the Queen of Egypt is a Cleopatra, and Pamela is a Griselda. Nevertheless, some of Pamela's critics accuse her of nearly as good management of her man as Cleopatra's; better, if tragedy be disaster. In the beginning her master might agree with the critics, for he is cynical enough to imply that her first fainting fit is a trick. In her fifteenth letter she specifies some "freedoms" which he "offered" her, says that she broke from him

by a sudden spring, and ran out of the room! and the next chamber being open, I made shift to get into it, and threw to the door, and it locked after me; . . . I just remember I got into the room; for I knew nothing further of the matter till afterwards; for I fell into a fit with my terror, and there I lay, till he, as I suppose, looking through the keyhole, 'spyed me upon the floor, stretched out at length, on my face; . . .

Surely he saw that the thing was genuine. She did not totter to a sofa and sink in a becoming attitude, but went down on her face. But it suits his purpose to say of it, "But since she is so apt to fall into fits, or at least pretend to do so . . ." The next time he is not so cynical. We learn of it when "she gives the particulars of the worst attempt he had yet made." He has gone to extremes and is on the verge of the last extremity.

With struggling, fright, terror, I fainted away quite, and did not come to myself soon; so that they both, from the cold sweats that I was in, thought me dying.—And I remembered no more than that when with great difficulty they brought me to myself, she [Mrs. Jewkes] was sitting on one side of the bed . . . and he on the other

. . . but I fainted away once more, at these words, and at his clasping his arms about me again. And, when I came a little to myself, I saw him sit there, and the maid Nan, holding a smelling-bottle to my nose . . . I . . . have reason to bless God, who, by disabling me in my faculties, empowered me to preserve my innocence; and, when all my strength would have signified nothing, magnified himself in my weakness.

The full text of the passage assures us of Richardson's intent, that the reader shall believe that Mr. B. is genuinely frightened, truly concerned at last for Pamela. It is the very essence of the plot, for it is the measure of his feeling for her. Not until later do we have so much measure of her love for him. Not for love of him does she faint, but for love of her virginity, which is dearer to her, as yet, than is he. Her heart is divided, whereas his desire at this point becomes one with his love. The fainting spell in Act II of *Antony and Cleopatra* has a similar significance in that it is the measure of Cleopatra's love for Antony, the index of her undivided heart and of the division of his between love and glory, Egypt and Rome.

To very different effect is the wholesale fainting in the passage quoted from *Munster Abbey* in the last chapter. When "the fair" unexpectedly souses herself in the "humid space," the ladies and gentlemen faint by squads, the servant runs, and thus we know who's who. There have been gentlemen of romance who had the "art" of swimming, Leander, for example, and Lord Byron, but if a gentleman can't be a hero in the wide humid spaces and has to be a hero anyway, the best he can do is to faint and leave it to the dog. The fainting here is an act of fashion performed by mannequins. It is according to the code of romance in so far as the sensibility expressed by fainting is the property of aristocracy and servants are not susceptible to it. In both *Antony and Cleopatra* and *Pamela* there is enough of fashion to make the work acceptable to its time. Cleopatra acts like a lady in Act I, Scene 4, and faints like a woman in Act III, Scene 9. Her lady-

Boucher   Mme. de Pompadour

THE STAYS OF FASHION AND THE MOLD OF FORM

like acting is comedy, the other points straight to tragedy. Shakespeare uses the idea of fainting like a musical theme which sounded on the oboe makes us smile; sounded on the cellos it stirs us with all there can be of tragedy in music. Enobarbus plays it for comedy, but when he says, "she hath such a celerity in dying," one who knows the end may catch his breath in wonder whether it is tragic or comic foreboding.

The fashion was not new when Cleopatra demonstrated it on Shakespeare's stage. Literary fainting must be as old as literature; the most casual prospecting into former ages reveals it wherever we choose to look. Andromache at the sound of wailing rushes to the walls in time to see the corpse of Hector dragged after the chariot of Achilles. "Then dark night came on her eyes and shrouded her, and she fell backward and gasped forth her spirit," but not in death. Aeneas like Antony must for reasons of state leave Africa for Italy, and knows that Dido like Cleopatra will "die" at the least hint of it, and so she does.

> *Abrupt her utterance ceased . . .*
> *. . . Her swooning shape*
> *Her maidens to a marble chamber bore*
> *And on her couch the helpless limbs reposed.*

Very early in the Christian era we see it in the Sanscrit drama. In *The Little Clay Cart,* attributed to King Shudraka, Charudatta, a Brahman merchant, faints when he learns of the loss of jewels entrusted to his care; Vasantesena, a courtezan, faints at the thought of any harm coming to Charudatta; a courtier faints at sight of the body of Vasantesena. It appears in a Chinese story of the ninth century, A.D., translated by Arthur Waley. The heroine

was horrified to see her old lover standing before her so emaciated by hunger and disfigured by sores that he seemed scarcely human . . . with quavering voice she reproached herself, saying, "It is my doing that you have been brought to this pass." And with these words she swooned.

In *The Arabian Nights* of about the eleventh century, A.D., fainting is nearly as common as weeping to express emotion of both men and women. Chaucer makes use of it, not always in following his originals. As he tells Griselda's story, she faints at the good news of her restoration to her lord's favor, speaks for a stanza, and faints again. This is Chaucer's touch; Boccaccio does not have it. Troilus faints from sheer stress of love-longing at the bedside of Criseyde. As Malory tells the story of Elaine (about 1470), she offers herself to Launcelot to be his wife or even his mistress; when he refuses both offers "then she shrieked shrilly, and fell down to the ground in a swoon," and a gentlewoman bore her to her chamber. "What needeth it to sermon of it more?" It would be easy to collect examples in abundance from Chaucer to Shakespeare, from Shakespeare to Richardson; once begin to take note of them and you soon come to believe that literature is full of them in every country and in every age.

The daughters of Pamela must have inherited the tendency to faint from the daughters of Eve; literature must have taken it in the first instance from life. We have only to look about us to see that it is not a purely literary trait. Women do faint; yes, and men too. Hard-boiled soldiers will drop like sentimental heroines when jabbed with a hypodermic needle, or even while standing in formation. The silver screen is as deadly as the field of Mars; a United Press dispatch of 12 February, 1934, records the mortality.

The world's fainting record, heretofore held by the Philadelphia Auditorium, was broken recently by an humble newsreel picture house on the Boulevard des Italiens. An average of twenty women fainted daily for a fortnight-period during which was shown in realistic scientific detail an operation for appendicitis at Lariboisiere, leading Paris hospital. The grand total of 280 felled women is believed to surpass by a dozen or more the toll of the Philadelphia Auditorium where Lawrence Tibbett last year unintentionally mowed down club women by the scores singing the "Cuban Love Song."

But the statistics of fainting, whether they lie or tell the truth, need not detain us, for they do not concern the realistic novelists. Fainting is not conspicuous as a fashion in the realistic novel; it is mainly a trait of romantic heroes and heroines. It comes into the novel from the earlier ages of romance, first as a poetic formula to exhibit extreme emotion; second as a pattern of conduct for aristocracy according to the romance code of love. In the novel it undergoes some modification according to fashions in dress and conditions brought about by the rise of the middle class.

As a poetic formula for the expression of extreme emotion, fainting is still in daily use, if not in literature, at least in caricature. In the comic section of the newspaper, the victim of the atrocity registers stress of feeling in the second and third acts of his daily four-act drama by huge drops of sweat whirling from his forehead as if by centrifugal force. The climax demands even greater intensity of distress; what is there left but to faint? Fainting has thus become the inevitable commonplace of the last picture of the comic series. Such is its descent from high romance to low comedy. The device has long been so shopworn that it takes the highest genius to lift it to the plane of tragedy. Chaucer's Troilus weeps and mopes through a book of the poem until the last stanza, then abruptly snatches up his arms and in a few lines performs deeds of valor which the Greeks rue for many a day. On these alternations his emotions oscillate with some rhythmic regularity until the rise to the climax of Book III, in which his fainting at the bedside of Criseyde leads to her acceptance of his love. It is the cut and dried formula, but Chaucer lifts it on the breath of great poetry to the levels of high romance and tragedy. On lesser winds it cannot rise so high. In any hands feebler than the strongest it is merely an empty expression of emotion by formula that offers no inducement to the willing suspension of disbelief. And even the deliberate caricaturist cannot make it so funny as does the serious-minded novelist of

Munster Abbey, who seems to believe that the magic lies in the formula itself.

The formula comes from feudal times. Troilus's oscillations of spirit between love and warlike bravery are the same as those of Aucassin in the romance of two or three centuries earlier. Love and glory go in equal parts to make the spirit of a knightly hero, and his moods swing from the peak of one to the peak of the other as circumstances determine which shall dominate. In *Aucassin and Nicolette* the dramatization of this is at once sweetly romantic and quaintly absurd. Aucassin goes absent-mindedly into battle:

Now believe ye not that his mind was on kine, nor cattle of the booty, nor thought he how he might strike a knight, nor be stricken again: nor no such thing . . . rather he so dreamed of Nicolete, his sweet lady that he dropped his reins, forgetting all there was to do, and his horse that had felt the spur, bore him into the press and hurled among the foe, and they laid hands on him all about, and seized away his spear and shield, and straightway they led him off a prisoner, and were even now discoursing of what death he should die.

And when Aucassin heard them,

"Ha! God," said he, "sweet Saviour. Be these my deadly enemies that have taken me, and will soon cut off my head? And once my head is off, no more shall I speak with Nicolete, my sweet lady, that I love so well. Natheless have I here a good sword, and sit a good horse unwearied . . ." And he laid hand to sword and fell a smiting to right and left . . . making a murder about him like a wild boar when the hounds fall on him in the forest, even till he struck down ten knights, and seven he hurt, and straightway he hurled out of the press, and rode back again at full speed, sword in hand.

This represents the rise of the wave to the acute phase of the fighting spirit. Fainting represents the acute phase of love-longing. Both are essential elements of the pattern. To us the pattern may seem as remote from humanity as its day is far from ours. So it is if we take it in the abstract as a piece of pure design. Chaucer puts it still farther off in time but nearer in terms of human character. He makes Troilus emotionally real, so dramatized that when he behaves according to the romance formula we are convinced because we see him do it. Antony, too, like Aucassin is divided between love and war. Doubtless Shakespeare chose the theme because for once he saw a synthesis between the romantic formula and authenticated history. Once or twice genius inspired the formula with life. Others who used it were mere craftsmen who stuffed it and mounted it in conventional attitudes.

A chain of such craftsmen formed the line which conducted the pattern from medieval romance to modern novel. They were the romance writers who in metre and prose trace before Chaucer the patterns of chivalric behavior, most of those who between Chaucer and Shakespeare conduct those patterns into the Elizabethan drama, and those who carried them on through the seventeenth century till they appear in their modified forms in the novel. Their names and the names of their heroes and heroines, once household words, are now less familiar; they are the tales of Arthur and the Round Table, Merlin, Parisfal, Launcelot, Tristram, and the others; the tales of Charlemagne and his Peers, Huon of Bordeaux, Ogier the Dane, Milles and Amys and others. There is Amadis of Gaul, Partenopex of Blois—the list may run as long as one pleases. Their beginnings are uncertain; before Caxton and the English printers it is hard to tag them with authors and dates. There are few if any which scholars believe to be earlier than the eleventh century, and there are a few, perhaps more than a few, still active in one incarnation or another. Tennyson and Wagner gave them their chief vitality in the nineteenth century, and Edwin Arlington Robinson is not the only one in the twentieth century who has found in them names to conjure with. They have lived for nine centuries and the end is not yet. Read them in their earlier forms, omitting Chaucer and Malory, and you find yourself sifting load after load of inorganic dust for the sake of half a dozen germs of life. Yet life they certainly had, for minstrels sang them and scribes recorded them all over Europe; the earliest printing presses were busy with them, and linotypes and rotary presses have known their words.

In their earlier stages they were probably highly popular as expressions of the interests and aspirations of most of their hearers. What is more they had no competitors; there was nothing else to listen to, or to read if you could read and get hold of books. We may guess that the minstrels offered naught else because naught else was so profitable. In this they were like radio broadcasters, and their hearers, like radio audiences of today, found it easier to sit and listen to what came than to forage for themselves. In a society in which there was no important middle class between prince and peasant, war and religion were the big businesses to which tended all educational propaganda. If literature reflects life, the time was a training corps for the army and the church, upholding a military-ecclesiastical pattern of the gentleman, and a pattern for the lady which best subserved the propagation, maintenance and morale of the fighting man. His interests must be war, love and religion; his exercises jousting and hunting; his qualities bravery, courtesy and devotion. The damsel must be beautiful, well-born, faithful, chaste, submissive and dutiful. These fashion-figures the minstrels literally harped upon, and listeners absorbed their words as docilely as twentieth-century listeners gulp down pseudo-science about tooth paste and cigarettes. For the purpose there was no need that the figures have life; in fashion drawings a certain conventional resemblance to the human figure is all we need; vivacity and verisimilitude we do not demand. If now and then a drawer of fashion figures is also a costume designer and an artist, like Watteau, so much the better. So much the better, too, for literature when the minstrel happens to be also a poet.

This fashion pattern of the Middle Ages included weeping and fainting as indications of aristocracy for both men and women, weeping always for sorrow and sometimes for joy (how else could the minstrel tell us that they felt anything?) and fainting at important crises (how else could the minstrel tell us that it was a crisis?). The code for fainting scarcely differs from that for weeping; seldom do they faint without weeping first. Men and women weep and faint on receipt of bad news, or no news when that means bad news, most often when the news is of misfortune or death coming to a relative, friend or lover. They may drop in a faint without finding time to weep if the disaster occurs in their sight or presence. They are less apt to faint, but sure to weep, at misfortune to themselves. At parting from relatives, friends or lovers, they are sure to weep and more apt than not to faint. At lovers' meetings they may faint from stress of love-longing. At least one instance there is of fainting in prompt repentance for an irrevocably foolish deed. A woman may faint at a dangerous threat to her chastity or at an immediate prospect of a forced undesired marriage.

These patterns the romances preserve unchanged for centuries. Caxton printed them in the fifteenth century. Copland printed them in the sixteenth century. Of these periods are the earliest copies we have of some romances which we know originated much earlier. Chivalry by then was dead and did not know it, and the romances are the sweet odors in which it was embalmed. By Shakespeare's time it was deader yet and still more vocal; like the little choir boy in the legend it kept on singing long after it had been murdered by capitalism and gunpowder. Sir Philip Sidney gave it what life he could in his daily acts and in the pages of *The Countess of Pembroke's Arcadia.* This is the best representative of the fashion of the day in prose romances (the day was that of Elizabeth), for it has enough of true romance in it to give some vitality to the fashion. By then, the exercise of chivalry, jousts, tournaments, chivalric pageants and the literary courts of love, were mere exercises of fashion. The *Arcadia* weaves them into a beautiful decorative pattern, as did the Flemish weaver of the two large tapestries now in the Uffizi which show a fiesta of Henri II and Catherine de Medici, a superb pageant of chivalry, the men engaged in warlike exercises under the eyes of fair ladies. Such also is the design of the *Arcadia,* on even grander scale, and even more widely varied. It shows two pairs of royal lovers, Pyrocles and Philoclea, Musidorus and Pamela. They are gaily painted in romance colors. Either prince is a match for any number of opponents when he has his mind on his work, but when his fancy turns to love he is easily snared. Musidorus and Pamela set out on an elopement, but are so interested in one another that they forget to keep moving, and are captured and brought back. Pyrocles in Philoclea's chamber where she is in bed, at a time when discovery would seem fatal, like Troilus lets his feelings overcome him.

. . . hee did abandon the succour of himselfe, and suffered griefe so to close his heart, that his breath fayling him, with a deathfull shutting of his eyes, he fell down at her bedside, having had time to say no more, but Oh! whom dost thou kill *Philoclea?*

Philoclea recovers him:

She that little looked for such an extreme event of her doings, start out of her bed, like *Venus* rising from her mother the sea, not so much stricken down with amazement and griefe of her fault, as lifted up with the force of love and desire to help, she laid her faire body over his breast, and throwing no other water in his face, but the streame of her teares, nor giving him other blowes, but the kissing of her well formed mouth . . .

but loses herself:

At that word with anguish of mind and weakness of body, encreased one by the other, and both augmented by this fearfull accident, she had faln down in a sound, but that *Pyrocles* then first severing his eie-lids, and quickly apprehending her danger, to him more than

death . . . staied her from falling: and then lifting the sweet
burthen of her body in his armes, laid her again in her bed.

Philoclea is quite the model princess as depicted by a gentleman-
author, "sweet minded Philoclea whose consideration was limited
by his [Pyrocles'] words, and whose conceit pierced no deeper
than his outward countenance." She can nurse him, but it is not
her business to make decisions. So she goes placidly to sleep by his
side. He ponders for half a page without doing any thinking,
then he too goes to sleep, and there they lie chastely at the mercy
of their enemies. But through many such perils Sidney brings
them to the double marriage.

Did Richardson take the name of one princess and the fainting fit of the other to furnish forth the homely tales of a serving-
maid and a rake? He knew all about English serving-maids, all
their minds and hearts. He knew all about the heroines of
romance. Their hearts are factitious and their minds are absent;
know their names and you know all. In spite of civil war and
puritan austerities, they swarm through the seventeenth century,
and are scarcely less numerous and conspicuous in Richardson's
time than they were in Sidney's. We may trail them through
the innumerable pages of the hosts of folio and quarto volumes
that were the "long-winded romances," the *roman à longue
haleine*, repeated, adapted and imitated from the old models.
Many of them were English, *Parismus, Arcadia, Amadis of Gaul,
Urania, Argenis, Parthenissa, Bentivolio and Urania, Pandion and
Iphegenia, Guy of Warwick*. Many more were translated from
the French, with such titles as *Polexander, Ibrahim, Cleopatra,
Cassandra, The Grand Cyrus (Artemenes), Clelia, Astrea, Grand
Scipio, Belinda, Pharamond*. Romances of all sorts were printed
in all sorts of forms for all sorts of readers. *Tatler* No. 95 tells
us that they were adapted for children in Richardson's time. Mr.
Bickerstaff is interviewing his little godson:

I found upon Conversation with him, though he was a little noisy
in his Mirth, that the Child had excellent Parts, and was a great

Master of all the Learning on t'other Side Eight Years old . . .
I found he had very much turned his Studies for about a Twelvemonth
past, into the Lives and Adventures of Don *Bellianis* of *Greece, Guy*
of *Warwick,* the *Seven Champions,* and other Historians of that
Age . . . He would . . . find Fault with the passionate Temper in
Bevis of *Southampton,* and loved St. *George* for being the Champion
of *England* . . .

Book dealers' catalogues testify that such romances were still
popular a hundred years later; for example:

CYNTHIA: With the Tragical Account of the Unfortunate Loves of
Almerin and Desdemona. Crude Woodcut frontispiece. Twelfth
Edition. Dublin, N. D. (circa 1800) Chap. Book. 10/6

Between Mr. Bickerstaff's little godson (1709) and Pamela
(1740) we can show a realist, Defoe, whose heroine faints like a
woman, and a romanticist, Mrs. Aubin, whose heroine faints like
a lady. Defoe's Moll Flanders may be a sentimentalist, but she
is no lady. Early in her life, she is seventeen or eighteen at the
time, she is in a situation much like Pamela's, serving-maid
educated somewhat above her station, exposed to the solicitations
of her master's elder son. Into the space of a dozen pages Defoe
concentrates what Richardson tells in a volume, the strategy of
the attack; serving-maids and beginning rakes may learn from
it what they will. At length she tells us, "I made no more resistance to him, but let him do just what he pleased and as often
as he pleased"; but this is not until he has solemnly promised to
marry her when he comes into his estate. In the face of this
promise, he attempts to pass her on to his younger brother, who
has fallen in love with her and is trying to get his parents' consent
to marry her. When the elder brother coolly advises her to marry
the younger if she can, she says:

I gave him a look full of horror at these words, and turning pale
as death, was at the very point of sinking down out of the chair I
sat in . . . it was a good while before I fully recovered my senses,
and was not able to speak for several minutes.

This is very nicely in character with herself and her pretensions. As a child she amused all about her by expressing her intention to be "a gentlewoman." Her lover has gained her mainly by bribery, and she tells us herself that he might have had her for less money and less strategy. The reader may judge for himself whether the fainting fit is genuine, but it is what any gentlewoman would do if she had done all for love. What is more, it is what any devout churchwoman would do if she believed that to marry her lover's brother was incest. Some such, indeed, is the occasion of the next recorded attack of faintness, after she is hardened in wrongdoing, when her mother-in-law's story convinces her that

this was certainly no more or less than my own mother, and that I had now had two children, and was big with another by my own brother, and lay with him still every night . . . I thought I should have sunk down in the place. She perceived I was out of order, and asked me if I was not well, and what ailed me.

Thereafter nothing causes her to feel faint but actual fear. On the morning after a bigamous marriage she looks out of the window and sees three gentlemen in the innyard.

It was not to be concealed, nor did it leave me any room to question it, but the second of the three was my Lancashire husband. I was frighted to death; I never was in such a consternation in my life; I thought I should have sunk into the ground; my blood ran chill in my veins, and I trembled as if I had been in a cold fit of an ague.

Toward the end of the story she is caught stealing, and is liable to a death sentence if convicted.

The sight of a constable indeed struck me, and I thought I should have sunk into the ground. I fell into faintings, and indeed the people themselves thought I would have died . . .

She has fits of terror while in prison—"it threw me into fits and swoonings several times a day"—and faints when informed that she has been indicted—"I sank down when they brought me news of it, and after I came to myself I thought I should have died with the weight of it." This is what a realist does with fainting in the dawn of the modern novel. Moll's first attack may be aspiration to gentility, or idleness; the others puritan emphasis on the terrors of evil-doing. As such, and in every other aspect, they contrast with romance. The incest motif, to be sure, does appear here and there in romance, and legitimately entitles any lady to a fainting fit, but what have ladies to do with bigamy, felony and the prospect of hanging?

Moll Flanders' contemporary of the romantic school we have seen for a glimpse in an earlier chapter; she is Ardelisa, heroine of Mrs. Aubin's *Count of Vinevil*, 1721. She offers fair contrast to Defoe because she challenges comparison on the title page. Ardelisa's father is a count, albeit engaged in a commercial venture in Constantinople, where the "curs'd Mahometans" murder him. Ardelisa, directly unaware of the murder, perceives it in a dream. As she wakes from it, her hostess comes in to tell her the tragic news.

. . . the Consul's Lady, entering the Chamber all in Tears, said, 'Dear *Ardelisa,* I have News to tell you, that a Vertue less than yours could not support. Now summon all your Reason and Religion to your Aid, and to that God submit, who has this dreadful Night preserv'd you.' 'Alas! Madam, I too well understand you, *she reply'd,* my Father's murdr'd.' She at these words fell into a Swoon, out of which, with difficulty they recover'd her; . . .

See romance taking fresh tints from the color of the times: virtue the universal protector; reason the universal cure; the new trinity, Virtue, Reason, God, with God for the third person.

Ardelisa faints again in Chapter VII. In the familiar romantic disguise of a boy, she, with two disguised servants, seeks to escape her enemies, but the "lustful Turk," Osmin, takes them as runaway slaves, and compels them to march in chains in the middle of his troop. "They had not gone far before Ardelisa fainted, being unable to support her inward Grief, and the Fatigue of the March," which calls Osmin's attention to her, and leads to his bold discovery "that she was of the soft sex" (cited in Chapter III). Is her "inward Grief" apprehension for her virtue? She does not save it by fainting, but by the more active device of setting fire to Osmin's palace and escaping through the flames. Fainting is not a safeguard to bodily chastity unless the aggressor is so far in love that he is more concerned for the lady than for his own gratification. As a rule, heroines do not faint at attempted rape unless the author intends the ravisher to succeed, or does not wish to record any, or any more, of the protests of the outraged lady. So it is in Chaucer's version of the Rape of Lucrece. The story is that she succumbed to Tarquin's threat of killing her and a servant and showing the bodies in bed together, which calls forth Sarah Fielding's epigram: "Lucretia, whose chastity nothing but the fear of losing her reputation could possibly have conquered." Chaucer has Tarquin speak the threat, whereupon Lucretia passes out and leaves the decision to the next bidder.

> *Thise Romain wyves loveden so hir name*
> *At thilke time, and dredden so the shame,*
> *That, what for fere of slaundre and drede of deeth,*
> *She loste bothe at-ones wit and breeth,*
> *And in a swough she lay and wex so deed,*
> *Men mighte smiten of her arm or heed;*
> *She feleth no-thing, neither foul ne fair.*

Then, too late to save her body, she proceeds to a measure which to an orthodox Christian would mean the loss of the soul also, suicide. This is not rare among pagan heroines—Chaucer gives us elsewhere a long list of those who have used it—but it is not the usual protection of Christian maidens. They have a trick they must have learned from saints and martyrs. Le Bone Florence of Rome practises it with notable success. When the villain is about to do his worst, she prays to God and the Virgin Mary, and straightway his desire and his power leave him. She plays this on him twice, which annoys him so much that he hangs her by her hair to a tree, strips her and whips her. Sometimes the Christian virgin converts the ravisher to Christianity and marries him; sometimes she melts his heart by tears and entreaties. In one version of the story of Apollonius of Tyre, the Lady Lucina in captivity and sold to the keeper of a brothel softens the hearts of a dozen patrons one after the other. Often when the heroine is aboard ship at the mercy of an amorous captain, the ship cracks up on a rock just in time to save her virginity. On land she may be rescued by the hero who happens to be strolling by the scene of the attempt. In general, then, our heroines have felt that fainting at such a crisis was not good protective diplomacy. To be sure, an experienced and epicurean rake prefers full consciousness and co-operation, and will go through chapter after chapter of stratagem to get it, but no heroine can trust him not to take her at the opportunity whatever it is; he will even drug her as Lovelace did Clarissa if he can't get her by other means. No, it is not the best time to faint.

The fact that Pamela did faint at the crucial moment offered to Fielding an opportunity for satire which he did not take advantage of in *Joseph Andrews*. What might he not have done with Lady Booby and a fainting Joseph? Are we to reverse the picture and think of Lady Booby as Pamela? Lady Booby did not faint to dodge responsibility for Joseph's opportunity, however chagrined she may have been that he did not take advantage of it. If Fielding had shaped the action thus, he would have distorted Pamela as it seems he wanted us to see her, prudish, insincere, "sick of self-love," all that a woman should not be. Woman as she should be, "generous, guiltless, and of free disposition," he exhibits in the person of Sophia Western. The formula is spoken by the noble Countess Olivia, proffered as a cure for Malvolio's sickness of self-love; but it was Shakespeare who created Olivia on that very pattern, and on the same pattern Fielding created Sophia Western. Is it, then, any more a man's pattern for a woman than a woman's pattern for a man? Virtue does not have to rise above humanity to become sexless; the best of men are tender as well as brave; the best of women are brave as well as tender. Fielding explains this first, then dramatizes it in a single situation. Sophia has gone boldly out of her father's house alone at midnight.

Notwithstanding the many pretty arts which ladies sometimes practise to display their fears on every little occasion, (almost as many as the other sex use to conceal theirs) certainly there is a degree of courage which not only becomes a woman, but is often necessary to enable her to discharge her duty. It is, indeed, the idea of fierceness, not of bravery, which destroys the female character; for who can read the story of the justly celebrated Arria, without conceiving as high an opinion of her gentleness and tenderness as of her fortitude? At the same time, perhaps, many a woman who shrieks at a mouse or a rat, may be capable of poisoning a husband; or, what is worse, driving him to poison himself. Sophia, with all the gentleness that a woman can have, had all the spirit which she ought to have. When, therefore, she came to the place of appointment, and, instead of meeting her maid, as was agreed, saw a man ride directly up to her, she neither screamed out, nor fainted away: not that her pulse then beat with its usual regularity; for she was at first under some surprise and apprehension . . .

This shows clearly enough that Fielding is putting Sophia's conduct in deliberate contrast with that of any sort of heroine who would have fainted under the circumstances, be it Sidney's Pamela or Richardson's. Her later behavior indicates what Fielding thinks should make a proper woman faint. Tom has saved her a fall from an unruly horse at the expense of a broken arm.

Sophia, seeing his left arm dangling by his side, while he was using the other to lead her, no longer doubted of the truth: she now grew much paler than her fears for herself had made her before; all her limbs were seized with a trembling, insomuch that Jones could scarce support her; and as her thoughts were in no less agitation, she could not refrain from giving Jones a look so full of tenderness, that it almost argued a stronger sensation in her mind, than even gratitude and pity united can raise in the gentlest female bosom, without the assistance of a third more powerful passion.

We infer that if she had lost consciousness completely, Fielding would not have accused her of sentimentality. She does so at a report of Tom's death. She is at the whist table with Lord Fellamar, Lady Bellaston and Tom Edwards. Tom Edwards concludes his report:

". . . I saw the lad lie dead in a coffee-house. Upon my soul, he is one of the finest corpses I ever saw in my life."

Sophia, who had just begun to deal as Tom [Edwards] had mentioned that a man was killed, stopped her hand, and listened with attention, for all stories of that kind affected her; but no sooner had he arrived at the latter part of the story, than she began to deal again; and having dealt three cards to one, and seven to another, and ten to a third, at last dropped the rest from her hand, and fell back in her chair.

Fielding's intention seems clear enough. Sophia is never sick of self-love. Being guiltless, she has no fear for herself; being generous, she fears for others. Her fainting fits are not the only index of her character, but they mark it clearly, and Fielding uses them consistently.

The heroine who would have fainted where Sophia Western does not is she who inhabits the Gothic romance of forty years later. Although her Gothic habitation was yet to come in Fielding's time, she was already on her way. The unknown author of *Leonora,* 1745, derived her from Sidney and passed her on to Ann Radcliffe. Traces of the *Arcadia* are the names Musidorus and Philoclea; names of other figures suggest a most comprehensive reading in romance on the part of the author, Pastorella, Cleora, Amoret, Florimel, Zara, Fidelia, Alexis, Lycidas, Arpasia. In such company no heroine could faint by falling flat on her face like Pamela, or could misdeal her cards like Sophia. Leonora faints in the embellished style:

Surprized she started back, and gave a loud Shriek, a shivering Coldness at that Moment seem'd to threaten her dissolution, a Death-like Paleness succeeded; no Signs of Life appear'd, the unhappy Lover caught her in his Arms, shewing all the Signs of Grief that could possess a Mind robb'd of Hope.

Here we may know that Leonora was a lady because the author takes fifty words to say of her what Shakespeare said in four of the Queen of Scotland and in six of the Queen of Egypt. On another occasion the author uses even more violent means to heighten her effect. Areatta is stealing out to meet Manly to elope with him:

. . . with Fear and Love of Companions of her Flight, she wing'd her Way through the well known Apartments, till she arriv'd at the Garden-Door, which opening she discover'd a very tempestuous Night; the Lightning seem'd to split the Clouds from Pole to Pole, which struck her with Horror and Amazement: What could she do! To return was dangerous. After a little Pause, Love determin'd her to venture, tho' almost dead with Fear. At last she spied her Lover, when endeavoring to mend her Pace, she found her trembling Limbs unable to sustain her long. Manly rather flew to her than walk'd; he caught her in his Arms where she fainted: No Signs of Life for some Time appear'd, which almost drove him to distraction: He call'd her often in vain, at last his well known Voice Lur'd back the fluttering Soul to her almost forsaken Mansion.

In this passage the hodge-podge of the author's reading has brought together two flavors that later made a famous blend, love and thunder. In the romances of the former age, thunderstorms are no customary accompaniment to lovers' meetings; rarely are they used for anything but shipwrecks, though here and there we find imitations of the cave scene in the *Aeneid*. Shakespeare uses them for orchestral effects to tune his audience to the key of his scene. Perhaps the Weird Sisters brought thunder, lightning and rain to the birth of the infant Romance of Terror of which Hamlet was the literary father.

Cruikshank's plates illustrating Fielding's novels show no figure of Sophia Western, but exhibit Amelia in several plates in which we may see that her waist at its narrowest is precisely the width of her neck at its widest. All the ladies in these plates cut the same figure, which is an exaggeration of the fashion of the time when Cruikshank drew the plates, about 1830. In Amelia's time waists were fully as narrow, even narrower, than in 1830, but the breasts were suppressed rather than emphasized. Amelia is of the mammalian order, as the passage quoted above on page 91 makes quite obvious. Fielding is not the man to endorse any fashion which suppresses the breasts; for approval or for disapproval he never fails to mention them whenever he describes a woman. Was it tight lacing that pushed Amelia's "protuberances" up to her "neck" and made her faint four times to Sophia's once? The silhouette of fashion did not change much between Sophia's time and Amelia's, between 1749 and 1752. It was one which had been much in fashion in the sixteenth century, held favor with some modifications in the seventeenth century, and prevailed through much of the eighteenth. It makes of the body an inverted cone, or, when the breasts are flattened, a triangle, the pubic triangle extended by running its side lines up to the arm-pits or the points of the shoulders. Boucher's portrait of Mme. de Pompadour shows it; so does Lancret's of Mlle. de Sallé, Nattier's of Madame Adélaide, and many of the drawings and paintings of Watteau. Here is pressure enough on the "sides of nature" to excuse fainting without additional stress of emotion. Perhaps Sophia Western did not wear so strict a costume of fashion as did Amelia; she lived much more in the country. Perhaps she was young and carefree as Amelia was not. Perhaps her vigor and freedom are gifts of Fielding's youthful imagination. His biographers tell us that he drew both figures from the same model, his first wife. If so, we may be justified in thinking of Sophia as the "phantom of delight," and of Amelia as "the very pulse of the machine," and consider Amelia's tearfulness and tendency to faint the result of poverty, child-bearing and anxiety.

Contemporary with Fielding's heroines is Smollett's Emilia Gauntlet, who graces the pages of *Peregrine Pickle,* the only female figure to whom Smollett gave humanity enough to make her seriously interesting. Smollett's customary formula for extreme feeling is gross hyperbole. Fear at the sight of a supposed ghost makes the teeth of an intrepid old naval officer chatter so violently that they shatter like glass. Such emotions as rage and disappointment not only make Peregrine Pickle faint, but foam at the mouth or bleed copiously from the nose. Occasions of minor vexation make other women in these novels faint, but not Emilia Gauntlet. She has cause enough to do so in the many chapters through which she has to restrain and govern the conduct of the unruly Peregrine. When he has safely won her love and his road is smooth to marriage, he basely attempts to take her as Lovelace did Clarissa, by carrying her off in a coach after a ball. She does not faint, but vigorously tells him what she thinks of his conduct, calls a chair, and goes safely home. She faints but once, when Peregrine has rescued her from a dangerous fire, and that is not because she is tightly laced, for at the moment she has nothing on but her shift. Smollett is the implacable foe of the sentimental view of life.

In direct contrast to Smollett is the nameless writer of *The Rival Mother,* 1755, cited above in Chapter III, who has such faith in the charms of unconsciousness that she (impossible to think that a man wrote it) gives the hero and the reader their first glimpse of her two heroines when one of them is stretched on the ground in a dead faint. The other is that Julia who the astute surgeon perceived by her "neck" was a woman when she was disguised as a man. Julia doesn't faint; she thriftily saves the cutting of laces by removing her stays when she thinks they will be in the way.

I then shut my door, and taking off my stays, with a trembling hand, I open'd the Baron's letter.

Julia, before she sat down to Table, went into her chamber to undress, and her maid had but just taken off her Stays, when the Chevalier entering her Room, took her in his Arms, which so terribley frighted her, that she screamed out aloud.

Doubtless she would have fainted if she hadn't had her stays off. Did she take them off because she wanted to eat a square meal, or because she expected the Chevalier?

A widely popular and influential romance of the second half of the eighteenth century was *Caroline of Lichtfield,* which Thomas Holcroft translated from the French. At one stage of this three-volume agony the Canoness of Rindaw might have brought Caroline and Walstein together by a straightforward letter or by plain-speaking.

But all this was much too simple for the Canoness of Rindaw, too trivial for the end of a romance, in which she was quite in raptures to be one of the *dramatis personae.* Surprise! Gratitude! Tears! Faintings! If these were wanting the scene must have been insipid.

She goes about it more theatrically, and the result is more than she bargained for.

Poor Caroline scarcely hears the end of the phrase: sense and feeling have forsaken her, and she drops, motionless on the shoulder of her imprudent friend! . . . And now the Canoness, in despair, repents, too late, of what she has done. Caroline continues lifeless, moves not, breathes not, betrays not the least sign of existence! [Walstein comes on the scene.] The first object he beholds is Caroline, senseless, with her lace cut, her hair loose, her bosom bare . . .

This is an interesting device to heighten the effect of tears and fainting in a romance by making the reader feel first their customary romantic artificiality.

Mrs. Ann Radcliffe uses a less ingenious device. In her first novel, *The Castles of Athlin and Dunbayne,* 1789, the fainting fits come early and often. The Countess Matilda hears that her son is captured and sentenced to death, and her fortitude faints, which is nearly fatal.

The fortitude of Matilda fainted under the pressure of so heavy a calamity; she was attacked by a violent illness which had nearly terminated her sorrows and her life, and had rendered unavailing all the tender cares of her daughter. These tender cares, however, were not ineffectual; she revived . . .

The hero's sister is captured:

. . . Mary . . . had fainted in the arms of the villain who had seized her . . . her terrors may easily be imagined, when she revived and found herself in the hands of unknown men . . . despair seized her mind, and she lost all signs of existence: in this state she remained some time; . . .

The Baroness learns that her long-mourned son is not dead after all:

The Baroness could hear no more; she was carried insensible from the apartment.

Mary is kidnapped again:

. . . she had been overtaken by a party of armed men who carried her off senseless.

After all this, what can one do to register a new agony? Just nothing at all.

There is a certain point of misery beyond which the mind becomes callous, and acquires a sort of artificial calm. Excess of misery may be said to blast the vital powers of feeling, and by a natural consequence consumes its own principle. Thus it was with Matilda: a long succession of trials had reduced her to a state of horrid tranquility, which followed the first shock of the present event.

Of all Pamela's daughters, these heroines of Mrs. Radcliffe's are the most habitual fainters. They inherited the trait from

Pamela; it is not "one of the best features of the old romance" which Walpole and his followers sought to revive. In Pamela and in them it is an index of the trait that has been most obnoxious to readers of all times since Richardson's, particularly to the twentieth century. Pamela is all things to all men, but seldom more than one thing to any one critic. The Pamela who faints from self-esteem at the attack on her virtue is she who is unpopular with Richardson's readers, and it is she who is the ancestress of the fainting heroines of the Gothic romance. In the truly "old" romances, this is the rarest of all causes for fainting. In the Gothic romance an expurgated version of Pamela's situation is the commonest of causes for fainting. Pamela is naked in her bed in the hands of the ravisher whose every motion she specifies. In the passage quoted above from *Athlin and Dunbayne,* "Mary is in the arms of a villain who had seized her; her terrors may easily be imagined." May they? Or would a "young person" of 1789 have to know more than she was supposed to if she were to imagine them? Did Mrs. Radcliffe suppose that the young reader knew more than she was supposed to know? And how much are we supposed to suppose that Mary knew? Whatever the terror presupposed, it was for herself. Mary and all her numerous tribe were sick of self-love when they fainted. The heroines of the old romances were more apt to faint for the love of others. Fielding's best attack on *Pamela* is not the distortions of *Joseph Andrews,* but the truer lines with which Sophia Western is drawn, "generous, guiltless, and of free disposition," who faces alert any danger to herself and faints only when she is helpless to undo misfortune which has already befallen one she loves.

There is no reason to suppose that there was any more fainting in real life during the vogue of the Gothic romance than in any other; indeed, the fashions in clothes would suggest that there should have been less. Mrs. Radcliffe was born in 1764, the year of *The Castle of Otranto,* and she published her first

novel, *The Castles of Athlin and Dunbayne* in 1789, the year of
the storming of the Bastille. With the fall of the Bastille, in-
flated skirts and elevated head-dresses fell also. The Committee
of Public Health commissioned Louis David, painter of monumental scenes of Greece and Rome, to design a costume in the
spirit of the time. He turned out something on classic lines, from
which extremes of fashion took license and veered toward effects
of nudity. A fashion plate of 1799 shows a lady who seems to
wear nothing but a long filmy chemise, a pair of stockings and a
turban; probably she wore also a skin-colored *maillot* from the
waist to the top of the stockings. We may guess that few went
so far toward nudity, though there is evidence that some did,
and caricatures of the time would have us think that all did.
Those whose figures showed to advantage in clinging diaphanous
draperies were lucky. Obese dowagers were victims of the
caricaturists; Rowlandson's plates pitilessly show them doing
their best with the aid of such devices as they could command
to follow the pitiless fashion. The corsets of the time were somewhat like the dress reform "waists" of the later decades of the
nineteenth century, upholding the breasts and restraining the
waist, but doing little for any redundancies below that. The
one period between the fourteenth century and the twentieth
when women's bodies were by fashion unconfined was the time
when the novel made its strongest bid for "the world's fainting record."

To understand this, we may think of fainting as a symptom
of a sort of aristocracy complex, and of the Gothic romance as
a dream of feudalism by way of escape from an inevitably rising
tide of democracy. Of course, fainting gathers frequency enough
to look like a habit in literature long before the outbreak of the
French Revolution, but not before the Cromwellian revolution.
And if we choose to look even farther back, we may note that as
soon as democracy began to act on feudalism, feudalism began
to react on literature; the process had been going on for

centuries before the Castle of Dunbayne and the Bastille fell in the same year. In France so long as it was dangerous to look like an aristocrat, fashions were conspicuously plebeian in style. The neo-classic styles in clothes were anti-aristocratic in so far as they sought to abolish social distinctions. In real life, corsets were in the discard, but the feminine chivalric exercise of fainting passed the Gothic novel along with tilts and tournaments.

Fainting was, of course, a part with liquid sorrow of the literary hysteria which was the novel of sensibility; its diagnosis leads to the same underlying conditions. Both these ghosts of aristocracy received the attack of Jane Austen's keenly edged shafts as ghosts would; they were riddled but they never knew it. Reassemble the titles of dead romances and you have the muster roll of a whole limbo of such ghosts testifying that publishers found them profitable, in spite of Scott's better example, until Dickens dressed many of their absurdities in early Victorian costume and made them at home in the London of his day. Sentimentality is the hardiest perennial of all literature; "the more it is trodden on, the faster it grows." Smollett was its implacable foe. His attack on sentimental romance carried him into the romance of humor, the farce of hyperbole. Jane Austen opposes romance with sense of fact. In *Sense and Sensibility* she denies the fainting habit of the romantic heroine by showing the most romantic girl possible to real life consciously practising romance wherever it can be consciously practised. The fashionable mood of grief can be encouraged and induced.

Elinor saw with concern the excess of her sister's sensibility; but by Mrs. Dashwood it was valued and cherished. They encouraged each other now in the violence of their affliction. The agony of grief which overpowered them at first, was voluntarily renewed, was sought for, was created again and again. They gave themselves up wholly to their sorrow, seeking increase of wretchedness in every reflection that could afford it, and resolved against ever admitting consolation in the future.

Costume Parisien—Fichu—Turban, 1799

"THE SIDES OF NATURE" UNCONFINED

But Marianne cannot faint at will, and, sentimental as she is, is not hypocrite enough to pretend it. She does not faint when she sprains her ankle; that was not necessary to induce Willoughby to pick her up and carry her home in his arms. She does not faint when she learns of Willoughby's baseness of character; neither real nor pretended fainting could remedy that. She does not faint at all. A heroine who never faints is even more obviously the antithesis of the romantic heroine than is the burlesque figure who faints when she breaks a teacup or treads on a worm. Even *Northanger Abbey* is too realistic for either burlesque or satire. It is satire in so far as it makes romance ridiculous, but it does not distort its subject. Others who made game of romance overshot the mark. *The Heroine,* by Eaton Stannard Barrett, 1813, exhibits in Cherubina an ultra absurd heroine who has perished with the type it burlesques, for Barrett was a lesser artist than the best of those he parodied. Jane Austen's satire of ephemerids takes rank with the greatest, and commanded the respect of the greatest romancer in the history of the English novel.

In *Northanger Abbey,* Catherine Morland opposes the romantic heroine in every trait without going to any inhuman extremes; in fact it is her very human qualities that most sharply point the contrast.

No one who had ever seen Catherine Morland in her infancy would have supposed her born to be an heroine . . . She had a thin awkward figure, a sallow skin without colour, dark lank hair, and strong features . . . She was fond of all boys' plays, and greatly preferred cricket, not merely to dolls, but to the more heroic enjoyments of infancy, nursing a dormouse, feeding a canary-bird, or watering a rose-bush . . . She was, moreover, noisy and wild, hated confinement and cleanliness, and loved nothing so well in the world as rolling down the green slope at the back of the house. Such was Catherine Morland at ten. At fifteen . . . it was not very wonderful that Catherine should prefer cricket, base ball, riding on horseback, and running about the country, to books . . . She had reached the age of seventeen without having seen one amiable youth who could call forth her sensibility: without having inspired one real passion, and without having excited even any admiration but what was very moderate and very transient.

Almost the only mention of fainting in *Northanger Abbey* is satirical only by contrast. Catherine sees Mr. Tilney after he has been out of town for a week.

He looked as handsome and as lively as ever, and was talking with interest to a fashionable and pleasing-looking young woman who leant on his arm, and whom Catherine immediately guessed to be his sister; thus unthinkingly throwing away a fair opportunity of considering him lost to her forever by being married already . . . therefore, instead of turning of a deathlike paleness, and falling in a fit on Mrs. Allen's bosom, Catherine sat erect in the perfect use of her senses, and with cheeks only a little redder than usual.

In *Mansfield Park,* 1814, Fanny Price does not faint, though the state of her health would seem to warrant it. Indeed, the only out-and-out fainting fit in all Jane Austen's serious novels is that of Henrietta in Chapter XII of *Persuasion,* when she thinks that Louisa has been killed by a fall. If Jane Austen is a trustworthy observer and reporter, we may infer that fainting in life was merely normal at a time when it was at its height in fiction. She testifies, too, as to its height in fiction in a novel that is not at all serious, *Love and Freindship* [*sic*], written in 1792. It is a burlesque on the novels of fainting; in it she put all the fainting fits she might have put in the other novels, like Lord Timothy Dexter's marks of punctuation, in solid blocks for the reader to season his dish with according to taste.

Never did I see such an affecting scene as the meeting of Edward and Augustus . . . It was too pathetic for the feelings of Sophia and myself— We fainted alternately on a sofa. [Augustus is imprisoned for debt.] Ah! what could we do but what we did! We sighed and fainted on the sofa. [Edward and Augustus are killed by the overturn of a carriage.] Sophia immediately sunk again into a swoon.

—My grief was more audible. My voice faltered, my eyes assumed a vacant stare, my face became as pale as death, and my senses were considerably impaired . . . For two hours did I rave thus madly and should not then have left off, as I was not in the least fatigued, had not Sophia who was just recovering from her swoon, intreated me to consider that night was approaching and the damps began to fall.

The difference between the wild raver and the passive fainter turns out to be that between life and death. Before long Sophia

complained of a violent pain in her delicate limbs, accompanied with a disagreeable head-ake. She attributed it to a cold caught by her continued faintings in the open air as the dew was falling the evening before. This I feared was but too probably the case; since how could it be otherwise accounted for that I should have escaped the same indisposition, but by supposing that the bodily exertions I had undergone in my repeated fits of frenzy had so effectually circulated and warmed my blood as to make me proof against the chilling damps of night, whereas Sophia, lying totally inactive on the ground must have been exposed to all their severity.

"My beloved Laura (said she to me a few hours before she died) take warning from my unhappy end and avoid the imprudent conduct which had occasioned it . . . Beware of fainting fits . . . Though at the time they may be refreshing and agreeable yet believe me they will in the end, if too often repeated and at improper seasons, prove destructive to your constitution . . . My fate will teach you this . . . I die a martyr to my grief for the loss of Augustus . . . One fatal swoon has cost me my life . . . Beware of swoons, dear Laura . . . A frenzy fit is not one quarter so pernicious; it is an exercise to the body and if not too violent, is I dare say conducive to health and its consequences— Run mad as often as you chuse; but do not faint."

"One of the finest corpses I ever saw in my life," says Tom Edwards of Tom Jones. No doubt he was a connoisseur in corpses. People may well have been so at a time when the sentimental view of death stood in the way of the understanding of tragedy. It was an age that avoided the realistic view of death, and could make no better romance of it than appeared in either the chill of terror or the smirk of sentimentality; anything but the reverence of awe. A beautiful heroine in a faint was the most ideally beautiful corpse imaginable, but when Mary of Athlin faints in the arms of a villain, no one says of her in the mood of tragedy, "cover her face; mine eyes dazzle; she died young." Death in the Gothic novels has the romance of terror, which is low tragedy. Death in high tragedy has not the romance of pity and terror, but that of sympathy, awe and reverence; it is "eloquent, just and mighty," and its mood is that of supreme authority. Such feeling would be to Mrs. Radcliffe's time sublime but not beautiful; she makes her scenes beautiful in Burke's sense of the word, and leaves them greatly lacking in authority of mood to us. Byron after an illness said to his mirror, "How pale I look! I should like, I think, to die of a consumption; because the women would all say, 'See that poor Byron,—how interesting he looks in dying!'" The fainting of Mrs. Radcliffe's heroines is practising dying before the mirror, reading their own flattering obituaries in the faces and comments of the "interested" bystanders. Even in the mood of high tragedy, fainting may be a rehearsal of death, as Enobarbus says of Cleopatra, but there it rises to a climax which rings with the authority of tragedy:

> *Give me my robe, put on my crown; I have*
> *Immortal longings in me; . . .*

But the heroines of the Gothic novel rehearse it so often and to so little effect that we think of them as of the young man in the limerick who "thought he should die, and he did, and nobody cared."

CHAPTER VI

THE LASS WITH THE DELICATE AIR

Young Molly, who lives at the foot of a hill,
Whose fame every virgin with envy doth fill,
Of beauty is blessed with so ample a share,
Men call her the lass with the delicate air.

One evening last May as I traversed the grove
In thoughtless retirement, not dreaming of love,
I chanced to espy the gay nymph, I declare,
And, really, she had a most delicate air.

By a wandering brook, on a green, mossy bed,
A chaplet composing, the fair one was laid.
Surprised and transported, I could not forbear
With rapture to gaze on her delicate air.

A thousand times o'er I've repeated my suit,
And still the tormenter affects to be mute.
So tell me ye swains who have captured the fair
How to win the dear lass with the delicate air.

RICHARDSON was not the only one in his day who was interested
in pretty maids of low degree. Thomas Arne who wrote of sweet
Molly with the delicate air was a contemporary of his. So was
Henry Carey who wrote *Sally in Our Alley,* and John Gay,
author of *Black-Eyed Susan,* the lass who loved Sweet William,
the sailor. Carey is said to have written *Sally in Our Alley* after
walking on a holiday afternoon behind an apprentice and a
servant-maid to observe their plebeian love-making. In *The Beg-*
gar's Opera Gay used these low-born figures as they had long
been used, for purposes of comedy and satire. But in the ballad
Arne and Gay take Molly and Susan a shade more seriously, and
sentimentalize them in their way as completely as Richardson
does Pamela. And in just so far as this sentimentalizing of the

169

plebeian is more serious than comedy or satire, it is a step toward bourgeois tragedy which was even then seeking a real tragedian to make it an acceptable form. If Richardson had been a dramatist he might have done it. *Pamela* is sentimental comedy, and *Clarissa* is tragedy of the upper middle class, but not for the stage.

In order to be in line for promotion to the middle class, if she is below it, or to the aristocracy, or to tragedy, the low-born damsel must have the delicate air as a minimum requirement. Sally (of our alley) hasn't it, and must remain a comedy figure. Black-eyed Susan is good enough for anybody:

> *The noblest captain in the British fleet*
> *Might envy William's lips those kisses sweet.*

even were he Sir Joseph Porter, K.C.B. And we know her air is delicate:

> *"Adieu!" she cries, and waves her lily hand.*

We may suppose a less delicate girl would have hollered, "Bye, Bill!" and waved a bandanna. Pamela, too, has a lily hand; we have seen her blister it in trying to scour a pewter platter. It is a hand of little employment save in ladylike tasks about her indulgent mistress, and we have Hamlet's word for it that the hand of little employment hath the daintier sense. Hamlet knew the delicate air when he saw it.

God hath given you one face and you make yourselves another: you jig, you amble, you lisp, and nickname God's creatures, and make your wantonness your ignorance.

Enobarbus notes it in Cleopatra, and suggests a reason for the affectation:

> *I saw her once*
> *Hop forty paces through the public street;*
> *And having lost her breath, she spoke, and panted,*
> *That she did make defect perfection,*
> *And, breathless, power breathe forth.*

We may fairly take this to be but a part of her infinite variety, for we have seen her put forth energy enough to knock a man down, drag him about by the hair, and draw a knife to stab him. If the dynamic Queen of Egypt and Daughter of all the Ptolemies is to be out of breath at forty paces, it behooves lesser lights of fashion to be even more delicate. Regina Maria Roche shows in *The Children of the Abbey* what it had come to in 1796.

Art and fashion were exhausted in adorning her, and she entered the room with all the insolence of conscious rank and affectation of beauty. As she walked she appeared scarcely able to support her delicate frame, and her languishing eyes were half closed.

Some two centuries before the Christian Era, Terence noted the delicate air as fashionable in Roman society.

The girl is not like those in our society whose mothers try to fit them with falling shoulders and flat bosoms to make them sylphlike. If one is a bit plump, she's called a boxer and has her rations cut down. Though she's all right by nature, treatment makes her like a bulrush. So suitors come.

The lines remind one of Fielding's approval of Fanny Andrews in his description of her (quoted in Chapter III), as "not one of those slender young women, who seem rather intended to hang up in the hall of an anatomist than for any other purpose." Fielding derided Richardson's attribution of the delicate air to the serving-maid, and ridiculed Pamela's exhibition of it by conferring it on Joseph:

. . . his hair . . . was displayed in wanton ringlets down his back: his forehead was high, his eyes dark, and as full of sweetness as of fire: his nose a little inclined to the Roman: his teeth white and even: his lips full, red and soft: . . . Add to this the most perfect neatness in his dress, and an air, which, to those who have not seen many noblemen, would give an idea of nobility.

And we learn elsewhere that he has a very white skin. The phrase, "to those who have not seen many noblemen," seems to score a direct hit on Richardson. Fielding came of the family of the Earl of Denbigh, and was cousin to Lady Mary Wortley Montagu. No doubt he knew more about noblemen than did Richardson, but how about servant girls? Perhaps he knew them too, but did not care to boast. Examination of the details of the portrait of Fanny indicates that most of the anti-Pamela of *Joseph Andrews* is in the character of Joseph, for Fanny, though she does not set up to be a heroine, has much of the quality that Fielding derides in Pamela, almost enough to give her the delicate air. She has not the lily hand, but barring that, a little tan, a pock-mark, and something less than regularity in the teeth, she is quite ladylike. She is robust and of full figure, but none the less "delicately shaped," white of skin where the sun does not touch it, possessed of sensibility, and above all of a "natural gentility" which, like Pamela's, surprised all beholders. Note, too, the phrases nearly repeated from the description of Joseph in the earlier chapter—Fielding does not describe Fanny till nearly halfway through the tale.

With this compare his portrait of one who is a lady in so far as she is the daughter of a country gentleman, a squire, a landed proprietor:

Sophia [Western] . . . was a middle-sized woman, but rather inclining to tall. Her shape was not only exact, but extremely delicate; and the nice proportion of her arms promised the truest symmetry in her limbs: her hair which was black, was so luxuriant that it reached her middle, before she cut it to comply with the modern fashion; and it was now curled so gracefully in her neck, that few could believe it to be her own: if envy could find any part of the face which demanded less commendation than the rest, it might possibly think her forehead might have been higher without prejudice to her: her eyebrows were full, even, and arched beyond the power of art to imitate: her black eyes had a lustre in them which all her softness could not extinguish: her nose was exactly regular; and her mouth, in which were two rows of ivory, exactly answered Sir John Suckling's description in those lines:—

SOPHIA WESTERN

"Generous, Guiltless, and of Free Disposition"

Her lips were red, and one was thin
Compared to that was next her chin;
Some bee had stung it newly.

Her cheeks were of the oval kind; and in her right she had a dimple which the least smile discovered: her chin had certainly its share in forming the beauty of her face; but it was difficult to say it was either large or small, though perhaps it was of the former kind: her complexion had rather more of the lily than of the rose; but when exercise or modesty increased her natural colour, no vermilion could equal it: then one might indeed cry out with the celebrated Dr. Donne,

—her pure and eloquent blood
Spoke in her cheeks, and so distinctly wrought,
That one might almost say her body thought.

Her neck was long and finely turned: and here if I was not afraid of offending her delicacy, I might justly say that the highest beauties of the famous Venus de Medicis were outdone: here was whiteness, which no lilies, ivory, nor alabaster could match: the finest cambric might indeed be supposed from envy to cover that bosom which was much whiter than itself: it was indeed, *nitor splendens Pario marmore purius:* 'A gloss shining beyond the purest brightness of Parian marble.'

We have no portrait of Pamela to hang beside that of Fanny, but Lovelace's description of Clarissa affords us a companion piece to Sophia.

Her wax-like flesh (for after all, flesh and blood I think she is) by its delicacy and firmness, answers for the soundness of her health. Thou has often heard me launch out in praise of her complexion. I never in my life beheld a skin so *illustriously* fair. The lily and the driven snow it is nonsense to talk of: her lawn and her laces one might indeed compare to those; but what a whited wall would a woman appear to be, who had a complexion which would justify such unnatural comparisons? But this lady is all glowing, all charming flesh and blood; yet so clear, that every meandering vein is to be seen in all the lovely parts of her which custom permits to be visible.

Thou has heard me also describe the wavy ringlets of her shining hair, needing neither art nor powder; of itself an ornament, defying all other ornaments; wantoning in and about a neck that is beautiful beyond description.

Her head-dress was a brussels lace mob, peculiarly adapted to the charming air and turn of her features. A sky-blue ribband illustrated that. But although the weather was somewhat sharp, she had not on either hat or hood; for, besides that she loves to use herself hardily (by which means and by a temperance truly exemplary, she is allowed to have given high health and vigor to an originally tender constitution) she seems to have intended to show me, that she was determined not to stand by her appointment. O Jack! that such a sweet girl should be a rogue!

Her morning gown was a pale primrose-coloured paduasoy: the cuffs and robins curiously embroidered by the fingers of this ever-charming Arachne, in a running pattern of violets and their leaves, the light in the flowers silver, gold in the leaves. A pair of diamond snaps in her ears. A white handkerchief wrought by the same inimitable fingers concealed— O Belford! what still more inimitable beauties did it not conceal!—And I saw, all the way we rode, the bounding heart (by its throbbing motions I saw it!) dancing beneath the charming umbrage.

Her ruffles were the same as her mob. Her apron a flowered lawn. Her coat white sattin, quilted: blue sattin her shoes, braided with the same colour, without lace; for what need has the prettiest foot in the world of ornament? neat buckles in them: and on her charming arms a pair of black velvet glove-like muffs of her own invention; for she makes and gives fashions as she pleases.—Her hands velvet of themselves, thus uncovered the freer to be grasped by those of her adorer . . . the fire of her starry eyes began to sink into a less dazzling languor. She trembled: nor knew she how to support the agitations of a heart she had never found so ungovernable. She was even fainting when I clasped her in my supporting arms.

Here are two portraits in the best manner of the mid-century, 1748 and 1749, one the daughter of a country gentleman, the other of a wealthy city merchant with nearly equal claim to gentility. Richardson describes Clarissa Harlowe's family as "very rich," "uncommonly prosperous." The money is as respectable as possible; it comes from mines and East India traffic; in the background are estates in England and Scotland. Clearly there might be a knighthood or a baronetcy on the King's next birthday. It is as if the portrait showed a window opening on a dimly distant prospect of a gentleman's park, and the insignia of the Order of the Bath lying carelessly on a table. A part of this aura of gentility is the unmistakably delicate air of the portrait. If Boucher had painted it we should have seen just about what Richardson shows us, which is, of course, mainly costume; "the lovely parts of her which custom permits to be visible" are only face and hands and what one may perceive through the kerchief which fills the square opening of the decolletage. Boucher painted Mme. de Pompadour without the bourgeois prudery of the kerchief, displaying the fact that her tightly laced corset held her breasts high and covered them only just over the nipples. Did she sit to the same painter for his *Diane Sortant du Bain?* One guesses it is the same model, and enjoys the sight of various lovely parts invisible in the other picture, the round young breasts which need no compression to hold them high, the long body which would come as near as anything nature makes to fitting the Louis XV corset, long hands and fingers, long feet and toes, long legs with the feet pointed down to emphasize the taper from the full thigh to the tip of the second toe. It is a perfectly healthy, slender but rounded girl of sixteen, a *"fausse maigre"*; Stratz shows a photograph from life of such a girl in almost the same attitude, which corresponds exactly to the painting. These paintings of Boucher's have sense of fact no less than sense of fashion. They express the feeling of the moment, and yet they are lasting works of art. They are Louis XV, rococo, in its very best manner. Study them attentively side by side with the word portraits by Richardson and Fielding, and you must feel that they are the same fashion set forth with equal artistry. These artists turn fashion into lasting art, and from these examples we may breathe the delicate air like a perfume.

Note the number of details from the word portraits of Richardson and Fielding that apply to Boucher's young Diana. She is rather inclining to tall; one guesses that those taper legs provide a trifle more than half her height. The delicacy and firmness of her flesh answers for the soundness of her health. Her shape is not only exact but extremely delicate, rounded enough, that is, to afford agreeable proportions, but not beyond the slenderness that connotes youth. The legs, now that we may see them, carry out the promise of the arms. She loves to use herself hardily; we see her here bathing in a snow-cold spring after running through and through the rough forest in pursuit of the hares, now lying at her feet, which she or her arrows have overtaken—no doubt her flesh is firm, these delicate rondures are the index of athletic muscles. If she had chosen to use them instead of her divine powers she might have punished Actæon as Cleopatra did the messenger of ill-tidings. If her constitution was originally delicate, her exercises have given it high health and vigor. Her neck is long and finely turned, and when fashion or taste prefers Diana to Venus, the Venus de Medici is indeed outdone. The delicate air is perhaps too ethereal a perfume for laboratory analysis, but the attempt may teach us one or two things that will help us. If Boucher's paintings are in the Louis XV fashion called rococo, Clarissa and Sophia represent the rococo fashion in heroines. The fashion calls for a combination of robust health and fragile delicacy which taxes the word-painter's ingenuity to balance between the two, to emphasize the white skin (even in a black-haired heroine) and the slender body to the verge of ill-health, and still leave the impression of an entirely healthy girl. Only the best of them succeed.

Fielding's taste is, as a matter of course, more robust than Richardson's; Fanny is in (literally) exuberant health, and Sophia scarcely less. Clarissa is sound when we see her but there is a background of fragility—"a constitution originally tender," "she was even fainting when I clasped her in my supporting arms." Does this give Richardson the lighter touch? His picture seems closer to Watteau than to Boucher; we may think of the *Em-*

barcation for the Isle of Cythera. The end of Clarissa's voyage
is tragic, but so it may be with Watteau's figures for anything we
know. One must believe that Richardson knew French art of
his time, Greuze, Watteau, Lancret, Boucher, even the erotic engravings. If so, the English novel owes to French painting more
than it has acknowledged, for this portrait of Clarissa is the first
serious full-length portrait of any heroine of the novel, and its
style was followed for so long that Pamela's daughters prevailingly take after their Aunt Clarissa. Richardson had little precedent for it, only Fielding's portrait of Fanny (hardly serious
and not exactly a heroine) and what he might have gathered
from romances in prose and verse, which would have yielded him
only "a gray eye or so, but nothing to the purpose." In the metrical romances there are a number of recurrent phrases, hair like
gold wire, eyebrows like silk threads, eyes gray as glass, nose
straight and well formed, long straight sides, breasts small,
round and high, small waist, but rarely do we find more than two
or three of these applied to any one lady. The best of the sort is
in a prose portion of the *cante-fable* of *Aucassin and Nicolette:*

Her locks were yellow and curled, her eyes blue and smiling, her
face featly fashioned, the nose high and fairly set, the lips more red
than cherry or rose in time of summer, her teeth white and small;
her breasts so firm that they bore up the folds of her bodice as they
had been two apples; so slim was she in the waist that your two hands
might have clipped her, and the daisy flowers that brake beneath
her as she went tip-toe, and that bent above her instep, seemed black
against her feet, so white was the maiden.

Chaucer in the fabliau manner gives us sharply etched little
vignettes of women with incomparable realism, but they are
not heroines, they have not the delicate air. In describing his
serious or dignified women he echoes the metrical romances
("hir nose tretys, hir eyen gray as glas"). The most conspicuous
full-length portrait in his gallery is that of Blanche the Duchess,
doubtless the most successful thing of the sort before the novel;

successful, too, in spite of the fact that it is a mosaic of all the medieval details and clichés. It loses by concentration and paraphrase, but it can hardly be presented otherwise, for it is the major part of the poem of 1300 lines.

> She was steadfast of countenance, noble of carriage and behavior. Her hair was gold, her eyes debonair, good, bright, serious, straightforward, well-proportioned, not too large. Her look was not aside but straightforward, and took in all details of what she looked on. Her color was ruddy, fresh and lively. Her neck was white, smooth and straight like a round tower of ivory, fair shoulders, long body, arms well rounded, white hands, rosy nails, round breasts, hips of good breadth, a straight flat back, legs in perfect proportion.

Here are the dead details; the breath of life is in the poem, and there Blanche the Duchess lives immortally. They are worth exhibiting only as a summary of the medieval standard of beauty, a concentrate of all one could get from the romances before Chaucer, and of all that the romanticists had for precedent before the time of the realists. What it had come to by 1721 we may see from Mrs. Aubin's introduction of her heroine, the fair Ardelisa, whom we have met but not scrutinized.

> She was then Fourteen, and the most charming Maid Nature e'er form'd; she was tall and slender, fair as *Venus,* her Eyes blue and shining, her Face oval, with Features and an Air so sweet and lovely, that Imagination can form nothing more compleatly handsome or engaging. Her Mind well suited the fair Cabinet that contained it; she was Humble, Generous, Unaffected, yet Learned, Wise, Modest, and Prudent above her Years or Sex; Gay in Conversation, but by Nature Thoughtful; had all the Softness of a Woman, with the Constancy and Courage of a Hero: in fine, her Soul was capable of everything that was Noble.

If this were anonymous we should still know that a woman wrote it, for throughout the eighteenth century the men novelists give their heroines physical and emotional charms, whereas the women add to these mental attainments. Ardelisa puts prodigies of scholarship to shame; she is "learned" at four-teen without benefit of high school, seemingly by sheer intuition. Aside from this we observe that the best the author can do for the physical appearance of the most charming maid that Nature had achieved up to 1721 was to tell us that she was tall, slender, blonde, and had blue eyes. The rest is an attempt at persuasion. Richardson tells us scarcely so much, yet he persuades us so much the more. Is Clarissa blonde or brune? She is snow white and rose red, has "shining" hair, and wears blue and silver. Most of us would image a blonde, but black hair may shine, and set off a skin of lily and driven snow. Richardson, with the air of careful detail, leaves us free to enshrine here what image we will, an example which many of his successors have followed with success—but not Fielding.

Smollett, implacable foe of sensibility, creates a heroine well endowed with common sense, but still gives her the fashionable delicate air. Peregrine Pickle is "just past his fourteenth year" when he meets Emilia Gauntlet at a ball.

She seemed to be of his own age, was tall, and though slender, ex-quisitely shaped; her hair was auburn, and in such plenty, that the barbarity of dress had not been able to prevent it from shading both sides of her forehead, which was high and polished; the con-tour of her face was oval, her nose very little raised into the aquiline form, that contributed to the spirit and dignity of her aspect; her mouth was small, her lips plump, juicy, and delicious; her teeth regular, and white as driven snow; her complexion in-credibly delicate, and glowing with health; her mien was at the same time commanding and engaging, her address perfectly genteel, and her whole appearance so captivating, that our young Adonis looked and was overcome.

This is three years after Clarissa and two years after Sophia, still the rococo heroine, tall and though slender, exquisitely shaped, complexion incredibly delicate and glowing with health; the details of the face, too, check with Boucher's paintings with the exception of the lift of the nose toward the aquiline. The Lass with the Delicate Air is obviously the favorite with the novelists in the beginnings of the novel, and so she was for a century, from Mrs. Aubin to Miss Ferrier, before we come upon any noticeable attempt to rationalize her. The heroine of Susan Ferrier's *The Inheritance,* 1824, slips out for a walk before breakfast, and returns to find that she has committed an impropriety in a household in which impropriety is crime. Lord Rossville pronounces judgment; his peroration is as follows:

> But before dismissing this subject—I trust forever—let me here state to you my sentiments with regard to young ladies walking before breakfast—a practice of which, I must confess, I have always disapproved. I am aware it is a practice that has the sanction of many highly respectable authorities, who have written on the subject of female ethics; but, I own, I cannot approve of young ladies of rank and family leaving their apartments, at the same hour with chamber-maids and dairy-maids, and walking out unattended at an hour when only the lower orders of the people are abroad. Walking before breakfast, then, I must consider as a most rude and masculine habit—as the Right Honourable Edmund Burke observes, 'an air of robustness and strength is highly prejudicial to beauty' (that is, as I apprehend, female beauty,) 'while an appearance of fragility is no less essential to it';—and certainly nothing, in my opinion, can be more unbecoming, more unfeminine, than to behold a young lady seat herself at the breakfast-table with the complexion of a dairy-maid and the appetite of a ploughman.

If Lord Rossville were to "state" his "sentiments" in more modern form, he might say that women do well to assume fragility because it emphasizes a supposed sex-characteristic in a way that is flattering to men. He chooses not to support his sentiments by evidence but by the authority of Burke's *Our Ideas of the Sublime and the Beautiful.* The Right Honourable Edmund does not support them by evidence so much as assert them.

> There is [a] notion current . . . that perfection is the constituent cause of beauty. This opinion has been made to extend much farther

than to sensible objects. But in these, so far is perfection, considered as such, from being the cause of beauty, that this quality, where it is highest in the female sex, almost always carries with it an idea of weakness and imperfection. Women are very sensible of this; for which reason they learn to lisp, to totter in their walk, to counterfeit weakness, and even sickness. In all this they are guided by nature. Beauty in distress is much the most affecting beauty.

In other words, women affect weakness because it makes a flattering appeal to the "strong" man. Enobarbus told us that of Cleopatra; Barrie calls it what every woman knows; you can read it in any pulp magazine you choose to pick off the newsstand. Burke has other opinions on feminine beauty for which he might have found evidence if he had felt he needed it.

A great beautiful thing is a manner of expression scarcely ever used; but that of a great ugly thing, is very common. There is a wide difference between admiration and love. The sublime, which is the cause of the former, always dwells on great objects, and terrible; the latter on small ones, and pleasing; we submit to what we admire, but what we love submits to us; in one case we are forced, in the other we are flattered into compliance. In short, the ideas of the sublime and the beautiful stand on foundations so different, that it is hard, I had almost said impossible, to think of reconciling them in the same subject, without considerably lessening the effect of the one or the other upon the passions. So that attending to their quantity, beautiful objects are comparatively small.

[A] property constantly observable in [beautiful] objects is smoothness. A quality so essential to beauty, that I do not now recollect any thing beautiful which is not smooth. In trees and flowers, smooth leaves are beautiful; smooth slopes of earth in gardens; smooth streams in the landscape; smooth coats of birds and beasts in animal beauties; in women, smooth skins; and in several sorts of ornamental furniture, smooth and polished surfaces. A very considerable part of the effect of beauty is owing to this quality; indeed the most considerable. For take any beautiful object, and give it a broken and rugged surface, and however well formed it may be in other respects, it pleases no longer . . . any ruggedness, any sudden projection, any sharp angle, is in the highest degree contrary to that idea [*i.e.,* the idea of beauty].

Among colors, such as are soft and cheerful, (except perhaps a strong red which is cheerful) are unfit to produce grand images. An immense mountain covered with shining green turf, is nothing in this respect, to one that is dark and gloomy; the cloudy sky is more grand than the blue; and night more sublime and solemn than day.

A woman, then, to be beautiful according to Burke's specifications, must be imperfect, small, smooth, and not too deeply colored; if she is otherwise, she is either sublime or ridiculous. If these standards are universals, they were and are true for all time; if they are fashions, they are only of the day.

She must be imperfect; not only "make defect perfection," but in order to have perfection must assume defect if she have it not. The affectations of defect tend toward the delicate air. Pope signals to it in 1732 with his famous line, "Faine by defect, and delicately weak." Steele and Addison satirized various fashionable assumptions of bodily imperfections among the men of their time, notably the monocle and the cane, which for more than two centuries have been under fire as affectations of aristocratic helplessness, the delicate air of aristocracy intended to suggest that you do not know how to do anything for yourself because you have always had hosts of servants, and that never having had to lift a finger you have never developed the muscles that would enable you to do so. The slender waist is the weakness of those who have never developed the muscles of the torso by pitching hay or bending over the washing or lifting children. The small foot is the weakness of those whose feet have never had to carry them about. Even the hard-boiled horsemen of the American plains sought to distinguish themselves from ploughmen and other pedestrians by boots which made their feet look small. Long trains and high heels emphasize helplessness and inability to work. By all standards of normality they represent deformities and imperfections. By the standards of fashion they are beauties. Why short-sightedness should be a fashionable affectation is not so easy to say. Perhaps it affords a supercilious gesture; quizzing-glass was once a name for the monocle. Perhaps it indicates wealth enough to buy lenses and gold frames. Perhaps we may throw it in with all other bodily weaknesses and take Swift's suggestion that the true mark of aristocracy is bodily weakness caused by diseases of luxury and vice, and that aristocracy would soon extinguish itself were it not for infusions of plebeian blood from ladies' unions with their footmen and coachmen. In France about 1785, between the Convention and the Directoire, those who sought to lead the fashions by aping the extinguished aristocracy found nearly their whole stock in trade the affectations of bodily imperfections and weaknesses. They peered through single-barrelled spy-glasses, leaned on canes, and could not pronounce the *r* because it "scorched" their tender throats, which had never been hardened by unbolted flour, husks or other rough food. A century and a quarter later the disappearing *r* was still held an affectation of superiority in some parts of the United States.

She must be small. Steele suggests this too, forty-seven years before Burke. "The foremost of the whole rank of Toasts," he says, "and the most undisputed in their present Empire, are Mrs. *Gatty* and Mrs. *Frontlet:* The first an Agreeable, the second an Aweful Beauty." Burke's whole thesis of the sublime and the beautiful is a sort of elephantine elaboration of this airy suggestion. Miss Ferrier quizzes Burke by sounding him with variations on the lips of the pusillanimous Lord Rossville, but others took him more seriously. The author of *Emmera* might be Lord Rossville himself in his fear lest his heroine who tills the soil should have the complexion of a dairymaid and the appetite of a plough-boy.

Have you not some idea, my friend, of a hale, close-fisted, country milk-maid in England, when I talk of my Emmera's hoeing and other laborious employments? Certainly you have—but much are you mistaken—never was woman of greater delicacy of person than this elegant girl—not a *fashionable* delicacy, an affectation of brittleness and nicety—but a clear glowing and animated complexion, fine as a painting can express, and her hands and arms of the most lovely form and hue I ever beheld—Indeed she has something of the woman in her—and being excessively cleanly, extends it to the care of her hands—which show not one trace of labour. Her person is all native grace and elegance! She moves through her little creation like the queen of grace and beauty, diffusing a fresh vegetation on all the beauties of nature—What rays of beauty shoot from each moving limb!—

Here are all the catchwords of the delicate air and all the invigorations of the return to nature churned together into an emulsion. Frances Brooke puts Steele's distinction into the mouth of Arabella Fermor in *Emily Montague,* 1767, with a turn of phrase that seems to refer it to Burke.

If beauty, as I will take the liberty to assert, is given us for the purpose of pleasing, she who pleases most, that is to say, she who excites the most passion, is to all intents and purposes the most beautiful woman; . . . but my first aversion is your fine women; don't you think a fine woman a detestable creature, Lucy? I do; they are vastly well to fill public places; but as to the heart—Heavens, my dear! yet there are men, I suppose, to be found, who have a taste for the great sublime in beauty.

If to be smooth is to be comparatively hairless, and colored like the day means blonde, the delicate air may seem less like a fashion than like a biological preference, an evolutionary factor. How else have we derived our bare skins from forefathers and foremothers who, science would have us believe, were covered with serviceable suits of fur? Probably the first lass with the delicate air was a female ape with scanty pale hair and blue eyes. She discovered that the anthropoid gentlemen about her preferred blondes, especially those who exhibited least hair below the scalp. We may guess that after this discovery the less preferred ladies of that time went to work with lye and deer-hide scrapers, and there began the history of depilatories and bleaches which have never since been wanting to those who were born without the delicate air.

"Either eyebrow like a silken thread"; the phrase certainly gave the delicate air to the lady in the Middle Age romance which so described her. Ladies in ancient Egypt plucked their eyebrows for the sake of the delicate air. They did so in Chaucer's time. One of the most indelicate of his fabliau heroines, Alisoun, the Carpenter's wife, had the requisite silhouette, her body was slender "as any weasel"; her eyebrows were arched, and "black as any sloe," and plucked "full small." Ladies today follow her example. It is in no wise indelicate for a lass to have a vigorous growth of hair on the head, but there is no record of a time when it was allowable anywhere else. We need no Edmund Burke to tell us that this smoothness is an essential of the delicate air. It is romantic, more or less contrary to fact, a process of idealization, a carrying over of pleasure of the sense into the aesthetic. And as we follow its history in works of art through the ages we find it a mark of differentiation between realistic and romantic. By this test, very little of the art of which we have examples has ever been realistic. In general "primitive" comic and erotic art is most nearly so. Unsophisticated or "primitive" art seems to concern itself single-mindedly with representation; later stages are concerned with "effects," aesthetic effects to the exclusion of those which are incompatible with them, disgust, for example, or sexual stimulus. This tends to modify or eliminate the appearance of the primary organs of sex in the representation of nude figures, and makes it common in painting or sculpture to show the body of a Hercules with the genitals of a twelve-year-old boy, and that of a Venus with none whatever, and as hairless as the marble in which she is wrought. This has been so long and so universally a convention of art that it seldom occurs to us to ask why it is so. We may accept it as the delicate air, but if we push the inquiry further, we may understand the delicate air the better for the analysis.

To represent the female body as hairless is realistic when and where women prevailingly practice depilation, but to represent it without the primary marks of sex is not realistic, and we can hardly more than guess why so romantic an idea ever became so universally acceptable, unless it is just because it was romantic. Why should we accept an image of the goddess of fertility which conspicuously lacks the organs of generation? Perhaps because the abstract idea of fertility is beautiful but the organs through which it works are not so to the eyes of false modesty; their appearance would destroy the delicate air. It might suggest other functions less easily idealized. So it might in the representation of the bodies of boys and men, which are customarily shown with much more realism than are those of women and girls. But men are not supposed to have the delicate air; if the artist wishes to give it to them he must restrain his sense of fact as best he can. Even if he does not restrain it, he may feel safe in assuming that he will not arouse feeling contrary to aesthetic pleasure in either men or women, for men will not be interested and women (he might assume) should not be. If he represents female bodies realistically, both men and women might have feelings inimical to the feeling of beauty; the men might feel erotic stimulus, and the women disgust or shame. Even the Church seems to grant this to a certain extent. The Christ child is allowed to flaunt his sex. Should we have had a different tradition if the Church had had a female saint or divinity of equal importance? Probably not. The Church has been very chary about exhibiting the physical charms of female saints and martyrs. Nude figures are rare in frescoes and paint-

ings in the churches, and when we do find an Adam and Eve
it is not always easily apparent which is which.

Primitive Christian art may have acquired its modesty from
the Book of Genesis and the symbolic art of the catacombs.
Renaissance art had all this behind it reinforced by the tradition of Greek art, which was the art of ancient Rome. Greek
art was not prudish, but it had its reticences, which it passed
on to the whole of Europe. We may believe that the Greeks
were accustomed to the sight of nude people of both sexes.
They were sometimes more and sometimes less realistic in
representing the bodies of men and boys, but few indeed are the
instances in which their representations of nude women show
even so much as the pubic hair. It seems probable that this
is not in spite of the fact that nudity was a comparatively familiar
spectacle to them, but because of it. In that age as in any other,
beautiful objects must be smooth, women must have the delicate air. In the nineteenth century women wore long sleeves
and thick black stockings, not to conceal nudity, but to conceal
hairy forearms and shins. When shoulders are bare too the
axillary hair must go also. When we find a Greek vase painting
of a woman who shows the pubic hair, archeologists are likely
to tell us that it represents a priestess of Astarte who retained it
as in some sort a badge or symbol of her order, and that it
was customary for other women to pluck or shave it. Women
are likely to do so in the twentieth century who appear on the
stage in degrees of nudity which seem to demand it.

Woodcuts and other engravings of the sixteenth century
and perhaps a little earlier, German and Flemish for the most
part, show naked women in the public baths with hairless
bodies. A few of these pictures are more or less salacious in
intent, but most of them seem merely naïve. They belong to
the period before or in the early beginnings of the Reformation, before nudity *per se* was generally considered a sin in the
Germanic parts of Europe, and confirm the idea that when and

where nudity in public is a possibility, depilation is a practice. We have contemporary evidence from Clément Marot, who derides barbers come down in life haunting the baths like lost souls to "raser priapus." Sauval tells us that the Comtesse d'Auge received a razor every year from her vassals the use of which is unspecified. He goes on to say,

It is certain that among the people and the bourgeoisie the fashion of depilation disappeared along with the habit of going to the baths. A passage in the "Facétieuse Paradoxes de Bruscambille," a passage which I do not wish to quote, shows clearly that by the sixteenth century most women had given it up . . . But in the *grande monde* [*sic*] it remained in esteem until the end of the eighteenth century. In 1786, when the Duc d'Orléans married Mme. de Montesson, the bridegroom received his shirt on the eve of the marriage with the customary ceremonial of the court. The Marquis de Valancay handed it to him, and the Prince, taking off the one he had on, showed those present an example of complete depilation, according to the rules of the most brilliant gallantry of the time. "Princes and courtiers," declares Soulavie (Mémoires du Regne de Louis XVI, II, 99) "did not consummate a marriage or receive the first favors of a mistress without undergoing this operation as a necessary preliminary."

There are, however, indications that the practice continued longer than he says among the people and the bourgeoisie. We find two fabliau-like bits said to be of the seventeenth century in the *Anciennes Poesies Françoises,* one indicating that female barbers were at the service of women who preferred them to men, the other telling of three maidservants, Ysabau, Perrette and Alizon, going to the baths where a female attendant with an old knife shaves the belly to the very skin; Ysabeau thought she should die under the process, but when it was over had much pride and delight in the result. Both cleanliness and smoothness, however, gave way to godliness; the baths were suppressed as iniquities, and all who could not afford private baths had to go dirty. Meanwhile people had begun to read the Bible in the vernacular and found faith in the word of God against nudity. The fashion for pubic depilation waned in European manners, but not in European art.

Its persistence in art sets us hunting for causes deeper than the mutations of fashion, traits of human nature of which the whims of fashion are freakish surface manifestations. Many an adolescent girl uses the scissors on the first appearance of the pubic hair, thinking it "isn't nice." She could not tell if she would anything more definite by way of reason. We may guess that there is a vague underlying dread of the change of which this is an outward and visible sign. We may think of it as an instinctive move to emphasize a sex difference; men are hairy and virile, women smooth and feminine. Boys emphasize it too; at the swimming hole puberty progresses with boasting and envy. But the boys who boast at the swimming hole will shave the first sign of a beard. This is mainly a matter of fashion; however we may refer it to cleanliness. Generalization here is especially unsafe, for of all human experience the basic one of sex takes on most individual variations; none the less one inclines to say that boys are apt to welcome and be proud of the signs of advancing puberty, girls to fear them or to resist or conceal them. "Keep that schoolgirl complexion," might be the eternal expression of the delicate air in so far as it is the wish of the woman to have the charm of an impubic child, a charm most highly esteemed in a sophisticated period when men seek in women the air of the twelve-year-old girl with the face of a child and a body with the contours of womanhood and the smoothness of childhood. The index of this in the lovely parts of her which custom permits to be visible would be the eyebrows. A girl may pluck her eyebrows down to silken threads because it is the fashion, or regardless of fashion because she feels it "isn't nice" to have hairy brows, quite unconscious of the fact that from the days of *The Thousand and One Nights* (and doubtless ages before that) to those of Freud, eyebrows have been read as the index of the body-hair. Depilation may be conscious or unconscious conformity to a racial pattern or ideal of beauty, *rassenschönheit,* a standard of beauty in each race which tends to emphasize racial characteristics of body. Depilation of face and body for both men and women is frequent among yellow and red peoples, who naturally have scanty beards and body-hair. It is said to be a Persian custom of long standing, and as such may have had its influence on· the Greeks, and so on European art. As a fashion, depilation springs recurrently from perennial roots.

The representation of the goddess of love with no outward appearance of organs of generation is a similar romantic idealization. Love would have a much more delicate air if it were all of the spirit and nothing of the body. Such a symbol is a universal expression of the feeling that many a girl has when her first glimpses of the actualities of bisexual generation revolt her while yet she is dreaming of her ideal lover. She wishes she could make love a communion of pure spirits and leave the baby business to the stork, but even so she finds that kisses are sweet, and she is glad she has a body, a "figure," that may be admired. This leads us to think of the development of the race as parallel to that of the individual. The stage of direct sex-worship is like the childish one of curiosity, exploration, exhibitionism; its representations are like the scrawls on the schoolhouse fence, the sex organs without the body. The flowering age of Greek art is like adolescence, flowering of spirit and body, idealization, outpouring of emotions; of this a beautiful body without organs of sex is an intelligible symbol. Myriads of readers have accepted such a symbol in the women of Dickens' novels, who are obviously equipped for lactation but not for generation. This appearance has even been formulated as a canon of female beauty and rationalized anatomically. In almost all times the pattern of feminine beauty has striven in some way to express fertility and youth; sometimes emphasis on one tends to minimize the others; now Venus prevails, and now Artemis, but most often

Boucher

Diane sortant du bain

ROBUST HEALTH AND FRAGILE DELICACY (See page 175)

we see fashion, as in the rococo heroine, trying to worship at both shrines at once. But on the whole the pattern of fertility prevails in determining standards of beauty; the "boyish figure" is not so frequently recurrent in the annals of fashion as is the figure with the wider pelvis. This tends to bring the body down to a wide angle between the thighs, to make the lines between the mons veneris and the thighs more nearly horizontal. Where this angle is wide, the vulva tends to stand farther back and under, and those who like to make generalizations of taste into "laws" of female beauty proclaim that the lower body is the more normal and therefore the more beautiful the less the vulva shows from the front. Whether we are conscious of such a canon or not, it might, if sound, have its weight in accounting for the artistic convention. It would to some extent justify the representation of the goddess of fertility depending mainly on wide hips to suggest her function. Perhaps we unthinkingly accept the convention with a subconscious feeling that "it wouldn't show." Perhaps we accept it because we unconsciously carry over visual images of baby girls in the first "filling out" stage, three years old and under, when, however fat the mons veneris may be, its cleft shows very little from the front. This makes more realistic than is sometimes admitted the familiar nude figure of the child in art whom we accept as a girl because it obviously is not a boy.

"Mothers," said Terence, "try to fit their daughters with falling shoulders and flat bosoms to make them appear sylph-like," and a German commentator gives us the clue, "Sloping shoulders and small breasts give, in Terence's opinion, the delicate air [*zarte anmut*]." The fashion was not new in the time of Terence. God himself has sloping shoulders, if we may accept the testimony of a mosaic in San Miniato in Florence, and we may learn from a thirteenth-century statue in the Bamberger Dom that he conferred them on Eve. Her daughters who inherited them from her were favorites with artists in most places and times.

Painters and sculptors show them in early and later periods in China, Japan, India and Egypt. They are not characteristically an item of the Greek ideal, but Greek art shows them, perhaps more in later than in earlier periods. As in Greece, so in Rome; Terence notes the fashion and Pompeian wall-paintings exhibit it. As soon as Christian art shows human figures that are anything more than symbols, their shoulders, those of men, women, saints, sinners and angels, have the slope of the delicate air. We see them in frescoes in San Clemente in Rome from the seventh to the eleventh centuries. The mosaic in San Miniato, Florence, is said to be of the thirteenth century. Artists of the Low Countries, Germany, France and Italy represented them with increasing persistence in the thirteenth, fourteenth and fifteenth centuries, many unnamed artists of wood and stone, and painters whose names are known, Jan van Eyck, Hans Memling, Joos van Cleve, Lucas Cranach, Konrad Miet, Jean Fouquet. Following them, Dürer, in the early sixteenth century, in his Eve and his Lucrece, shows shoulders that slope to the verge of deformity, at the same time declaring that he finds his ideal in the real. From Dürer's time nearly through that of Victoria we may trace the silhouette through works of art and works of fashion and hardly find a decade when sloping shoulders were out of fashion. They are set off with falling sleeves and falling ruffles, or accented by decolletage perilously below the shoulder-line. We may see them with short necks and rounded with fat on the full rounded figures of the seventeenth and of the mid-nineteenth centuries. We may see them with flat bosoms and narrow waists in the rococo figures of the eighteenth century, and with the hourglass figures and bustles of the seventies and eighties of the nineteenth century. The bicycle-golf-tennis girl of the "gay nineties" does not affect them, nor are they a part of the boyish silhouette of the second decade of the twentieth century. They would seem to belong, then, to the delicate air wherever we find it, whether in languorous voluptuousness and the full figure,

or delicate sprightliness and the slender figure, but not to
the athletics of masculinity. The student of fashions might more
easily accept this than might the student of anatomy. The slope
of the line from the base of the skull to the beginning of the
rise of the deltoid which rounds the angle of the shoulder and
arm, is that of the trapezius muscle which controls most of the
motions of the head and shoulders. It often shows conspicuously in the figures of men of great bodily strength whose
exercises develop it, oarsmen, pugilists, axemen and sawyers and
tumpline packers. But fashion does not study anatomy. In its
canon, broad square shoulders denote masculine strength; therefore the opposite, narrow sloping shoulders, must denote feminine
delicacy. These will merge gracefully into the lines of a long
"swanlike" neck without disagreeable angularity. It must be
for some such reasons that sloping shoulders have been so
much in favor through so many centuries, and that mothers
sought to "fit" their daughters with them, however they contrived that.

Life sets its patterns for art, and art in turn sets its patterns
for life. Art idealizes the patterns of life; life seeks its ideal
patterns in art. The senses are the gates of the spirit; the artist
must win them if he would go within. The artist cannot reach
the spirit if he forgets the body, nor yet if he does not go
beyond it. Of love also it is true that to satisfy the body leaves
the spirit athirst, but the spirit may not drink unless the body
drink too. The woman who would put love on a higher plane
than that of the body alone must make of the body a work of
art. By effort and through change she makes of herself what
she can to suggest effortless, changeless beauty. Of such beauty
the patterns that have been most steadily before our eyes for
a thousand years are those of the Greek statues. In these the
Greeks bequeathed us their ideals of form in the human figure,
and perhaps of texture or "tactile values." If they exhibited
color too, little of it has come down to us. We may infer it,

however, from other expressions. The Judgment of Paris is an episode of far-reaching importance in their mythology and in significance to us. The competing goddesses were three, "golden" Aphrodite, "ox-eyed" Hera, and Athena, who was the very brain of Zeus until she outgrew her quarters. If Aphrodite deserves her epithet, she was a blonde. If Hera was ox-eyed, she was a brune (unless she was peroxide), for who ever heard of a blue-eyed ox? If Athena was wise, she was a fool to compete, for who cares whether a learned lady is blonde or brune? One of the things every woman knows is that if she has charm it matters little what else she has, and if she hasn't, nothing else will help. Paris may have been a shepherd, but he was the first gentleman, for with a blonde, a brune and a bluestocking come to judgment, he preferred the blonde.

This important event took place when history was in the myth-making stage, when the past was preserved in the epic memory of men, which recorded only significant matters without superstitious fidelity to mere facts and dates. In Rome the first expression of preference for blonds is recorded as history. We are told that it occurred in the sixth century when Gregory the Great was a young deacon. He saw fair-haired slaves in the market place and was told that they were Angles. "Not Angles but Angels," was his comment, and a few years later he was in a position to send missionaries to make good his pun. Long afterward the Italian painters carried his idea of Nordic superiority into their imagery of Heaven, and angels have had golden hair ever since. So have the saints, and it is a rare thing to find a dark head except on an enemy of the children of light—Roman soldiers in paintings of the Crucifixion usually wear dark hair and beards. Fra Angelico put two or three dark-haired saints into the golden glory of his *Coronation of the Virgin* only because he wanted a few dark spots just there for his decorative pattern. Are these indeed historic times? If you answer yes, we may ask whether history has ever gone beyond myth-making, for it is easy to see here the same process that makes the sun-god the "golden" Apollo. With the eye of the body we can see the coloring of the sky, and that is about all we can see with the eye of the spirit of the glory of Heaven.

The blonde's color scheme seems to set her pattern of behavior; she looks like an angel, and we seem to expect her to behave like one. An instructor asked a girl-student whether Jane Bennet was blonde or brunette. "A blonde," said the student. "What makes you think so?" "She behaved like a blonde." The undergraduate is not the only one who takes the pattern of blonde behavior easily for granted. Maggie Tulliver finds it a convention of the novel, and is impatient with it. She is telling Philip Wakem why she did not finish reading *Corinne*.

As soon as I came to the blonde-haired young lady reading in the park, I shut it up, and determined to read no further. I foresaw that that light-complexioned girl would win away all the love from Corinne and make her miserable. I'm determined to read no more books where the blonde-haired women carry away all the happiness. I should begin to have a prejudice against them. If you could give me some story, now, where the dark woman triumphs, it would restore the balance. I want to avenge Rebecca, and Flora MacIvor, and Minna and all the rest of the dark unhappy ones.

Persons with more pretensions to science than Maggie have accepted such patterns as actual. One writing in the twentieth century of the ethnology of Germany says that we find "in the oldest sagas and histories the gold-blond Kriemhild and the dark Brunhild." A German studio made a film of them showing Kriemhild as the passive blonde whose coloring made mental or physical activity unnecessary, for her beauty brought all gifts to her; the heroes preferred her. Brunhild was shown as the dark woman who must use her brain and her body against Kriemhild's beauty. The fact is that the old saga does not indicate the complexions of these heroines, nor show any pattern of blonde behavior. The names have nothing to do with "brown" and "cream." Brunhild is the mailed warrior by her name, and Kriemhild the masked warrior, and neither in the *Volsunga Saga* or the *Nibelungenlied* is there much to choose between them as fighters with brain and muscle. The pattern does appear, however, in Germanic folklore of a somewhat later stage, when *kindermärchen* show traces of dwindled myth and legend. In the Grimm collection it appears in the story of *The White and the Black Bride,* which has a tint of Christianity. The Daughter rebuffs an angel in disguise, but the Stepdaughter is kind to him, whereupon he turns the Daughter "black as night" and the Stepdaughter "beautiful and spotless as the sun." Immediately Daughter and Mother begin to plot against her. They throw her into the river as if she were a sack of meal—it would not be the part of a blonde to resist—and if at last she comes into her kingdom it is not through effort of her own. Of Snow-White and Rose-Red we learn, "they were two as good, pious, industrious, and amiable children, as any that were in the world, only Snow-White was more quiet and gentle than Rose-Red." In these we have rudimentary forms of the "double heroine" device, the Rowena-Rebecca situation, which is frequent in the novel. In *The White and the Black Bride,* the pagan symbolism would be the explicit contrast between the delightful day and disagreeable night; the Christian symbolism is like that of the Church painters, the fair complexion is implicitly conferred as the outward and visible sign of the inward and spiritual grace. In *Snow-White and Rose-Red,* the white skin is the index of behavior; Rose-Red may have had fair hair for anything we know. In *The Man of Iron,* fair hair is a sure mark of gentility, gentlemen are blonds: "I saw long ago," says the Princess, "that he was no gardener's boy from his golden hair."

A few of the British and Scottish ballads show similar indications: *The Twa Sisters,* for example.

There were twa sisters dwelt in a bower,
There cam a knight to be their wooer.
He courted the eldest wi' glove and ring,
But he loved the youngest above a' thing.

Read so far and you perceive that because he was a knight, he was a gentleman, therefore the younger sister must have been a blonde. So, indeed it is. The elder sister leads the younger to the water and shoves her in like a log of wood; being a blonde she can neither resist nor remonstrate, only beg plaintively to be pulled out. The elder sister refuses.

Your cherry cheeks an' yallow hair
Gars me gae maiden forever mair.

And so we know that her cheeks are olive and her hair dark in harmony with her behavior. The brunette pattern of behavior appears clearly in *The Brown Girl.*

I am as brown as brown can be, my eyes as black as a sloe;
I am as brisk as a nightingale, and as wilde as any doe.
My love has sent me a love-letter, not far from yonder town,
That he could not fancy me, because I was so brown.
I sent him his letter back again, for his love I valu'd not,
Whether that he could fancy me or whether he could not.
He sent me his letter back again, that he lay dangerous sick,
That I might then go speedily to give him up his faith.
Now you shall hear what love she had then for this lovesick man;
She was a whole long summer's day in a mile a going on.
When she came to her love's bedside, where he lay dangerous sick,
She could not for laughing stand upright upon her feet.
She had a white wand all in her hand, and smooth'd it all on his
  breast;
In faith and troth come pardon me, I hope your soul's at rest.
I'll do as much for my true-love as other maidens may;
I'll dance and sing on my love's grave a whole twelvemonth and a day.

Here brown and brisk are the colors of mischief and witchcraft. Shakespeare softens the pattern in *Midsummer Night's Dream.*

In a situation where no differentiation of character is necessary between Hermia and Helena—indeed, more than a shadow of it would spoil his plot—he makes only this distinction between them, that Hermia is small, dark and shrewish, whereas Helena is tall and fair, a "painted maypole," and more inclined to weep than to fight. The Brown Girl in real life may have been as timorous as a brown mouse, and the tale merely her wishful reverie, but as it comes to us, "eyes black as sloe" clearly connote boldness. In the eighteenth century the black eye may be downcast; Black-Eyed Susan has the delicate air. Sophia Western is black-eyed, perhaps because Fielding wished to lend her outward charm a suggestion of the bravery which he stresses in her character. An anonymous novel of 1755, four years earlier than *Tom Jones,* tells us plainly that black eyes suggest boldness. Of one of the two heroines, Felicia, we are told, "her black, lively, and speaking Eyes, gave her a spirited Look but far from any appearance of Boldness." Her nose, too, was slightly aquiline, a feature which both Fielding and Smollett use to index initiative in character. This novel, *The Rival Mother,* quoted in earlier chapters, suggests the double heroine in the appearance of the two sisters, but makes nothing of it in the plot. Julia has brown hair and "dark-coloured" eyes. The black-eyed Felicia has hair the same color as her sister's, "and coloured without the help of art." Felicia is hardly more the brunette in behavior than in complexion; she differs from her sister only in a few degrees more of liveliness, and for even this we must take the author's word.

Charlotte Smith in *Celestina,* 1791, opens with the ballad situation, and suggests an origin in race characteristics for the literary blonde-brunette behavior-pattern. Celestina is a blonde.

Her countenance, with that blooming delicacy which the French distinguish by calling it *"le vrai teint Anglois,"* had all that animation which is more usually found among the natives of the south of Europe; yet this spirited expression often melted into softness so insinuating, that it was difficult to say whether pensive tenderness or sparkling vivacity was the most predominant; . . .

The hero, Willoughby, like the knight in the ballad, loves her above all, but economic pressure and his promise to his dying mother hold him pledged to the heiress Matilda, a stodgy brunette.

Her complexion was brown, and as her hair was not dark, the want of contrast produced a muddy and heavy effect, which nothing could have relieved but two dark eyes, whose powers were assisted by a greater quantity of rouge than unmarried ladies are, even by the French customs usually allowed. What expression they naturally had however was not pleasing, and what they borrowed from this addition added more to their fierceness than their lustre.

And so we know what to expect if we have been properly brought up on fairy tales; toads and vipers will issue from her lips when she speaks. But the outcome of the tale is of less moment than the suggestion that vivacity is characteristic of the Mediterranean peoples, who are racially dark of skin and hair, and impassivity of the blond northern races. Is this fact or prejudiced international generalization? "The French are a frivolous people, fond of dancing and light wines," says the old-fashioned English geography. We discredit an elaborated system of criticism of English literature based on a view from across the Channel of a London fog. But if the Romanic peoples look upon the Nordics as phlegmatic, they must consider themselves as at least somewhat mercurial, and if English, Germans or Scandinavians think of French or Italians as shamelessly emotional, they must pride themselves on some degree of stoicism. We may be justified, then, in accepting a judgment in which we agree with our opponents, and in believing that the tellers of tales in prose and verse have written something more than fiction.

It remained for Scott to reconstruct the device of the double heroine from the fragmentary outlines of it in the ballads. His first novel, *Waverley,* 1814, is a true example, for it shows two female figures keeping so even a pace in the forefront of the action that the reader hardly knows which Scott intends should most engage his sympathy. The blonde is Rose Bradwardine, aged seventeen.

She was indeed a very pretty girl of the Scotch cast of beauty, that is, with a profusion of hair of paley gold, and a skin like the snow of her own mountains in whiteness. Yet she had not a pallid or pensive cast of countenance; her features as well as her temper had a lively expression; her complexion, though not florid, was so pure as to seem transparent, and the slightest emotion sent her whole blood at once to her face and neck. Her form, though under the common size, was remarkably elegant, and her motions light, easy, and unembarrassed. She came from another part of the garden to receive Captain Waverley, with a manner that hovered between bashfulness and courtesy.

The other figure, Flora Mac-Ivor, is well contrasted with Rose. Scott begins his description of her with her dress,

which was in texture elegant, and even rich, and arranged in a manner which partook partly of the Parisian fashion, and partly of the more simple dress of the Highlands, blended together with great taste. Her hair was not disfigured by the art of the friseur, but fell in jetty ringlets on her neck, confined only by a circlet, richly set with diamonds.

Flora Mac-Ivor bore a most striking resemblance to her brother Fergus; . . . They had the same antique and regular correctness of profile; the same dark eyes, eye-lashes, and eye-brows; the same clearness of complexion, excepting that Fergus's was embrowned by exercise, and Flora's possessed the utmost feminine delicacy. But the haughty and somewhat stern regularity of Fergus's features, was beautifully softened in those of Flora. Their voices were also similar in tone, though differing in the key. That of Fergus . . .

> *was heard around,*
> *Loud as a trumpet with a silver sound.*

That of Flora, on the contrary, was soft and sweet,—"an excellent thing in woman"; . . .

Scott follows this comparison and contrast between Flora and her brother farther than we need follow him. His purpose is clear, to show the brunette as a feminized version of the man. The blonde is every inch the woman in her own right. The anthropologist rationalizes this for us:

The feminine skin is of finer grain and lighter tint than the masculine . . . The white skin of the blonde deserves higher esteem than the darker shades because it is farthest from the male sex-character, and gives a secondary female sex-characteristic its strongest expression.

Scott said it long before in much more agreeable terms. He indicates, too, that boldness and initiative are in the same category as the dark skin. Fielding and Smollett would throw in the aquiline nose for good measure. Such is the formula for the active heroine. Its observance is good economy of effort for the novelist. After a few generations he evolves a Freshman reader who can tell from the heroine's behavior whether she is blonde or brunette.

The literary tradition is that the fair-haired maiden is an angel, and if anything less than angelic is to be done, the nut-brown maiden must do it. Scott does not follow the tradition so closely in *Waverley* as he does in *Ivanhoe*. Rose Bradwardine, the blonde, does not faint nor weep. Flora, the dark-haired beauty, faints, with good cause enough, when she thinks herself responsible for her brother's execution. For herself, according to the heroic tradition, she feels no qualms. She does not faint when a bullet grazes her forehead; instead she makes an epigram. Except for this bit of soldierly fortitude, she is nearly as mild as Rose. The gentleman in the case, Captain Waverley, does not definitely prefer the blonde. He offers himself first to Flora, but in the end marries Rose. We are told that Scott's first love was a blonde, but he married a brunette. Would this account for the contrary experience of one and another of his heroes?

In *Ivanhoe*, 1820, the situation as between blonde and brunette runs truer to form. Rowena, the Saxon heroine, is the true "snow-white" of the fairy tale. Scott describes her as she enters her guardian's hall, the target of every eye at the board.

Formed in the best proportions of her sex, Rowena was tall in stature, yet not so much so as to attract observation on account of superior height. Her complexion was exquisitely fair, but the noble cast of her head and features prevented the insipidity which sometimes attaches to fair beauties. Her clear blue eye, which sate enshrined beneath a graceful eyebrow of brown sufficiently marked to give expression to the forehead, seemed capable to kindle as well as melt, to command as well as to beseech. If mildness were the more natural expression of such a combination of features, it was plain, that, in the present instance, the exercise of habitual superiority, and the reception of general homage had given to the Saxon lady a loftier character, which mingled with, and qualified that bestowed by nature. Her profuse hair, of a colour betwixt brown and flaxen, was arranged in a fanciful and graceful manner in numerous ringlets, to form which art had probably aided nature. These locks were braided with gems, and, being worn at full length, intimated the noble and free-born condition of the maiden. A golden chain, to which was attached a small reliquary of the same metal, hung round her neck. She wore bracelets on her arms, which were bare. Her dress was an undergown and kirtle of pale sea-green silk, over which hung a long loose robe, which reached to the ground, having very wide sleeves, which came down, however, very little below the elbow. This robe was crimson, and manufactured out of the very finest wool. A veil of silk, interwoven with gold, was attached to the upper part of it, which could be at the wearer's pleasure, either drawn over the face and bosom after the Spanish fashion, or disposed as a sort of drapery round the shoulders.

The companion piece to this is the brilliant picture of the Jewess, Rebecca:

Her form was exquisitely symmetrical, and was shown to advantage by a sort of Eastern dress, which she wore according to the fashion of the females of her nation. Her turban of yellow silk suited well with the darkness of her complexion. The brilliancy of her eyes, the superb arch of her eyebrows, her well-formed aquiline nose, her teeth as white as pearl, and the profusion of her sable tresses, which, each arranged in its own little spiral of twisted curls, fell down upon as much of a lovely neck and bosom as a simarre of the richest Persian silk, exhibiting flowers in their natural colours embossed upon a purple ground, permitted to be visible—all these constituted a combination of loveliness, which yielded not to the most beautiful of the maidens who surrounded her. It is true, that of the golden and pearl-studded clasps, which closed her vest from the throat to the waist, the three uppermost were left unfastened on account of the heat, which something enlarged the prospect to which we allude. A diamond necklace, with pendants of inestimable value, were by this means also made more conspicuous. The feather of an ostrich, fastened in her turban by an agriffe set with brilliants, was another distinction of the beautiful Jewess, scoffed and sneered at by the proud dames who sat above her, but secretly envied by those who affected to deride them.

Here is Scott's version of the delicate air, two copies, one bound in white and gold, the other in olive and black, brilliant impressions both. Rowena suggests the rococo, delicacy and health, tall (but not too tall) and (if it were "permitted to be visible") long-legged. Scott makes quite plain the popular ascription of mildness to blondes, but he accepts it with the cautious condition—"if mildness were the more natural expression" of the blonde complexion, aristocracy and the habit of command made Rowena enough of an exception to save her from insipidity. One guesses that a long run of blonde sweetness was beginning to cloy. Rebecca's delicacy shows in such phrases as "exquisitely symmetrical," and "lovely neck and bosom," and the fact that she is cast for the more active part shows in her brilliant black eyes, superbly arched eyebrows, and aquiline nose.

Such are Flora Mac-Ivor and Rebecca, two of the "dark unhappy ones" whom Maggie Tulliver would wish to avenge. Is Maggie spokesman for her author? George Eliot was dark of complexion and commanding of mien. Her profile was that of Savonarola, and should, if there be any virtue in physiognomy, have brought her to leadership and martyrdom. She was "advanced" and "emancipated" in thought, and challenged conventional morality in one act of her private life, but conformed to it sedulously in her novels. Her gallery of heroines presents two types, the less intelligent who conform, and the more intelligent who inwardly rebel. The two are indifferently blonde and brunette. Hetty Sorrel, in spite of dark hair and eyes, suffers because she follows the path of least resistance. Romola, golden-haired and scholarly, suffers because she does not. Dinah Morris, a pale saint, wins her husband because of Hetty's downfall, not because she is a blonde, nor yet because she behaves like one. Mirah, the Jewess, wins Daniel Deronda because he happens to be on hand when she is in despair, not because of any brunette pattern of action; her eyes are black as sloe, but she is neither brisk nor bold. If George Eliot resented the gentlemanly preference for blondes, she was very ladylike about it.

In the popular novel of the nineteenth century, the double heroine device runs true to the type of the popular poetry, the ballad. In *The Broken Wedding Ring* of Bertha M. Clay, the elder sister, Leah, is a brune,

just sixteen, and beautiful as the opening bud of a June rose; grace, dignity and passion were marked in every line of her face. The brow was somewhat low and broad, full of ideality and thought, the eyes were dark, the eyebrows straight, with a proud but sensitive mouth— a face difficult to read. The lightness and brightness of girlhood were not on it; it was slightly mystical and dreamy, and the lustrous eyes had a shadow in them. The noble head, the graceful figure and its movements, the mass of dark waving hair . . .

The younger, Hettie,

though only one year younger, seemed still a child. She was tall, slight, and unformed . . . Hettie had hair of pale bright gold, that was like an aureole round her head; she had eyes blue as heaven . . . The chief expression of Leah's face was of pride; it did not lack beauty, but it certainly lacked tenderness; while the chief loveliness of Hettie's face lay in its softness.

This gives us a nearly perfect expression of the concept. The blonde is the angel child, the brunette has the pride which is the first of the deadly sins, for it caused the angels' fall and the rebellion against Heaven. The hero, Martin Ray,

> *Courted the eldest wi' glove and ring,*
> *But he loved the youngest above a' thing.*

In *Her Only Sin,* by the same author, Katherine Brandon "was just seventeen, and a more perfectly lovely ideal of an English girl could not have been found." The description of her plays ding-dong on the words "perfect," "lovely," and "perfectly lovely." Her eyes were like pansies steeped in dew. "She was a blonde beauty, but she had more color, greater vigor"; more and greater, for a guess, than a blonde might be expected to have. Her stepsister, Veronica, "looked like a Roman empress . . . dark, tender, passionate eyes . . . hair black as night." In Laura Jean Libbey's *Pretty Rose Hall,* "Lillian was sweet and good with the fair beauty of an angel, but Rose—ah, how shall I find words to describe the dark, passionate, glowing beauty of Rose Hall—the young girl whose life held so tragic a story?" Yet find them she does, as follows:

A dark, piquant, dimpled face; cheeks and lips as crimson as the glowing heart of the flowers whose name she bore; great, dark, velvety, Oriental eyes shaded by the longest and silkiest of lashes, a low, broad brow crowned with rings of curling love-locks, darker than a raven's plume, and a saucy smiling mouth that seemed made only for love's sweet kisses and rippling laughter.

Of these three novels the plots are similar, a melodramatic concatenation of lost wills and secret marriages, with none of the simple, tragic inexorability of the ballad, and through it all behavior of blonde and brune run true to type.

Thus spake the nineteenth century; the twentieth century uses other terms. Science makes a study of the facts, and decides that pigmentation is no index to behavior-patterns, that a blonde woman is quite as apt to show initiative and energy in action as a brunette. This leaves us free to infer that if she doesn't show it so often as the brune, it is merely because she doesn't have to. She has the delicate air by gift of nature, and if because of it we endow her not only with all worldly goods but all the graces of heaven, we do so at our own risk, not by the mandate of God. The scientist spoke only to the few; the satirist spoke to us all. For one who heard what science said there were a million who heard Anita Loos proclaim, *Gentlemen Prefer Blondes*.

Goldsmith treated the delicate air with mild-mannered ridicule. He displays the Vicar's robust daughters with romantic names from popular novels, aspiring to be heroines, brewing cosmetics over the kitchen fire, trying to go to church in a coach and arriving on a plough-horse, and generally aping the manners of supposed aristocratic ladies who turn out to be "anything but." Sheridan in *The Rivals* makes of it a type character with a type name, Lydia Languish, but his wit is more rakish than Goldsmith's. Lydia is hastily making up her delicate air to receive visitors:

LYDIA. Here, my dear Lucy, hide these books. Quick, quick.—Fling *Peregrine Pickle* under the toilet—throw *Roderick Random* into the closet—put *The Innocent Adultery* into *The Whole Duty of Man*—thrust *Lord Ainsworth* under the sofa—cram *Ovid* behind the bolster—there—put *The Man of Feeling* into your pocket—so, so—now lay *Mrs. Chapone* in sight, and leave *Fordyce's Sermons* open on the table.

If the delicate air had been as truly delicate as it set up to be, we should have heard no more of it after the rough treatment Mary Wollstonecraft gave it in her *Vindication of the Rights of Woman*, 1791 or 92. Her sturdy mind makes her completely contemptuous of it as a "weakness of mind and body which men perpetuate." She calls "the amiable Dr. Gregory" to account for "his celebrated Legacy to his Daughters."

. . . he actually recommends dissimulation, and advises an innocent girl to give the lie to her feelings, and not dance with spirit, when gaiety of heart would make her feet eloquent, without making her gestures immodest. In the name of truth and common sense, why should not one woman acknowledge that she can take more exercise than another? or, in other words, that she has a sound constitution; and why to damp innocent vivacity, is she darkly to be told, that men will draw conclusions which she little thinks of? Let the libertine draw what inference he pleases; but, I hope, that no sensible mother will restrain the natural frankness of youth, by instilling such indecent cautions.

To what base levels do such counsels sink us!

Bodily strength from being the distinction of heroes is now sunk into such unmerited contempt, that men as well as women, seem to think it unnecessary: the latter as it takes from their feminine graces, and from that lovely weakness, the source of their undue power; and the former, because it appears inimical with the character of a gentleman.

She quotes Dr. Fordyce: "I will use," she says, "the preacher's own words."

Let it be observed, that in your sex many exercises are never graceful; that in them a tone and figure, as well as an air and deportment, of the masculine kind, are always forbidding; and that men of sensibility desire in every woman soft features, and a flowing voice, a form not robust, and demeanor delicate and gentle.

Dr. Fordyce develops this idea into a character which Mary Wollstonecraft calls "the portrait of a house-slave," and pours her scorn on it.

Such a woman ought to be an angel—or she is an ass—for I discern not a trace of the human character, neither reason nor passion in this domestic drudge, whose being is absorbed in that of a tyrant's.

But you can't wound the delicate air with an arrow, nor crush it with a steam-roller. Mrs. Radcliffe carried on with it as if nothing had happened. Here is Adeline from *The Romance of the Forest*, 1791:

Her features [they were bathed in tears] had gained from distress an expression of captivating sweetness: she had

> *"an eye,*
> *As when the blue sky trembles through a cloud*
> *Of purest white."*

A habit of gray camlet, with short slashed sleeves, shewed, but did not adorn her figure; it was thrown open at the bosom, upon which part of her hair had fallen in disorder, while the light veil hastily thrown on, had, in her confusion, been suffered to fall back.

Ellena Rosalba, from *The Italian,* 1797, is her twin sister.

The sweetness and fine expression of her voice attracted his attention to her figure, which had a distinguished air of delicacy and grace; . . . The breeze from the water caught the veil . . . and . . . wafting it partially aside, disclosed to him a countenance more touchingly beautiful than he had dared to image. Her features were of the Grecian outline, and, though they expressed the tranquillity of an elegant mind, her dark blue eyes sparkled with intelligence. She was assisting her companion so anxiously, that she did not immediately observe the admiration she had inspired; but the moment her eyes met those of Vivaldi, she became conscious of their effect, and hastily drew her veil.

All Mrs. Radcliffe's heroines are the same model, varying only slightly in pose and tint. One would think there could be no further refinement, but Sydney Owenson, Lady Morgan, attempted the impossible, and carried the delicate air to the *nth* degree of rarefication in *The Wild Irish Girl,* 1806.

[Glorvina had] a form so almost impalpably delicate, that as it floated on the gaze, it seemed like the incarnation of some pure etherial spirit, which a sigh too roughly breathed would dissolve into its kindred air; yet to this sylphid elegance of spheral beauty was united all that symmetrical *contour* which constitutes the luxury of human loveliness.

For atmospheric air the sky is the limit, but for the delicate air we may go beyond the atmosphere, beyond the stratosphere, beyond the ether—"spheral" is the word! Will anyone say ultra-spheral?

Not Jane Austen. She brings the delicate air back from its spheral excursion and sets its feet (of human loveliness) on the ground. When Elizabeth Bennet walks to Netherfield on a rainy day it is with weary ankles and muddy stockings and petticoat. Bodily weakness is more apt to give rise to suffering than to chivalry. In *Mansfield Park*, Fanny Price is really frail in health. While she is walking round the park at Rushford with Edmund and Miss Crawford, her strength gives out. Does Edmund carry her home in his arms and declare his love? Not at all. He deposits her on a bench and proposes to walk on with Miss Crawford.

Fanny said she was rested, and would have moved too, but this was not suffered. Edmund urged her remaining where she was with an earnestness which she could not resist, and she was left on the bench to think with pleasure of her cousin's care, but with great regret that she was not stronger. She watched them till they had turned the corner, and listened till all sound of them had ceased.

And that, girls, says Jane Austen to her "fair" readers, is as far as the delicate air gets you in real life.

Scott was a romantic, but he was a great artist, which means that he balanced his imagination with sense of fact. He loves the delicate air, but he does not rarefy it so far that it will not sustain life. His notion of aristocracy has more in it of vigor than of languor. The Countess of Leicester would be a match for Elizabeth herself if her husband's treachery had not stricken her heart and dissolved her spirit. There is, to be sure, Mary

Avenel, pallid and thin as the ghost of the White Lady that flits with her through the pages of *The Monastery,* but for one such in Scott's gallery there are a dozen who are full-bodied, clothed with human flesh, and briskly human in action and feeling.

Dickens is quite otherwise. He sentimentalizes the sentimental heroines of Mrs. Radcliffe, and nearly equals Lady Morgan in his etherealization of the delicate air. *Dombey and Son* appeared when Victoria had been on the throne ten years, but if Florence Dombey is Victorian, so also are all of Mrs. Radcliffe's heroines.

. . . Florence grew to be seventeen. Timid and retiring as her solitary life had made her, it had not embittered her sweet temper, or her earnest nature. A child in innocent simplicity; a woman in her modest self-reliance, and her deep intensity of feeling; both child and woman seemed at once expressed in her fair face and fragile delicacy of shape, and gracefully to mingle there;—as if the spring should be unwilling to depart when summer came, and sought to blend the earlier beauties of the flowers with their bloom. But in her thrilling voice, in her calm eyes, sometimes in a strange ethereal light that seemed to rest upon her head, and always in a certain pensive air upon her beauty, there was an expression, such as had been seen in the dead boy; . . .

Here the child-woman of innocent simplicity is of the sentimentality of the painter Greuze of the century before. The strange ethereal light that "seemed" to rest on her head is a wild bid for religious sentimentality. Her resemblance to the corpse of her little dead brother is a shameless resuscitation of the sentimentality of his most notoriously sentimental chapter earlier in the same book, the death of little Paul, a bid for the parlor funeral sentimentality of the same period in America; American anthologies of the mid-century are full of it. When Dickens says that Florence Dombey has self-reliance, he belies her. When the stern decree of alienation of affection is handed down to her from Dombey through Carker and Edith, she sobs and begs, but she does not challenge or rebel. When the tyrant issues a milder order to Edith, she defies him to his face; Florence trembles, weeps and obeys. She faints, she feels a sense of powerlessness, she does not dare go to Edith's room. Edith dares anything and everything, but Edith is a bad girl; Florence is a heroine. Edith goes when she is commanded to stay, leaving a magnificent devastation behind her. It takes a blow in the face to indicate to Florence that she isn't wanted, then she makes an exit like a kicked dog. She has to sustain the delicate air, whereas Edith, as any Freshman could tell from her behavior, must have been a brunette.

They are the White and the Black Bride. What does Dickens do but transplant plots and characters from fairy-tales and romance to the London of his childhood (before Victoria) and put them through their stock repertory in hoop skirts and chimney-pot hats? *Nicholas Nickleby* is the old romance in terms of the London of 1825. Nicholas is the knight-errant, without a flaw to make him either human or tragic, wandering about the country rescuing helpless women and children who are oppressed by ogres and giants, the vague powers of unspecified evil. He delivers Smike, and rescues the troop of children that the ogre has in confinement, like Jack the Giant Killer, or Hop-o'-my-Thumb. He rescues Kate from the giant Ralph Nickleby and Madeline from the loathsome dragon Gride. Kate trustingly goes to the wicked giant, Ralph, as little Red Ridinghood to the wolf, and confidingly goes from one den of iniquity to another at his bidding. Madeline Bray faints at the crisis of her misfortunes, and is handled like a sack of meal for a page and a half to the end of the chapter. She seems as useful to the purposes of the plot in this state as in any other, for her only function is to be rescued. In *David Copperfield,* Dora Spenlow and Agnes Wickfield are only slight variations of the same model. Dora is intended to be charmingly vivacious and touchingly childlike. She can only achieve this combination by shaking her ringlets, teasing her little dog, talking baby talk, and pleading that she is such a child that she can't be expected to know any better. On her death-bed she shows her one gleam of rationality; she declares that it is "better so" because her attributes which may be charming in youth would not be so graceful or agreeable as she grew older. Not every woman is intelligent enough to die because she is too stupid to live. Agnes Wickfield is no more real than Dora; she has, indeed, less of vivacity in that she has less of motion. Her delicate air is that of the pale saint in the faded fresco, drawn in flat colors and fixed attitudes of adoration and being adored. She is supposed to exert a tremendous influence for good over David's whole life, but it is not through any act of hers, for she does nothing from one end of the book to the other but to exist in her pale colors and fixed attitudes. Then suddenly between chapters at the end there are children; there are none in chapter 52, and in chapter 53 there are several. It must be that they unfolded like paper dolls.

Thus the delicate air wafts into Victorian times. Just before the accession of the Good Queen, about 1834, one of Praed's ballroom belles is vexed by a scoff at sentiment.

> He sneers,—how my Alice would scold him!—
>   At the bliss of a sigh or a tear;
> He laughed—only think!—when I told him
>   How we cried o'er Trevelyan last year;
> I vow I was quite in a passion;
>   I broke all the sticks of my fan;
> But sentiment's quite out of fashion,
>   It seems, in a talented man.

Shall we say, then, that Dickens was not "talented"? Not *Trevelyan,* not the works of Dickens, were the last of the sentimental novel; a hundred years later did not see the end. And the lass with the delicate air carried on sturdily. See her in Tennyson's early poems; the table of contents lists her varied names, the poems display her poses and colors, her sentimental attributes: Claribel, a lyric grave, sentimental death; Lilian, airy-fairy, innocent-arch, cunning-simple; Isabel, eyes not downdropt nor over bright, pure vestal, stately flower of female fortitude; Mariana, he cometh not, my life is dreary, I would that I were dead; Madeline, ever-varying, delicious spites and darling angers; Adeline, mystery of mysteries, faintly smiling; Margaret, sweet, rare, pale like moonlight on a falling shower; Rosaline, frolic falcon, bright-eyed, wild-eyed, careless of both wind and weather; Eleanore, swanlike stateliness, luxuriant symmetry, nourished on the sweet influences of nature. We know that this is the poetry of fashion, for we can trace the vogue of these figures during the very years of Tennyson's early volumes, 1827 to 1847, through the pages of Keepsakes, Annuals, and notably Heath's *Book of Beauty,* edited through most of this time by the Countess of Blessington. Here in suave steel engravings appear all the graces of the delicate air which custom permits to be visible. Not an item from the novelists' descriptions is missing, yet there are only four models varied by attitude, costume and accessories, blonde and brunette, plain and ringlets. For two decades the delicate air carried publisher and editor on a trade wind of prosperity. In the next decade the weather shifted.

CHAPTER VII

AUNT TABITHA

My aunt! my dear unmarried aunt!
  Long years have o'er her flown;
Yet still she strains the aching clasp
  That binds her virgin zone;
I know it hurts her,—though she looks
  As cheerful as she can;
Her waist is ampler than her life,
  For life is but a span.

My aunt! my poor deluded aunt!
  Her hair is almost gray;
Why will she train that winter curl
  In such a spring-like way?

. . . . . .

. . . one sad ungathered rose
  On my ancestral tree.

OLIVER WENDELL HOLMES.

PAMELA married and lived happily ever after; at least, the three and three-quarters volumes of her married life have seemed forever to many an impatient reader. In so far as such an ending is typical of the English novel, there would seem to be little space in a parade of its heroines for a regiment of old maids. But there is a regiment of them, and they demand representation. The novel was still young as a type when Charlotte Palmer made a heroine of Adeline, who in spite of solicitations numerous and protracted, steadfastly remained a spinster. Before that a major novelist depicted an old maid who stands as a main support of his reputation as a humorist. After that for a hundred years the old maid as a secondary figure in the novel furnished many chapters of comedy and episodes of tragedy for innumerable novels. Then with the last decade of the nineteenth century she takes a new title and importance, and steps to the front as a major type of heroine. Her vicissitudes are not mere matters of chance, but are of a piece with the social changes of the times in which we find them.

Richardson has much to say about virginity, but he does not stand as an advocate of the lifelong practice of it as a profession. The reward for hoarding virginity, "virtue," is to part with it for the price of honor. Hoard it thriftily for the accumulated interest it brings, but do not hold it miserly till it is past its market. One figure he shows who held it too long, Mistress Judy Swynford, whom Pamela describes as she says, "because she is a character that is in a manner new to me."

She is a maiden lady, as you know madam; and though she will not part with the green leaf from her hand, one sees by the gray goose on her brows and her head, that she cannot be less than fifty-five—But so much pains does she take, by powder, to have never a dark hair in her head, because she has one half of them white, that I am sorry to see, what is a subject for reverence, should be deemed by the good lady matter of concealment.

She is often in conversation, indeed, seemingly reproaching herself, that she is an *old maid,* and an *old woman;* but it is very discernible that she expects a compliment, that she is *not so,* every time she is so free with herself: And if nobody makes her one, she will say something of that sort in her own behalf.

She takes particular care, that of all the public transactions which happen to be talked of, her memory will never carry her back above thirty years; and then it is, About thirty years ago when I was a girl, or, when I was in hanging sleeves; and so she makes herself, for twenty years of her life, a very useless and insignificant person. . . . But, poor lady! she is so *young,* in spite of her wrinkles, that I am really concerned for her affectation; because it exposes her to the remarks and ridicule of the gentlemen, and gives one pain for her.

This type can never be a heroine because she cannot have any sympathy from the reader. A heroine must have "charm" and be followed by hosts of adorers. In most novels the woman who has never had a proposal of marriage is unsought because she is undesirable, usually repellent, for qualities which we feel are her own fault. She is usually considered fair game for the satirist. This is the old maid who makes the term one of opprobrium. But it is possible to make a heroine of the virgin who remains so from choice in spite of frequent and urgent solicitation, from fidelity to an ideal, usually an early love affair, a dead lover. Of this the monumental prototype is *Female Stability,* quoted extensively above in Chapters III and IV, in which Adeline stands unwaveringly true to the memory of the lost Augustus, an immutable fountain of tears at the altar of love, without variableness or shadow of turning through five long volumes while oceans of lovers cast themselves in hopeless waves at her feet. One may be quite sure that Charlotte Palmer when she finished writing this book was confident that the *varium et mutabile semper* doctrine of female behavior would never hold up its head again. This was in 1780.

The major of the eighteenth century battalion of old maids is Smollett's Tabitha Bramble, whose portrait runs to full length through the pages of *Humphry Clinker,* 1771, the most memorable figure in the book, and in the opinion of some critics and readers the most striking portrait in Smollett's whole gallery. Her nephew describes her.

. . . Mrs. Tabitha Bramble is a maiden of forty-five. In her person she is tall, raw-boned, awkward, flat-chested, and stooping; her complexion is sallow and freckled; her eyes are not grey, but greenish, like those of a cat, and generally inflamed; her hair is of a sandy, or rather dusty hue; her forehead low; her nose long, sharp, and, towards the extremity, always red in cold weather; her lips skinny, her mouth extensive, her teeth straggling and loose, of various colors and conformation; and her long neck shrivelled into a thousand wrinkles. In her temper she is proud, stiff, vain, imperious, prying, malicious, greedy, and uncharitable. In all likelihood her natural austerity has been soured by disappointment in love; for her long celibacy is by no means owing to her dislike of matrimony; on the contrary, she has left no stone unturned to avoid the reproachful epithet of old maid.

He goes on to specify some of her attempts to get a husband; others she carries on before our eyes in the course of the tale. She cherishes an ill-tempered dog as ugly as herself, "malicious, greedy, and uncharitable." Her credulity is such that she accepts the suit of a young gentleman to her niece as to herself.

This is the type figure of the old maid as it appears in the English novel, complete in all of its details. Smollett did not invent it or its main traits; he is responsible merely for the vigorous dramatization. He did not invent the name; Mistress Bramble is named Tabitha because she is an old maid. Tabby was the type name for the old maid before it was the name of the striped cat, and it was the name of the striped cat before it was the name of the female cat. But perhaps it is not safe to infer that the term old maid was applied to the cat as a term of contempt before the old maid was contemptuously called a cat. Smollett found the name no less ready to his purpose than the figure itself. He put the two together and gave the novel a type figure with a type name, the sort of thing which has been the mainstay of low comedy from its beginning. Ben Jonson gave the device especial recognition and prestige under the name "comedy of humors," comedy made of the reactions on one another of a set of grotesque figures of only one trait of character apiece, caricatures like cardboard figures painted only on one side, useful in only one groove of the toy theatre. These figures are as old as European comedy. They are the basis of the Greek comedy on which the Roman comedy grew, and their introduction into dramatic parts of the church services marks the beginning of the English comedy. But the comedy of humors figure of the old maid, thoroughly English as she seems when Smollett displays her in his novel, comes in on a side wind from France.

In 1692, ninety-nine years before *Humphry Clinker,* Molière dramatized the caricature of the old maid as Bélise, the maiden aunt of Armande and Henriette, in *Les Femmes Savantes*. Bélise is a very different figure from Tabitha Bramble, but the contrast is in traits arising from environment; they are basically of the same stock. Bélise's affectations are those of the courtly delicacy of the time. Her misunderstanding of the lover who applies to her for the hand of her niece is as persistent as Aunt Tabitha's, but very different in terms.

You mustn't open your soul to me too freely. If I consent to admit you to the ranks of my lovers, you will have to confine yourself to your eyes as your only means of expression, and never reveal to me by any other language desires which to me are an outrage. Love me, sigh, burn for my charms, but never let me know it. I can shut my eyes to secret flames so long as you confine yourself to mute expression, but if your lips take any part, I must banish you from my sight.

Clitandre explains as well as he can that it is Henriette for whom he burns, but Bélise imperturbably applauds the delicacy of the device which will allow her to listen to his praises of Henriette and accept them as for herself.

Smollett imported his marionette from France, stripped it, painted it in English colors and dressed it in English manners. Before Bélise we have in English drama instances of virgins of marriageable age and beyond to furnish forth in sum total of their features an Aunt Tabitha, but nobody added them up. The earliest example that comes readily to hand of a female character of any importance who remains unmarried at the end of the play is Julia, sister of the Marquis of Saluzzo, in *The Pleasant Comodie of Patient Grissel*, 1603, ascribed to Dekker, Chettle and Haughton. The date ascribed to it is the year in which Queen Elizabeth died, an old maid of seventy. The play represents marriage as a field of battle, and Julia's function in it is to sing the praises of the peace of celibacy. Dekker's Roaring Girle, Moll Cutpurse, declares against marriage in a dozen or more of pungent lines, but if she is a virgin (and so she may be for any direct evidence to the contrary) she hasn't the reputation of one. Delia in *The London Prodigal,* 1605, is more like an old maid. "She hath refus'd seven of the worshipfulst hous-keepers this day in Kent" before she comes on the stage, and turns away two more before our eyes. For a time it looks like religious celibacy, but in the end she gives a practical enough reason:

> *Not that I doe condemn a married life,*
> *For tis no doubt a sanctimonious thing:*
> *But for the care and crosses of a wife,*
> *The trouble in this world that children bring,*
> *My vow is in heaven in earth to live alone,*
> *Husbands, howsoever good, I will have none.*

So far we have no reproach attached in literature to protracted spinsterhood. Naturally, with an elderly unmarried queen on the throne, the fashion was for elaborate, conceited praise of virginity. Shakespeare followed the fashion in *Midsummer Night's Dream* with Oberon's superb lines on the "fair vestal throned by the west," the "imperial votaress . . . in maiden meditation, fancy free." But in the same play he gives us Theseus' lines scarcely less familiar:

> *But earthlier happy is the rose distill'd*
> *Than that which withering on the virgin thorn*
> *Grows, lives, and dies, in single blessedness.*

and we may give our allegiance to King or Duke, Oberon or Theseus, as we choose. In such a time the term "old maid" scarcely appears in print, though there is reason to think it occurred in speech. Its use is a sort of index of the changes in woman's status brought about by the economic changes of the time described in Chapter II. The important change in woman's condition that came between the time of Elizabeth and that of Anne began to register in the time of Charles II. It shows first in 1673 in an anonymous work, *The Ladies' Calling,* which is,

like other Puritan expressions, religious in purpose and scathing
in terms. Times have changed, it would seem, since the days of
the Virgin Queen.

An old Maid is now thought such a Curse as no Poetic fury can
exceed, look'd on as the most calamitous Creature in Nature . . .
[If] these superannuated Virgins would behave themselves with
Gravity and Reservedness, addict themselves to the strictest Vertu and
Piety, they would give the world some cause to believe 'twas not
their necessity, but their choice, that kept them unmarried; that
they were pre-engaged to a better Amour, espoused to the Spiritual
Bridegroom: and this would give them among the soberer sort at
least the reverence and esteem of Matrons . . . But if, in the other
side, they endeavour to disguise their Age by all the impostures and
gaieties of a youthful dress and behaviour, if they still herd themselves
amongst the youngest and vainest company, and betray a young
mind in an aged body, this must certainly expose themselves to
scorn and censure.

There are no old maids in the comedy of the Restoration because its world is a "Utopia of gallantry" in which it would
be derogatory to the charms and powers of the gallants to suppose that any female should retain her virginity long enough
to become one. Truly it is no place for an old maid. If the plot
of the play demands it, the heroine keeps her virginity long
enough to surrender it to a bridegroom just after the curtain.
The others are all in the way of frailty, mistresses, bawds, jilts
and orange girls—if any are virgins when the curtain rises, none
are so when it falls. Then came Molière and the Parisian conquest of English comedy, which assembled and wound up the
figure of the old maid so successfully that it has performed its
more or less mechanical antics on the stage and in the novel
for something like two and a half centuries. It is significant that
William of Orange and *Les Femmes Savantes* came to England
at so nearly the same time, the King in 1688 and the comedy
in 1692. Both represent conditions which for centuries had been
working upward and now came to the top. Poets hailed Wil-

liam King of Commerce and his merchants as merchant princes:

> *Commerce gives learning, virtue, gold!*
> *Ply Commerce, then, ye Britons bold . . .*
> *View, emulate, outshine old Tyre;*
> *In scarlet rob'd with gems on fire,*
> *Her Merchants princes, every deck a throne!*

And as for the high-brows,

> *And are there, then, of lofty brow,*
> *Who think trade mean, and scorn to bow*
> *So far beneath the state of lofty birth?*
> *Alas! these chiefs but little know*
> *Commerce how high, themselves how low,*
> *The sons of nobles are the sons of earth . . .*
> *Merchants o'er proudest heroes reign . . .*
> *Accomplish'd merchants are accomplish'd men.*

The long slow change which turned the princes of feudalism into princes of commerce made the social changes which evolved the old maid. If unmarried women had always been economically independent, we should never have had old maids, for wealth would have commanded respect which would have protected unmarried women from the odium which begets the caricature. The caricature represents a type figure which appears in literature as soon as old maids become numerous enough in society to be recognized as typical. In England this came about as a focus of several social and economic conditions working together, a complication of causes such as does not arise in a simpler society.

One need not delve far into the lore of the anthropologists to learn that there are no old maids in the organizations of society which we call "primitive" or "savage." There the state of affairs would be that expressed by the negro woman who explained to Agnes Repplier, "Laws, Honey, we's no old maids. Some's married and some isn't, but we's no old maids." In the simplest organizations of society every woman is born in the purple in so far as her "three kingdoms," the husband, the job and the baby, are concerned. Whatever her unhappiness, it does not arise from having nothing to do or from lack of opportunity to fulfill her biological function. It is society organized for commerce that denies these things to women and makes old maids. The old maid does not exist as a type in the Middle Ages; no finger of scorn was then pointed at the unmarried woman. Malory tells of the three knights who met three damsels, and

the eldest had a garland of gold about her head, and she was three score winter of age or more, and her hair was white under the garland. The second damsel was of thirty winter of age, with a circlet of gold about her head. The third damosel was but fifteen year of age, and a garland of flowers about her head.

Sir Uwaine speaks for age and experience:

I am the youngest and most weakest of you both, therefore I will have the eldest damsel, for she hath seen much, and can best help me when I have need, for I have most need of help of you both.

Then there was open to the unmarried woman a way of life that commanded esteem; the Church welcomed her as the bride of Christ and offered her a vocation independent of family or fortune. Whatever we may have to say against the religious orders of that time, we may give them honor where it is due; at least they provided an established place for the woman who did not marry. History does not tell us of any conspicuous excess of women in the Middle Ages. Probably women were for the most part, either as housewives or workers in cottage industries, an asset rather than a liability to the householder, to society, and to themselves.

The breaking up of the monastic establishments of England was a rapid process of the last dozen years of the reign of Henry VIII, 1534-1547. From that time till the twentieth century, some three hundred and fifty years, there was no economic or

intellectual place in English life for the unmarried woman.
During these years the view of society was like that of the law,
which regarded every woman as either married or about to be
married, and had no view at all of the woman who was neither.
Still it took time for the surplus of unmarried women to ac-
cumulate enough to develop the type. In the time of Elizabeth
industry was not so far organized but that there was plenty for
women to do, and an old maid on the throne reflected prestige
on spinsterhood. Through most of the seventeenth century the
numbers of unmarried women formerly regimented in nunneries
was accumulating in civil life, but there was still work for them,
for England was not even then completely organized for commerce. Commerce came to the throne with William of Orange,
and it was in his time that the unmarried woman became a
type figure in society, and literature noted and reflected the fact.
It was not Puritanism which made the change unless it were
by default. The Catholic Church, Roman or Anglican, held
virginity high as an ideal, and provided for women who held
to it. The Puritans also esteemed it, but made no provision for
women who practised it. They were hardly more tolerant of any
condition other than virginity than were the severest of their
predecessors; they would admit sourly with St. Paul that it was
better to marry than to burn, but not much more. It was not
the old maid's virginity that made her a scoffing in Puritan
times. She might lay up her treasure in heaven to any amount,
but when she interfered with the laying up of treasure on earth
she became an obstacle to the great Puritan virtue of thrift. The
Puritan-commercial organization of society deprived her of
every opportunity for productive activity, and then found fault
with her because she was unproductive. What could the poor
girl do? We have seen how the capitalistic organization of industry deprived her twice over of her chances of happiness. It
deprived her of her opportunity of productive work. This took
away the other chance by making marriage the only legitimate

career open to her, at the same time enormously reducing her hope of attaining it by placing it on an economic basis, the dowry system. In any age this would make the unmarried woman a burden on her family and on society at large, and therefore an "odious creature," victim to the satirist. At that time there was an aggravating cause, the scarcity of men brought about by protracted wars. We have seen that the tendencies of the eighteenth century were to make the situation worse rather than better. One was the increase of population. Another was the dominance of Puritanism, of which the quintessence is individual responsibility rather than social co-operation or duty. The Church, then, offered no outlet for the energies of women, neither did society organize any altruistic social and charitable works. Such projects were initiated by individual women and taken over by society when they were in working order.

In the fact that the comedy figure of the old maid is first dramatized as a learned lady there is the clear implication that any woman who knows more than enough to suckle fools and chronicle small beer cannot hope to marry. There is much of interest in the background no less than in the foreground of this idea; its background is magic, and its foreground is sociology. A woman cannot know too much unless she knows more than you do. If she knows more than you do, you necessarily use your imagination on the nature and extent of the margin, and the deeper the ignorance, the wilder the effort. In the former age the result was magic; perhaps in the present age we are more apt to call it science, but the outcome is the same. It was dangerous once for a woman to allow experience and knowledge (even though it came from life and not at all from books) to work together through the years toward wisdom. For a time she might pass as a "wise old woman," but if she did much beyond the limited brains of her neighbors they might burn her at the stake. A figure like Morgan le Fay in the legends of Arthur suggests that if science or magic were practised on a high enough scale it might command more prestige but scarcely less of fear. In the twentieth century we have an instance of a man who murdered his wife and put the body in a sewer because she knew more than he did. Mme. Curie managed it better in France. For women the science of today is the magic of yesterday. For centuries stupidity has kept itself stupid by telling girls, "If you know too much you will never get a husband." Fortunately intelligence too has a biologic urge, and women have fought their way to degrees, and higher degrees, in growing numbers. But the question whether these degrees are gateways to the realm of spinsterhood is a never-lacking accompaniment to their performances. In Molière's time it was not a question; it was an assumption.

Almost as soon as the old maid came into being as a type in society and literature, champions came forward with plans for relieving her distress. The first was one of her own kind, an old maid with the reputation of a bluestocking, Mary Astell, whose *Serious Proposal to the Ladies for the Advancement of their True and Greatest Interests* appeared in 1694, Part II in 1697. The prosposal was to erect

a religious retirement and such as shall have a double aspect, being not only a retreat from the world for such as desire that advantage, but likewise an institution and previous discipline to fit us to do the greatest good in it, and such an institution as this (if I do not mightily deceive myself) would be the most probable method to amend, preserve and improve future age.

As she describes her project we see the retirement to be more religious than monastic, and more Anglican than Puritan. She wished to fortify religion against the world, but not to imprison it or its practitioners. The members of the institution were to return to the world as occasion called them, either for marriage or for good works. She will have the sacraments and feasts of the established Church, and its music, "neither God nor

wise men will like us [women] the better for an affected severity
and waspish sourness." The advantages of the institution were
to be to provide a refuge for heiresses who were hunted for their
fortunes, to educate daughters of large families where dowries
were limited, and to provide for daughters of decayed gentlewomen by giving them opportunity to teach in the institution.
The author does not claim that life in such an order would be
better than marriage, but it would be better than a bad marriage,
and might help a woman to make the best of marriage bad or
good. She calls upon women to refute by demonstration the
prejudices of society against the possibility or advantages of the
education of women. She proposes to cultivate understanding
and judgment, and to strengthen religious faith on a rational
basis by a course of philosophy and useful modern languages.

The scheme seems fairly well considered, even as we look at
it down a perspective of more than two centuries of time, and
several generations of experience with education for women.
It received respectful consideration and financial support in its
day. Queen Anne was so far interested that she subscribed ten
thousand pounds to it anonymously. Probably it would have
been realized if it had not been for the opposition of Bishop
Burnett, who saw it as a monastic establishment and scented
popery. If it had been effected, it might have set the world a
century and a half ahead in the collegiate education of women.
It received the disrespectful attention of the satirists, and it is ten
or a dozen years before we hear the last of it in periodicals and
pamphlets. There was social rank and prestige in the group that
promoted the plan. There was Lady Anne Coventry, Lady
Elizabeth Hastings, of whom Steele said "to love her was a
liberal education," and Lady Mary Wortley Montagu. There
was learning, too, in the person of the scholar, Elizabeth Elstob.
"A group of these ladies who were of quality," as Steele calls
them, naturally omit the middle class in their project. Their
proposal is to ladies for their true advancement, and goes no

farther beyond them than some suggestion of training for working girls. Though it never came to fruition it is worth attention
as a sign of the times, and as a landmark in the history of the
old maid, since it proposes activities and occupations other than
marriage as worthy of a gentlewoman. It is a coefficient, too, of
the relation of the novel to social conditions, for if it had come
to fruition the occupation of many a heroine might have been
changed from bewailing her helpless state to something more
profitable. If Clarissa had had such a refuge, where would
Richardson have looked for material for a tragedy? If women
could have been educated to meet life as it comes, what would
Mme. D'Arblay have found to furnish forth five volumes of
"FEMALE DIFFICULTIES"?

From Molière's time to Smollett's, the old maid, with or
without the attribute of learning, flits through the scenes of
minor comedy, but in only a few does she show vitality enough
to attract our attention. Steele has her in *The Tender Husband,*
1705, in the person of Mistress Bersheba Tipkin, aunt to the better
known Biddy. Steele is neither puritan enough nor rake enough
to be very severe with the character. He gives her the characteristics of the type in mild form, and uses them to work out
the plot. Mistress Bersheba is chaperon to her niece, and seeks
to bring about Biddy's marriage to her country cousin, Humphrey
Gubbin, but Clerimont, wooing Biddy, diverts Mistress Bersheba's
attention by setting Pounce to play upon her old-maid traits,
credulity, love of flattery, and cupidity. Pounce is sure he can
turn the trick.

The antiquated Virgin has a mighty Affection for Youth, and is a
great Lover of Men and Money—One of these, at least, I am sure I
can gratify her in, by turning her Pence in the Annuities, or the
Stocks of one of the Companies; some way or other I'll find to entertain her, and engage you with the young lady.

Her love affairs are not so farcically discreditable as Tabitha
Bramble's.

My dear, I was very cruel thirty Years ago, and no Body ask'd me since. Yet, I assure you, there were a great many Matches propos'd to me—There was *Sir Gilbert Jolly,* but he, forsooth, could not please; he drank Ale and smok'd Tobacco, and was no fine Gentleman, forsooth—but, then again, there was young Mr. *Peregrine Shapely,* who had travell'd, and spoke *French,* and he smil'd at all I said; he was a fine Gentleman—but then he was a Consumptive: And yet again, to see how one may be mistaken; Sir *Jolly* died in half a year, and my Lady Shapely has by that thin Slip eight Children, that should have been mine.

Isabella in *The Conscious Lovers,* 1772, is also chaperon to her niece.

I once had almost as much love for a man who poorly left me to marry an estate, and I am now, against my will, what they call an old maid—but I will not let the peevishness of that condition grow upon me, only keep up the suspicion of it, to prevent this creature's being any other than a virgin, except upon proper terms.

Steele touches on old maids here and there in his periodical papers, as in his suggestion for a tax on bachelors to provide dowries for them, but always as kindly as they may deserve, without reprehension of their spinsterhood as such, only for such faults as it may have engendered. In Steele's work the old maid scarcely appears as a type, and receives no new traits as a stock character for fiction.

Defoe is not so forbearing. He writes in 1723 of the old maid with more of the zeal of the Puritan than the suavity of the Cavalier.

But I happened the other Day to get Intelligence of another class of these Lady-Inquisitors, which I must Confess, alarmed me much, because I was told they were of another Species of Women, and particularly such, as were more Cruel and Merciless than the other, being a Furious and Voracious kind of Females; nay, even a kind of Amazonian Cannibals, that not only Subdued, but Devoured those that had the Misfortune to fall into their Hands. I say, I was much alarmed at the Account I had of this new Sort of Inquisitors, for I thought that in a free Nation, as this is, we should never have such unlimited Power, such Cruelty unmixed with Mercy, such unrelenting hard Heartedness Suffered to be Practised . . . this tea-Table Court, . . . consists of a Bench of Old-Maids. These, having made themselves Judges, and clothed themselves with a Self-made Authority, are so Cruel, and so Voracious, that no mercy is expected from them; it is not in their Nature, they are a sort of people who have no Compassion . . . their very diversions savour'd of those Sour, and acrimonious Liquids which flowed in their Veins, instead of Blood; and . . . Venom and something noxious was mingled with their animal Spirits . . . if an OLD–MAID should bite any body, it would certainly be as Mortal as the Bite of a Mad-Dog . . .

As an economist, Defoe should have known better, and perhaps he did, but wrote this as a Puritan, a newspaper man, a cartoonist. Is Steele's manner milder because he is a sentimentalist, or because he is a gentleman? Either one has a heart that softens to a damsel in distress. Even if she is an old maid distressed by that very fact? Well, Steele's own definition of a gentleman tells us "that the height of good breeding is shown rather in never giving offense than in doing obliging things." He has ever an eye to his female readers; he could not afford to offend those who were elderly and unmarried. Steele's wit is in this sense well-bred. Defoe's is the mood of caricature, the mood which will punish a man for being what he is if it is something which the caricaturist doesn't happen to like. Between this spirit and that of the puritan there is sometimes little to choose.

Just before the old maid appeared in the novel, there came another plan for relieving, or abolishing her. It was propounded "by a Lady" in the *Gentleman's Magazine* for September, 1739, under the comprehensive title, *A New Method for Making Women as Useful and as Capable of Maintaining Themselves as the Men are, and Consequently Preventing Their Becoming Old Maids or Taking Ill Courses*. This was as definitely calculated for the meridian of the middle class as Mary Astell's was for the upper class. The author first points out the need for reform.

> 'Tis the misfortune of this Nation that the most Part of our Gentlemen and Tradesmen bring up their Daughters at a *Boarding-School,* where Miss is taught to work a Cushion, or a Picture, in seven years, a little Drawing and French, with English and Writing, which she is never made perfect in. [The result is that] when she is afterwards forced to shift for herself in the world, she is looked upon as a poor helpless Creature and despised by Mankind. . . . [To] make ourselves as useful, valuable, and even desirable as may be, I have formed the following easy scheme. Let all the Gentlemen who have several Daughters, and Tradesmen, who can give about 1000 or 1500 pounds a-piece to their Daughters, and some who are able to give no more than two or three hundred pounds, on the interest of which no woman can live genteelly . . . take care their Daughters be taught the most useful part of Needle-work, all the arts of Oeconomy, Writing, and Bookkeeping, with enough Dancing and French to give them graceful easy Freedom both of Discourse and Behaviour: . . . let them at the age of fifteen or sixteen be put Apprentices to genteel and easy trades, such as Linen or Woollen Drapers, Haberdashers of small Wares, Mercers, Glovers, Perfumers, Grocers, Confectioners, Retailers of Gold and Silver Lace, Buttons, etc. Why are not these as creditable Trades for the Daughters of Gentlemen as for their Sons; and all of them more proper for Women than Men?

This last question the writer argues vivaciously, and sums up, "By this means a single woman may get a handsome and reputable living, and not be forced to a disagreeable match, or even to marry at all." The plan was even more practical than Mary Astell's but it brought no comment nor any steps toward fulfillment.

Dr. Johnson gives us a new type-name for the old maid in the 119th *Rambler,* 7 May, 1751. In two previous papers he has represented a bachelor describing by way of apologia for his bachelorhood the impossibility of finding an acceptable wife among the worthless society women of the time. As a companion piece to this he shows Tranquilla, a satisfied, even complacent old maid, who demonstrates the impossibility of building any structure of matrimonial happiness out of the unsound masculine timber within the range of her choice. Tranquilla is not so much a person as a satirical device for passing in review types of men of whom Johnson does not approve, but the drawing of the figure for the purpose is a step in the history of the old maid in literature, for it brings out the idea that there may be earthly happiness, at least content and tranquillity, for the rose that withers on the virgin thorn. Tranquilla admits the thorn, but declares that it need not be allowed to infect character. She says that she is

one who has been subject for many years to all the hardships of antiquated virginity; has been long accustomed to the coldness of neglect, and the petulance of insult; has been mortified in full assemblies by inquiries after forgotten fashions . . . been long considered by the airy and gay as too venerable for familiarity, and too wise for pleasure. It is, indeed, natural for injury to provoke anger, and by continual repetition to produce an habitual asperity, yet I have hitherto struggled with so much vigilance against my pride and my resentment, that I have preserved my temper uncorrupted. I have not yet made it any part of my employment to collect sentences against marriage; nor am inclined to lessen the number of the few friends whom time has left me, by obstructing that happiness which I cannot partake . . . It is, indeed, not very difficult to bear that condition to which we are not condemned by necessity but induced by observation and choice; and therefore I, perhaps, have never yet felt all the malignity with which a reproach, edged with the appellation of old maid, swells some of those hearts in which it is infixed.

In *Pamela,* Richardson gave the old maid a sort of negative tolerance. Judy Swynford's fault was not that she was an old maid, but that she was an old maid was clearly her own fault. In *Sir Charles Grandison,* 1753, Harriet Byron analyzes the situation a little; had she been reading *The Rambler?*

I believe there are more bachelors now in England by many thousands than were a few years ago: and, probably, the numbers of them (and of single women, of course) will every year increase. The luxury of the age will account a good deal for this; and the turn our sex take in *un*-domesticating themselves, for a good deal more. But let not those worthy young women, who may think themselves destined to lead a single life, repine over-much at their lot; since, possibly, if they have had no lovers, or having had one, two, or three, have not found a husband, they have had rather a miss than a loss, as men go. And let me here add, that I think, as matters stand in this age, or indeed ever did stand, that those women who have joined with the men in their insolent ridicule of old maids, ought never to be forgiven: . . . An old maid *may* be an odious character, if they will tell us, that the bad qualities of the persons, not the maiden state, are what they mean to expose: but then they must allow, that there are old maids of twenty; and even that there are widows and wives of all ages and complexions, who, in the abusive sense of the words, are as much old maids, as the most particular of that class of females.

This says it again; it is not a fault to be an old maid unless you are an old maid by your own fault. Here as in Molière, celibacy is connected with mental attainments. Miss Byron sets forth the intelligent woman's dilemma in an age of fops.

What can a woman do who is addressed by a man of talents inferior to her own? Must she throw away her talents? Must she hide her light under a bushel, purely to do credit to the man? . . . it is said women must not encourage fops and fools. They must encourage men of sense only. And it is *well* said. But what will they do, if their lot be cast among foplings? If the men of sense do not offer themselves? And pray, may I not ask, if the taste of the age, among the men, is not dress, equipage, and foppery? Is the cultivation of the mind any part of their study? The men, in short, are sunk, my dear; and the women but barely swim.

She goes on to speak of Mr. Grandison, not the peerless Sir Charles, remember, but his brother, and if you choose to think him one of the fops you have this justification; he is, Miss Byron says, so near being handsome, that he may be excused . . . for thinking himself so; because he is liable to make greater mistakes than that. He dresses very gaily, too . . . He dances, he sings, he laughs; and values himself on all three qualifications: and yet certainly has sense; but is not likely to improve it much . . .

and more of the same sort to the extent of a paragraph, ending with, "What a captious, what a supercilious husband, to a woman who should happen to have a stronger mind than his would Mr. Grandison make!" This exclamation introduces the paragraph quoted above about bachelors in many thousands and the luxury of the age. In Volume I, you may see Miss Byron hold her own, though with wise modesty and diffidence of expression, in an argument with a university pedant, in which she demonstrates the degree of intelligence which Richardson thinks correct for the young lady who is to marry the perfect gentleman, Sir Charles. She is not acquainted with "the learned languages," but well understands their use and abuse, she knows her English poets well from Milton to Pope, she profits from listening to discussions among wise men. Her retentive memory plants her fertile mind, and she is adroit in argument, but very diffident in using her skill, lest she should incur the odium that attaches to learning in women. For that she turns an apt phrase in denying her knowledge of Latin and Greek, "I know but one lady who is mistress of both; and she finds herself so much an owl among the birds, that she wants of all things to be thought to have unlearned them." To this the pedant replies, "I should rather choose to marry a woman whom I could teach something, than one who would think herself qualified to teach me." All this goes far to translate Molière's caricature into terms of character.

The subject comes up again in the eighteenth letter of the fourth volume. Sir Charles has suggested that an unmarried woman of thirty may look back, "and sometimes repent and sometimes rejoice that she has gained that summit *sola.*" Thereupon Mrs. Reeves sententiously runs over the familiar complaint, the disadvantages endured by the unmarried woman contrasted with the freer condition of the unmarried man. Sir Charles, never to be found wanting, has the remedy at hand.

We want to see established in every county, *Protestant Nunneries,* in which single women, of small or no fortunes, might live with all manner of freedom, under such regulations as it would be a disgrace for a modest or good woman not to comply with, were she absolutely on her own hands, and to be allowed to quit it whenever they pleased . . . such a society as this . . . might become a *national* good; and particularly a seminary for good wives, and the institution a stand for virtue, in an age given up to luxury, extravagance, and amusements little less than riotous . . . numbers of young women, joining their small fortunes might be able, in such a society, to maintain themselves genteelly on their own income; though each singly in the world would be distressed . . .

This in its general plan, and in phrasing, particularly the term *Protestant Nunneries,* suggests that Richardson knew two similar schemes which had been put forward some fifty-five years before, that of Mary Astell and that of George Wheeler. Did Richardson make the plot of *Sir Charles Grandison* of imagined situations which would dramatize the contents of his commonplace book?

Fielding has little mercy on women who do not attract men sexually. In *Joseph Andrews,* Mistress Slipslop is an old maid by courtesy. "She was a maiden gentlewoman of about forty-five years of age, who, having made a small slip in her youth, had continued a good maid ever since . . ." Fielding is merciless in his description of her person.

She was not at this time remarkably handsome; being very short, and rather too corpulent in body, and somewhat red, with the addition of pimples in her face. Her nose was likewise rather too large, and her eyes too little; nor did she resemble a cow so much in her breath, as in two brown globes which she carried before her: one of her legs was also a little shorter than the other, which occasioned her to limp as she walked.

He is merciless, too, in translating the old maid's credulity about lovers into plain terms of thwarted sexual desire.

The truth is, she was arrived at an age, when she thought she might indulge herself in any liberties with a man, without the danger of bringing a third person into the world to betray them. She imagined that by so long a self-denial, she had not only made amends for the small slip in her youth above hinted at, but had likewise laid up a quantity of merit to excuse any future failings. In a word, she resolved to give a loose to her amorous inclinations, and to pay off the debt of pleasure which she found she owed herself, as fast as possible.

Fielding has a more authentic example of the old maid in *Tom Jones,* Mistress Western, whom he sketches with the hand of the writer of comedy and farce. She is in the line of descent from Bélise, for it is her learning no less than her masculine appearance and six feet of height that prevents men from thinking of her as a woman.

Smollett's first version of the old maid is a coarse-grained caricature of the learned lady in *Roderick Random,* 1748, the aunt of the heroine.

Her forehead was high and wrinkled, her eyes were large, grey, and prominent; her nose was long, sharp, and aquiline; her mouth of vast capacity; her visage meagre and freckled, and her chin peeked like a shoemaker's paring knife; her upper lip contained a large quantity of plain Spanish, which, by continual falling, had embroidered her neck that was not naturally very white, and the breast of her gown, that flowed loose about her with a negligence truly poetic, discovering linen that was very fine, and to all appearance, never *washed but in Castalian streams.* Around her lay heaps of books, globes, quadrants, telescopes, and other learned apparatus. Her snuff-box stood at her right hand, at her left lay her handkerchief sufficiently used, and a convenience to spit in appeared on one side of her chair.

If Smollett set out in pursuit of Molière, his vigor of hyperbole has carried him far from the trail.

In 1785, a third-rate poet, William Hayley, put the fixed features of the conventional type elaborately on record in a work of entertainment and erudition, *A Philosophical, Historical, and Moral Essay on Old Maids.* "By a Friend to the Sisterhood. In Three Volumes." He proposes to devote himself "with a new species of Quixotism to the Service of Ancient Virginity," to "redress all Wrongs of the Autumnal Maiden." Part I has a chapter on each of the conventional traits of the caricature: curiosity; credulity; affectation of youth, of censorial importance, of extreme sensibility, of superlative delicacy; envy; ill-nature. In Part II the chapters are on qualities which the satirists have ignored, ingenuity, patience, charity. Volumes II and III are the history of old maids, beginning with "Conjectures Concerning the History of Old Maids before the Flood," and running on discursively with more authentic lore of ancient times, "Christian and Other Modern Old Maids," compilations from the Church Fathers, legends, lives of saints, American Indian legends, Scandinavian tradition, through chivalric times and down to Spenser, concluding with a "Sermon to Old Maids," and a "Plea to Readers." As a landmark on the path, this book is monumental, but it is nothing but a marker. The first part is no improvement on the work of the journalists, for it has nothing of first-hand observation. It may account for Hayley both as a poet and as a scholar to say that his industry is better than his imagination.

Much more important and less voluminous is Mary Wollstonecraft's comprehensive *Vindication of the Rights of Woman,* 1792, which concerns the old maid first because she is a woman, and second because the changes, economic, mental and physical (omitting those moral and spiritual) which the author calls for, in so far as they have come about, have practically eliminated old maids as a class, and left us only women, married and unmarried, as are men. In her dedication, Mary Wollstonecraft briefs the core of her argument succinctly.

Contending for the rights of women, my main argument is built on this simple principle, that if she be not prepared by education to become the companion of man, she will stop the progress of knowledge, for truth must be common to all, or it will be inefficacious with respect to its influence on general practice.

In her introduction, she defines her audience by addressing it in terms.

I shall first consider women in the grand light of human creatures, who, in common with men, are placed on this earth to unfold their faculties . . . I wish also to steer clear of an error, which many respectable writers have fallen into; for the instruction which has hitherto been addressed to women, has rather been applicable to ladies . . . I pay particular attention to those in the middle class, because they appear to be in the most natural state. . . . My own sex, I hope, will excuse me, if I treat them like rational creatures . . .

Did the middle class open its eyes at seeing its name here for the first time in print? Mary Wollstonecroft's declaration of independence comes most clearly in a refutation of Rousseau. "Rousseau declares that a woman should never for a moment feel herself independent . . . What nonsense!" She has a "theory of the leisure class" that seems quite modern in its classification of idle women with the idle rich. She classes unmarried woman and unmarried men together:

"He that hath wife and children," says Lord Bacon, "hath given hostages to fortune; for they are impediments to great enterprises, either of virtue or mischief. Certainly the best works, and of greatest merit for the public, have proceeded from the unmarried or childless men." I say the same of women.

One of the evils of economic dependence which she points out has served the novelists well; indeed, her exposition of it wants little to be an outline of the plot of many a novel.

. . . Girls who have been thus weakly educated, are often cruelly left by their parents without any provision; and, of course, are dependent on . . . the bounty of their brothers. These brothers are . . . good sort of men, and give as a favor, what children of the same parents had an equal right to. In this equivocal humiliating situation, a docile female may remain some time, with a tolerable degree of comfort. But when the brother marries . . . from being considered as mistress of the family, she is viewed with averted looks as an intruder, an unnecessary burden on the benevolence of the master of the house, and his new partner.

Who can recount the misery, which many unfortunate beings, whose minds and bodies are equally weak, suffer in such situations—unable to work and ashamed to beg? The wife, a cold-hearted, narrow-minded woman, and this is not an unfair supposition; for the present mode of education does not tend to enlarge the heart any more than the understanding, is jealous of the little kindness which her husband shows to his relations; and her sensibility not rising to humanity, she is displeased at seeing the property of *her* children lavished on an helpless sister.

These are matters of fact which have come under my eye again and again. The consequence is obvious, the wife has recourse to cunning to undermine the habitual affection, which she is afraid openly to oppose; and neither tears nor caresses are spared till the spy is worked out of her home, and thrown on the world, unprepared for its difficulties; or sent, as a great effort of generosity, or from some regard to propriety, with a small stipend, and an uncultivated mind into joyless solitude.

This is the situation which left many an eighteenth-century heroine exposed to the cruelties of the world; there is much of it in *David Simple;* the characters of the brother and wife are those which make the opening situation of *Sense and Sensibility;* there is much of it in Trollope's *Miss Mackenzie,* and many another novel of the nineteenth century.

Mary Wollstonecroft declares independence of a host of tyrannies. "I declare against all power built on prejudices, however hoary." This is something like an ultimatum, followed by contention for independence. "It is not empire — but equality, that they should contend for." The road to opportunity should be opened to them, and government without representation is tyranny.

I cannot help lamenting that women of a superior cast have not a road open by which they can pursue more extensive plans of usefulness and independence. I may excite laughter by dropping a hint, which I mean to pursue, some future time, for I really think that women ought to have representatives, instead of being arbitrarily governed without having any direct share allowed them in the deliberations of government.

Lives are wasted for lack of opportunity to work.

How many women thus waste life away, the prey of discontent, who might have practised as physicians, regulated a farm, managed a shop, and stood erect, supported by their own industry, instead of hanging their heads surcharged with the dew of sensibility that consumes the beauty to which it at first gave lustre . . .

What women need is liberty, equality and sorority.

Let an enlightened nation then try what effect reason would have to bring them back to nature, and their duty; and allowing them to share the advantages of education and government with man, see whether they will become better, as they grow wiser, as they become free. They cannot be injured by the experiment; for it is not in the power of man to render them more insignificant than they are at present.

Then she outlines a simple plan of education which should go far to bring all this about. It is only an outline, she says, and not very original; "I have borrowed some hints from a very sensible pamphlet written by the late Bishop of Autun on Public Education." The topics of her plan in modern terms make details unnecessary and show how far we have followed the trail which she and the Bishop of Autun blazed for us. She calls for free education, free for all without class distinctions, coeducation, physical education, and student self-government. Here she drew the plans for the tower which with babel of tongue has long been a-building. Fifty or sixty years afterward the foundations were secure, fifty or sixty years more and the structure was well toward completion. The first quarter of the twentieth century saw her main requirements in everyday practice, and the old maid, strictly so called, a museum specimen embalmed in literature and caricature.

Jean Paul Richter has a paragraph on the old maid in his novel, *Hesperus,* of 1794. If his purpose is sympathy, the effect is reversed by the unendurable sentimentality of the passage, which is not mitigated by the clumsiness of an unknown translator.

Forsaken but patient one! misknown and mistreated! Think not of times when thou hadst hope of better than the present are, and repent the noble pride of thy heart never! It is not always our duty to marry, but it is always our duty to abide by right, not purchase happiness by loss of honour, not to avoid unweddedness by untruthfulness. Lonely, unadmired heroine! in thy last hour, when all life and the bygone possessions and scaffoldings of life shall crumble to pieces, ready to fall down, in that hour thou wilt look back on thy untenanted life; no children, no husband, no wet eyes will be there; but in the empty dusk, one high, pure, angelic, smiling, beaming Figure, godlike. . . will hover, and beckon thee to mount with her, mount thou with her, the Figure is thy Virtue.

The caricatures are so severe that they make us sympathize with the old maid; here the sympathy is enough to make us despise her. Malthus, who tried to oppose the vague optimism of perfectibility with hard realities, is scarcely less sentimental than Richter in praise of the old maid who opposes the increase of population with a lifelong virginity which, whether voluntary or involuntary, seems to him "virtue."

There are very few women who might not have married in some way or other. The old maid, who has never formed an attachment, or has been disappointed in the object of it, has, under the circumstances in which she has been placed, conducted herself with the most perfect propriety; and has acted a much more virtuous and honourable part in society, than those women who marry without a proper degree of love, or at least of esteem, for their husbands; a species of immorality which is not reprobated as it deserves.

In 1816, Thomas Love Peacock gives us in *Headlong Hall* an old maid who is little more than a name, but the name is voluminous, Miss Brindle-mew Grimalkin Phoebe Tabitha Ap-Headlong. The name speaks as much for her as she speaks for herself in the brief time she is on the stage. As if to make amends for this caricature a year later, he introduces Miss Evergreen in *Melincourt,* seemingly to say a good word for the calumniated.

. . . Miss Evergreen was an amiable and intelligent woman, and was single, not from having wanted lovers, but from being of that order of minds which can love but once. Mr. Fax took occasion, during a temporary absence of Miss Evergreen from the room . . . to say he was happy to have seen so amiable a specimen of that injured and calumniated class of human beings commonly called old maids, who were often so from possessing in too high a degree the qualities most conducive to domestic happiness.

Jane Austen shows the old maid for the first time with nothing extenuate and naught set down in malice. Miss Austen lived in and depicted a world in which marriage was quite as much a market as a game of love. She was an old maid herself, and thought about her situation with a keenly analytic mind. She was between thirty-five and forty when she drew and shaded the figure of Miss Bates in *Emma,* the outstanding exemplar of the old maid in her novels. Her exposition of Miss Bates's status is a bit of economic analysis worthy of Defoe or Malthus. We have it from the lips of Emma herself.

. . . it is poverty only which makes celibacy contemptible to a generous public! A single woman with a very narrow income must be a ridiculous, disagreeable old maid! the proper sport of boys and girls; but a single woman of good fortune is always respectable, and may be as sensible and pleasant as anybody else! And the distinction is not quite so much against the candour and common sense of the world as appears at first; for a very narrow income has a tendency to contract the mind, and sour the temper.

And apropos of her prospect of herself being an old maid:

. . . mine is an active, busy mind, with a great many independent resources; and I do not perceive why I should be more in want of employment at forty or fifty than one-and-twenty. Woman's usual occupations of eye, and hand, and mind, will be as open to me as they are
now, or with no important variation.

The figure of Miss Bates is comedy of manners developed out
of comedy of humors by the addition of fine line and brush work
to the coarse outlines of caricature. It is comedy of humors in
so far as the figure always exhibits one trait, garrulity. But it is
more than this in so far as it always exhibits garrulity in combination with other traits. Miss Bates is, as Emma says, "so silly,
so satisfied, so smiling, so prosing, so undistinguished, and so apt
to tell everything to everybody . . . but in general she is very
much to the taste of everybody . . . I really believe, if she had
only a shilling in the world, she would be very likely to give
away sixpence of it; and nobody is afraid of her: that is a great
charm." This is high comedy because the figure is so far shaded
with sympathy as to round it into a solid, a three-dimensional
figure rather than a one-sided flat. This, too, in spite of the
difficulty of the task. Is there anyone besides Shakespeare and
Jane Austen who has succeeded in dramatizing boresome garrulity so as to make it continuously entertaining?

In *Pride and Prejudice* there is an intriguing hint by indirection
of the origin of the old maid species. Mary Bennet, one feels,
stands no chance in the marriage game so briskly playing about
her. Nothing is explicit, but the reader knows by the clearest
implication that Mary feels this. She is the plain one of the
five sisters, and her mind is as plain as her face. She demonstrates
this fact by her unconsciousness of it. She may be aware that
she cannot do much for her face, but she naïvely thinks that
by means of second-hand decorations from second-rate literature
she can beautify her mind and thereby attract men. It is the

situation of the old maid and the learned lady deftly dramatized in an unobtrusive background figure.

Hang the portrait of Miss Bates beside Scott's of Miss Barbara Yellowly, in *The Pirate*, 1821, and we can see what Scott meant by his gallant bow to Jane Austen:

> That young lady had a talent for describing the involvements and feelings and characters of ordinary life, which is to me the most wonderful I ever met with. The Big Bow-Wow strain I can do myself like any now going; but the exquisite touch, which renders ordinary commonplace characters and things interesting, from the truth of the description and the sentiment, is denied me. What a pity such a gifted creature died so early!

Miss Yellowly can hardly be exhibited in any passage brief enough to quote. She is much closer to the comedy of humors than is Miss Pratt. Her dominant quality is stinginess. She is farcical—angular, strident and scolding—but not altogether unhuman, for caricature is touched with character to just the right degree for a background figure, and to just that degree she is woven into the plot. Such fine brushwork as Jane Austen's would be lost in so large a canvas as this of Scott's.

The same novel presents us a convenient example of another type of figure, which, though actually a lifelong old maid, hardly registers as such in the reader's mind. It is Minna Troil, one of Maggie Tulliver's "dark unhappy ones," whose blonde sister Brenda "carries off all the happiness." Minna loves the pirate, Cleveland, whose crimes are pardoned at the last extremity for an earlier act of gallantry to some highborn Spanish ladies. Thus his endearing crimes are whitewashed, but he doesn't come out quite white enough for a "nice" girl like Minna to marry, so he is exported to a death of military glory, leaving Minna to wither among the autumnal maidens. Her single state is blessed by the poor; her celibacy is like that of a religious devotee, a long life of austere devotion, but we hardly know it. During all the time she is before our eyes, she is the heroine of a romantic love affair with a Byronic hero; the vista of the celibate years is a glimpse in the last few paragraphs of the last chapter. As a heroine she is not an old maid, and as an old maid she is not a heroine, but she is an essential link in the history of the old maid as a literary character. In so far as she is a heroine, she does, by definition, command the sympathy of the reader, and she can hardly be said to alienate it by becoming an old maid in the last paragraph. This type of heroine we last saw in 1780 disappearing into the tomb of the lost Augustus in a fog of dewy sorrow. Perhaps we might have had glimpses of her again if we had sought them, but in such an impersonation she is not worth watching for. Here in *The Pirate* she emerges as an acceptable heroine who holds a reasonably well-assured place in the gallery of fiction. She has had sympathy enough from generations of readers since 1821 to keep her alive. The next step is the type of plot in which the tragedy, be it major or minor, is determined earlier. Of this an American example is *The Gayworthys,* by Mrs. A. D. T. Whitney, 1865. The earlier chapters present the thwarted love affairs of the Gayworthy sisters, Rebecca and Joanna, of whom it is said in the middle of the book,

Rebecca was thirty-one; Joanna just beyond her in years; they had crossed the line of their youth into old maidenhood; nobody looked any longer for change in them; they would count their years out as people did here among the hills; they would be the "old Miss Gayworthys" as Joanna had prophesied to herself.

Rebecca's love affair is permanently thwarted. She must tragically make the best of a broken life. It is in a sense a minor tragedy, but the old maid has enough of the sympathy of the reader to sustain a tragic rôle—indeed, Minna Troil's thwarted love had in it the feeling of tragedy to Maggie Tulliver's mind. The old maid, then, has passed from the coarsest of caricature through low comedy and high comedy to the steps of the throne.

A generation after Rebecca Gayworthy came Mary E. Wilkins Freeman, who copyrighted *A New England Nun* in 1891, and played the theme with variations through many pages of her stories. The New England nun is Louisa Ellis, not a tragedy of thwarted lives; thwarted lives would have come from her marriage, which is prevented by a happy chance of eavesdropping. Louisa was engaged to Joe Daggett, who kissed her and went off to make his fortune. " 'It won't be for long,' poor Joe had said huskily; but it was for fourteen years." Through that time Louisa lived tranquilly alone in her own house and her own way of life, developing a trait which in the nineteenth century became as essential a part of the old-maid character as was amorous credulity in the eighteenth, the love of scrupulous order and cleanliness. She picked some currants and "sat on the back doorstep stemming them, collecting the stems carefully in her apron and afterwards throwing them into the hencoop. She looked sharply at the grass beside the step to see if any had fallen there." Joe Dagget comes to see her.

Presently Daggett began fingering the books on the table. There was a square red autograph album, and a Young Lady's Gift Book which had belonged to Louisa's mother. He took them up one after the other and opened them; then laid them down again, the album on the Gift Book.

Louisa kept eyeing them with mild uneasiness. Finally she rose and changed the position of the books, putting the album underneath. That was the way they had been arranged in the first place. . . . "I always keep them that way," murmured she.

And after he has gone,

Then she set the lamp on the floor and began sharply examining the carpet. She even rubbed her fingers over it and looked at them.

"He's tracked in a good deal of dust," she murmured. "I thought he must have."

Louisa got a dustpan and brush, and swept Joe Daggett's track carefully.

Yet with the inflexible will which made New England what it was (and nine-tenths of Mrs. Freeman's stories what they are) she holds to her word to Joe until the chance of an overheard dialogue tells her that it is his will only that holds him to his plighted faith to her; his heart is elsewhere. Then she releases him without telling him what she knows.

Louisa, all alone by herself that night, wept a little, she hardly knew why; but the next morning, on waking, she felt like a queen, who, after fearing lest her domain be wrested away from her, sees it firmly insured in her possession . . . That afternoon she sat with her needlework at the window, and felt fairly steeped in peace . . . Serenity and placid narrowness had become to her as the birthright itself. She gazed ahead through a long reach of future days strung together like pearls in a rosary, every one like the others, and all smooth and flawless and innocent, and her heart went up in thankfulness . . . Louisa sat, prayerfully numbering her days, like an uncloistered nun.

There are many New England nuns in Mrs. Freeman's tales; they have their sorrows and their anxieties, at times their psychology approaches the morbid, but the torment of sex never disturbs their serenity. There is no desire under the elms of her villages.

Meanwhile the caricature, or comedy of humors, type of old maid continued without change except for minor adaptations to the purpose of the artist. An early American example is in the *Salmagundi Papers,* of Washington Irving and James Kirke Paulding, a periodical of the Tatler-Spectator kind. Miss Charity Cockloft furnishes material for the whole number of April 25, 1807. She has most of the conventional traits of the type, and nothing more. She affects youth: "My Aunt Charity departed this life in the fifty-ninth year of her age, though she never grew older after twenty-five." She was not beautiful: when young "she was as knotty a little piece of humanity as he ever saw; and . . . if she had been possessed of the least sensibility, she would . . . most certainly have run mad at her own figure and face . . . in a looking-glass." She affected delicacy: "My good aunt prided herself on keeping up this buckram delicacy . . ." She set her value in the marriage market too high: "she never met with a lover who resembled Sir Charles Grandison, the hero of her nightly dreams and waking fancy." She was charitable: "Was any acquaintance sick? In vain did the wind whistle and the storm beat; my aunt would waddle through mud and mire . . . but what she would visit them." But she would have it her own way: "Woe be to the patient that came under the benevolent hand of my aunt Charity; he was sure to be drenched, willynilly, with a deluge of decoctions . . ." And she died at last of curiosity: "no one could expound the history of this mysterious stranger: she never held up her head afterward—drooped daily, took to her bed . . . being the seventh Cockloft that has died of a whim-wham." Here the type is drawn for its own sake with no purpose but delineation.

Susan Ferrier in 1824 employed three old maids to pad out her three necessary volumes of *The Inheritance* with comedy of humors scenes. Lady Betty St. Clair is of the dull stupid type.

She was chiefly remarkable for the quantity of worsted work she executed, which, for a person of her time of life, was considered no less extraordinary than meritorious. She was now employed on her fifth rug. She also read all the novels and romances which it is presumed are published for the exclusive benefit of superannuated old women, and silly young ones; such as "The Enchanted Head". . ."The Miraculous Nuptials." She was now in the midst of "Bewildered Affections, or All is not Lost," which she was reading, unconsciously for the third time with unbroached delight. Lastly, she carefully watched over a fat, pampered, ill-natured lapdog, and asked a great many useless questions which few people thought of answering.

Miss Pratt is the gossiping busybody,

a person from whom nothing could be hid. Her eyes were . . . active, brisk, busy, vigilant immoveable eyes, that looked as if they could not be surprised by anything—not even by sleep . . . Her . . . ears might evidently be classed under the same head with the eyes—they were something resembling rabbit's—long, prominent, restless, vibrating ears,—forever listening, and never shut by the powers of thought. Her voice had the tone and inflexions of one accustomed to make frequent sharp interrogatories. She had a rather neat compact figure, and the *tout ensemble* of her person and dress was that of smartness.

Miss Becky Duguid's name and appearance speak for her.

Miss Becky's dress did require an apology, for the marks of children's fingers were upon her gown—her cap looked as if it had been sat upon, and her shawl even bore symptoms of having served to play at bo-peep! In short, Miss Becky had the *tout ensemble* of a poor elderly maiden aunt . . . every parent levied the most unconscionable taxes upon her time and capabilities . . . But even the labours imposed upon her by her own relations were nothing compared to the constant demands made upon her by the world in general . . . When in town, her life was devoted to executing commissions from the country—inquiring the character of servants—hiring governesses and grooms—finding situations for wet nurses—getting patterns of pelisse cloths from every shop in town—trying to get old silks matched with new—gowns made—gauzes dyed—feathers cleaned—fans mended, etc., etc., etc.

And for good measure Miss Ferrier throws in the Misses Black, who are so religious that we might call Christianity their dominant trait. Two years later Lady Morgan put two Irish old maids into *The O'Briens and the O'Flahertys* for farce-comedy effect. They are the Misses McTaaf, twin sisters in their sixty-first year.

Tall, stately, and erect, their weather-beaten countenance and strongly marked features were neither faded nor fallen in. The deep red hue of a frosty and vigorous senility still coloured their unwrinkled faces. Their hair, well powdered and pomatumed, was drawn up by the roots from their high foreheads . . . and their long, lank necks, rose like towers above their projecting busts; which with their straight, sticky, tight-laced waists, terminating in the artificial rotundity of a half-dress bell-hoop, gave them the proportions of an hour-glass. They wore grey

camlet riding-habits, with large black Birmingham buttons; . . .
while petticoats, fastened as pins did or did not their office, shewed
more of the quilted marseilles and stuff beneath, than the precision of
the toilet required . . . Their large, broad silver watches, pendant
from their girdles by massy steel chains . . . were still without those
hands which it had been in the contemplation of the Miss McTaafs
to have replaced by the first opportunity, for the last five years. High-
crowned black-beaver hats, with two stiff, upright, black feathers, that
seemed to bridle like their wearers, and a large buckle and band, completed the costume . . .

In the following decade appeared Dr. Holmes's poem, *My Aunt*,
quoted at the head of this chapter, which again is portrait for
portrait's sake in the mood of the periodical essayist. In 1853,
J. T. Trowbridge put three old maids into *Burrcliff*, and in spite
of the good word he says for the class, the effect of the episode
is that of coarse-grained farce, with the old maid as the victim.

Trowbridge's is the sort of farce that Whittier deprecates in
Snow-Bound, 1866. Among the members of the household he
introduces "the dear aunt,"

> *The sweetest woman ever fate*
> *Perverse denied a household mate, . . .*
> *Who, lonely, homeless, not the less*
> *Found peace in love's unselfishness,*
> *And welcome wheresoe'er she went . . .*
> *For well she kept her genial mood*
> *And simple faith of maidenhood; . . .*
> *All unprofaned she held apart*
> *The virgin fancies of the heart.*
> *Be shame to him of woman born*
> *Who hath for such but thought of scorn.*

Mary Wollstonecraft had the courage of conviction and the
energy of an untrammeled mind. Few of those who came after
her in the path were anything but timid followers. Even in the
land of the free and the home of the brave, there was for long
little of either bravery or freedom in any motions toward inde-

pendence for unmarried women. William A. Alcott, a zealous educational reformer, believed in physical education for women if it could be attained without unladylike violence of motion, but would close to them most doors to gainful occupations for sentimental reasons.

> . . . I must omit, of course, in a work like this, intended for young women, the mention of any motion more rapid than walking. Running, to those who have passed into their teens, would be unfashionable, and . . . who could risk the danger of being regarded as a romp?
>
> Nor can I wish to see young women trained to do the "buying and selling" instead of the men, in order to give energy to their character; although I do not doubt that such a course is often successful. . . . young women should love domestic life, and the care and society of the young, because it is, without doubt, the intention of Divine Providence that they should do so, and because home, and the concerns of the home, afford the best opportunities of moral improvement.

No chance here for Aunt Tabitha except as mother's helper! This was in the United States in 1840. In England in 1849, Miss Mitford wrote in a letter to a friend,

> You are quite right about the want of objects for single women. In France the rank just below the gentry is made at once useful and happy by keeping the shop books. In England even that resource is wanting, and that class is added to the idle and wretched worsted-working young ladies. Among the other evils, too, the want of better occupation drives girls to write bad verses.

Perhaps there were more occupations open to women than Miss Mitford knew or Mr. Alcott could wish to see. A writer in *Chambers's Journal* in 1853 lists thirty-five or more, from button manufacturing and pin making to artificial flowers and envelope-folding, but it has to do with working-class women rather than with the genteel old maid, though we can see in the article an apparent effort to make the occupations seem attractive —"the labour cannot be very badly paid, or the girls would not look so plump in their neat summer dresses, or show such a neat foot as some of them do glittering in shining pumps." Probably the labor conditions of women rising from the industrial revolution were making the classes above the workers conscious of women's work. This leaven seems to work through and appear higher up about the middle of the nineteenth century.

That was about the time when England began to catch up with Mary Astell and the lady projector of the *Gentleman's Magazine*. As early as 1833, Oberlin College in the United States opened its doors to women together with men, but England opened the first college for women, Queens College, in 1848. Bedford opened in 1849, and North London College School in 1850. In 1856 a writer in *Chambers's Journal* describes as in operation a plan much like that suggested in the *Gentleman's Magazine* in 1739, for profitable employment and education.

Within the last few years, it has been seen that there are many arts of an elegant kind which women might pursue, to the securing of their independence, and the saving of themselves from the usual evils of idleness, were it not that these arts in general require to be prosecuted under factory or workshop arrangements . . . Can ladies work under such circumstances without any injury to their dignity? Well, a pretty fair experiment has been tried, and, as far as yet appears no one has been at all the worse of it, but on the contrary, a moral elevation has clearly resulted . . . The Ladies Guild, as it is called, is a true manufacturing company, by which the different processes of the business are carried on by groups of ladies . . . a new employment for educated women, upon the principle of their sharing the profits . . . The things that have struck me most in the Guild are the great happiness and interest of manual work . . . the beautiful feeling among the workers to one another . . . the nice social amusements, the reading aloud, the parties, the excursions, and the earnest feeling we had about our classes in French and vocal music.

A reviewer in the *North British Review* has an article in February, 1857, covering eight books on women, their "sphere," condition, duties and work, including three by American writers, Margaret Fuller, Thomas Wentworth Higginson and Theodore Parker. The reviewer calls for fewer words and more acts.

What we want is something plain-spoken and practical . . . Women have been told already, during too many centuries what it becomes them to be. Now in this nineteenth century it is time that something should be done to teach them what to do, and to help them to do it . . . There is abundant employment for women, if we will only let them have it.

It was in this period that Mrs. Gaskell's *Cranford* appeared in Dickens' *Household Words,* between December, 1851, and May, 1853. The date is not significant, for its scenes and costumes are of the middle thirties, when *Pickwick Papers* was appearing in parts, and itself belongs to all time, for although it shows prettily the lines of period costume, it is not a work of fashion but one of lasting art. The old ladies of Cranford might have known Jane Austen's Miss Bates if they had visited at Highbury, for they are very nearly of the same generation, though their chronicles are forty years apart. Jane Austen blended her tints with a crude caricature trait to give vigor to her portrait. Susan Ferrier made half a dozen old maids out of a third of a dozen of stock traits of the old caricature. Mrs. Gaskell furnished a whole village of old maids, and old maids in very truth they are in every word and thought and deed, but there is hardly a stock trait in the whole village. There is a fineness of texture in the drawing of these figures that Mary E. Wilkins Freeman did not attain, and that Jane Austen did not surpass. *Cranford* is the highwater mark of the old maid in art. Mrs. Gaskell touched the subject again in her *Life of Charlotte Brontë,* 1857, with a practical comment.

I speculate much on the existence of unmarried and never-to-be married women now-a-days; and I have already got to the point of considering that there is no more respectable character on this earth than an unmarried woman, who makes her own way through life quietly, perseveringly, without support of husband or brother; and who, having attained the age of forty-five or upwards, retains in her possession a well-regulated mind, a disposition to enjoy simple pleasures, and fortitude to support inevitable pains, sympathy with the sufferings of others, and willingness to relieve want as far as her means extend.

And in the same year Charles Kingsley's *Two Years Ago* returns to the sentimental.

Ah, true sisters of mercy, whom the world sneers at as "old maids," if you pour out on dogs and cats and parrots a little of the love which is yearning to spend itself on children of your own flesh and blood! As long as such as you walk this lower world, one needs no Butler's Analogy to prove to us that there is another world, where such as you will have a fuller and fairer (I dare not say a juster) portion.

A writer in the *Dublin Magazine* in 1860 returns to the economic aspects of the situation. He finds old maids most abundant in the middle class; in the working class it is still an advantage to a poor man to marry, and in the upper class wealth makes celibacy usually no hardship to women. His solution is one we have met before. He urges middle-class parents who cannot provide money for their daughters to teach them trades and professions by which they can earn it for themselves. Two years later an article in *Fraser's Magazine* raises the question, "What shall we do with our old maids?" and answers it, "Give them work to do."

. . . it is only on the standing-ground of a happy and independent celibacy that a woman can really make a free choice in marriage. To secure this standing-ground, a pursuit is more needful than a pecuniary competence, for a life without aim or object is one which more than all others, goads a woman into accepting any chance of a change.

He cites an expression of the Convocation of Canterbury for that year in which he finds

the subject of Protestant Sisterhoods or Deaconesses, discussed with an unanimity of feeling almost unique in the history of ecclesiastical parliaments. High Churchmen and Low, Broad Churchmen and

Hard, all seemed agreed that there was good work for women to do, and which women *were* doing all over England; and that it was extremely desirable that all these lady guerillas of philanthropy should be enrolled in the regular disciplined army of the Church, together with as many new recruits as might be enlisted.

Here, in so far as the Protestant sisterhood is concerned, we have fallen in step with Mary Astell. *Chambers's Journal* returns to the subject in 1871, marking time just where it was in 1856, which is just where the *Gentleman's Magazine* was in 1739. But an article in *Blackwood's* the following year brings us back to the nineteenth century. The writer sorts out various types of old maids by their prevailing qualities, then generalizes.

There have been a great many speculations on the number, large and increasing, of the class which has been our topic. We have no doubt that growing refinement is one great cause of this increase. In the working classes, where congeniality of tastes is little thought of, an old maid is a rarity, though the proportion of the sexes must be the same. Marriage even among the less fastidious of a higher class, cannot now be owned the one object of life, as it was understood to be on all hands a hundred and fifty years ago . . . It is clearly less intolerable to be an old maid than it has been . . .

Here are open hints that at last the spread of education and enlarged opportunities for work, something at least more than slushy sympathy, are bringing about the metamorphosis of the old maid into the bachelor woman. Noteworthy is the declaration that not every woman is fit to be an old maid. She, in her highest manifestation, is "the woman who has never met with her ideal, and who has never been cunningly persuaded to accept anything short of it . . . The woman who has shown herself equal to the charge of herself is the woman to do credit to the single state." The old maid of literature does not rate the title. "No woman without a certain independence and force of character is fit to be an old maid." Mere conformists are good enough for mere wives; "the woman who does not mean to conform to the rules of society should keep single." And we salute the martyrs to the cause:

It has been one of the achievements of spinsterhood to advance the cause of education, to make women as a body less ignorant, to infuse into them at least some smattering of intellectual accomplishment; and this was done under an amount of discouragement which constitutes the blue-stocking a true if somewhat obtrusive martyr to the cause of mind. . . .

which makes one think of Mary Wollstonecraft's quotation from Lord Bacon, and perhaps of Trollope's figure of Miss McNulty in *The Eustace Diamonds,* 1872, an excellent characterization of a woman who is not up to the job of being an old maid.

On both sides of the Atlantic the discussion runs on through the magazine of the seventies—and on both sides of the question, the sentimental and the practical. Some of the writers are a century behind their time. Others reflect the beginnings of the active agitation for "woman's rights." At the same time women were forcing their way into the medical profession, and an old maid, if she were worthy to be one, might become something more than a nurse. She might be more than a working woman too, for the newly introduced typewriter was beginning to pass women through the previously unpassable door between the shop and the executive office. In the eighties we begin to hear of shop-girls rising to executive positions. "Jenny June" writes of "The Business Girl" in *Demorest's Monthly Magazine* in 1883. "Jenny June" was Mrs. David G. Croly, herself a landmark on the path of woman's progress. Sorosis, the mother of the Federated Women's Clubs, is said to have been founded because Mrs. Croly was not invited, on her own demand, to a stag dinner of a club of which her husband was a member. Her article is noteworthy for its early recognition of business girls, not shop girls or working women, as a class, and its record of the fact that they are rising from the ranks to executive positions. She finds many girls behind the counters who have been gently nurtured and tenderly reared, not specially trained for any pursuit, not exceptionally well educated at all, but sent to school after the desultory fashion of fifteen or twenty years ago, after the fashion of many struggling and not very clear-sighted people now-a-days . . .

To one of these who was floundering and complaining, she says she gave a bit of advice:

Be ambitious to be a merchant instead of a clerk; but be a good clerk while you are one, and interest yourself in learning all you can about your department, and particularly all that is possible in regard to the goods you sell, and the changes of fashion, so that you can talk about them to your customers.

Some years later she met the girl on a steamer for Liverpool, and heard the story of her rise, ending, "and—well to make a long story short, . . . I was made the buyer, and this is the third year I have been abroad for the house." In another article in the same series, "How We Live in New York," Jenny June tells of four business girls who keep house together in a "flat." With these the bachelor maid is complete in all but the title.

The term "old maid" is hopeless; it is indelibly stamped on the caricature and all attempts to redeem it are hopeless. "Business Girl" is a step in the right direction, but it is pitched low and doesn't reverberate. *Macmillan's* in 1888 tried to launch *The Glorified Spinster*—"An old maid is a woman *minus* something; the glorified spinster is a woman *plus* something."— But spinster, however buoyed with glory, wouldn't float. Nobody heard of the glorified spinster, but everybody knows the Bachelor Girl, though not all who know her know that her successful title was not the least noteworthy of the many achievements of the versatile William Hosea Ballou. The novel itself is not so significant as the title, and even that does not apply directly to the old maid, nor yet to the business woman. She is "the girl of the plutocracy, the bachelor girl." "Miss Lily . . . is a modern bachelor girl. She lives a club life, though exclusively in her own home." She is a bachelor girl because she leads a life that in some respects resembles that of a bachelor man. Her life is "fast," though its actual speed is only that of a saddle-horse in Central Park, and a wild excursion in a non-dirigible balloon. Champagne and an occasional cigarette are the limit. The moral tether is short; twice she is nearly compromised by being out after sunset with a man and without a chaperon, but luckily no one hears of it. The divine fire is not in the book, but the title had a spark that kindled and spread; twenty or more novels in forty years played the few possible variations on Mr. Ballou's title. Better known than the original, and more to our purpose, was Mrs. Burton Harrison's *A Bachelor Maid,* 1894. This is the first noticeable appearance of a hardy perennial, the "marriage *vs.* career" plot, a stock on which more recent blossoms are A. S. M. Hutchinson's *This Freedom* and Storm Jameson's *Three Kingdoms.* Mrs. Harrison's heroine breaks her engagement with a super-eligible young man, and goes from her father's house to live in an apartment with another girl. She finds, however, that she can't make a career out of living in an apartment, so she ends by marrying after all. Read it today and it seems a faded flower whose tints could never have been anything but pale, but in its day it was a cry of freedom, and it was the end of the old maid. It was no longer necessary to be old to be a maid when a girl could be a bachelor. Mr. Ballou tried to make his heroine the topmost bubble in the wave of fashion; it is none too convincing, but the intent is clear. Mrs. Harrison's heroine moves quietly in the best circles. And that is what "bachelor" meant then, however it may have descended later. It was a simple and obvious change, from "old" which meant everything opprobrious to "bachelor" which represented the heart's desire. Mr. Ballou abolished the old maid by coining a title which women who could not or would not marry were ready to claim. It is not the least of his many services to society.

The next step was toward the abolishment of the distinction expressed in the term "maid." The question was "what price virginity?" The topics were the right of the unmarried woman to motherhood and even to sexual experience on the same terms as the bachelor man, the "single standard." These are topics for other chapters. Enough to say here that not all women in our novels are like Louisa Ellis, content without a man, and not all wish for motherhood or sexual experience without marriage; some do, some don't.

CHAPTER VIII

SOME DO

1766

When lovely woman stoops to folly,
And finds too late that men betray;
What charm can soothe her melancholy?
What art can wash her guilt away?—

The only art her guilt to cover,
To hide her shame from every eye,
To give repentance to her lover,
And wring his bosom, is—to die!

GOLDSMITH.

1929

When lovely woman stoops to folly and
Paces about her room again, alone,
She smooths her hair with automatic hand,
And puts a record on the gramaphone.

T. S. ELIOT.

SOME do, but few of those who do are heroines, for the sufficient reason that few of our novelists have been tragedians. The history of the novel in England covers the two centuries when the law which Goldsmith framed so epigrammatically (but did not originate) was in force in fiction. The penalty in the kingdom of the novel for a woman's surrendering, or losing, her virginity on any terms but marriage, was death. Occasionally by act of executive clemency the sentence was commuted to life imprisonment, lifelong penance in seclusion. Sometimes sentence was suspended because of a flaw in the indictment; the marriage supposed to be fraudulent turned out to be binding after all, and the frail damsel became by the accidental discovery of accidental validity, an honest woman. The enforcement of such penalties on secondary characters makes the lesson a secondary one. We identify ourselves with the major characters of the fiction we read, and if the penalties do not befall them, nothing happens to us. If the ethical operation is painless, it is ineffective. Practically all the novelists are moralists, truly or professedly; but few of the moralists are great surgeons. Not daring a major operation, they give us a sugar-coated pill with the comforting assurance that it is "just as good." The verdict of tragedy is guilty; its sentence is death. The verdict of melodrama is "not guilty, but don't do it again." Goldsmith's law of capital punishment for a fault which he denominates "folly" makes melodrama of the novel, much as laws calling for capital punishment make juries with more conviction than courage acquit prisoners they believe guilty. The death penalty for folly may be according to nature, but it is not human justice. Tragedy speaks with high seriousness to minds and feelings that can scale its heights and breathe its rare air. Melodrama tries to bring all this to lower levels, and succeeds only in reducing it to sentimentality. Death, inevitable in high tragedy, low tragedy imposes trivially on unworthy characters under warrant of Goldsmith's law, furnishing abundant material to the fashion of sentimental death, and opening, as we have seen, abundant spigots of liquid sorrow.

Richardson, the first of our novelists to deal with the matter as a major subject, made of it a major tragedy. But in so far as what Goldsmith calls "folly" is a trait of the women whom we meet in the pages of our fiction, Pamela cannot be held responsible; obviously they cannot have inherited any such trait from her. Most readers are willing enough to find the trait in Richardson's other and greater heroine, Clarissa. Clarissa fell into the snare spread for her by the seducer, Lovelace; no marriage made her an honest woman, and she died. A reader who knows only so much of her story as this might well believe that Richardson originated the law which Goldsmith made famous.

Most readers will never learn more, for there is no way to learn
Clarissa's story save to live it with her page by page through
all its eight volumes, and few there are in the twentieth century
who are willing to dwell so long in pages that are two hundred
years old. Page for page, *Clarissa* will stand as close analysis as
Hamlet, yet a format that would give *Hamlet* one hundred and
fifty pages would need more than four thousand for *Clarissa*.
No summary can do justice to the subtle shading of the motivation arising out of character, yet some comprehension of it we
must have if we are to discuss the relation of Clarissa to the host
of women in fiction who followed her in time, and whom we
find outside of narrow paths of conventional morality.

Clarissa is eighteen when we meet her, and not much older when
she dies; it is hard to tell the exact extent of the seemingly long period
covered by the many volumes of the story. Her family stands topmost in the middle class on the verge of promotion to the peerage.
There is great wealth made in the most respectable commerce, the
East India traffic, and there are estates in Scotland and in England.
Clarissa has inherited a fortune from her grandfather, and has prospect
of princely legacies from other relatives if she becomes a peeress by
marriage. The long story is told in letters, many of them exchanged
between Clarissa and her devoted friend, Miss Anna Howe. Miss
Howe opens with an inquiry about a duel between Clarissa's brother
James and a Mr. Lovelace. She has heard that young Harlowe insisted
on fighting, and that Mr. Lovelace behaved with forbearance and
discretion. Clarissa tells her the whole story, beginning with Mr.
Lovelace's first acquaintance with her brother at the university, where
the similarity of their domineering tempers made them quarrelsome
rivals. Then, at a time when James was in the north, looking after
estates in Yorkshire and Scotland, Mr. Lovelace's aristocratic family
put him forward as a suitor for the hand of Clarissa's sister Arabella.
He, however, did not surrender to Arabella's charms quickly enough
to please her, and she tried a fit of the sullens which did not please him.
He obtained his dismissal by a trick cleverly adapted to Arabella's
character. By making her angry he drew from her expressions of her
displeasure with him, then proposed at a time when she could not
accept him without belying and stultifying herself, so she must needs

reject him. He withdrew, and reported that she had rejected him after mature deliberation, and did not renew his suit. This left her no choice but to express disapproval of him, in which James heartily agreed with her. Before long, Lovelace returned and renewed his application for alliance with the Harlowe family by offering for Clarissa. Mr. Harlowe would not decide without James's consent. James peremptorily refused any consideration of the offer, insulted Lovelace when he came to the house, involved the whole family in the quarrel, and let all the blame for the occurrence fall on poor Clarissa.

Clarissa's conduct at this time is such that no reasonable person could find fault with it. She has no leanings toward Lovelace, rather the contrary. "I did not like him at all;" she says, "he seemed to have too good an opinion both of his person and parts to have any regard to his wife, let him marry whom he would." But as her family become increasingly revengeful in temper toward Lovelace, she fears the effect on him, and she and her mother decide that to prevent further bloodshed she may carry on a secret correspondence with him, for such placating effect as it may have. She goes for a short visit to Miss Howe, and on her return finds the whole family, instigated especially by James and Arabella, arrayed against her in proposing to marry her to a Mr. Solmes. In appearance and character Solmes seems contrived as the exact antithesis of Lovelace. He is old, wrinkled, repulsive; Clarissa calls him a monster, a toad. His only recommendation is the exact opposite of Lovelace's most conspicuous fault; he has not, credibly enough, been a pursuer of women. He is a miser, and has gained his great wealth by meanness and trickery. His offers in marriage settlements do injury to all his relatives. He has let some relatives live on the verge of starvation. He inhumanly disregards all Clarissa's attempts to reject him, and for the sake of financial advantage will marry her even if she is under compulsion by force. "He has," she says of him, "a very ordinary share of understanding, is very illiterate, knows nothing but the value of estates and how to improve them, and what belongs to land-jobbing and husbandry." Richardson spares no pains to make us feel that for Clarissa to submit to such a marriage would be worse than suicidal.

Compulsion by force is essentially what Clarissa has to face in the efforts of her family to promote this marriage; they are inflexibly set to gain at once revenge on Lovelace and wealth which will further their active chance for a peerage. These motives especially animate James, who influences the other members of the family. He is of a "haughty and morose temper" and exceedingly ill-natured. As the prospective head of a very important family he feels that he should have all in his own hands, and should himself be heir to his grandfather and his two uncles, which would give him a fortune which would make him sure of a peerage. He holds it against Clarissa that his grandfather's fortune went to her. All that girls need is a few thousand pounds each for dowry; "daughters were but encumbrances and drawbacks upon a family," one must get them off one's hands, and that impairs the family fortune. This notion of his own importance he succeeded in impressing on his mother and his uncles, and even his father treated him with deference. James's plan for self-aggrandisement is the root of Clarissa's trouble. He seeks her marriage with Solmes to put marriage with Lovelace out of the question, because her uncles plan to endow her with a suitable fortune should she become a peeress, as she probably would if she married Lovelace. Her father is fully as stubborn and even more violent. His is a nature prone to obstinacy and violence, inflamed by gout. He defers to no one but James, whom he looks upon as his successor. He is incensed to the verge of apoplexy by the thought that a daughter of his should resist his will, and commands her to marry Solmes.

Clarissa at first cannot believe that they will actually condemn her to any such horrible fate. When she perceives that it is even so, she seeks in every way to escape. She disclaims any inclination toward Lovelace, but that only makes matters worse; they tell her that since she does not care for Lovelace, she has no reason for refusing Solmes. She puts her estate and fortune completely, but not irrevocably in her father's hands. She offers to give up all thought of Lovelace if she may be free of Solmes. All in vain.

Meanwhile, Lovelace, incensed by the hostility of the Harlowe family and by Clarissa's readiness to renounce him, begins to spread his snares. If he could gain Clarissa without marriage it would be a "rape worthy of Jove." He establishes a spy, Joseph Leman, as a servant in the Harlowe household, learns all that goes on there, introduces wild inflammatory rumors of his own hostile intentions, and suggestions of harshness to Clarissa on the part of her family, which will and do tend to drive her to him for refuge. He goes elaborately round about to bring to her ears reports of his kindness, generosity and trustworthiness as if accidentally by way of Miss Howe. Thus inflamed unconsciously by Lovelace, Clarissa's family proceed step by step in cruelty and oppression till she is virtually imprisoned, cut off one by one from every resource and every hope of relief or sympathy from uncles, aunts, cousins or friends. They dismiss her old nurse Mrs. Norton and her good servant Hannah, and set over her as spy and executioner her sister's confidential servant, Betty Barnes; they forbid her to come into the presence of her father or her mother, who seem to fear the effects of her persuasion and her logic. They confine her to her room and the garden, and so far as they can, completely as they believe, cut off her communications outside the house, but she still communicates with Miss Howe and with Lovelace by leaving and taking up letters from a secret place in the wood house. She offers to give up Lovelace and vow never to marry; she offers to give over her fortune to Arabella, who may marry Solmes for the advancement of the family, but nothing will serve. Her father goes on with preparations for her marriage with Solmes, and sets the date. She has every reason to believe that they will use force to bring it about. She overhears James and Arabella planning to keep up her parents' resentment against her. In despair she writes to Lovelace that she will meet him and throw herself on the protection of the ladies of his family unless she lets him know before the appointed time that she has changed her mind. She leaves a letter telling him that she has changed her mind, but he does not take it up, and she feels that she must meet him to tell him so. While they are debating her refusal, she is terrified by clash of arms and shouting which she thinks is her people attacking those of Lovelace—really it is a contrivance of his. She runs with Lovelace, who pulls her into the coach and carries her away. Lovelace makes the Harlowe family think she went with him of her own will. Clarissa writes to Miss Howe "in the utmost anguish of mind" when she realizes something of what has happened to her.

She perceives that she is in a very serious predicament, and sets bravely to work to try to extricate herself. Immediately she writes to her family, for above all she wishes reconciliation with them. She asks to be allowed to return to them or to retire to her own estate on condition that she comply with all their requirements except marriage with Solmes. She assures them that no promise binds her to marry Lovelace. She urges them to be lenient because her reputation is suffering, and her reputation is dearer to her than life itself. They, however, are not only obdurate but actively hostile. They succeed in arousing Anna Howe's mother against Clarissa so that she can find no refuge there, and declare that they will not accept the mediations of the ladies of Lovelace's family. Next she asks Lovelace to take her to some place of safety where she will be independent, and leave her to try again for a reconciliation. He agrees, and seems to be seeking a suitable abode for her; actually he sees to it that rumors reach her to the effect that James is planning to capture her and force her marriage with Solmes, which makes it seem necessary for him to stand by for her protection. Miss Howe urges Clarissa to marry Lovelace at once; it is the only solution, for her family will not relent. Clarissa is of the same mind, not realizing that it is no longer for her to choose. Lovelace now has the power in his own hands; he may marry her if and when he likes. He decides to try to gain her without marriage, to try her resistance to the utmost. If it holds out, he will marry her; if not, they will live together on his terms. His game with Clarissa thereafter is like that of a superior chess player who forces his opponent's every move, but he does it so skilfully that she does not perceive it. He seems to urge marriage, but he does it as he proposed to Arabella, always in some way to which she cannot quite assent. Or again he will suggest that he would urge it were it not for the terms which she imposed on him when she put herself under his protection, that he should keep his distance at all times. These injunctions which she laid on him in her resentment at the trick by which he carried her off, he ingeniously uses now for his purpose instead of for her protection, and she is quite unable to declare that they are all to be laid aside. Miss Howe urges her to swallow so much of her modesty as may be necessary to bring him to terms. Clarissa replies that marriage is not now in her power. She does not understand why Lovelace should be so bashful. He seems to be doing everything in his power to make her situation easy and to gain her esteem; for example, to have her maid Hannah and Mrs. Norton come and live with her at a time when he knows that the effort to get them will be vain. Meanwhile Clarissa's overtures to her sister and to her Aunt Hervey meet with cruel rebuffs. Arabella informs her that they will receive no further letters from her; they will send her clothes; they have given up all thoughts of bringing her back; they consider her irretrievably ruined. Her father has laid upon her a terrible curse, "that you may meet your punishment both here and hereafter, by means of the very wretch in whom you have chosen to place your wicked confidence." Clarissa is shocked by this into a dangerous nervous breakdown which frightens Lovelace into urging immediate marriage, but she defers it pending her recovery.

Thus Lovelace's feelings alternate between tenderness and childish

resentment at Clarissa's ability to resist his charms; her "coldness" as
he calls it. At length he arranges a stratagem; he takes a dose which
produces symptoms of violent illness. Her concern brings both Lovelace and herself to the conviction that she loves him, but this does not
bring him any nearer to his goal, and he attempts still more wiles and
stratagems, the most elaborate he has yet attempted, to bring her to
his will by love and gentleness. The attempt fails, and he, despairing
of gentle methods, and feeling that his reputation as a rake is in the
balance, plans something more harsh. He has a fire set in one of the
servants' rooms at night, and in the alarm and confusion rushes into
Clarissa's room. In her resistance she attempts suicide, which he
prevents. The next morning he goes out to get a marriage license, and
while he is absent she escapes from the house, convinced of his baseness. After some search, Lovelace discovers the place of her retirement, and sets himself patiently and ingeniously to work to allay her
fears and regain lost ground. It is a long process, but at last he gets
her back into his own hands by having two women in his pay im-
personate his aunt and his cousin. Promptly he proceeds to extreme
measures; he has her drugged, and ravishes her. She is stupefied and
delirious for more than a week afterwards; then tries to escape again,
but is prevented. Lovelace declares that he will make amends by
marriage, but she indignantly rejects the suggestion; "thinkest thou
that marriage will satisfy for guilt like thine?" She considers herself
"a lost creature to this world," and asks Lovelace not to withhold her
from entering on a life of severe penitence to secure the only hope she
has left, that for eternity. He refuses to release her, and she tries to
escape, unsuccessfully once or twice, but at last she gets away. Her
heart is broken; she suffers hardship, poverty and persecution, including cruel insults from Arabella. At the end her only friend besides
Miss Howe is Lovelace's correspondent, Belford. After Clarissa's
death, Lovelace has alternate fits of repentance and swaggering. He
falls in a duel with Col. Morden, Clarissa's cousin, and is repentant
when he dies.

While the story of Clarissa was appearing in parts, many
were the pleas that came to Richardson to "save" her, first from
violation, second from death. They are better tributes to the
hearts than to the heads of his readers. If he had heeded their
pleas, his work would have been the merest melodrama. As it

stands, it is high tragedy. It puts our spirits to the tests of sympathy and awe. It poses the unanswerable problem of sin and suffering. To Clarissa the problem is insoluble; no move that she can make is in every sense right; anything she can do is in some sense wrong. Like the protagonists of the greatest tragedies, she strains the theory of the "tragic flaw" to the breaking point, for she has no tragic flaw except that she is human, she is a woman, she is what she is. Of such a story death is the only possible ending. Yet generation after generation of readers have known it no better than to see in it only a bald allegory teaching that the wages of sin is death, that when lovely woman stoops to folly she can do no better than to die. And if we may read the English novel as an index of conventional morality, we might well believe that this idea originated with Richardson and prevailed unchanged and almost unchallenged from his time through the nineteenth century. The idea may have grown out of Richardson's work, but it is not what he tells us in *Clarissa*. Clarissa lost her virginity, and her death was one of the consequences of the loss, but nowhere does Richardson seem to suggest that death always has been and always will be the inevitable consequence of such a loss.

Clarissa's death is inevitable as a sign that the earthly drama is closed, that there is no earthly recompense, no earthly sequel to her suffering. Clarissa has not stooped to folly. Her death is not to cover her guilt, for guilt she has none; not to give repentance to her lover, for he has repented and begged to make such atonement as he sees it in his power to give. She is tainted by misfortune with a stain that she and society feel to be ineradicable. It makes her earthly life to her hopeless in so far as usefulness and happiness are concerned. Logically, then, she turns her mind to the life eternal. Of that, her prospects, she feels, would not be improved by her marrying Lovelace, and the penance of living with him. Most of those who have found it a sermon on the text, "The wages of sin is death," have understood the text as little as the sermon. St. Paul used the phrase as an epigrammatic summing up at the end of an exposition of the effect of sin on the human mind and spirit. His point is that if sin has not dominion over you, then neither has death dominion over you. He says the same thing in the following epistle, that to the Corinthians: "The sting of death is sin," he says, and again, "when this mortal shall have put on immortality . . . death is swallowed up in victory. O death, where is thy sting? O grave, where is thy victory?" Is not this very much what Richardson means? Death must come to Clarissa and to Lovelace, but her integrity swallows it up in victory, its sting is for him. Death is thus not a punishment to Clarissa for her sin, but the consummation of the tragedy, its necessary finale.

Beside all this, Goldsmith's little song from *The Vicar of Wakefield*, "When lovely woman stoops to folly," seems absurdly frivolous, a *vers de société* version of a tragedy, *Hamlet* served up in a triolet, *Lear* in a limerick. In its context, it is merely a rococo touch of pathos in an Arcadian romance; Rowlandson drew a plate to illustrate the episode which he entitled "The Fair Penitent." Yet it has been the standard expression of a standard of conduct for Pamela's daughters from Richardson's time through Thomas Hardy's. Prevailingly, too, it has been the conventional code of morality, and too prevailingly society has acted on it by relentless ostracism and persecution of any woman who willingly or unwillingly, actually or reputedly, has lost her virginity without marriage. In various times and places, society has prescribed death as the legal penalty, but not so often for fornication as for adultery. But where can we find before Richardson an example of a heroine who is doomed to perish according to Goldsmith's law? Heroines have died before 1740, and worms have eaten them, but not for loss of virginity.

Among many tribes and nations premarital virginity has not been, perhaps is not, much esteemed; some codes call for its

ritual or deliberate destruction. Among the Hebrews in biblical times it was esteemed, and there is much to say in various
books of the Old Testament against fornication. The Church
Fathers carried the principle to extremes, and had much ado to
reconcile the injunction "be fruitful and multiply" with St.
Paul's predilection for virginity. In the early ages of Christianity, and in the Middle Ages, the officers of the Church preached
against all forms of unchastity, but kept the source of their authority, the Bible, to themselves in languages which few of their
hearers could read, and at times, if we may believe reports, some
of them set a bad example. In feudal times, the response of
courtly listeners to these exhortations on conduct was the code
of courtly love, according to which a married woman might
have as many lovers as she chose so long as she was instigated
by love and by no other consideration, so long as she was off
with the old love before she was on with the new, and so long
as she successfully hoodwinked her husband. "Better death
than dishonor" as an item in the chivalric code, if it had anything to do with women, applied to married women in the eyes
of their husbands, who were the interested parties because they
did not wish to see titles and estates go to other men's sons.
As for virgins, a gentleman might offer his daughter to an
esteemed guest as an accommodation for the night without noticeably damaging her chances of marriage. There is no reason to
think that the peasants and workers took the doctrine of chastity
very seriously. Doubtless their sexual life was according to their
code; if they confessed their peccadillos to the priest, they did
their penance and received their absolution, and no one died
of shame or grief. But when the Bible came out in the vernacular and people could read it for themselves, respect for the biblical injunctions grew up with puritanism, with the middle class,
and with notions of the sanctity of property, including property
rights in women and in their virginity. And by the time the middle class rose to the level of self-expression in literature, it had

evolved the Goldsmith law, that a woman who stooped to folly, or to whom folly stooped, was of no further use to herself or to the world, and might as well get out of it. When the middle class attained self-expression in literature, its own peculiar medium was the novel, and it is the novel that most conspicuously promulgates the doctrine.

Before the novel the doctrine is not conspicuous. Goldsmith's law is an outgrowth of puritanism and middle-class manners. The biblical law is severe on all forms of sexual uncleanness, but it does not suggest that a damsel who is victim of rape or seduction should have no will to live, or that she can settle any scores by dying of grief or shame. Lucretia was a victim of rape, and she committed suicide, but she was a wife, not a virgin; her responsibility was to her husband. She decided to surrender her wifely chastity in order to live long enough to vindicate her reputation. She was successful; she is known as the "chaste" Lucretia. Medieval tales of the sort seldom have to do with virgins, but are such as come under the rulings of the courts of love. Criseyde is a widow, and when she yields to Troilus, all is as it should be. Chaucer's infinite pity flows out to her when she is unfaithful to Troilus, and it is this trespass, not against propriety but against love, that she expiates pitifully in Henryson's poem.

In Elizabethan drama, the theme we are following is by no means common; almost the only example at all to our purpose is Shakespeare's *Measure for Measure*. The core of this play is sexual experience, about which Shakespeare arranged his characters in their various attitudes to round out his treatment of the theme. Of these attitudes, those of Isabella, Juliet, Angelo and Mariana are most significant here. Isabella's is that of the fastidious girl maturing to that of the normal woman. Juliet plays the fair penitent, Angelo the puritan, and Mariana the pattern of courtly love, or the lady of the Renaissance. "Lord Angelo is precise";

> *Stands at a guard with envy; scarce confesses*
> *That his blood flows, or that his appetite*
> *Is more to bread than stone.*

He values his reputation,

> *my gravity,*
> *Wherein, let no man hear me, I take pride.*

In public he is unswerving in demanding the severest penalty of the law for an offense to which he is tempted at the first private opportunity. At the very outset the Duke gives him kindly warning to the effect that ingrowing virtues lose themselves and their uses.

> *Angelo,*
> *There is a kind of character in thy life,*
> *That to th' observer doth thy history*
> *Fully unfold. Thyself and thy belongings*
> *Are not thine own so proper, as to waste*
> *Thyself upon thy virtues, they on thee.*
> *Heaven doth with us as we with torches do,*
> *Not light them for themselves; for if our virtues*
> *Did not go forth of us, 'twere all alike*
> *As if we had them not. Spirits are not finely touch'd*
> *But to fine issues, . . .*

Angelo is not finely touched. His mind is not large enough to hold more than a line or two of what the Duke says; he gathers only that if virtues do not go forth of us, 'twere all alike as if we had them not, and all he makes of it is that if they do seem to go forth of us it is not necessary to have them at all. This is just about the way the great words of the leaders dwindle to fit the narrow minds of the followers. Moralists of the eighteenth century who tell girls to guard their "honour" (reputation) for when it is blemished all is lost, remind us of Lord Angelo who prides himself on outward and visible signs when the inward and spiritual grace is lacking. We are justified, then, in thinking of him as a puritan, though Shakespeare does not name him so.

Isabella, in the beginning, is intolerant, but her intolerance is not that of puritanism but of purity; her inflexibility is not that of the formalist but of youthful high ideals. Immediately she is forced to plead for her brother's life who has committed the sin to her most repugnant. Such experiences lead her in the end to plead for the life of Angelo himself, who has refused her plea and tried to involve her in the repugnant sin. She feels that Claudio should gladly surrender his life on the scruple of her virginity, but there she asks no sacrifice that she would not give. Her feeling of "better death than dishonor" is sincere adherence to a high ideal. If she did not feel it she would not act on it because a puritanical society told her she ought to feel it. Juliet is pregnant by her affianced lover, Isabella's brother, Claudio, withheld from marriage by lack of dowry. She has given all for love, and seems to feel the world well lost; she does not challenge the price of what she has had in view of its value. She is ready to pay. Her conscience is not very sore.

> I do repent me, as it is an evil,
> And take the shame with joy.

Here is penitence of a sort, but not shame enough to be fatal. Juliet's love is quite as human as it is spiritual; she begins where Isabella ends.

Isabella, on her way from hyper-fastidiousness to normality, leads Mariana into just such a situation as Juliet's. If Juliet's act is sin, and so Isabella regards it at the time, it is virtue which she induces Mariana to sacrifice to save her (Isabella's) virginity. But she has for it a sanction which she takes to be that of the Church, for it is pronounced by the "good friar," though it is actually that of the supreme political authority, the Duke. Mariana, too, trusts the friar,—

DUKE: Do you persuade yourself that I respect you?
MARI.: Good friar, I know you do, and oft have found it.

who assures her that she does nothing wrong in going to Angelo:

> *Nor, gentle daughter, fear you not at all.*
> *He is your husband on a pre-contract:*
> *To bring you thus together is no sin . . .*

Mariana feels no puritanical or Protestant sense of personal responsibility for her conduct. She suggests the Renaissance feeling in that precedents for her behavior are in the pages of Boccaccio, and in that her case which would get a verdict of death under Goldsmith's law would be dismissed in a court of love.

The earliest record we have of *Measure for Measure* is a note of its performance in 1604. Milton's *Comus* appeared in 1634. The thirty years between saw the death of the greatest Elizabethan and the dawn of the mightiest Puritan. *Comus* stands first in the chronological list of Milton's works. It is a court masque; he wrote it when he was young and under the spell of poetry, before he was oppressed with the duties of Puritanism and had subdued his pen to their uses. Its basis is Puritanism; its color and perfume are of the Renaissance. Comus, god of pleasure, offers his cup of beauty and enchantment to the virtuous virgin, who rejects it with scorn. Comus threatens her with the power of his enchantments, and is about to work them on her body—her mind and spirit have declared their independence—when her brothers, warned by her attendant spirit, rush in and save her. The Elder Brother has much to say of the power of true chastity.

> *My sister is not so defenseless left*
> *As you imagine; she has a hidden strength,*
> *Which you remember not.*

SEC. BRO.   *What hidden strength?*
> *Unless the strength of Heaven, if you mean that?*

ELD. BRO. *I mean that too, but yet a hidden strength,*

Which, if Heaven gave it, may be termed her own.
'Tis chastity, my brother, chastity:
She that has that is clad in complete steel,
And, like a quivered nymph with arrows keen,
May trace huge forests, and unharboured heaths,
Infamous hills, and sandy perilous wilds;
Where, through the sacred rays of chastity,
No savage fierce, bandite, or mountaineer,
Will dare to soil her virgin purity.
Yea, there where very desolation dwells,
By grots and caverns shagged with horrid shades,
She may pass on with unblenched majesty,
Be it not done in pride, or in presumption.
Some say no evil thing that walks by night,
In fog or fire, by lake or moorish fen,
Blue meagre hag, or stubborn unlaid ghost,
That breaks his magic chains at curfew time,
No goblin or swart faery of the mine,
Hath hurtful power o'er true virginity.

This looks towards the Renaissance, Spenser's Una wandering through perils guarded by the lion which her innocence commands, virgins whose virginity can tame deadly unicorns, theme of Renaissance tapestries, and all the powers of virginity in the late romances. It looks no less to puritan novels of the eighteenth century which seem to owe as much to Milton as to Richardson for their frequent scenes of damsels rescued from the ravisher in the nick of time. The supernatural device of the Attendant Spirit omitted, this appears more often a matter of mere chance than of heavenly intervention.

Milton does not suggest what would have happened if the Lady had fallen victim to the enchantment, but there is a possible inference that might have had its effect in shaping Goldsmith's law. Heaven protects the chaste; chastity protects itself, chastity protects her who has it; the theme sounds insistently on the mightiest instrument of Puritan music. If, then, the girl falls victim to Comus, what can we infer but that her armor of chastity was not so complete as we supposed? Steele tells us this in plain terms without allegory. It is in the story of Jenny Distaff, cited above on p. 51. She has so far overcome her inclination to a gentleman who attempted her chastity as to refuse him when he offers her marriage. "The conquest of passion," she concludes, "gives ten times more happiness than we can reap from the gratification of it, and she that has got over such a one as mine, will stand among beaux and pretty fellows, with as much safety as in a summer's day among grasshoppers and butterflies." The true chastity that protects itself is that founded on inclination conquered by will. The armor of chastity is not effective till it has been heated by passion and cooled by resistant will. Steele's figure is a *vers de société* expression of *Comus* thoroughly characteristic of its author, the sternest doctrine of puritanism in terms of beaux and butterflies. It is enough to make us think of Steele as the father of Pamela and the grandfather of most of her daughters, so clearly does this sentence show the protoplasm of all the puritan and anti-Roussellian novels from the will-against-passion of Richardson to the sense-against-sensibility of Jane Austen.

Where does the Milton-Steele doctrine of protective chastity leave Clarissa? First off, one would say that her situation is that of the Lady in *Comus,* and its outcome is what would have befallen her if the brothers had not intervened. The draught which Lovelace administered is the working of the enchantment on her body; when he exercises its power he forfeits all hope of attaining dominion over her mind and spirit. Before that, he was justified in entertaining the hope, for she loved him, and he her; nothing but "his libertine reasons," his pride in his reputation as a rake, stood in the way of their ultimate happiness. If she had married him and been prosperous she would have loved him dearly; she confessed to Miss Howe that she loved him before she saw his design fully revealed. Humanly she was perfect, but in the eyes of heaven, or in the view the puritan thought he got by looking through such eyes, her armor of chastity was not perfectly tempered.

If the flaw in Clarissa's armor of chastity was her inclination to Lovelace, it would seem that no armor of chastity is serviceable if a woman have the slightest first motion of desire toward any man whatsoever. No doubt the source of this idea is St. Paul, whose doctrine is subject to the same difficulty of adjustment to actual life as is that of the puritans. St. Paul had to compromise the counsel of perfection; man being what he is, it is better to marry than to burn. So it is in the puritan sermons of the eighteenth century. Steele made *The Ladies Library* of essays "supposed to be collected out of the several writings of our greatest divines, and are disposed under proper heads, in order to fix in the mind general rules for conduct in all the circumstances of the life of woman." The sermon on chastity tells us by way of definition that chastity is

a triumph over a desire which nature has imprinted in the heart of man, fierce and unruly . . . Chastity suppresses whatever is unlawful in this passion; and all desire is unlawful, which is not warranted by marriage, which is not within the order of nature, and the moderation of Christian modesty.

Such is the influence of St. Paul on the English novel. The puritans use his doctrine as heavy artillery against their opponents, and inject it as preventive serum into the veins of their daughters. No wonder no self-respecting heroine can admit that she has the slightest inclination to any man until she is warranted by marriage. It is easy to believe that centuries of this Christian modesty have given us generations of frigid women; some of these were novelists whose frigid heroines were praised for self-control. Even if carnal copulation be warranted, can it ever be within the moderation of Christian modesty? The Church raised the question long ago, but we did not take it to heart till we began to read the Bible for ourselves, and we forgot it as soon as we stopped reading the Bible for ourselves. Two centuries of that Bible-reading time were those of the English novel. Its heroines were girls with the doctrine of St. Paul in their veins; its frail ones were those whose inoculation did not "take." The good girls must not know they are in love until they are warranted safe by marriage, lest they should cause the little rift in the armor of chastity which will impair its completeness of strength and forfeit the favor of heaven. The importance of being a prude in the novel is the demonstration of the application of this doctrine to life. The puritan preacher who defines chastity in *The Ladies Library* tells his "fair" hearers that modesty is the means by which chastity preserves itself and them. Rakes are dangerous enemies;

It is a melancholy reflection that, . . . our age has arrived to as compendious arts of this kind as industrious vice can suggest . . . Wherefore the best way for women to countermine those stratagems of men, is to be superciliously vigilant even of the first approaches. He who means to defend a fort must not abandon the outworks: and she who will secure her chastity must never let it come to a close siege, but repel the most remote insinuations of a tempter.

Modesty, then, preserves chastity like paint; "Save the surface and you save all."

The number of *The Tatler* in which Jenny Distaff tells her story is dated June 5, 1709. Between that and the time of *Pamela* and *Clarissa* we have other examples of more and less unfortunate heroines. Ardelisa in Penelope Aubin's *Count of Vinevil* does not trust to Heaven to protect her virginity, nor in her chastity to protect itself, but protects them by direct measures, assassination and arson. These measures also release Violetta who has been for a year or two in Osmin's harem, to which she came a maid "but out a maid never departed more." She escapes to Europe where the first effect of the experience is melancholy.

Violetta only seemed melancholy: the loss of her Honour, and the dismal Impression the way of Life she had led with *Osmin* had made in her Soul, no Change of Condition could perfectly efface; she thought only of retiring to a religious House, to weep for a Sin, of which she was in reality altogether innocent.

She condemns herself:

. . . till I saw *Ardelisa,* I found my Conscience undisturb'd . . . But that noble Lady's heroick Conduct has convinc'd me, I did not what I ought: she never would have permitted a lustful *Turk* to possess her, but, by his Death would have preserv'd her Honour; or, resisting to Death, would not have surviv'd it. I am no longer friends with myself, and long to hide my Face in a Convent, where Tears shall wash away the Stains of his Embraces:

But a priest consoles her:

The Priest answer'd, "Madam, you are deceiv'd: in *Ardelisa,* who was marry'd to another, it would have been a horrid Crime to suffer another man to possess her; but as you were single, a Virgin, and made his by the Chance of War, it was no Sin in you to Yield to him, and it would have been wilful Murder to have kill'd him, or but conspir'd his Death: nay, a sin not to have been faithful to his Bed, whilst he is living you ought not to marry, you might have been a means of his Conversion; you ought to pray for him, and consider he acted according to his Knowledge and Education." *Violetta* thank'd him, and seem'd much reviv'd.

A suitor for her hand soon comes forward, Capt. Mons. de Feuillade, who, she admits when he declares himself, is acceptable to her. He dismisses the harem experience as no obstacle to their marriage.

. . . no Circumstance remains to bar me from being happy; . . . You are not pre-engag'd, the Villain who possessed that lovely Person, had no Title to it but lawless Force; he neither was a Christian nor a

Husband; he us'd you as his Slave, and, doubtless would, whene'er
his brutish Lust inclin'd him to a Change, have bestow'd you on some
Favourite-Slave to use or poison you.

Violetta rehearses the priest's argument; she cannot be his while
Osmin lives. Then opportunely, as such things happen in romances, a ship arrives bringing news of Osmin's death. Violetta stipulates six months' interval for decency's sake, and at
the end of that time marries de Feuillade. All this is contrived for its purpose, which is to echo the courtly love procedure of the old romance with enough flavor of Christianity
to suit the palate of the time. The judgment that a virgin
enforced may be accepted in marriage for the virginity of her
mind savors of the old code. It is according to the newer code
that she feels contamination, and saves her face by professing
some regard for Osmin and by treating her connection with him
as if it had been a Christian marriage. We note that the judgment which would have been that of a court of love in the
former age is here pronounced by an officer of the Church,
and that Violetta compares Ardelisa's experience with her own
on nearly the basis of the Milton-Steele test of true chastity.
Ardelisa's chastity came through intact; it must have been the
real thing. Probably Violetta's scarcely acknowledged regard
for Osmin was the weakness in her armor.

The Count of Vinevil is hardly more than a chap-book; it
has only 138 pages of large type. A chap-book too is *The Perjured Citizen,* 1732, a pamphlet of fifty-five pages printed to sell
for a shilling. It is a rather bald tale of illicit love ending
in murder, offering itself as "a warning to the youth of both
sexes." We might accept it as fact without the elaborate
protestations of the preface, were it not for the romantic contrivances to bring in unromantic bits of puritanical moralizing.
The preface announces it as a "dreadful example of ungov-
ern'd passion," and the very first words of the narrative are,
"The dreadful consequences which have attended giving way to

the passions . . ." The passion is sexual desire masquerading as love. Matilda is a rich merchant's daughter who seduces her master's clerk to be her paramour, and murders him when he leaves her to marry a virtuous maid. The tale leaves her under the shadow of the gallows. Her stooping to folly is merely the first step on the way to dusty death, but death is not the result of the stooping except as both come from the character of ungoverned passion. But the brief tale is a direct step toward the long ones of Richardson, and in the development of Goldsmith's law.

An interesting indicator of fashions in morals before and after Richardson is Mrs. Eliza Haywood. Two of her shorter romances or chap-book-novels are *Lasselia,* 1724, and *The Unequal Conflict,* 1725, shilling pamphlets of less than a hundred pages each. Mrs. Haywood calls *Lasselia* a novel, and, like the author of *The Perjured Citizen,* anticipates Richardson in announcing her purpose.

> My design in writing this little novel (as well as those I have formerly published) being only to remind the unthinking part of the world, how dangerous it is to give way to passion, will, I hope, excuse the too great warmth, which may perhaps appear in some particular pages, for without the expression being invigorated in some measure proportionate to the subject, 'twould be impossible for a reader to be sensible how far it touches him, or how probable it is that he is falling into those inadvertencies which the examples I relate would caution him to avoid.

But if her purpose is puritanical the effect is (as one guesses from her announcement of it) quite cavalier. The King seeks Lasselia for his mistress, a station which would seem to be one of glory rather than of infamy. She avoids it for reasons not specified, flees to the country, where she falls in love with a married man, and seeking to flee to him, feels guilty when her friends praise her virtuous avoidance of the King.

[They] applauded her resolution; and told her they could not enough extol her bravery of soul, who, to preserve her honour, could be blind and deaf to all the enchanting charms of power and grandeur, and chuse rather to be buried in an innocent obscurity, than shine the envy of the world in guilty greatness.

Lasselia, however, has enough conscience to feel that she is guilty in intent, though not yet guilty in act.

These encomiums were not perhaps so pleasing to Lasselia as they imagined; a consciousness of not meriting what they said, embittered all the sweets such praises, if deserved, would have bestowed: therefore waving [*sic*] all that might remind her of how criminal she really was . . .

Mrs. Haywood's profession that Lasselia is really criminal is more clearly expressed than dramatized. She tells us, too, that Lasselia was taking long chances in becoming de l'Amye's mistress.

. . . it was but a chance whether by putting herself under his protection she should not fall into the most miserable circumstance to which a fond believing woman can possibly be subjected; and in such a venture there were ten thousand blanks to one prize. But fortune in this particular was on her side . . .

This is not at all according to the puritan law of probabilities, which, if the chances were ten thousand to one in her favor would have thrown the game against her. In the same passage Mrs. Haywood declares herself as not of the puritan party. In speaking of the lover's trustworthiness, she says,

. . . Such a ruin (as by the nicely virtuous the sacrifice she made him of her honour could be called no other) was too pleasing to permit her to repent it.

The term "nicely virtuous" is clearly the cavalier characterization of the puritan, and the attitude toward what the puritan calls "ruin" is that of the Restoration comedy. Whatever her professions, then, it is clear that Mrs. Haywood's code is that of courtly love; whatever is lost for love, though it be the world (which Lasselia renounces in the end by taking the veil), is well lost.

So it is in *The Unequal Conflict* and its sequel, in which two heroines are both transgressors. Antonia, unhappily married, is deeply and secretly in love with Coeurdemont, and inadvertently substitutes for her maid in an assignation with him in a dark room, so secretly that he does not know that he has had the mistress and not the maid. Philenia is courted by Fillamour, once affianced to her but now married to another, who gains her in a propitious moment by a combination of surprise, persuasion and force. Separated from her, Fillamour afterward lives with another mistress, Misimene. Philenia, Misimene, and Antonia's husband perish in the course of their wild adventures, leaving Fillamour to a life of mourning, and Antonia and Coeurdemont to married bliss. This tale Mrs. Haywood moralizes as follows:

> Thus was the crime of giving way to unwarrantable passion, punished in the persons of Philenia and Misimene, and that of perjury and ingratitude in Fillamour; while the constancy of Antonia, and the honour of Coeurdemont, received the reward their virtues merited, and they continued, to their lives end, great and shining examples of conjugal affection.

What Mrs. Haywood says here is that she has shaped her story to the ends of poetic justice, but if she knows what justice is she belies it, as the most cursory examination shows. If Fillamour is guilty of adultery, Antonia's act, voluntary or not, is no less. If Philenia's lapse from virtue was by surprise and force, she was as innocent as Antonia. Either both are equally innocent or equally guilty, yet Antonia lives happily ever after and Philenia dies in the manner of tragedy. Coeurdemont is perhaps a shade less guilty than Fillamour; he committed adultery unwittingly when he "intended only fornication."

Yet the one is rewarded and the other punished. Mrs. Haywood rewards what she calls the "constancy" of Antonia. This is according to the code of the courts of love, the courtly-chivalric code, not that of the bourgeoisie or the puritans. She is a married woman in love with a man not her husband. Her constancy is merely her secrecy and her persistence in the pursuit of her amour. Her secrecy is such that though she is fairly burning with love, no one guesses it, and she enjoys her lover so secretly that not even he, much less her husband, knows it. Clearly enough, all this is more in the vein of Chaucer or Boccaccio than that of John Milton or John Bunyan.

Both Milton and Bunyan, however, echo distinctly in a later work of Mrs. Haywood's, for after *Pamela* had set a new fashion in fiction Mrs. Haywood changed her style to follow it. In 1751 she came out with *The History of Miss Betsy Thoughtless,* a full-length novel in four volumes, an early example, perhaps the first, of the faulty heroine. The fault is that for which she is named, thoughtlessness, as a result of which she is giddy, vain of conquest, vain of her power over men, a coquette; otherwise she has every virtue, for she is essentially innocent and good at heart. Her fault leads her into many perilous situations, her reputation suffers, she loses the best of her lovers, marries the worst, suffers cruelly in his hands, but survives him, and marries Mr. Trueworth, whose old passion for her revives in time for him to marry her and have in her chastened behavior the benefit of the severe penance she had undergone for her thoughtlessness. In twenty-five years, then, a change has come over the spirit of Eliza Haywood's dream. In 1725, heroines may depart from the path of chastity, marry and live happily ever after. In 1751, for the sin of levity a heroine is condemned to penance by which she learns sobriety. In *Lasselia,* Mrs. Haywood spoke slightingly of "the merely virtuous." The whole lesson of *The History of Miss Betsy Thoughtless* is to teach girls to be just that. One of Betsy's advisers is Mr. Goodman, a name that might have come from *The Pilgrim's Progress,* as might that of Mr. Trueworth, and others in the book. After one of Betsy's escapades has nearly ended in the maid's tragedy, Mr. Goodman tells her

> that the honour of a young maid like you, is a flower of so tender and delicate a nature, that the least breath of scandal withers and destroys it.—In fine, that it is not enough to be good, without behaving in such a manner as shall make others acknowledge us to be so.

"Honour," it seems, is not only "virtue" but reputation also. But the use of having our virtues go forth of us is not, as the Duke said to Angelo, to kindle the torch in others, but as Angelo seems to understand it, merely for the advantage of good name to ourselves in this world. Fanny Burney, whom *Betsy Thoughtless* may have inspired to write *Evelina* on the same theme, accepts solemnly this utilitarian narrowing of the Duke's principle. Reverend Mr. Villars writes to Evelina, "Remember, my dear Evelina, nothing is so delicate as the reputation of a woman: it is at once the most beautiful and most brittle of human things." When Jane Austen came on this line, she giggled, and in *Pride and Prejudice* she shed on it the silvery laughter and the oblique light of the Comic Spirit.

When Mrs. Haywood was about sixteen years old, she might have read the 126th *Tatler* in which Steele characterized the Prude and the Coquette as having each "the distinction of sex in all her thoughts, words and actions," the Coquette the Cavalier woman, the Prude the Puritan. Forty-two years later she dramatized the character of the coquette, ran her through four volumes of penitential training, and turned her out a Puritan. Is it an allegory of her own change of literary fashion? Her heroine escapes the power of Comus through the opportune arrival of her elder brother. Betsy is not deserving of the protection of Heaven, for she has walked deliberately into her perils "in pride and in presumption" (her coquetry and vanity of conquest), and has dallied with danger in heedless love of pleasure. This conduct leads her straight into the power of the rake, where "her ruin had certainly been completed, if a loud knocking at the door had not prevented him from prosecuting his design." As in *Comus* it is her brother who saves her, but there is no indication that it is anything more than luck that he arrives in the nick of time, unless it be in Betsy's account to him of the matter afterwards, which she "ended with saying, she was sure it was heaven alone that gave her strength to prevent the perpetration of the villain's intentions." Such are the steps by which Milton's great allegory descends into the theory so often expressed in the nineteenth-century melodrama, that heaven will protect the working girl. The phrase would characterize a host of facile novels in which the bodily chastity of the heroine is preserved by unmotivated devices, mostly undeserved luck, merely to be provocative of further pursuit and attack.

Coeval with some of Mrs. Haywood's earlier romances are Defoe's two novels, *Moll Flanders,* 1722, and *The Fortunate Mistress,* 1724. We have seen how Moll first stooped to folly, and how she once stood under the shadow of the gallows, but she did not die then, nor at last as a consequence of her "folly." Roxana began with marriage, and her transgressions thereafter led her rather towards riches than towards death. There is much puritan moralizing along the way in both narratives, but nothing worth mentioning that derives from Milton or Steele, or points to Richardson or Goldsmith. We have seen that where the choice is prostitution or death, these women do not choose death. Neither does Goldsmith's law condemn them, for it applies to "lovely woman," and these women make no pretensions to loveliness. Moll Flanders and Roxana are not trying to soothe any melancholy, wash any guilt, or give repentance to any lover; death beckons not to them.

One of Richardson's commentators, E. A. Baker, remarks that

the plot of *Pamela* "was not one which required any very daring effort of imagination at that period." It could have been founded on news reports with little change. Even as Pamela's story was going through the press the editor of the *Gentleman's Magazine* printed an account of an experience strikingly like hers, as a lesson to the female sex; "as a high Sense of Virtue and Honour is a Woman's greatest Safeguard, it cannot be too often inculcated." The story is of a young girl brought up to be virtuous by her mother, who is beseiged with dishonorable intentions by the brother of the young lady to whom she acts as a companion. When he became "rude and boisterous" in his attack, she resolved to leave, and gave notice to her mistress, the young man's mother, who forced her to tell the cause. On learning it, she sent for him and gave him her permission "to make Reparation for the Injury he had offered" by accepting her with honor. Like Pamela, the young lady tells her own story; unlike Pamela, she cuts it short: "Farther Description of my Behaviour would be tedious; I could not give a denial to such a Proposal. I shall in Gratitude endeavour to make his Life a continued scene of Felicity and Content." Heaven protected the working girl—this time. At other times, according to the *Gentleman's Magazine,* it was not so propitious.

December 26, 1763

A destitute girl applied for assistance at a public house, and three young fellows under pretence of helping her to a lodging decoyed her into a hayloft, where they all severally lay with her and robbed her of what little she had. The three were committed to gaol.

May 11, 1765

"A most shocking scene of brutal passion near Bath." A band of thirteen or fourteen miscreants fell on a young man and his sweetheart on the road. They beat him, and carrying her to a by-lane, about nine or ten successfully used her ill, when she was rescued by two gentlemen. The unhappy girl has since made oath against them, but they have escaped.

July, 1773

At session of Old Bailey, John Leonard, a bailiff's follower, received sentence of death for ravishing Miss Ann Boss, who was a lodger in a house into which he had carried an execution. When the maid went out, he was first rude to Miss Boss, then, being repulsed, behaved to her in a manner too shocking to be mentioned. She screamed out, and made all the resistance in her power, seized the villain by the throat and struggled until she lost her senses. A neighbor hearing and suspecting knocked and inquired the cause of the noise; Leonard stuck his head out of the window and said it was only a drunken woman. [Note the resemblance of the stratagem to Lovelace's successful one.]

And working girls were not the only ones who needed the protection of Heaven.

January, 1772

Late at night, a gentleman and his sister having taken a hackney coach at Temple Bar to go to Moorfields, were obstructed by some fellows who pretended to have taken the coach before; and while the gentleman was endeavouring to bring the watch to their assistance, three of them entered the coach to the lady, ordered the coachman to drive on, and, notwithstanding the cry of murder, vehemently repeated, one of them attempted to abuse her while another held a knife to her throat. They have since been apprehended, and the two principals committed to gaol.

February, 1740

The Court of the King's Bench gave judgment against some persons committed for seducing a young lady of 16, and marrying her without consent of her guardians. The husband was fined £500, the son of a noble person concerned £500; two men-servants to be imprisoned one month each, and a maid-servant to suffer six months' imprisonment and pay a fine of one mark.

One report, history, to be sure, rather than news, reminds us of *Clarissa*.

September, 1764

Account of the trial of Ford, Lord Grey and others for seducing and ruining Lady Henrietta Berkeley. [The trial took place in 1682.]

Lady Henrietta was Lord Grey's sister-in-law, which aggravated the crime. Evidently she loved him, for she ran away alone, later meeting him, and at the trial tried to exonerate him by testifying that he had nothing to do with her running away. None the less, all concerned were declared guilty, but the next vacation the case was compromised and no sentence passed. When Lady Henrietta's father attempted to take her home, she revealed that she was married to one of Lord Grey's sycophants. Afterwards they accompanied Lord Grey to Holland. Lady Henrietta died much later in obscurity and retirement, "while her name was prostituted by one of the most licentious writers of her own sex [*i.e.,* Mrs. Manly] in that collection of letters pretended to pass between her and her gallant during the course of their criminal amour."

These reports offer us few details; we examine them in vain to discover how, or whether, Goldsmith's law worked in real life. From the *Gentleman's Magazine* we learn that the preacher speaks of ruin, shame, guilt, sorrow, repentance, but not of death; Edward Cobden preached a sermon on chastity before the King, reported 11 December, 1748.

"Alas! that virgin innocence, which once was her comfort and her glory, which was her brightest ornament, and most valuable dowry, is lost, irrecoverably lost; and shame, guilt and sorrow are to her continual attendants." What can she do? Her betrayer will not deal with her on terms of honor and no other man will venture to marry a woman who he cannot think will be faithful to him. "The best and wisest course she can take is, to endeavour to wash away the stain she has contracted, with the tears of unfeigned repentance, and to take off her reproach in the eyes of the world by giving the regularity of future conduct, as an evidence of the sincerity of her contrition . . . There is no reflecting on so wretched an object, without the deepest compassion for her misery, as well as the utmost detestation for her guilt."

One suspects that in the eyes of the society which this sermon represents, her "guilt" is mainly unthrift in wasting her dowry of virginity without gaining a marriage which would have provided for her without making her a burden on her family or on society. We have testimony in a letter to the editor from a seducer that the ruin is irretrievable because "the betrayer will not deal with her on terms of honor," and his exquisite reasons therefor.

December, 1773

The writer has succeeded in seducing his loved one, but now is tortured by the fact that he cannot marry her, for he will always suspect that where he conquered, others can too; and yet, he still loves her and hates to continue to ruin her. "I am doomed, in spite of reason, to entertain suspicions of that virtue which melted before the flame of my love." He presents his dilemma as a lesson to other gallants, never "to ruin a reputation, which never, alas! can be repaired."

As might be expected, good citizens wrote frequently to the editor declaring that "there ought to be a law," and suggesting penalties and means of enforcement. There are recorded cases of violent rape beyond anything the novelists dared use. In one or two instances the victim died of the violence, but no one, in these reports from life died of grief or shame, or because society had no further use for her.

Romance, meanwhile, draws its counsels of perfection from philosophy rather than from life. The anonymous *Leonora,* which has already drifted within view on the currents of liquid sorrow, furnishes an example of a lady who declares that so long as she is blameless she cannot be unhappy. She is Camilla, second only to Leonora as heroine of this patchwork romance. She tells that she was engaged to Rinaldo till her father's loss of fortune made it impossible for him to supply the stipulated dowry. Rinaldo then asks her to become his mistress,

nor think the omitting a little Ceremony can rob us of Innocence, our Minds fore-ever united will compleat our Marriage; . . . Let me on my Knees persuade you to dry these falling Tears, and banish all those little Scruples which Education stamps on the ductile Mind, training it up to the narrow Rules impos'd by Custom: These may make you wretched, but they can never set you above the misfortunes in which you are involv'd.

To this I answer'd with great Warmth, I am free from Guilt, therefore cannot be unhappy. Impious Rinaldo never see me more. From this moment I shall view you as a Wretch fit only to be the scorn of virtuous Minds. . . . My constant soul could bear Poverty or Death but not Disgrace.

This looks vaguely toward Plato; more definitely, perhaps, toward the Lady in *Comus:*

> *Fool, do not boast.*
> *Thou canst not touch the freedom of my mind*
> *With all thy charms, although this corporal rind*
> *Thou hast immanacled while Heaven sees good.*

But it is not necessary to think that Milton turned up the idea in the process of unsphering Plato, for it would be a commonplace to anyone whose idea of happiness was founded on an untroubled conscience.

Smollett's first novel, *Roderick Random,* came the same year as *Clarissa,* 1748; Fielding's *Tom Jones* the year after, and Smollett's *Peregrine Pickle* and Fielding's *Amelia* in 1751. Their heroines, Narcissa, Sophia, Emelia and Amelia, do not stoop to folly, but secondary female characters do in all four novels, and though they suffer consequences, some comic and some distressing, they do not feel constrained to die. None of these transgressors are virgins when we first meet them. Fielding's comment on the conventional concept of sex morality we saw in *Joseph Andrews.* He makes the opening situation the converse of that in *Pamela;* as in the Bible story the virtuous manservant is named Joseph, and the wicked aggressor is a woman. Most readers go through *Tom Jones* without observing that the same theme sounds there with variations. Tom falls from grace three times that the reader is definitely given to observe, with Molly Seagrim, with Mrs. Waters, and with Lady Bellaston. Each time the woman makes the advances in

a way of which the reader is fully conscious even when Tom
is not so. And in the affair with Lady Bellaston Tom does the
thing that in his day and in many a day before and since has
been the unforgivable sin in woman; he does for money what
he would not do for love. Is Fielding asking our sympathy for
the "fallen" hero as some since have asked it for the "fallen"
heroine? If this is Fielding's way of calling for the single standard, he did not call loud enough, for where is there reader
or critic who has heard his voice?

Smollett has only one heroine worth noting, Emilia Gauntlet
in *Peregrine Pickle*. She is a mere schoolgirl, about fourteen,
when she first comes on the scene, but she has a slightly
aquiline lift to her nose, and she lives up to it. Her experiences
with the headstrong Peregrine mature her rapidly; she has need
of strength and ability to hold a modicum of control in dealing
with him. She soon shows as a fine, high-spirited girl with
plenty of common sense and no languishments. Peregrine has
secured her love, and has only to hold a straight course to
matrimony and he will attain his desire. But he is just then
flush in fortune and is playing the gentleman; he must needs
attempt seduction in the fashionable aristocratic manner. His
first attempt is to take Emilia to a tavern as they are going
home one evening from the opera, but she succeeds in declin-
ing the invitation without seeming to take it too seriously.
The next time he manages to get her into a bagnio before she
is fully aware where she is, and there offers her a small fortune to
be his mistress. This Emilia is unable to pass off as a joke.
She gives him a stinging rebuke.

". . . Sir, your behaviour on this occasion is, in all respects, low and
contemptible; for, ruffian as you are, you durst not harbour one
thought of executing your execrable scheme while you knew my
brother was near enough to prevent or revenge the insult: so that
you must not only be a treacherous villain, but also a most despicable
coward." Having expressed herself in this manner, with a most

majestic severity, she opened the door, and walking down stairs with surprising resolution, committed herself to the care of a watchman, who accommodated her with a hackney-chair, in which she was safely conveyed to her uncle's house.

Emilia is genuinely in love with Peregrine, fully intends to marry him up to this juncture, and does so in the end when he has expiated his folly. But her inclination to him makes no flaw in her armor of chastity. She does not "sink" or faint. She does not look to Heaven to protect her virginity, but protects it herself by resolute and prompt action, and such assistance as she needs from a watchman and a hackney chair. Smollett, it seems, did not think Pamela should have refused to marry the man who attempted her virtue. Had *Clarissa* come off the press in time for him to have read it before he wrote the scene quoted here? Did he think that Clarissa left too much to God and neglected the police? Many a reader has thought that if Clarissa had tried what Emilia successfully did, she might have saved herself. They have not read Clarissa's story carefully enough to learn that she tried just that, and that Lovelace outwitted her. Emelia was dealing with a headstrong but very silly and unintelligent boy. Clarissa had to match her wits against those of a very, very clever man.

Mrs. Haywood's change of literary style suggests that she may have found the puritan fashion more profitable, but Smollett's vigorous campaign against romance indicates that the old style was by no means dead. Examples of it in this period are not far to seek. There is *Patty Saunders,* 1752, whose adventures are all in the realm of romance, however the geographical names may seek to keep her in the island of Britain. The heroine comes through *virgo intacta;* is it under guardianship of Heaven, or by sheer luck? Her companion stays long in captivity, victim to the wicked ravisher, but is romantically held uncontaminated by the experience because it was enforced. Here again speaks the judgment of a court of love, not that of a puritan

society. *The History of Lucy Wellers,* "by a lady," 1754, if it had
been named in the nineties of the nineteenth century might have
been called "Better Death than Dishonor, or, Heaven will protect
the Working Girl." Lucy, to be sure, was not born in the
working class; she was brought up and educated in a sort of
middle-class gentility, but thrown on her own resources by the
death of a spendthrift father. Attacks on Lucy's chastity are
frequent enough; the account of them takes up the main part
of her history. She trusts in Heaven, but she doesn't leave it to
God. She exhausts every resource of energy and ingenuity
before she resorts to tears or takes refuge in prayer. At one
time she wears her captors down by her resistance till they
lock her by herself in a room where, "having given vent to
her grief by tears and lamentations, she fell on her knees and
fervently implored the protection of Heaven." At another time
she tells the rake who has her in his power that she puts her
trust in Heaven, and says, "I freely resign my life into your
hands, but will never consent to part with my honour, which
is much dearer to me." This is to the same effect as the response
of the Lady in *Comus,* and it wins the protection of Heaven,
for she escapes by what the worldly would call luck; but it
has come down in the social scale, for Lucy is not a lady
by birth, and at the time is in the working-girl class by occupation.

If Lucy had been a lady she might have been harder put to
it than she was, for assassination and arson were no longer in
fashion as a means of convincing Heaven that you were in
earnest about your chastity, and, at least in the rosy pages of
romance, even so much as vigor of tongue, a slap in the face,
or activity in escape were not ladylike for the oncoming lass
with the delicate air. If, then, active self-protection is necessary
to assure Heaven that the heroine is worth protecting, the
authoress must resort to clumsy motiveless devices of sheer luck.
In *The Rival Mother,* 1755, the villain has Julia imprisoned,

but we learn that he "was obliged to open the door" to release her. Again for no apparent reason he grants her eight days' stay of sentence. At the end of that time he is about to carry out his wicked purpose, when the authoress can think of no cleverer device to save her than to have him "leave the room" at the crucial moment. If it is thus that Heaven protects virginity, truly it moves in a mysterious way. Here, too, it would seem that not even a husband has power over true virginity, for on the bridal night Julia's paragon of a husband perceives that she is in terror of what is to come, and assures her that he will be a brother to her until she is ready for something more. We do not need the title page to assure us that this was written by a lady.

Next comes the "fair penitent" herself, Olivia in *The Vicar of Wakefield*, 1766. After her fall, her father finds her in misery and want, and hears the details from her own recital. She tells him that a priest married her to Thornhill. Then all is well! Not so, for he had been married before; she had seen his earlier wives living in "contented prostitution." She loved him dearly and tried to please him, but he soon tired of her, and offered her to a profligate companion. Thereupon she left him, flinging in his face the purse of gold he put into her hand. The Vicar takes her to his bosom, and assures her of his trust and love, and his faith that there are yet happy days in store, but her mother is less forgiving; there is reserve and a touch of acerbity in her reception of the errant daughter. "Honest Farmer Williams," who courted her in better days, renews his suit, and would marry her, but she refuses him. She is nervous, melancholy, penitent, and in this mood sings the little song. Soon her health seems impaired. Before long the Vicar "sees the hand of death upon her," and next, while he is in prison, he is told that she has died. Up to this point, if you are reading the book for the first time, you feel that Goldsmith has the courage of his convictions, and condemns his heroine

to death under his own law. But next we learn that she is not
dead after all; the Vicar's family have been deceiving him to
make him give in to Thornhill and to get him out of prison
in spite of himself. Then, when "the villain gets his flogging at
the gangway," it transpires that of all his marriages this is the
only valid one. She is an honest woman after all, and her
mother takes her to her bosom. Thornhill becomes a pensioner
on his wife's bounty; a long term of repentance and good works
may gain her forgiveness. Can Goldsmith be serious, or is this
satire on the conventional view of such cases? His successors
took him seriously, and it was long before any novelist dared
impose any sentence less than death or life imprisonment on any
heroine who fell into any such situation.

The author of *Emmera, or The Fair American,* 1767, read
Milton; we know it from his quotations, and from his fancy land-
scapes woven of details from *Paradise Lost,* and arranged in convenient but indeterminate situations in colonial Pennsylvania.
Emmera is like the Lady in *Comus,* like Una, like the virgins
in the romances and the lives of saints. She is clad in chastity
like complete steel, and may trace huge forests, infamous hills
and perilous wilds, where no savage fierce will dare to soil her
virgin purity. We may realize the value of such armor to
a maiden in the American colonies when we think of the un-
nameable atrocities perpetrated by the fierce savages on their
female captives. These savages are as tame to Emmera as the
fierce unicorn to the legendary virgin; they save her and serve
her as her needs arise. On Englishmen, too, her chastity has
power; Chetwin says:

The astonishing awe and reverence I have for the native innocence
and simplicity of this angelic creature, works so powerfully with me,
that, so far am I from harbouring a thought injurious to her honour,
I dare not explain the situation of my mind to her; the words *I love
you,* are forever quivering on my tongue—but I tremble too much to
drop them.

It is hard to decide whether Emmera's virtue is Roussellian or puritan. Her father has had full experience with "the orgies of voluptuousness." He protects his daughter from them not by repression but by removal. His reaction from a society like that of the Restoration drama is an expression of Rousseau in terms of Milton, which to the sterner moralists of his day must have seemed like an attempt to reconcile Satan and God. There is more of Rousseau and less of Milton in Mrs. Frances Moore Brooke's *Emily Montague,* 1769. Mrs. Brooke expresses repeatedly, in the voice of one character after another, the idea that puritanical severity of conduct, manner, precept, on the part of virtuous women drives men to the society of women of less virtue, that to make a bogey-man of the rake is one of the puritanical affectations, and that even a virtuous wife may learn something from women whose profession is to please. We have seen in an earlier chapter that Mrs. Brooke was a disciple of Rousseau; that she was anti-puritan we may see here. No doubt many of her readers considered her books dangerous, and attributed the danger to infection from the *Nouvelle Héloïse.*

Charlotte Palmer, in *Female Stability,* 1780, gives us three views of the "fallen" woman, puritan, sentimental, and rakish. The incomparable Adeline, seeking to be severe on the vice, is perhaps unwittingly severe on the victim. In an argument with Sir Harry, a rake, against gallantry, she says of the wife and children of the seducer, "Must the cries of unprotected innocence plead in vain; and the virtuous mother of those infants be abandoned for a vile and infamous female?" This however is a general argument. Later she meets a concrete instance, Emilia Ayscough, victim of that same Sir Harry, and becomes sentimental about the infamous female, and makes a virtue of relieving her distress. The author presents the fair penitent in sentimental terms.

"Affection," repeated she, her eyes streaming; "no, Captain Montague, he has long ceased to have any affection for the unhappy

Emilia: but does he mention his wretched children? May I not be permitted to go to London to see my innocent infants?"... "Cruel man!" exclaimed she, "will he then deprive me of every comfort? but tell him, Captain Montague, I will comply. Entreat him to take care of my helpless boys and I will obey him in every respect. But," continued she with a modest blush, "I am shocked, sir, to be obliged to expose myself to you. Sir Harry should have had more delicacy than to have made my fall from virtue known to you; but it does not signify; I hope my life and my sufferings will quickly end; and I shall then be happy."

And then, as her hard-boiled seducer sees her:

. . . if she was a sensible woman she would think herself happy: but that is the misfortune of your sentimental females; they think it necessary to act the farce of repentance, and by their soft sorrow recall the faithless wanderer. I had a great regard for Emilia Ayscough once: indeed she was a fine woman; but she had a whining way that always displeased me: in my days of fondness for her, she was so continually lamenting her deviation from virtue, that she lost my heart much sooner than she would have done had she behaved with any spirit.

The purpose here is apparent enough: first, to exhibit Adeline's virtue and her ability in argument; second, to get sentimental effect from the sorrows of the discarded mistress; third, to exhibit the villainous character of the rake. We need not take them seriously; they are no more than literary devices for the purpose of the tale, fashions of the time in thought and feeling which people would assume and change as occasion demanded.

Robert Bage suggests clearly enough that these attitudes, as well as the whole Milton-Steele-Goldsmith standard, are mere poses of literary fashion. In his *Mount Henneth,* 1781, one of the situations in his loosely organized plot is that of a young officer of the East India Company military service entering the house of an English resident as it is being plundered by natives, just too late to save a lady and her maids from rape. He falls in love with the lady and wishes to marry her, but she protests that by all English standards she knows, she is unfit to be his wife:

> . . . And let it be remembered also, (the sweet sad air with which she spoke this is inexpressible), that though he saved my life, he came too late to save my honour.
>
> Honour, Cara! Is there upon earth a man so absurd, as to associate the idea of dishonour to thy sufferings?
>
> I know not, sir. In all those English books your goodness has procured for me, I find it is the leading idea: women who have suffered it must die, or be immured forever; ever after they are totally useless to all the purposes of society; it is the foundation of an hundred fabulous things called novels, which are said to paint exactly the reigning manners and opinions: all crimes but this may be expiated; no author has yet been so bold as to permit a lady to live and marry, and be a woman after this stain.
>
> By heaven, a woman is more dishonoured by a wanton dream! What say you, Foston, is Cara a painter after truth?
>
> We have enthusiasts, sir, in points of honour as well as in religion; but things like this, which cannot stand the test of reason, seldom take strong holds of the minds of a people. It is to be found in books, sir, and I hope for the honour of the human intellect, little of it will be found anywhere else.
>
> You renounce it, then?
>
> I cannot, sir, I never entertained it.

The proposal for the more or less hypothetical community at Mount Henneth is of the nature of a satirical device in criticism of society, a list of types of persons whom society discourages but the author approves. It includes any lady who after a lapse from virtue shows by a sufficient interval of continence that she is not an habitual offender. Bage has no patience with solemn prudery. Quite respectable young ladies in his novels are able to laugh where puritans would draw long faces. In *Mount Henneth* Laura Stanley gives a vivacious account of a hoydenish schoolgirl's escapade with a boy of her own age which a strait-laced aunt took for a major disaster. Laura tells the story with laughter to Julia Foston, adding,

. . . But I must tell you that I put on no *badinage* to Miss Thompson, but have mingled the little wisdom I have with a soothing tenderness, that I hope has already produced a change: . . .

Julia Foston finds that she can talk freely with Mr. Cheslyn.

. . . Yes, Laura, this gentleman and I have found the secret of talking over your whole catalogue of generations, without exciting an immodest idea.

But these girls are inclined to poke fun at a woman who makes a point of conscience about a freedom which does not sit easily on her; perhaps she seems to them a plebeian assuming aristocratic freedom of manners.

Yesterday nearly our whole society were enjoying the cool air of the evening on the terrace. In the beautiful hanging pastures beneath, amongst other quadrupeds, was your little roan mare, employed, as females sometimes are, in attending to the love of an ass. This animal was in love *à la folie;* had broke through three several barriers, and was eager to reap the fruits of his bold enterprise. To the philosophic eye all things are equal. Miss Caradoc was first struck with the view, and drawing Julia and Laura to the wall, see, cries she.—Fie, Laura, said Miss Foston, walking on.—Brother, says the contemplative Miss Caradoc, you have constantly asserted that copulation betwixt animals of different species is unnatural, and always committed by a rape of the female—see the contrary.—Miss Melton and Mrs. Tyrrell turned across the area. Harriet followed something unwillingly. . . . A learned dispute followed between these two originals in which the whole science of generation was discussed. The brother maintained the egg system; the sister, Lewenhoeck's. They ended at last with an enquiry into the political cause of circumcision.

Besides the *novelty* of hearing these things from the mouth of a woman, we were extremely amused by the superficiality displayed on both sides. . . . The old baronet applauds himself for having given his children so very proper an education.

In *Barham Downs* Kitty Ross falls victim to the Hon. Mr. Corrane,—"Kitty, unable to resist the flood of tumultuous sensations, gave herself up to be plundered without resistance; his honour's penitence and virtue were lost in the conflict, and the scene was—ruin." A letter brings the story to Henry Davis and a group of his friends in the country, who make conventional and unconventional comments.

This little story of Miss Ross, as far as it goes, I have taken the pains to write over again, just as I suppose Miss Ross herself would have told it; and calling it a fact of the last century, read it to Miss Whitakers and Miss Delanes.

The two first honoured it with their tears. Miss Amelia Delane, vain of her intellectual accomplishments, (for her father has taught her Latin) observed, that in favour of this young lady, nothing could be alleged; no arts of seduction were used; no train of dark contrivances. She fell at the first attack.

Unfeeling pedantess, says I to myself; thou art no wife for me.— That, replies Annabella, is, in my opinion, precisely the circumstance which most entitles her to compassion. She sunk under the full force of her own strong sensibilities. Can any other possible compulsion be half as powerful? A few minutes time for recovery might have saved her, and saved her forever. . . .

Amelia replied, she did not very well understand what was a want of virtue, unless yielding to desire might be called so. . . . And what signifies after all from what motive a woman loses her virtue? When it's gone, it's gone. Who considers anything but the fact itself? . . . and this is right, Mr. Davis, is it not?

It is not . . . when I consider the young lady's youth,—her inexperience, her respect and even affection for the gentleman, the novelty of her emotions, the unguarded moment, all together, in my eyes, do away the fault to almost nothing.

The experience exposes her to, and arms her to resist, many further attempts. This redeems her according to Bage's standard defined in the proposal for the Mount Henneth community, and he marries her to the principal narrator of the complicated tale.

This is revolutionary doctrine, open defiance of Goldsmith's law. Perhaps in those revolutionary times it may have been a shade more acceptable to society than it was to Scott some forty years later when he wrote the introduction to the three novels of Bage which Ballantyne published in his *Novelists' Library*. After an urbane dismissal of Bage's political doctrine, Scott turns to a more serious matter.

This misrepresentation of the different classes of society, is not the only speculative error Bage has indulged in during these poetic narratives. There is in his novels a dangerous tendency to slacken the reins of discipline upon a point, where, perhaps, of all others, society must be benefitted by their curbing restraint.

Fielding, Smollett, and other novelists, have, with very indifferent taste, brought forward their heroes as rakes and debauchees, and treated with great lightness those breaches of morals, which are too commonly considered as venial in the male sex; but Bage has extended, in some instances, that license to females, and seems at times even to sport with the ties of marriage, which is at once the institution of civil society most favourable to religion and good order, and that which, in its consequences, forms the most marked distinction between man and the lower animals. All the influence which women enjoy in society,—their right to the exercise of that maternal care which forms the first and most indelible species of education; the wholesome and mitigating restraint which they possess over the passions of mankind; their power of protecting us when young, and cheering us when old,—depend so entirely upon their personal purity, and the charm which it casts around them, that to insinuate a doubt of its real value, is wilfully to remove the broadest corner-stone on which civil society rests, with all its benefits, and with all its comforts. It is true, we can easily conceive that a female like Miss Ross, in *Barham Downs,* may fall under the arts of the seducer, under circumstances so peculiar as to excite great compassion, nor are we so rigid as to say, that such a person may not be restored to society, when her subsequent conduct shall have effaced recollection of her error. But she must return thither as a humble penitent, and has no title to sue out her pardon as a matter of right, and assume a place as if she had never fallen from her proper sphere. Her disgrace must not be considered as a trivial stain, which may be communicated by a husband as an exceeding good jest to his friend and correspondent; there must be, not penitence and reformation alone, but humiliation and abasement, in the recollection of her errors. This the laws of society demand even from the unfortunate; and to compromise further would open a door to the most unbounded licentiousness. With fault in principle is connected an indelicacy of expression frequently occurring in Bage's novels, but which, though a gross error in point of taste, we consider as a matter of much less consequence than the former. It is in some degree chastened in the present edition, and where it exists must find such shelter as it can, under the faulty example of the earlier novelists.

Bage has faith in reason; his ideal man is guided by that alone. From this doctrine Scott dissents. Reason, he thinks, is humanly imperfect; we must look to higher and external authority for ethical standards. In Bage's own time a clergyman, Martin Madan, wrote vigorously to the same effect in a comprehensive treatise, of which the title page "presents a tabular view of the volume's contents" somewhat as follows:

Thelyphthora; or, a treatise on FEMALE RUIN, in its CAUSES, EFFECTS, CONSEQUENCES, PREVENTION, AND REMEDY: Considered on the Basis of the DIVINE LAW: Under the following Heads, viz. MARRIAGE, WHOREDOM and FORNICATION, ADULTERY, POLYGAMY, DIVORCE; with many other INCIDENTAL MATTERS; particularly including AN EXAMINATION of the principles and Tendency of Stat. 26 Geo. II. c. 33. Commonly called the MARRIAGE ACT. London . . . M. DCC. Lxxxi.

It is truly according to its promise a discussion on the basis of divine law; its basic assumption is that the Bible is the word and the law of God. God's law, he declares, is unalterably fixed; "What God doeth, it shall be forever; nothing can be put to it, nor anything taken from it; and God doeth it that men should fear before him. Eccl., III, 14." This is, of course, the axiom on which the bourgeois code rests, but there is much indirection in the growth as it has come up in the minds of generations of laymen. God spoke Hebrew, and most of his hearers in Europe knew other languages better. Interpretations varied and were reflected waveringly in the minds of multitudes of hearers through many centuries. If the light was ever clear and single, the troubled minds of those who have faced it, innumerable points of reflection, have shattered it into millions of indirections, till it is only a blurred reflection in a darkened glass. Madan seeks to reassemble it. He delves much after Hebrew roots, and complains of the instability of later tongues. He follows inevitable inferences wherever they may lead him, and is satisfied with the results as unalterable truth. The whole is interesting for its seeming to present a clear-cut picture of the original of the blurred composite which stands as the bourgeois code of sexual morality. Madan dedicates his work to the "Governors of those well-intended charities" that seek to reclaim and benefit fallen women. He points out that

as our laws are at present framed, women are exposed to *seduction, prostitution,* and *ruin,* almost without controul;—they seem to be looked upon as lawful prey to the lust, treachery, cruelty, and mean artifices of licentious and profligate men, who can seduce and abandon them at their will.

and declares his purpose

to exhibit a system far different from this—to set forth the *divine law* as the contrivance of infinite wisdom, for the security, peace, preservation, and protection of the female sex . . .

He will show us, then, the very law of God by which Heaven protects chastity as a model for human laws to the same effect.

Were this to be made the basis of our *municipal laws,* it would prove an adequate remedy for all those mischiefs, which, in comparatively few instances, can now only find a partial palliation from benevolence . . . but which must in general still be the portion of those, whom God's law was formed to protect.

"The alarming increase of *female prostitution* and *ruin,*" he declares, "calls loudly for some remedy." The cause of it is rendered effectual, by restoring the *wisdom* of God to its due place in our esteem, and by making it, as it is found revealed to us in the scriptures, the *basis* of our *municipal* laws . . . the *line* of our conduct . . . the *rule* of our obedience.

He believes that marriage is a divine institution, but finds in God's law no least hint or most distant allusion to any outward rite or ceremony of marriage. He infers that in God's sight marriage consists in the personal union of the man and the woman as one flesh, and no outward form or ceremony of man's invention can add to or diminish from the effects of this union in the sight of God. As evidence he cities Exodus 22: 16, 17:

If a man entice a maid that is not betrothed, and lie with her, he shall surely endow her to be his wife. If her father utterly refuse to give her to him, he shall pay money according to the dowry of her virginity.

and also Deuteronomy 22: 28, 29: "the man that lay with her shall give unto the damsel's father fifty shekels of silver, and she shall be his wife; because he hath humbled her, he may not put her away all his days." Unlike some of the Church Fathers, he does not feel that the sexual act is in itself contaminating, but the terms in which he expresses this idea suggest those of the preacher on chastity. He reminds us of the injunction to increase and multiply, and goes on to say:

. . . It could not be but that the act whereby mankind was to be propagated must be totally *innocent* in itself: otherwise it could not have been consistent with the state of *innocence* in which man was when *marriage* was first ordained. But this *act,* innocent in itself as any other function of the body, might be kept within due bounds of *order* and *decency,* and all confusion and disorder avoided; God enacted certain *positive* laws for this very purpose, to confine within such bounds as seemed good to himself to limit, that *natural,* but *violent* passion, which, for the great purpose of propagating the *human species,* was made an inseparable adjunct to the *human frame.*

Those who imagine that this appetite is in itself *sinful*, either in the *desire* or *act, charge* God *foolishly*, as if He could ordain the increase and multiplication of mankind by an *act* sinful in itself: an absurdity little short of *blasphemy*.

But for violations of God's law, the penalty should be that which God dictates.

God expressly commanded that there should *not be a whore of the daughters of Israel*, Lev. xix, 29. Deut. xxii, 27; and ordained that a woman *playing the whore*, if the daughter of a common person, should *be stoned to death*, Deut. xxii, 21; but if the daughter of a priest, she was to *be burned with fire*, Lev. xxi, 9. I mention these things as proofs of the sinfulness of an act, innocent in *itself*, when committed against a divine positive law. No human power or custom can alleviate its guilt, or make it less offensive to God than His word has made it; . . .

"What art can wash her guilt away?" asks the poet. "No human power or custom," replies the preacher. Is there here something like Biblical warrant for something like Goldsmith's law? The fair penitent is not a prostitute, but harsh-spoken judges would be likely to call her whore, and, though they would neither stone her nor burn her to death, they would be willing enough to see her die.

The preacher has his ideals, but he is not wholly impractical. He does not profess to believe that the penalty for "playing the whore" should be death unless all of God's laws should be revived. And his comment on the attempt to make it so shows that he is not of the puritan sect.

In the year 1650, when the ruling powers found it for their interest to put on the semblance of a very extraordinary strictness and purity of morals; not only *incest* and wilful *adultery* were made capital crimes but also the repeated act of keeping a brothel, or committing fornication, were (upon a second conviction) made felony without benefit of clergy. But at the restoration, when men, from an abhorrence of the hypocrisy of the late times, fell into a contrary extreme of licentiousness, it was not thought proper to renew a law of such unfashionable rigour. And these offenses have ever since been left to the feeble coercion of the *spiritual court,* according to the rules of the canon law; a law which has treated the offense of incontinence, nay even *adultery itself,* with a great degree of tenderness and lenity; owing perhaps to the celibacy of its first compilers. The *temporal* courts therefore take no cognizance of the crime of *adultery* otherwise than as a private injury.

Madan, to be sure, quotes this passage from Blackstone, but his very citation of it marks him non-puritan, and the remark itself from so grave an authority is interesting evidence on many of the social situations that shape the novel. Puritan or not, Madan is thoroughly bourgeois when he comes to explain why adultery is so heinous a sin. All its evils cannot be reckoned, he thinks, but he will mention a few.

. . . It must introduce a total confusion as to the offspring, a defeating of rightful heirs, an utter obscurity as to family descents and pedigrees; for where *adultery* is, no man can know his own children, or even ostensible brothers and sisters ascertain their relation to each other: for which, as well as for many other wise causes, doubtless it was (as well as to preserve the sanctity of the marriage institution) made *capital* by the Divine Lawgiver. This we may humbly presume to be the case; for this offense is introductory of that kind of disorder, which must, in the very nature of it, tend to destroy every bond of *civil* and religious society, and make the world, in a moral sense, a mere chaos. . . . The wise, holy, uniform and connected scheme of God's moral government, with respect to the *commerce of the sexes* has *two* principal ends in view. The *one,* to prevent all *confusion of issue*—the *other* to secure the *female sex* from that which must lead to it.

Prevention of confusion reminds us of Dr. Johnson's comment on the value of chastity quoted above in Chapter III. In so far as Madan is right in thinking it a conspicuous item in the Hebrew code, we might attribute it to the jealousy of the Jews for the purity of their race. But when we add to it such phrases as, "he shall pay money according to the dowry of her virginity," and, "the man that lay with her shall give unto the damsel's father fifty shekels of silver, and she shall be his wife," it turns our thoughts to marriage by purchase; the price of virginity is fifty shekels, and we think again of Dr. Johnson's evaluation of chastity on the basis that on it depends all the property in the world. If Johnson's bourgeois code was the code of shopkeepers, were the Hebrews already shopkeepers in Biblical times?

Madan sees no such inference. He believes that we should be much better off if our customs and statutes were in accord with God's laws. God does not condemn polygamy, but allowed, owned, and even blessed it. Madan discusses concubinage, ancient and modern, at great length, and decides that

If such a custom as this prevailed among us, and was inforced on men of *rank* and *fashion,* who are now turned loose on the *lower order of females,* and debauch them at *free cost,* without being under the least responsibility towards them . . . it would not only prove a happy check to the most mischievous licentiousness in many instances, but be also a means of preventing the utter ruin of *thousands,* who, under the present *system* of things, are seduced, abandoned, and destroyed, without any *remedy* whatsoever, or almost any possibility of *escape.*

The real trouble, then, would seem to be that God makes laws which, in this world at least, he leaves to man to enforce.

Dr. John Moore is unsparingly severe on the conventional attitude toward the "fallen" woman. In *Zeluco,* 1789, the third chapter announces its theme with a couplet from Pope:

> *Virtue she finds too painful an endeavour;*
> *Content to dwell with decencies forever.*

and introduces the Countess Brunella, of whom the author says that "it was impossible to account for the marriage which had raised her to both rank and fortune, but by supposing that, at the time it took place, she was handsome."

She was chaste, without being virtuous; because in her it proceeded from constitution, not principle. Guarded by the breastplate of frigidity, which like the aegis of Minerva, repels the shafts of love, she walked through life erect, and steady to the dictates of decorum and self-interest, without a slip or false step.

Inexorable to all helpless females who, from the frailty of nature, or the perfidy of man, were observed to totter, or even to stoop, in their progress, she insisted that they should be forever excluded from the society of the upright: and if any person shewed a disposition to palliate their errors, this vulture of chastity quitted, for a moment, the frail bird on whom she had pounced, and turned her envenomed beak against those who were for shewing the smallest degree of mercy; and being freed by nature from any propensity to one particular frailty, she indulged, without bounds, in the gratification of envy, hatred, slander, haughtiness, and other vices of the same class, for which, from her childhood, she had discovered a decided taste.

The Countess "fixed her eyes" on Zeluco "as a commodious match for her niece," but,

Whilst the aunt . . . was artfully planning what she considered an advantageous match for her niece, the unwary young woman granted, without marriage what her aunt in similar circumstances had carefully preserved.

When the Countess learned of this, she

. . . expostulated with Zeluco, attempting to obtain by threats, what integrity and a sense of honour ought to have inclined him to perform. He treated her threats with derision, and . . . in the mean time, added he sarcastically, it is to be hoped you will make your own niece an exception from your favourite maxim, that all who have made a single false step should be forever excluded from respectable society.

Inasmuch as it is not Zeluco, "veteran in iniquity," nor any character in the tale, who characterizes the Countess, it is safe to infer that Moore, like Bage, was intolerant of intolerance. In a later chapter, Moore shows with approval a contrasting picture, that of Signora Sporza, who "contrary to the advice

of her friends, . . . had relinquished great part of the funds
appropriated for the security of her own jointure, to relieve
her husband's difficulties," and, "although her husband had left
no money to maintain her, yet he contrived to leave a child by
another woman for her to maintain." Her friends "exclaimed
against the indecency and folly of her supporting an adulterous
bastard and its wicked mother. . . . All the answer which Signora Sporza made . . . was desiring them to find out some
other woman or man, if they pleased, who would maintain the
unhappy woman and her child, in which event she was willing
to yield up her claim." There is a suggestion forty years earlier
of a similar liberality in Smollett. Narcissa in *Roderick Random*
protects the "unfortunate" Miss Williams, and even associates
with her. It is not wholly revolutionary; is it because they are
men that Bage and Moore are more liberal than Mrs. Hofland
and Mrs. Opie, or shall we say that this is a gesture of aristocracy that makes Goldsmith and Scott seem bourgeois? Moore,
indeed seems ultra-revolutionary in that he goes beyond even
Bage, and oddly suggests Milton in the same passage.

There is a dignity and elevation in virtue which overawes the most
daring profligate. No man of sense, however free in his morals,
ever attempted a woman till he imagined she had some inclination
he should. Let him use what delicate terms he pleases, to what purpose can he be supposed to express his own wishes, if he does not
suspect she has the same wishes with himself? This is the true
point of view in which women ought to consider addresses of this
nature.—In what other point of view can they be considered? A
woman is solicited to grant what dishonours herself. Well, her
solicitor, if he is not a fool, will not, in conscience, expect she will
stoop to this without a motive, or merely to please him. What then
does he expect? Why, that she will consent to please herself.

Here he subscribes to the theory of the self-protective power of
flawless chastity. None the less he is charitable to those who
depart from it, and that without seeking excuses for them;
his charity is for those who please themselves.

Fairly liberal, too—at least for a woman—is Charlotte Smith. She writes in the romance tradition, with views more courtly than puritanic. Her heroines, though often on the brink of disaster, come through unscathed, but minor characters are not so well guarded. Emily Cathcart, a very minor character in *Celestina,* 1791, is sister to Mrs. Elphinstone, a figure of only slightly more importance. Poor Emily confides in a specious promise of marriage, elopes, and disappears from the tale for so long as suffices her sister to go through a series of severe and undeserved misfortunes which reduce her to the last extremity. She is seeking frantically for a physician who will without fee, for she hasn't a penny left, save the life of her dying child, when she accidentally meets Emily, glittering with the splendid wages of sin, who does everything for her that money and sisterly affection can do, though Mrs. Elphinstone wonders for a moment whether she ought to receive help that is tainted with her sister's shame. Having served this useful purpose, Emily disappears again till nearly the end of the fourth and last volume, where we are called upon to condone her sins because she makes such a beautiful corpse.

Emily sat in a great chair, supported by pillows—the extreme beauty which had been so fatal to its possessor, still remained, though its lustre was gone—Emaciated, and of a delicate fairness, her hands and her face had a transparency that gave an idea of an unembodied spirit, and her dress was such as favored the deception. The blood might almost be seen to circulate in her veins, so plainly did they appear; and her eyes had the dazzling radiance of etherial fire, to which the hectic heat of her glowing though wasted countenance, still added—A few locks of her fine light hair had escaped from her headdress; and played like broken rays from a receding planet, round a face, which only those who had hearts unhappily rigid, could behold, without feeling the sense of her errors suspended or overwhelmed by strong emotions of the tenderest pity.

Neither is Charlotte Smith one to call for the death penalty for adultery; she is more inclined to throw it in for good measure to show that her sentimental-rake hero can really transact business. Desmond, who plays the title rôle in the novel of that name, is for most of the time hovering sentimentally and protectively over his lady love, who is married to a despicable villain. Meanwhile he dallies a bit with the married sister of a friend in France. In the end it appears that this amour went so far as an illegitimate child, but the lady takes all the blame on herself; who could help loving Desmond? Clearly Charlotte Smith is Roussellian in feeling and revolutionary in sympathy; why should she condemn anyone who followed her heart?

In contrast with Charlotte Smith is Mrs. Jane West, who began to write moral tales a little earlier than did Miss Edgeworth. *The Advantages of Education; or, The History of Maria Williams,* 1792, exhibits the salvation of Maria Williams from the designs of Sir Henry Neville. Maria has been educated to confide in her mother, who is a pattern of all that a mother should be, a paper pattern, designed, cut and patented by Jane West. Maria, then, is fortunate in her parents; other girls who point the moral more than they adorn the tale are not so. One makes a showy marriage and leads a cat-and-dog life. Another falls victim to the seducer. Mrs. West believes that sound bourgeois virtues are better than what she calls "the pride and ignorance of feudal greatness." The seducer who attempts the chastity of Maria Williams wishes, after his plans have failed, to marry her, but Mrs. Williams snatches her back from such a fate, and bestows her on a parson of the Established Church. Maria's girlhood friend falls in for an "Honourable" through a few deaths in the family of her husband's father, but Mrs. West demonstrates that the title is a worthless gaud of Vanity Fair, tawdry beside the spiritual beauties of the parson, and anyway, the parson had relations who were no farther from a title than Mrs. Pierpont's, if anybody cared to boast of them. Is the scorn of aristocracy the betrayal of an inferiority complex? There is reason to think so. Homespun virtues Mrs.

West extols in language that apes aristocratic education. She
is trying to tell us that Mrs. Williams is a cheerful pessimist:

Mrs. Williams had ever, on the pressure of any great affliction, accustomed herself to a practice which she found very productive of
resignation and patience. Instead of permitting her mind to dwell
on those relative appendants that aggravate distress into desperation,
by a vigorous exertion of her powers, she turned her mental eye on
those alleviating circumstances, which Providence kindly allows in
every condition of misery, could we but permit ourselves to see them.

To be free and easy about money matters is, in her code, a vice
of fashion. The sensibility of a perfect mother is private and
devotional, not open, insincere and fashionable:

A tear stole down her face as she concluded this ejaculation; but accustomed to make no parade of feeling, she carefully obliterated every
trace of concern before she entered the dining-room.

No need to pile up evidence to show that Jane West is a bourgeois moralist. The sad tale of the errant damsel runs true
to type. Her brother is telling the story:

Judge then my horror, my inconceivable astonishment, when last
April a letter from my widowed mother, almost unintelligible with
tears, contained the soul harrowing tidings that the unworthy girl had
yielded to her seducer's arts—had eloped from her family—nay, lived
with him in the contemptible character of his mistress.

But soon "her penitence and sorrow have deeply affected her
health." Her family, "after the public disclosure of her frailty,
would not consider marriage as any reparation." Marriage is no
use; prostitution is a failure; there is no choice but death, and so,
"a hearse followed by two mourning coaches drove into the
yard," and the reader needs little cleverness to perceive that she
has died of repentance, "deeply sensible when too late, of an
error which only death could expiate." The bourgeois code
has accepted Goldsmith's law. The act gives repentance to her

lover and wrings his bosom. Sir Henry Neville goes out in a blaze of sulphur and brimstone, a sinner in the hands of an angry God. Vengeance is not for the hand of man; the victim's brother, Captain Seymour, who has up to this moment pursued the seducer with soldierly persistence, repudiates it.

"Thou mean deceiver!—thou base betrayer! . . . does this sight wring thy soul?—To aggravate thy agony, know that she forgave thee—her dying breath conjured me to spare thy life. Thy punishment then shall be to live—to live in infamy, execrated by all that deserve esteem, even shunned by the loose associates of thy less atrocious crimes. Thou shalt bear a hell in thy own bosom here, and despair shall plunge thee into endless misery hereafter."

After that the villain has only six and a half pages to live.

Neville, after rolling his wild eyes around the apartment, and darting them on the once lovely victim of his treachery, now senseless and inanimate, hurried down stairs . . . Here a violent scream, which evidently proceeded from Neville's apartment, terminated the debate . . . Herbert flew like lightning to the room where he had just left the miserable man; his fears had anticipated the horrid catastrophe. Sir Henry lay almost lifeless upon the ground, weltering in his blood, a pistol, the fatal instrument of destruction, was still grasped in his hand.

Here is the tragedy of Clarissa and Lovelace degenerating through loss of motivation and characterization into melodrama, low tragedy, the attempt to provide for the moron as nearly as possible the feeling that the highbrow gets from high tragedy. Such nineteenth-century melodramas as *Why Girls Leave Home* and *No Mother to Guide Her,* are direct descendants of the works of Jane West.

In 1792, Charlotte Palmer gave to one of her characters a view somewhat more liberal than was common. Miss Digby, in *It Is and It Is Not a Novel,* says,

In consequence of what I have asserted, do not impute to me a talent for universal censure on *all* whose attachments are not sanctioned by matrimony. There are many exceptions; and a man and woman of honour, who hold their word sacred, though given in private, when perhaps secret reasons put it out of their power to marry, are as virtuous, and perhaps *more* so, than some who boast of their *lawful* marriages: Yet it is incumbent that every individual should, (if possible) obey the ordinances of the legislature, for the general benefit of society.

Charity teaches us to compassionate the unsuspecting innocent, and credulous sisters of female weakness, who are led to imbibe the dangerous notions of those betraying language-masters, whose fair speeches almost make "Wrong appear the better reason!"—Yet what is to be said of their deceivers, who not only steal the heart of innocence, but like true *cowards,* first *mislead* that *judgment* which might have proved a guard!

This is not the word of a precisian, nor yet that of a revolutionary; it is not necessarily anything more than a touch of characterization. If there is calculation in it, it may be a slight trimming of the sails to the wind of the revolution.

Contemporary with Charlotte Palmer is the revolutionary Mary Wollstonecraft, whose voice rang trumpet-clear in her *Vindication of the Rights of Woman,* 1792. On one point she seems in agreement with Madan. She denies the necessity of polygamy,

yet when a man seduces a woman, it should I think, be termed a *left-handed* marriage, and the man should be *legally* obliged to maintain the woman and her children, unless adultery, a natural divorcement, abrogated the law. And this law should remain in force as long as the weakness of women caused the word seduction to be used as an excuse for their frailty and want of principle; nay, while they depend on man for a subsistence, instead of earning it with their own hands or heads. But these women should not in the full meaning of the relationship, be termed wives . . .

If we educate women for infamy, we may expect them to become infamous.

. . . highly as I respect marriage, as the foundation of almost every social virtue, I cannot avoid feeling the most likely compassion for those unfortunate females who are broken off from society, and by one error torn from all those affections and relationships that improve the heart and mind. It does not frequently even deserve the name of error; for many innocent girls become the dupes of a sincere affectionate heart, and still more are, as it may be emphatically termed, *ruined* before they know the difference between virtue and vice: and thus prepared by their education for infamy, they become infamous. Asylums and Magdalens are not the proper remedies for these abuses. It is justice, not charity, that is wanting in the world.

Goldsmith's law is a state of mind, fostered by

the state of idleness in which women are educated, who are always taught to look up to man for maintenance, and to consider their person as the proper return for his exertions to support them. Meretricious airs, and the whole science of wantonness, has then a more powerful stimulus than either appetite or vanity; and this remark gives force to the prevailing opinion, that with chastity all is lost that is respectable in woman.

To Mary Wollstonecraft no more than to Falstaff is "honour" synonymous with reputation.

When Richardson makes Clarissa tell Lovelace that he had robbed her of her honour, he must have had strange notions of honour and virtue. For, miserable beyond all names of misery is the condition of a being, who could be degraded without its own consent.

On this point she may be revolutionary, but she is not Roussellian.

. . . it were to be wished that superficial moralists had said less respecting behaviour, and outward observances, for unless virtue of any kind is built on knowledge, it will only produce a kind of insipid decency. Respect for the opinion of the world, has, however, been termed the principal duty of woman in the most express words, for Rousseau declares, "that reputation is no less indispensable than chastity." "A man," adds he, "secure in his own good conduct, depends only on himself, and may brave the public opinion; but a woman, in behaving well, performs but half her duty; as what is thought of her, is as important to her as what she really is. It follows hence, that the system of a woman's education should, in this respect, be directly contrary to that of ours. Opinion is the grave of virtue among the men; but its throne among women." It is strictly logical to infer, that the virtue that rests upon opinion is merely wordly, and that it is the virtue of a being to whom reason has been denied . . . This regard for reputation . . . took its rise from a cause that I have already deplored as the grand source of female depravity, the impossibility of regaining respectability by a return to virtue, though men preserve theirs during the indulgence of vice. It was natural for women then to endeavour to preserve what once lost— was lost forever, till this care swallowing up every other care, reputation for chastity, became the one thing needful to the sex.

Here is verification of our earlier suggestion that Rousseau may be quoted on either side of any argument. The strictest enemies of Rousseau might quote the "brittle and beautiful" qualities of a woman's reputation. Fanny Burney does so in *Evelina,* and makes a bogey-man of Rousseau in *The Wanderer.* It is at once the doctrine of Angelo the precisian and of Rousseau, the puritan's abomination; God and the Devil agree on it!

Mary Wollstonecraft has millions for love, but not one tear for sensibility.

. . . let pride whisper to them [men] that the victory is mean when they merely vanquish sensibility. The real conquest is that over affection not taken by surprise—when, like Heloisa, a woman gives up all the world, deliberately, for love. I do not now consider the wisdom or virtue of such a sacrifice, I only contend that it was a sacrifice to affection, and not merely to sensibility, though she had her share.

After this, the reader may wonder why her comment on Richardson quoted above does so little justice to him or to Clarissa, whose "honour" as Mary Wollstonecraft sees it would be restored by marriage with Lovelace, but as Clarissa sees it has no such ready salve. Clarissa's honor is not her standing with the world; she makes that clear again and again. It is her sense of personal integrity that has been violated; she answers to herself, not to what the world thinks of her.

American puritanism seems to accept Goldsmith's law, even to take it for granted, with the very beginnings of the novel in America. Not much American fiction preceded Susannah Rowson's *Charlotte Temple,* 1790, and Hannah Foster's *The Coquette,* 1791. Both these authors point out to the youth of both sexes that the path of folly leads but to the grave, without reflecting that the path of glory and all other human paths lead quite as inevitably to the same terminus. Both authors condemn the mother and the illegitimate child to death, causes unspecified. In both the seducer is guilty of all the compendious arts of vice, the victim is more to be pitied than blamed; she must die, but she is recommended to mercy in our thoughts of her. Susannah Rowson imagines a "daughter of youthful mirth" who, if she has a heart of sensibility, will stop not in contempt, but will address the victim of folly:

"Thou hast thy faults; but surely thy sufferings have expiated them: thy errors brought thee to an early grave; but thou wert a fellow creature—thou hast been unhappy—then be these errors forgotten."

Then in her own person she addresses the daughter of gloom who might reproach the daughter of youthful mirth.

"My dear madam, contract not your brow into a frown of disapprobation. I mean not to extenuate the faults of those unhappy women who fall victims to guilt and folly; but surely when we reflect how many errors we ourselves are subject to, how many secret faults lie hid in the recesses of our hearts, which we would blush to have brought into open day . . . I say, my dear madam, we surely may pity the faults of others.

"Believe me, many an unfortunate female, who has once strayed into the thorny paths of vice, would gladly return to virtue, was any generous friend to endeavour to raise and re-assure her; but alas! it cannot be, you say; the world would deride and scoff."

Both these novels are rather crude variants on *Clarissa,* and are interesting only as signals that the English tradition has carried over to the American colonies.

No heroine of Jane Austen's stoops to folly, but one has a sister who does. Lydia Bennet elopes with Wickham and lives with him for two weeks before her friends can purchase a marriage for her. Quite unobtrusively Jane Austen manages to shade this episode with various modulations of mild and severe opinion. Most of this is in character, nearly all comes to us as Elizabeth sees it, but one word we have from Jane Austen herself. One paragraph in Chapter XLV (Chapter XIII of Volume II) is directly author to reader by way of refutation of a hypothetical charge of lack of verisimilitude. Here where she is speaking for herself, Jane Austen makes casual mention of "Lydia's infamy," which tells us explicitly what she thinks of this particular instance of folly. Elizabeth gives a somewhat more emotional version of this cool judgment. She says in speaking to Darcy, "My youngest sister has left all her friends —has eloped;—has thrown herself into the power of—of Mr. Wickham. . . . *You* know him too well to doubt the rest. She has no money, no connections, nothing that can tempt him to—she is lost forever." It is not altogether Lydia's fault, if fault is all in intention; although Elizabeth "did not suppose Lydia to be deliberately engaging in an elopement, without intention of marriage, she had no difficulty in believing that neither her virtue nor her understanding would preserve her from falling an easy prey." In other words, Lydia does not have to stoop far to folly; she is her mother's own daughter, and it is this as much as anything else that shows the disaster to the realistic Elizabeth as irretrievable.

Jane Austen's view and that of Elizabeth are alike realistic and born of common sense, with no glamour of romance and little bias of convention. Various phases of the conventional show in the views of other figures in the drama. Lydia's sister Mary "came from her books" to hear the sad news, and we learn as soon as she speaks that her books are the works of the lady novelists, one of whom is Fanny Burney.

"This is a most unfortunate affair, and will probably be much talked of. But we must stem the tide of malice, and pour into the bosoms of each other the balm of sisterly consolation . . . Unhappy as the event must be for Lydia, we may draw from it this useful lesson:—that loss of virtue in a female is irretrievable, that one false step involves her in endless ruin, that her reputation is no less brittle than it is beautiful, and that she cannot be too much guarded in her behaviour towards the undeserving of the other sex."

Elizabeth lifted up her eyes in amazement, but was too much oppressed to make any reply.

Compare at this point the satirist with the controversialist, the use Mary Wollstonecraft made of this point with this comment of laughter. Mary Bennet is merely a type figure which Miss Austen uses here as a bowstring to shoot her needle-pointed darts at the romantics. Mr. Collins is as typically the empty-headed churchman. He sees Lydia's transgression as "A distress of the bitterest kind, because proceeding from a cause which no time can remove . . . The death of your daughter would have been a blessing in comparison of this . . . Let me advise you to throw off your unworthy child from your affection forever, and leave her to reap the fruits of her own heinous offence." Mrs. Bennet is at first alarmed lest Mr. Bennet fight Mr. Wickham,

And now here's Mr. Bennet gone away, and I know he will fight Wickham, wherever he meets him, and then he will be killed, and what is to become of us all?

and then chagrined because he has not, "Who is to fight Wickham and make him marry her? . . ." Her naïve behavior when the marriage is patched up is sheer parody of the "make an honest woman" theory. Elizabeth, too, feels that they must marry, but it is to her disgracefully the least of evils, not gloriously (as for her mother) the greatest good. Mr. Bennet is nearly of Elizabeth's way of thinking, and at first will not have Lydia and Wickham come to the house at all. He seems ready to obey Collins's injunction, but at length receives them, though without any show of affection at a time when Mrs. Bennet takes them effusively to her bosom. The village gossips are somewhat disappointed at the marriage.

The good news quickly spread through the house; and with proportionate speed through the neighbourhood. It was borne in the latter with decent philosophy. To be sure it would have been more for the advantage of conversation, had Miss Lydia Bennet come upon the town; or, as the happiest alternative, been secluded from the world, in some distant farm house. But there was much to be talked of in marrying her; and the good-natured wishes for her well-doing, which had proceeded before from all the spiteful old ladies in Meryton, lost but little of their spirit in this change of circumstances, because with such an husband her misery was considered certain.

They had made such a good beginning on Wickham when the news first broke—"All Meryton seemed striving to blacken the man, who, but three months before, had been almost an angel of light,—that it seemed a pity to spoil a good rake by allowing him to make an honest woman of his victim." But if Wickham is a good rake, his position is not what it would have been a century before. Elizabeth and Mrs. Gardiner at least raise the question whether the reforms instituted by William of Orange in the manners of the Army have not gone so far that an officer cannot be a gentleman and a rake at one and the same time; they speak of "such an affront to Colonel Foster," and "disgrace in the corps." Take them all in all, even laying aside the touches of satire, and we have here a view much the same as Scott's. The moderate view well tempered with common sense is much the same whether it come from realist or romantic.

As Scott refutes Bage, so Hannah More seeks to neutralize Mary Wollstonecraft. She sets her target high and shoots straight at it.

. . . among the innovations of this innovating period the imposing term of *rights* has been produced to sanctify the claims of our female pretenders, with a view not only to rekindle in the minds of women a presumptuous vanity dishonourable to their sex, but produced with a view to excite in their hearts an impious discontent with the post which God has assigned to them in the world.

This is from her *Strictures on the Modern System of Female Education,* 1799. Against "The Wrongs of Women" she is no less violent than against their rights.

About the time that this first attempt at representing an adulteress in an exemplary light [*i.e. The Stranger*] was made by a German dramatist, which forms an aera in manners, a direct vindication of adultery was for the first time attempted by a *woman* a professed admirer and imitator of the German suicide, Werter. The *female Werter,* as she is styled by her biographer, asserts in a work entitled "The Wrongs of Women," that adultery is justifiable, and that restrictions placed on it by the laws of England constitute one of the *Wrongs of Women.*

Here we have with more definition than in Miss Edgeworth and elsewhere the precise case against "German literature." No less exact is the formulation of the charge against Rousseau. She is speaking of literature which "serves to corrupt the public and undermine Christianity."

Rousseau was the first popular dispenser of this complicated drug, in which the deleterious infusion was strong, and the effect proportionably fatal, for he does not attempt to seduce the affections but through the medium of the principles. He does not paint an innocent woman ruined, repenting, and restored; but with a far more mischievous refinement, he annihilates the value of chastity, and with pernicious subtlety attempts to make this heroine appear almost more amiable without it. He exhibits a virtuous woman the victim, not of temptation, but of reason; not of vice but of sentiment; not of passion but of conviction; and strikes at the very root of honour, by elevating a crime into a principle. With a metaphysical sophistry the most plausible, he debauches the heart of woman, by cherishing her vanity in the erection of a system of male virtues, to which, a lofty dereliction of those that are her more peculiar and characteristic praise, he tempts her to aspire; powerfully insinuating, that to this splendid system chastity does not necessarily belong: thus corrupting the judgment, and bewildering the understanding, as the most effectual way to inflame the imagination and deprave the heart.

After this we are not surprised to come upon the dictum, "Girls should be led to distrust their own judgment." They must learn to submit, and must cultivate the submissive virtues, not "on the low ground of its being decorous, feminine and pleasing, . . . but let them be carefully taught to cultivate it on the high principle of obedience to Christ." Woman, then, must lay aside her judgment, but she must enlarge her understanding.

The more a woman's understanding is improved, the more obviously she will discern that there can be no happiness in any society where there is a perpetual struggle for power; and the more the judgment is rectified the more accurate views will she take of the station she was born to fill, and the more readily will she accommodate herself to it . . .

So it would seem that if we can lay aside the judgment, or mistrust it, and at the same time rectify it and use it, we may be soundly educated in submission to the station to which it pleases God to call us.

Meanwhile the lesser moralists turned the course of the "fallen" heroine straight into the melodrama. The first noteworthy instance of this is *The Father and Daughter* of Mrs. Amelia Alderson Opie, which comes conveniently at the landmark date of 1800. Mrs. Opie isn't sure she has written a novel; "I know," she says in the preface, "that *The Father and Daughter* is wholly devoid of those attempts at strong character, comic situation, bustle, variety of incident, which constitute a *novel,* and that its highest pretensions are to be considered a *simple, moral tale.*" This simple moral tale opens with a gambit—the pawn reputation is lost in the first move—which immediately became the favorite of hack writers for the rest of the century.

The night was dark,—the wind blew keenly over the frozen and rugged heath, when Agnes, pressing her moaning child to her bosom, was travelling on foot to her father's habitation. "Would to God I had never left it!" she exclaimed.

If this is, as it seems to be, the first appearance of this famous necessary scene, Mrs. Opie deserves a monument from the writers of melodrama of the nineteenth century. We who were brought up on it, scarcely need, as Mrs. Opie's readers perhaps did, to read the next seventy pages in order to learn that "Agnes Fitzhenry was the only child of a respectable merchant in a country town . . ." and so on to page seventy where we read, "But to return to Agnes, who, when she beheld in her insane companion her injured father, the victim probably of her guilt, let fall her sleeping child, and, sinking on the ground, extended her arms towards Fitzhenry, articulating in a faint voice, 'O God! My father!' then prostrating herself at his feet, she clasped his knees in an agony too great for utterance." This tale is worth citing because it is true melodrama growing directly out of Puritan moralizing, and marks what seems to be the beginning of the melodrama tradition of affirming at every performance the public code of morals by hissing the villain and applauding the virtuous hero and heroine when the characters are passed across the stage for the purpose. It is melodrama because the author is bold enough to impose a major catastrophe on her heroine, but not brave enough to enforce the full penalty. It shows the weakening of tragedy by sentimentality in that the attempt at clemency may seem to the reflective mind as the worst of cruelty when it commutes the penalty of death called for by Goldsmith's law into life imprisonment with an insane cell-mate. It is melodrama in so far as it is sensational; it calls in the terrors of the Gothic romance and the stage indecencies of insanity, indecencies that were expurgated from Shakespeare and rejected when Monk Lewis tried to stage them, to enforce the austere puritan code of morals. It shows us the beginnings of nineteenth-century melodrama in third-rate puritan moralizing, the attempt of the petty moralist to handle the thunder of Milton without killing anybody.

Even so Mrs. Opie preserved many decencies which one and another of her colleagues violated, the amenities of the English language, for example, of which Elizabeth Helme seems to have known little. Her *Farmer of Inglewood Forest,* 1796, opens with a picture of that pious peasant, Godwin by name, posed "with a dignity that might have graced a more distinguished rank" under an aged oak. "On his knee lay the Bible; on his right hand sat his wife, who, though gray hairs shaded her temples, the beam of youthful affection was not extinguished in her eye." In the picture also are his sons William and Edwin, "and at their mother's feet was placed [note that the author modestly disclaims responsibility for the pose] their sister Emma, trimming a straw hat with ribbons for the ensuing fair."

The lecture concluded, they adjourned to their humble mansion, which, though appertaining to some rich and highly cultivated land, was nothing more than a spacious and convenient farm-house; yet, to those to whom cleanliness and comfort constitute luxury, this dwelling possessed every attribute. The frugal meal was soon prepared, and seasoned with innocent mirth; and the happy cheerfulness of hearts unconscious of guile, might have outbalanced in pleasure far more sumptuous entertainments, for labour had given health, and health appetite; and for the corroding passions of envy, jealousy, pride, or malice, that so frequently embitter the feasts of the great, their hearts were too humble to entertain such overbearing intruders.

Clearly the stage is set for melodrama. Edwin, who is engaged to a neighbor's daughter, the virtuous Agnes, cannot wait for the appointed marriage. She protests, "Does not our parents think it wrong?—and you as well as me, Edwin, used to be satisfied with their decision; but you have grown strangely impetuous." Obviously this is written for the unthinking, and if it is tragedy, it is low tragedy or melodrama. Agnes hasn't grammar enough to stand off the strangely impetuous Edwin. Two pages more, and

Her gentle spirits were overpowered with the scene which had taken place; her head sunk on Edwin's bosom, and she could scarcely preserve herself from fainting. In that fatal moment the guardian angel of virtue and innocence, for a short time, left the unhappy and too susceptible Agnes,—and the villain Edwin succeeded in his infernal purpose.

Emma also goes to the bad. She falls victim to the gentlemanly seducer, who probably "possess every attribute." He is a married man, Whitmore by name, who promises to divorce his wife and marry Emma. One of his friends leaves a romance where Emma "carelessly" takes it up.

It was an elegantly written fiction, in which the hero, unable to combat his passion for a married woman, had terminated his existence. [Was it *The Sorrows of Werther?*] Emma's heart was not formed of unfeeling materials, and the catastrophe cost her many tears. The heroine was represented virtuous, yet she apparently loved the suicide; circumstances that Emma had thought incompatible; for how, had ever before whispered her innocent heart, can a good woman love any man but her husband? The hapless lover too was mentioned with pity and tenderness, sentiments in the humanity of which Emma coincided; but no one deplored what she had ever been taught to believe, that suicide was everlasting perdition; nor was she displeased at the omission of this circumstance, the tenderness of her disposition leading her to sympathise with the sufferer, and pity those errors her education had taught her to abhor.

Thus did the dangerous elegance of a pathetic tale at once undermine "all that the priest and nurse had taught," and which her father had never contradicted, leaving those ideas implanted on the mind which he thought might tend to the general good, or otherwise trusting to time and reason to develop, in the breasts of his children, sentiments which he found inexplicable, consonant with the philanthropy, that actuated all his thought and actions; . . .

No passage in the story shows more clearly than this the purpose of the whole, to glorify rustic and bourgeois virtues, standards of conduct, by contrast with novels which exhibit aristocratic manners without condemning them. Mrs. Helme's tale tries to be pathetic, but it flaunts no dangerous elegance. Whitmore plies Emma with elegance "until in an hour of unguarded folly, she bartered her honour for the gaudy and useless trappings of pride and vice." For the rest, it is hardly necessary to read the chapters, the tawdry copperplates tell the tale. There is "Edwin's surprise on Opening the Coffin." Edwin may be surprised, but you and I are not, to see therein the mother and the child in pale copperplate effigy. There is "Edwin at the Tomb of Agnes," in which the artist has not done justice to the text, for "Edwin threw himself on the ground and wept aloud for a considerable time" at that hallowed spot. There is "The Unfortunate Emma Discovered by Fanny," perhaps the most familiar melodrama scene which these plates exhibit. A careless stage hand has set the property lightning upside down—or is it a bare tree?—anyway, it denotes the conventional wild storm of the prodigal's return; "the wind blew a perfect hurricane, the rain and mingled snow beat against the window, and Fanny, in the charity of her heart had recommended to the protection of Heaven all who were exposed to the inclemency of the night, when, in the intervals of the tempest, a kind of hollow moan struck her ear." Even after that it takes nearly two pages to get to the situation shown in the picture. Agnes dies soon afterward of consumption. Her father forgives her: "What if thou hast been faulty, thou art not the first: God has forgiven thee, I am sure; and let him that hath no sin throw the first stone." The author in the same spirit forgave Agnes at the time of her fall: "Daughters of chastity, condemn not, but pity! May example warn you that Secrecy and Temptation are ever to be avoided." But Edwin, seducer of Agnes and at the same time paramour of the wife of Emma's seducer, spurns his sister Emma; "I have nothing to say to you, infamous girl; . . . How is it possible at your age to have so soon forgotten the precepts inculcated from your youth?"

This ensample teacheth us that it takes more than sin and death to make high tragedy. The verdict is guilty and the sentence is death, but the result is sure to be low tragedy so long as it is Elizabeth Helme and not Fate or God who does the preaching. Puritan earnestness is too complete to be high seriousness; the seriousness cannot be high if the preacher succeeds in bringing it down to what he believes to be the level on which his hearers walk. We may follow lovely woman, then, from the level of rococo folly to the level of Victorian melodrama without departing from the path of sentimentality.

CHAPTER IX

SOME DON'T

Duke Bailey greater wealth computes
 And sticks, they say, at no-thing,
He wears a pair of golden boots
 And silver underclothing.

Duke Humphry, as I understand,
 Though mentally acuter,
His boots are only silver, and
 His underclothing pewter.

"Two Dukes would Mary make a bride,
 And from her foes defend her"—
"Well, not exactly that," they cried,
 "We offer guilty splendour."

"We do not offer marriage rite,
 So please dismiss the notion!"
"Oh dear," said she, "that alters quite
 The state of my emotion."

The Earl he up and says, says he,
 "Dismiss them to their orgies,
For I am game to marry thee
 Quite reg'lar at St. George's."

(He'd had, it happily befell,
 A decent education,
His views would have befitted well
 A far superior station.)

His sterling worth had worked a cure,
 She never heard him grumble;
She saw his soul was good and pure,
 Although his rank was humble.

Her views of earldoms and their lot,
 All underwent expansion—
Come, Virtue in an earldom's cot!
 Go, Vice in ducal mansion!

SOME don't. Pamela didn't, and many, perhaps most, of her readers know no more of her than just that. To them she stands in a fixed attitude of categorical negative—Don't—Won't—Shan't—Mustn't—No!—No!!—No!!! To them her don'tness looms so big that they cannot see the real Pamela behind it. Most of her daughters, fortunately for their relations with their society, follow her lead so unobtrusively that one is not conscious of the choice. But there is a host also of those who must make the choice, and deserve credit for choosing as she did, because to them the choice between innocence and guilty splendor is that between ease and starvation. The true daughters of Pamela are the virtuous working girls, and they certainly do resemble their mother. The family resemblance is

obvious to the reader of elementary mind because it consists so
entirely of outward and visible traits and acts. These daughters
of Pamela are not intelligent, but they have their mother's
obstinacy, which determines the main lines of their behavior
pattern. Richardson set this pattern on the loom of fiction, and
it wove itself by rote for nearly two hundred years. It consists
of a simple combination of warp and woof; Pamela's situation
and Pamela's choice. Both are as old as human saga and story.
Richardson's bright idea consisted in adding a lively sex interest to the most popular of the fairy tales, and translating
it into the terms of his own day, the terms of puritanism, the
social compromise, and the everyday life of every servant girl.

If Richardson had known all the folk literature of the world,
and had deliberately searched it, he could hardly have chosen
a more popular theme. It is the fairy tale of the type we name
for its best known heroine, Cinderella. It is the scullion's dream
of escape from her slavery by flight in imagination into the
supernatural. Grimm's *Kinder- und Hausmärchen* has many
examples, and so have ballad, legend and myth all over the
world. If we chose, we might divide their heroines into two
classes, those who are born servants, and those who have servitude
thrust upon them, who when we find them in rags and ashes
are princesses in disguise. The choice may be taken as the
dreamer's idea of the validity of class distinction. If in your
mind there is an innate difference between a scullion and a
princess, your dream tells you that you were born upstairs. If
the only difference is in the clothes they wear, you have only to
wish for the clothes. If we think of the dream as a mild form
of insanity, we see in it delusions of grandeur and persecution
mania. Both find more indulgence when the heroine is a
princess in disguise. These two classes of heroines are the only
variations on the theme as it appears in the novel beyond the
circumstantial ones of time and place and setting.

Richardson did not search folk-lore and choose the theme

deliberately; he found it in life about him, and was drawn to it by affinity. It is a Richardsonian motif from the start. He is the mother or grandmother, telling soothing tales to children to keep them contented and quiet. The *hausmärchen* are tales for the house, the woman's kingdom where the entrance of the man is an invasion. In the Grimm version Cinderella's father is "a certain rich man," no higher than upper middle class unless the land be one "whose merchants are princes and whose traffickers are the honourable of the earth." She gains her fortune not by capricious gift of a fairy godmother, but by pious devotion at her mother's grave. Children, be good; honor your mother who tells you this tale, and you may rise a grade and a half above your present social rank. Thus did Pamela, and her virtue was rewarded by promotion to the gentry. Does anyone remember that Cinderella was born upstairs? Pamela was not, and Richardson gave himself the trouble of educating her above her birthright.

Not all his followers were so painstaking. The princess-in-disguise device is easier to manage, for the reader will swallow it eagerly at the outset and ask no inconvenient questions afterward. For generations before the time of the novel, folk-lore had taught people to accept the idea; the fields of myth, ballad and tale are so thickly sown with the motif that it is not worth while to pick out single instances nor possible to name all. It comes down to later times in the romance tradition in the drama with the Violas and Rosalinds of the Elizabethan stage, and into the novel by way of Sidney's *Arcadia* and Lodge's *Rosalind* through such romances as those of Eliza Haywood. In line with her tradition is *The Fair Wanderer,* anonymous, 1751, which inevitably calls for a glance back to *Twelfth Night,* and Shakespeare's source for the Viola story, the *Apollonius and Sylla* of Barnaby Riche. Sylla is a frank young animal who wants her man, and when he turns (or runs) away from her, disguises herself and goes after him till she gets him. Shakespeare turns

Delicacy Holds Her Helpless

Lured into the Thorny Path of Vice

FEMALE DIFFICULTIES

"My Honor Is My All"

this to the wistful, unselfish love of Viola, who wins by tactics as nearly as possible, under the circumstances, the opposite of Sylla's. Ethelinda, the Fair Wanderer, is in character more like Sylla; her passion for the handsome Mirabel "was more resemblant to Lust than Love." But she is not aggressive enough to win as Sylla did, though she follows far in disguise, attendant on Mirabel as his valet. Neither can she win as did Viola, so she ends in a convent. These stories stem back to such ballad tales as "Childe Waters and Fair Janet," in which the girl, pregnant by a lover who leaves her, runs after his horse over hill and dale, and swims after him through rivers. They are mentionable in a chapter on Pamela only through their cousinship to Cinderella.

Patty Saunders, 1752, "first began to understand" at about the age of four, that "she lived with one Thomas Saunders, a thatcher." This looks a bit like a Pamela pedigree, but the reader begins to understand no later than Chapter II that Patty's father is a duke, and Pamela dissolves into Cinderella, and in the subsequent wild adventures fades out of the picture. Patty does, indeed, stand out sturdily for her virginity, but, as we saw in Chapter VIII, more for the sake of adventure than for piety in so far as the author's contrivance of the resistance is concerned.

Lucy Wellers, who appears above in Chapter VIII, is directly in line with both Pamela and Cinderella. She was born upstairs; she comes of a genteel family. She was thrust into servitude by a reverse of fortune which in the novel takes the place of any fairy changeling device. Her father was a spendthrift who left her penniless when he died. Charlotte Lennox's Henrietta Courtney (1760) was not born to servitude; she achieved it. She was born in the shadow of a coronet; her father was the son of an earl. Her noble relatives gall her pride, and she resolves to establish her superiority to them by going into service; nothing higher than the station of a waiting-maid is lowly enough to satisfy her proud spirit and sufficiently humiliate her persecutors. Anne Hughes's Caroline Ashford (1787) is in a similar situation; she is the daughter of the youngest son of "an opulent baronet," who, like Henrietta's father, was disinherited for marrying without his father's consent. Miss Hughes's Juliana (1788) is branded with illegitimacy, and takes service as a governess; the familiar device of the "three-decker," "We shipped as able bastards till the wicked nurse confessed." So the loom clacks and the pattern repeats itself with unbelievable monotony on and on through the eighteenth century, through the nineteenth, and into the twentieth.

In the melodramatic working-girl novels of the late nineteenth and earlier twentieth centuries, gentility is as pat to Malvolio's formula as ever was servitude, some are born to it, some achieve it, and some have it thrust upon them. Agnes Renier, heroine of Dwight Tilton's *Miss Petticoats*, 1902, is clearly in the first category. She was an American mill hand who felt "that in some indefinable way" the mill "kept her from the better things of existence. She was different from the other working girls, and was determined to be a lady." She became one; it is quite simple. All you have to do is to discover that your grandfather is a French count, go to France and win him over, return to the mill town and triumph over those who despised you. Eric St. Ross, in *Only a Mill Girl, or, A Manchester Man's Revenge*, says of Kate O'Fulford that "somehow she is a perfect lady although only a mill girl." She can write "a fine Italian hand" and "speak like a lady," though she declares, "I'll never be ashamed o' my Lancasheer dialect." Clearly she must have been born that way. She was gifted, too, with exemplary table manners. The author says of her, when she is dining with the hero's family after she has saved his life,

We must confess that more than one well-bred person there expected some breach of table etiquette from Kate. Not a fault had she unless modesty and consummate ease are faults. Maude was annoyed. She would have been delighted if Kate had attempted to eat peas with her knife, so that she might have had an opportunity of championing her newly elected favorite.

She was born with the ability to play and sing "divinely." In the drawing-room after dinner they ask her to sing. The hero fears the worst, but she sings and plays her own accompaniment so as to charm all her hearers. Elsie Brandon, heroine of *A Working Girl's Honor,* 1911, also astounds her lover with her magnificent voice. The rival beauty mutters, "Working girl as she is, how can he help loving her madly when she is so beautiful and so gifted?" When all (including the reader) wonder how she could sing grand opera with the voice of a grand opera singer, Elsie tells us, "I was taught by a friend of our choir-master, who said I had a phenomenal voice. He wished me to go on the stage." Kate O'Fulford acquired the art of aristocratic dressing in Sunday School. Her neighbors found fault with her, "The loikes o' her dressin' up loike a foine lady." The author reassures us:

Kate's only offense was the aspiration after something better than the condition in which she found herself. Her earnings were sufficient to pay her way [Mark you, no guilty splendor!], attend night-school for years, and Sunday school. She had no drunken parents to rob her, and so was able to dress better than her fellow toilers, and lay something aside for a rainy day.

Maggie Pepper, heroine of Charles Klein's novel of the same name (1911), was quite business-like in her achievement of gentility.

She was minded to become a person of real importance in the world. It was borne in on her that to this end she should have health and beauty and the most possible of training in mind and manners. These things she sought to acquire as best she might by observation of the models that came within the range of her vision, and by reading such books and magazines as she could afford. She lived with the utmost simplicity, avoiding the usual recreations of those in her own walk of life, for the simple reason that they did not appeal to her. She was so amiable to her fellows in the store that this attitude of aloofness did not make her unpopular, although it provoked a mild wonder. And, since she was not out merry-making of nights, she had time for her reading and for those many personal attentions to which she came presently . . . She avowedly believed it her duty to be as beautiful as possible. Instinct taught her the supreme value of loveliness to a woman, and observation confirmed the truth . . . Since she was not born to the graces of deportment, she did her best to acquire them.

Even with all this she was dissatisfied with the results, though she "accomplished wonders in reality." Is the author writing a manual for shopgirls? If so, Maggie is a true daughter of Pamela.

Her habit of thought and life itself induced a refinement that reacted through her bearing at all times. Whether born with a strain of blue blood, or whether it was solely the result of her system of life, the girl had come into the possession of an instinct that many ladies might well have envied. Though she was totally unaware of it herself, an air of breeding went with her as an aura. Those who came into association with her felt the subtle influence instantly. There was about her ordinarily a poise that was worth any quantity of the merely formal attributes of good-breeding.

Was she born with blue blood? If so it was one hundred per cent American.

Finally, there was in her at its highest the American facility for adaptation and assimilation. The women of other countries follow the conventions come down to them from preceding generations. A certain conservatism is born in them, of the blood; it is common to peasant and princess alike. The American woman is restrained by no such hamper. Rather the instinct for change is born in her, the craving for new and better expression . . . In other lands, one may ape the duchess, and do it to perfection. It is most hazardous to assert the social position of any woman merely from the way she is garbed and bears herself . . . And Maggie possessed the quality of assimilation to a marvellous extent.

More illustrious writers than St. Ross and Klein do much the same thing. George Gissing endows Thyrza, a factory-girl, with a marvellous voice and a sensitive, highly imaginative nature. Like Pamela, she has soft white hands; her sister will not allow her to do any of the housework,

for she was sensible of refinements; numberless little personal delicacies distinguished her from the average girl of her class, and even from Lydia . . . Thyrza had repaid her sister's devotion with subtle influences tending toward a comely life.

Truly it is much easier for the heroine to be a princess in disguise, but the achievement is instructive to an aspiring reader.

In the fairy tale, Cinderella's only specified occupation is picking out of the ashes the beans that others have spilled. Most Cinderella-Pamelas have felt that people spilled beans only to make trouble for them, and have had neither pride nor joy in the work of picking them up. There are several varieties of beans, but none too many. We have seen that what the poor girl could do in the eighteenth century was limited by her necessity for keeping up her delicate air; if she could lay that aside her opportunities were before her to take or make according to the degree of her initiative. But if she must be a lady she must give way to FEMALE DIFFICULTIES; misfortune, it seems was no less feminine than Fortune herself. So it was still a century later. An occupational abstract of the census of 1841, the first systematic collection, probably, of statistics on occupations of women, shows a list of some four hundred occupations of astonishing variety engaging hundreds of thousands of women in England. At about the same period we find in a book of "characters" of English types a sketch by "Miss Winter" of "The Family Governess" in the form of a narrative of the woes of Miss Villars, whose father, like that of Cinderella, was not a very good business man. She did not want to teach, she was not qualified to teach, to instruct, however, was her fate: she could not remain dependent on her father; nor could she, as if she had been a son instead of a daughter, choose among different professions that which would suit her; nor marry a rich man she did not like, as she might have done, and as many do.

Why couldn't she choose as if she had been a son? First, because she was ignorant; second, because she needs must keep up her gentility; third, because there was nothing in the wide world, no gainful occupation in the whole four hundred, for which she had the slightest aptitude or the least training.

An occupational census of the heroines of novels of three centuries, somewhat more than a hundred, of which some ten per cent are of the eighteenth century, fifty per cent from the nineteenth and forty per cent from the twentieth, shows heroines hampered by their delicacy to about ninety-six per cent; that is, they take advantage of about four per cent of their opportunities. In the eighteenth century we find the ten are evenly divided between governesses and servant maids. In the nineteenth century we find fifteen governesses or teachers, seven factory girls, three apprentices to dressmakers, three shopgirls, three artists, three models, and one or two each of dairymaids, servant maids, nurses, bookkeepers, pit-girls, fishwives, and truck farmers. In the twentieth century we have twelve secretaries and stenographers, seven shopgirls, four models, two each of teachers, companions, beauty parlor operators, managers of large businesses, and one each of the following: personal maid, post girl, chorus girl, artist, farm girl, writer, famous dress designer, partner in a firm of accountants, partner in a bank—in all barely four per cent of the number of occupations in which women were engaged in 1841.

The difference between two occupations registered in the eighteenth-century novel and four hundred in the nineteenth-century census is a startling index of the changes of the century between *Pamela* and *Old Curiosity Shop*. We saw in Chapter II that the organization of industry worked in more than one way to take woman out of her position as producer and thrust her into a state of idleness or into the wage-earning class. The industrial revolution worked this change mainly in the cities by the end of the eighteenth century, and in the first quarter of the nineteenth had extended the change into the country. The "agrarian revolution" turned farming into a capitalistic manufacturing industry, and turned out of their positions the many women who were responsible proprietors or managers, into idleness, petty housekeeping, or wage-earning as day laborers. These last constituted a class to be reckoned with in life and in fiction through the greater part of the nineteenth century, from Mrs. Gaskell to Thomas Hardy. But further changes—machinery and men's labor unions—caused the disappearance of the class; Tess Durbeyfield is the last of them.

To Cinderella beans are beans, but you can sell them to Jack as opportunities of infinite significance.

"What do you call these?" he said.
"Beans," said Jack.
"Yes," said he, "beans, but they're the most wonderful beans that were ever known. If you plant them overnight, by the next morning they will grow up and reach the sky."

His mother, woman-like, does not see the opportunity, and throws the beans out of the window, but you can't keep a good bean down; they reach the sky just the same. Cinderella can't idealize a bean, but she can make a Rolls Royce out of a Hubbard Squash. Her poetic faith is all for princes; she can make one out of almost anything as readily as Jack can make a ladder to heaven out of a bean. If she is learned enough to read her Bible, she cons the Book of Esther and neglects the Book of Ecclesiastes. To her, happiness is social eminence and the luxury of material things; to her as to Agnes Renier work is not a means of attaining it, but an unjust barrier between her and it. Rank and luxury are debts the world owes her, and work only stops payment, an insult added to the injury. The distaste for work, and sometimes inaptitude for it, is, of course, the badge of the princess in disguise; reason enough why authors should insist on it for so long as social rank is the dream of servitude, or for so long as delusions of grandeur take shape as titles of aristocracy. This tradition does not begin to crumble in the Cinderella type of novel until nearly a hundred and fifty years after *Pamela*.

Almost the first suggestion that a woman might find in her work anything more than painful drudgery is that already quoted from Mrs. "Jennie June" Croly, 1882, whose article may have been fiction, but she did not offer it as such. In 1889, Merle, in Rosa Nouchette Carey's *Merle's Crusade,* cannot be a governess because she has not the ladylike accomplishment of spelling, cannot be a nurse because she has not money enough to enable her to go through the necessary training, so she becomes a nursery maid, and, oddly enough, finds so much satisfaction in the work that one might almost list her as the first of all the Cinderellas to find a "career" in the job of picking other people's beans out of other people's ashes. With Margaret Hale in Charles Garvice's *His Guardian Angel,* the circumstances are somewhat different. She develops into a talented painter, loves her work, and keeps it up after she marries the fairy prince, in this instance a noble lord. Such beans as these are her very own, and as truly a ladder to heaven as any the butcher could sell to Jack. So are those of an earlier heroine, Becky Sleeper in George M. Baker's *Running to Waste.* Becky begins as a tomboy, becomes a mill hand, and suddenly turns artist enough to make drawings on wood blocks for engraved illustrations. She is happy, too, in her work, whatever it is, but she is of a cheerful disposition. If there is a "career" here it is no more than implicit. Mrs. Humphry Ward's *Marcella,* 1894, is another early appearance in fiction of the idea that not every woman is a nurse because she was born a woman, that even "ministering angels" need hospital training. Even more significant is the fact that

Marcella after she qualifies as a nurse finds the work absorbing, not mere beans and ashes. This is the time of *The Bachelor Maid,* which suggests that it might be possible to prefer a "career" to an eligible marriage, but the career is vague, hardly more than separate maintenance provided by father, and the candidate weakens and returns to her lover's arms. If for the haughty damsels upstairs beans do not make ladders to the sky, small wonder that they throw them in the ashes for Cinderella, and small wonder that she can make no more of them than can her betters.

Even in the twentieth century Cinderella is still Cinderella; at least for the first ten years. In 1911 we find the novel arriving at the point which Jennie June signalled in 1882. Maggie Pepper wished to be a lady, but she did more than sit in the ashes and wish. By fifteen years of hard work she rose from shopgirl to assistant buyer, driven by ambition and sustained by enjoyment of her work, aided by the education which she determinedly acquired for herself. The heroine of *A Business Girl,* M. Allerton, 1918, is a stenographer who "loves" her work so much that she sets up an office of her own as a public stenographer.

The third decade of the century, that of the rediscovery of the old taboos, opens, appropriately enough, with a blast on Bernard Shaw's horn blown by Sir Harry Johnston, *Mrs. Warren's Daughter,* 1920. Has Mrs. Warren so far receded into ancient history that we need to be reminded that her profession is even more ancient, the most ancient of all for women? Is her daughter, then, a Cinderella? If so, she is a real come-outer. She is partner in a firm of accountants and an active worker in the suffrage and emancipation campaign. It is a rather self-conscious new pattern; a decade later it shows more poise. Ruth Suckow's Cora (1929) and Sinclair Lewis's Ann Vickers (1933) have their troubles, but they have also all the ease and sureness of efficient men in establishing their positions in their business and professional worlds. This new pattern does not obliterate the old one. The Cinderella-Pamela pattern weaves itself serenely on by rote as if there had been no change. In 1927 Kathleen Norris and Mary Pickford Fairbanks wrote it for the screen in *My Best Girl*. In the same year Phillips Oppenheim used it in *Miss Brown of X.Y.O.*, Berta Ruck in *The Mind of a Minx*, and Lola Jean Simpson in *Back Fire*. In 1929 Grace Livingston Hill used it in *Duskin*. In 1931 it appears unchanged in *Personal Maid*, by Grace Perkins, whose heroine is a serving-maid who

> *sees the moral beauty*
> *Of making worldly interest*
> *Subordinate to sense of duty.*

But like Pamela's her worldly interest does not suffer in the long run, for though she refuses guilty splendor she marries the millionaire.

Cora and *Ann Vickers* bring into the realm of art a type of fiction which in its magazine form is a mere work of fashion, the business story, in which business success is the basic ingredient and the love interest a sort of synthetic flavoring extract. Its development is apparent in the works we have been reviewing; it emerges as women, as a class, percolate through the barriers between work and business by means of their interest in their work, and their demand for, and attainment of, training and education for work, business and profession. Its emergence denotes the waning of the Cinderella interest in fiction as she learns to take more interest in the beans and less direct methods in the pursuit of Prince Charming. Baker's *Running to Waste*, 1874, is essentially of this type, and a very early example unless we include Charlotte Brontë's *Villette*, 1853, the first English novel, so far as these studies have gone, which deals with the heroine's work continuously and as an integral part of her life. It is less so in *Running to Waste*, for here a man is writing of a woman's work, if the author's name is a true one. This one is somewhat inclined to doubt because of the

Louisa-Alcott-like quality of the story. In order to make the story "wholesome" and the heroine healthy-minded, the author makes her a tomboy in childhood, fully conscious of boys, but as if she were one of them, and a hearty worker throughout; her love is man-fashion "of her life a thing apart." But her work is not her "whole existence," which is doubtless the reason why she no longer exists, for, one must believe, the author never was a mill hand or an illustrator. Neither, if we are to take his word, was he a woman. What is more, Becky Sleeper rises into the professional class without training, which suggests too clearly in spite of tomboyishness and the American background, the Old World device of the princess in disguise.

As early as 1814, Mary Brunton contrasted in *Discipline* the conscientious training girls receive for the profession of husband-getting with the inadequacy of their education for the profession of teaching. Thirty to forty years later Charlotte Brontë depicted three governesses whose training and education made them competent to fill their positions, Jane Eyre, Lucy Snow, and Frances Henri. The governess is the first of the wage-earners to rise to the professional class because she is in advance of the others to the extent of her birth, environment and education. She is always above the servant class in which her employer so uniformly (in fiction) tries to place her. For girls who are definitely in the working class the only training that appears in the novels is apprenticeship such as Mrs. Gaskell provides for Mary Barton and Ruth Hilton, nor does it seem likely that there is any instance earlier than those here recorded of promotion out of the working class by any other means than marriage. Apprenticeship seems to be the working girls' only training until the typewriter opens the door to business as a profession, the door between the outer office and the inner office. That opening is not dramatized in fiction till the last decade of the nineteenth century. Estelle Everett's (*Estelle's Millionaire Lover*) only qualification as a "typewriter" was her beauty, and the door which that opened led into the drawing-room. This was in 1893. Juliet Appleton (*The Typewriter Girl,* 1896) and Lois Cayley (*Miss Cayley's Adventures,* 1899) are better qualified, for both were Girton girls, and Juliet, at least, had studied typing and shorthand for four months. And unless we count Becky Sleeper, and unless Jennie June's little homily is fiction, Maggie Pepper (1911) is the first heroine we have met who promotes herself out of the working-girl class by hard work and no nonsense.

"I've worked my way up from cash-girl. I've been stock-girl; I've been saleswoman in every department. I've been on the job here since I was knee-high. So I thought I was entitled to ask for the place."
. . . Maggie found keen satisfaction in her work. Her intelligence was far beyond the ordinary, and she speedily found solace in the dreams of a lively ambition. She devoutly thanked heaven that she lived in a generation when woman is permitted to win for herself success in business life . . . Her ambition was too large to consider only the petty progress through the various departments of Holbrooke and Company's establishment.

But even so the paths of endeavor lead but to the Fairy Prince; Maggie marries her employer.

It is easy at this distance of time and change to make fun of Cinderella for directing her enchantments at the pumpkin instead of toward the beans, but what could the poor girl do? Even in this age we are not unanimous in believing that it is always better or wiser for a woman to seek a career rather than to bend all her energies to getting the right man. The sciences which counsel us on such matters, anthropology, psychology, sociology, psychoanalysis, psychiatry, seem to testify on both sides. We learn that thwarted sex-energy may be "sublimated" into higher achievements, that races or groups where full sex-expression is easy as soon as individuals feel its urge are not likely to rise to heights of achievement. On the other side they tell us that the psyche suffers when the bodily sex is thwarted—

that there is apt to be corrosive in the sublimate. Whatever you have, then, you miss the might-have-beens. So it is in the novel; the marriage-versus-career novel from J. G. Holland to H. S. M. Hutchison is apt to show women that their true career is their sex, and that achievement in art, business or profession is contrary to nature, the will of God, manifest destiny, or whatever each in the dialect of his generation chooses to call it. The Cinderella school which sees woman's true experience as the mating, and the gainful occupation as a mere means of subsistence till the end crowns the whole, is quite as easy to justify by science as the other, and it is much more popular because it is the common lot. The woman who can sublimate her energy into something of high worth, frequent as she may be in numbers, probably would not register high figures if we could reckon by percentages.

Pamela's master made her high offers if she would be "faithful and obliging," and when he first made his intentions clear he offered her a retaining fee:

". . . and here's something," said he, putting some gold in my hand, "to make amends for the fright I put you in."

"I won't take the money, indeed, sir," said I, "poor as I am: I won't take it . . . Oh, sir, take back your guineas! I will not have one, nor will my father, I am sure, till he knows what is to be done *for* them; and particularly what is to become of *me*."

The sentiment is immortal; its variations of phrase are many and amusing. The formula of the sentimental ballad of the Gay Nineties was "Take back your gold, for money cannot buy me." In the folk-ballad of "Childe Waters," long before Pamela's day it occurs in true ballad form:

> *"If the child be mine, Ffaire Ellen," he said,*
> *"Be mine, as you doe sweare,*
> *Take you Cheshire and Lancashire both,*
> *And make that child youre heyre."*

Shee says, "I had rather haue one kisse,
Child Waters, of thy mouth,
Then I would haue Cheshire and Lancashire both,
That lyes by north and south."

Lucy Wellers receives a proposition from her guardian almost in Mr. B.'s words, "I intend to make your fortune, child, if you will but be grateful." Her reply is not so humble as Pamela's, though to the same effect. "You infamous wretch," answered Miss Wellers, "how dare you make such proposals to me?" We have already seen (in Chapter II) how she sets the same idea to a different air, one of aristocratically embellished diction, when she has to sing it to a baronet. This is "Miss Wellers," not mere Pamela. In fact not often has a woman with any appearance of gentility a chance to use the Take Back Your Gold form of rejection, for to her a villain of any intelligence knows better than to offer it. Hargrave in *Self Control*, 1811, is not so stupid as to suppose that Laura Montraville would do for money what she would not do for love. He offers her love, and she talks innocently of marriage.

. . . he urged his suit in language yet more unequivocal. No words can express her feelings, when, the veil thus rudely torn from her eyes, she saw her pure, magnanimous Hargrave—the god of her idolatry, degraded to a sensualist,—a seducer. Casting on him a look of horror, dismay, and anguish, she exclaimed, "Are you so base?" and freeing herself, with a convulsive struggle, from his grasp, sunk without sense or motion to the ground.

In *The Wanderer* of Madame D'Arblay, 1814, Lord Melbury, convinced that "Ellis" (Juliet) is an adventuress, makes her a proposition, to which she replies:

"And is it then, from a brother of the pure, the exemplary Lady Aurora Granville, that I am destined to receive the most heart-rending insult of my life?"

Juliet is an aristocrat in disguise; Laura Montraville is upper middle class, a lady by virtue of refinement. Madame D'Arblay had lived at court; Mrs. Brunton was in spirit a daughter of Calvin. Neither (of the heroines or of the authors) is fully entitled to the working-girl's formula—indeed, "gold" is no conspicuous part of either offer. "Take back your gold, for money will not buy me," is an assertion from the plebeian of a pride equal to that of the aristocrat. The lady's reply is an expression less of pride than of shame. Each is dictated by conscious class distinction; their common denominator is something like, "What do you take me for?"

In Anne Hughes's *Henry and Isabella,* 1788, the heroine, Isabella alias Juliana, is dealing with a noble Earl, Lord Belford (even so long after Pamela as this it is still necessary to begin the name of the rake with B, or the reader might not recognize him). He offers her marriage, but she tells him she knows he is already married. He shows only a moment's confusion, then renews the offer:

. . . Let me likewise remind my adored Juliana that there is no person in the world known by the name of Lady Belford; that no one will ever dispute the title with her, nor will she injure anyone by assuming it. Hold, Sir, (exclaimed our heroine) were you unmarried and thought proper to offer me your hand and fortune; poor, unknown, and unprotected as I am, it is likely that I should reject them; do not then suppose that any proposals that you have now the power of making, can cost me even the hesitation of a moment.

She is entitled to an embellishment of diction at least equal to his, for when the wicked nurse confesses we learn that she is his daughter! But, although no one knows it but the author, she is not entitled to the working-girl's formula.

Comparable to the position of Isabella is that of Charlotte Brontë's Jane Eyre; each has an offer of marriage from a man already married. But Isabella's is prompted by lust, Jane's by love; Isabella's is an insult, Jane's is a temptation. Anne Hughes's scene looks toward sentimental melodrama; Charlotte Brontë's is in the realm of tragedy. In the tone of realism we have nothing noteworthy on the situation after Richardson until we come to Mrs. Gaskell. Her Mary Barton (1848) listens to the blandishments of young Mr. Carson, innocently believing that he wishes to marry her. At length she realizes, seemingly too late, that she loves Jem Wilson, and tries to break with Carson, but he makes a high bid to hold her, and in so doing betrays himself.

". . . I thought we could be happy enough without marriage." (Deep sank these words into Mary's heart.) "But now, if you like, I'll get a license to-morrow morning—nay, to-night, and I'll marry you in defiance of all the world, rather than give you up.". . .

"I am obliged to you, sir, for telling me what you have. You may think I am a fool; but I did think you meant to marry me all along; and yet, thinking so, I felt I could not love you. Still I felt sorry I had gone so far in keeping company with you. Now, sir, I tell you, if I had loved you before, I don't think I should have loved you now you have told me you meant to ruin me; for that's the plain English of not meaning to marry me till just this minute. I said I was sorry, and humbly begged your pardon; that was before I knew what you were. Now I scorn you, sir, for plotting to ruin a poor girl. Good night."

And with a wrench, for which she had reserved all her strength, she flew off like a bolt.

There is a suggestion here of Pamela in Mary's respectful demeanor, but it is only a hint. The situation is quite different. The paragraph before the one here quoted tells the reader that Mary

. . . had dreaded, now that she knew what true love was, to think of the attachment she might have created . . . it was a relief, to gather that the attachment was of that low, despicable kind which can plan to seduce the object of its affection . . . She need not be penitent to such a plotter! That was a relief.

There is real analysis here of the mind and feelings of a real girl. The phrase, "Now I scorn you for plotting to ruin a poor girl," may suggest the trite formula, but there is no melo-

drama in it where we find it. Verbally, however, it is a middle
term between Pamela and Nellie the Beautiful Cloak Model.

There is melodrama in the situation all along the line, where-
ever we find it in the work of the inferior practitioners. Mrs.
Radcliffe mingled the sweet sentimentalities of the lady author-
esses with sweet shivers of horror. This delicate blend was soon
fortified with fiery spirits distilled from Monk Lewis and
Byron. Such glimpses as we can get of the quality of the lost
and forgotten fiction between 1800 and 1850 indicate that it
went to the limit of the human imagination in pursuit of the
lurid. Penny dreadfuls and shilling shockers, they must have
perished by thousands, thumbed to dust by their addicts. Perhaps
thousands more perished by spontaneous combustion, their
sulphur and brimstone ignited by their own lightning, blown
up by their own thunder, drowned in their own blood. The
few that are left are collectors' items. One guesses that if we had
a plebiscite of all readers of the time the real "Victorian" novel
would turn out to be of this type, for it must have had thousands
of readers for every hundred who read Trollope or George Eliot.
Perhaps some who read it also read *Wuthering Heights* and did
not know the difference. Among these hectic scenes we find
heroines of humble birth, Peggy and Patty, Poor Mary, Father-
less Fanny, and others who scarcely own a name, the Kidnapped
Orphan, the Milliner's Girl, the Village Maid, the Cottage Girl,
the Clergyman's Daughter, and hosts of others if only we knew
them. These are in the direct line of descent from Pamela, and
the generation after them in the same line is the melodramatic
novel of later Victorian times, running even into the time of
Edward, *A Working Girl's Honor, The Curse of Beauty, Only
a Working Girl, Only a Mill Girl, Nellie the Beautiful Cloak
Model, Lotta the Cloak Model, Lil the Dancing Girl, Estelle's
Millionaire Lover,* and all the tribe they represent. Of these no
census has been taken. Since their descendants have become
shadows on the silver screen, their recorded annals have turned

their paper backs on us, and crept into the rear rooms of the older obscure book-shops on their way to the pulp mill. Let us take a look at some of the beautiful creatures before it is too late.

"Take back your gold!" they cry; the sentiment is unanimous; the words vary but little. Faith Marvin, shopgirl heroine of *For Gold or Soul* (Lurana Sheldon, 1900), says to the wealthy aristocrat who would corrupt her,

"Hush! Your words are an insult! I will not hear them. It is true that my knowledge of the world is limited, but this much I know . . . Working girl I am and may always be, but my lot is a queen's beside what you suggest! God pity the poor women who have not the wisdom to see it."

Estelle Everett is "the prettiest typewriter in New York." Her employer perceives that she is more than a mere machine, and offers her (not gold but) "diamonds, silks, horses." She tells him that his words are "an insult to any pure girl," and establishes the identification by promptly putting on her "hat and sacque." "Every word you utter," she says scornfully, "but betrays your utter baseness." Elsie Brandon, in *A Working Girl's Honor; or, Elsie Brandon's Aristocratic Lover,* reassures her mother, as does Pamela: "Mama, if I loved a man with all the passion of my soul, that love would turn to hate at the first breath of dishonor."—save that in Pamela's vocabulary the word "passion" does not occur in the feminine gender. Elsie's experience is Pamela's plus fifty per cent of Clarissa's multiplied by two, for she has to withstand siege from three men besides the hero, and finds herself three times in a house of prostitution. Inasmuch as it is always the same house, one must infer that in Elsie's makeup innocence plus ignorance equals stupidity. Her version of "Take back your gold," translates the formula into the dialect of the moron. Her employer, Mr. Harrison, makes her the offer.

"Wouldn't you like to have a dear little flat, all beautifully furnished, horses and carriages, silk dresses and jewels?"

"Yes," she answered, "I would like to have all those things, because then I would be rich, and mamma and Kate wouldn't have to work any more. But I guess there isn't much chance of my ever coming to that."

"My dear Elsie!" he panted, crowding her eagerly . . . "you shall have all those things, and more, too, if you will only be a good girl. Eh, my dear?"

He fumbled for her little hand as he spoke, and a sensation of utter horror overcame her, though even yet she did not comprehend what the wretched old man was proposing to her.

He was so old, so withered and tottering that her imagination stopped short of guessing that he was proposing infamy to her. She merely shuddered at his touch as she would have shuddered at contact with a snake . . .

"I—I will try to be good," she answered, "but I don't expect to get rich by it."

Can innocence continue to be alluring under the shadow of such black clouds of stupidity? A dim ray penetrates when Elsie discovers that she is in a house of prostitution.

"You horrid, wicked old man! Don't you dare touch me! Oh, if I had understood you! [Is the author suggesting "the moral obligation to be intelligent"?] I will tell them at the store; I will tell the whole world how wicked you are!"

"My dear, I am willing to give you your own price. Don't play virtuous; you won't get any more by it; and I hate the bother . . . Do you want a settled income?"

"I want nothing from you. I would not breathe the same air with you. You are a foul, wicked old monster. For shame! with one foot in the grave, to go about insulting defenseless girls."

The burlesque version, "Take back your gold, Reginald Montmorenci! Rather would I be the poor working-girl that I am than what your two-dollar bill would make me," is hardly an improvement on the density of Elsie Brandon's impenetrable innocence.

What can Heaven do to protect the priceless pearl of virginity when it is in charge of such a fool as Elsie Brandon? She has no mental agility, but she has physical strength which desperation increases. She

shut her little white teeth firmly together in the passionate resolve to defend herself to the last gasp ere she would permit herself to be detained a prisoner in that awful house.

And if flawless innocence must serve as armor to chastity, it cannot be too dense, too impenetrable. It protects Elsie in her sleep—from the hero, who, like Mr. B., later marries his intended victim.

. . . he fixed his eyes on the face, so pure and beautiful in its sweet unconsciousness.

A spasm as of pain crossed his features, and he drew back, murmuring hoarsely:

"She loves me now, and trusts me as she would Heaven. Dare I betray her trust, and dishonor her? If ever she should learn the truth, she will hate me. Could I bear her hate? Can I live without her love?"

He drew back step by step, as if he would put the width of the room between him and temptation; and at last, with his back against the wall he stood and gazed at her, while his conscience wrought within him. She was strangely, dangerously beautiful as she lay there, protected only by her innocence; and as his eyes wandered from her ravishing face to her rounded, perfect form, his broad chest heaved convulsively. . . . Great drops of perspiration started out on his brow and rolled slowly down over his face. . . .

"She is far, far above me!" he murmured. "She is too pure and good . . ." He crept softly from the room . . .

Milton had to call in an Attendant Spirit and two brothers to save a "lady." Heaven will protect the working girl all by itself. It is hopeless to expect a heroine to have more intelligence than the author of her being. Without mental agility these heroines can only use their legs, and leap for honor regardless of life. Sometimes it works, and sometimes it doesn't. Nellie Gray, the Beautiful Cloak Model (1906), is about to jump out of the window, but the villain considerately cries "Stop!" and she, with no consideration whatever, stops. Estelle Everett, the prettiest typewriter in New York, is not so docile. When the villain sees her on the window-sill poised for the plunge, he shouts, "Merciful Heavens! You will be killed!" "Better death than dishonor!" she retorts, and over she goes, not to a better world (she could not find a worse) but into the river, whence she is rescued by a narrow margin of coincidence. Thus does Milton's principle of the power of heavenly chastity come down in life, from the heights of poetry to the depths of melodrama.

These girls are looking ahead, but not to heaven. Whatever their religious professions, their main hope of happiness is in this world. Pamela sets the example to her daughters; pious as she is, she is no less shrewd.

He may condescend, perhaps, to think I may be good enough for his harlot; and those things don't disgrace men that ruin poor women, as the world goes. And so if I was wicked enough, he would keep me till I was undone, and till his mind changed; for even wicked men, I have read, soon grow weary of wickedness with the same person, and love variety. Well, then, poor Pamela must be turned off, and looked upon as a vile abandoned creature, and everybody would despise her; ay, and *justly* too, Mrs. Jervis; for she that can't keep her virtue, ought to live in disgrace.

A bystander in Caroline Hart's *From Want to Wealth* (1885) observes of working girls (or is it just girls?) "They have nothing but their good name to lose." It seems to be as true of them in the late nineteenth century as it was in the early eighteenth century that when they lose their "virtue" they have naught to hope for in this world; Goldsmith's law is still in force, at least in fiction. Elsie Brandon again translates Pamela into her dialect:

"I don't know how it may be with a man, but a girl's honor must be her most cherished possession as long as she lives . . . I am only a young girl yet, but I know that if I were not pure and virtuous, even though that virtue had been lost to you, the day would surely come when you would cease to respect or love me. Not even for you,

Harry, would I have yielded up my honor, for I should have known that there was no surer way of losing your love."

So it is also with heroines of more intelligence. One of Jane Eyre's reasons for leaving Rochester is that she feels that if she became his mistress he would eventually come to regard her as he does Madame Varens and his other mistresses on the continent. No more than Elsie Brandon is Jane a Cleopatra who scorns any means but her own charm to hold her man.

Not that they lack the charm; or if they do it is not because their authors did not try hard to endow them with it. They have a right to it, for Pamela was richly gifted with beauty, and she boasts of it as modestly as she can. Since it is essential to Richardson's plot, the reader must have it always in mind. There is no one to tell us of it but Pamela herself, and she is not to be found remiss in any duty; she conscientiously relays to us any reports of it that come to her, directly or by wireless, not omitting the becoming blushes appropriate to the recital. At the depth of her trial she might have called it a fatal gift, but in the end it was not so to her, for she added it to her virtue to make out a dowry which brought her a brilliant marriage. But to a few of her daughters it was indeed a fatal gift, for it brought them to their death. Such is the fate of Peggy and Patty in an anonymous novel of that name, 1783. In beauty there is little to choose between them, little to know.

> The eldest of these lovely young creatures [Peggy] could be barely seventeen . . . tall and full-formed for that early age . . . with the soft blue eyes of Lucy Collins! lips of coral, and a neck! but here imagination fails. The youngest of these angelic sisters . . . is a little lively brunette, about sixteen . . . a sweet rogue! with eyes so black and piercing that they deal death and destruction at every glance! cheeks glowing with the carnation bloom, a mouth! but how can I describe what is undescribable?

Here we have the double heroine, blonde and brune, but no significant distinction in behavior patterns, though of this there is a hint. Their father says of them,

Their dispositions are mild and good: . . . Peggy, my eldest child, is of rather a more sedate turn of mind than my little lively Patty, who is, however, equally good and dutiful.

It is not much of beauty, but its effects are lethal. Their fates are identical; hand in hand they tread the way to dusty death by way of rape and prostitution. It is as if the author, unable to make the reader visualize their charms (imagination fails at the neck) seeks to convince us by their fatal effect. So it is also with Mary Raymond in Mary Hays's *The Victim of Prejudice,* 1799. She, telling her own story, does not acknowledge the fatal gift, but she makes the most of her charms.

Tall, blooming, animated, my features were regular, my complexion a rich glowing brunette, my eyes vivacious and sparkling; dark chestnut hair shaded my face, and floated over my shoulders in luxuriant profusion; my figure was light and airy, my step firm, my aspect intelligent, and my mind inquisitive.

She is an early example of the athletic heroine—does the type originate here as an exaggeration of the behavior pattern of the brunette? Mary goes on to tell us that she had

a robust constitution, a cultivated understanding, and a vigorous intellect. I was early inured to habits of hardiness; to suffer without shrinking, the changes and inclemencies of the seasons; to endure fatigue and occasional labour; to exercise my ingenuity and exert my faculties, arrange my thoughts and discipline my imagination. At ten years of age, I could ride the forest horses without bridle or saddle; could leap a fence or surmount a gate with admirable dexterity; could climb the highest trees, wrestle with the children of the village, or mingle in the dance with grace and activity.

Even in her childhood these charms roused the passion of Sir Peter Osborne, who pursues her through years and chapters. Neither Heaven nor her athletic muscles can protect her from him. He catches her at a disadvantage at last and violates her. The results are hardships which leave her at the end in sight of death. In the course of them she has the satisfaction of refusing to marry her ravisher. But these are the daughters of Clarissa rather than of Pamela; few there were of Richardson's followers who had the courage to treat their heroines so harshly. With the others, beauty, be it gift or curse, is not fatal.

Pamela's father and mother feared lest Pamela's beauty should lead to her downfall. So in the nineteenth century it is less often the heroine herself who thinks of beauty as a curse than her family and friends. The sister of "the little beauty of the Passaic Cotton Mills," Hazel Esterbrook, had "one earnest prayer to Heaven"; it was that "little Gay's rare beauty would not prove a curse to her, for no man ever looked twice at that saucy, roguish, irresistible face whose heart was not conquered by it. She was only sixteen, yet she could count admirers by the score." Only by the score? There must have been hundreds, then, who looked but once. The mother and sister of Elsie Brandon "prayed fervently that her beauty would not be a curse to her." The idea is explicit in the title of *The Curse of Beauty; or, The Cloakmaker's Model* (1897). Can the author, Geraldine Fleming, make good the title? The first sentence of the heroine's beauty is a clean miss!

She was tall, with arms such as the famous Venus de Milo could not boast, and eyes and mouth and chin of which the sculptor never dreamed. Her eyes were like great velvet pansies before the sun has kissed all the dew from their exquisite depths—eyes that could grow soft with tenderness or black as night with passion. Hair that was like the softest threads of burnished gold crowned her brow. Her mouth, too, reminded one of the celebrated Venus, with its perfect curves, full lips, and exquisitely molded chin.

The arms, then, are anything or nothing, and one shudders to think of eyes and mouth of which the sculptor refuses to dream. Can velvet pansies and perfect curves redeem them and make them fatal?

The authors of these novels think that their readers prefer blondes. A check of many working-girl novels of the nineteenth century indicates that in every hundred heroines we have eighty blondes, ten brunes, and ten red-heads. The authors have little skill—one does not expect to find George Merediths in this class; for the most part their heroines appear only through raptures and ravings. Here, for example, is Carmen Deane, a creation of Geraldine Fleming's in *Only a Working Girl,* 1895. The hero tells us that he

> never had seen before so perfect a face. It was radiant and dazzling in the delicate hues of the skin; it was lit up by a pair of the most glorious blue eyes he had ever looked into; the little mouth was a perfect cupid's bow, with dimples dancing about the corners as if playing hide-and-seek with love; the cheeks were round and soft and peachy; the chin was molded by perfection's hand, and the brow was low, broad and white, with fluffy golden curls dancing about it in defiance of all attempts to confine them. He looked at her . . . and told himself that she was, face and form, the most beautiful creature he had ever looked upon.

Rose Hall is a fair example of the brunettes; we have already met her "dark, passionate glowing beauty" in Chapter VI. In general, too, these authors follow the age-old tradition of behavior-patterns, at least to the extent that the brunettes take a more active part in the action of the tale. Grant Allen is perhaps above this class, but he gave us a *Typewriter Girl,* and must take the consequences. Three of his novels, *The Woman Who Did, Miss Cayley's Adventures,* and *The Typewriter Girl,* have tall dark heroines who are forceful and self-reliant. Miss Cayley in describing herself suggests the theory of feeling and behavior.

> Nature had endowed me with a profusion of crisp black hair, and plenty of high spirits. If my eyes had been like Elsie's—that liquid blue which looks upon life with mingled pity and amazement—I might have felt as a girl ought to feel under such conditions; but having large dark eyes, with a bit of a twinkle in them, and being as well able to pilot a bicycle as any girl of my acquaintance, I have inherited or acquired an outlook on the world which distinctly leans rather towards cheeriness than despondency.

There is, then, a pretty definite way in which a girl with blue eyes "ought to feel," such eyes from their very pigmentation look upon life "with mingled pity and amazement"! Edgar Fawcett does not subscribe to this doctrine; his Claire Twining (*An Ambitious Woman,* 1883) has the infirmity of noble minds, and is active, in spite of fair skin and blue eyes, in seeking to gratify it.

Few indeed of these humble workers are inclined to use their beauty to improve their positions. It may be an asset to a "cloak model" now and then, but to shopgirls and mill hands it is a curse or a fatal gift. Eric St. Ross (*Only a Mill Girl*) puts a Greek goddess to work in a Manchester cotton mill. Kate O'Fulford has

> a pale face as sharply cut and as finely formed as that of any Grecian goddess. Her well-molded arms were, as is the fashion of mill girls, bare to the shoulders. Her bronze-brown hair rippled and waved, although tightly confined, and little coquettish curls peeped forth around her brow and neck. The former was broad and low; the latter magnificently poised, and as round and pure as an alabaster column.

Better men than he have done no less. Charles Reade in 1853 makes a Brunhild out of a "fish-wife." It is Christie Johnstone.

> She was fair, with a massive but shapely throat, as white as milk; glossy brown hair, the loose threads of which glittered like gold, and a blue eye, which being contrasted with dark eyebrows and lashes, took the luminous effect peculiar to that rare beauty.

George Gissing, too, gives to Thyrza, a factory hand, a face "so subtly modified, so refined, as to become a beauty of rare suggestiveness." Such beauty may bring its possessors love that releases them from the toils, but it does not get them promotion in business. In the ordinary run, beauty brings the heroine the persecutions of the villain and the chivalrous love of Prince Charming. When the villain is in the ascendant, the heroine's friends and family may speak of it as a curse or a fatal gift; she herself usually has other views.

Most of these toilers are as young as they are fair. Pamela is fifteen when we meet her and not much older when she marries. In the nineteenth century working-girl heroines average between fifteen and seventeen. At this rate, of one birthday a century, they will not be much older in our time. Whatever their years, it is the age of innocence. The authors do not fail to assure us of it. Richardson set the example; Mrs. Jervis says that Pamela is "a poor innocent young creature," and to innocence Pamela pins her faith; "innocence, I find, in a low fortune and a weak mind, has many advantages over guilt, with all its riches and wisdom." Mrs. Gaskell tells us that Ruth was "innocent and snow pure" in the beginning. Laura Jean Libbey says that fair-haired Lillian was "so pure, so true, so guileless" without telling us how pure, but for Lotta Marlowe she provides a standard; she is "as pure as a snow-drop or an angel," and even when she acts indiscreetly or wrongly she has an extenuating stanza ready from Moore:

> *Oh merry maid,—a spirit such as hers*
> *Is always pure, e'en when it errs.*
> *As sunshine, broken in the rill,*
> *Though turned away, is sunshine still.*

"Little hoydenish madcap Gay" (of the Passaic cotton mills) is "as tender as a white dove, and as guileless as one of the white angels in heaven"; the hero perceives it: "Little Gay is as pure as yonder fleecy clouds sailing across the blue of the heavens, and I love her better than my own soul." Estelle Everett (the prettiest typewriter in New York) shows that "if ever innocence and purity were written on a human face, they are written there." Carmen Deane (only a working girl) is "as pure as an angel," her soul "white, pure and unstained." Goldie Mowbray, factory-girl heroine of *Love at the Loom*, 1895, is "too good and pure to need anybody's warning," her nature is "so pure and innocent as to feel without being conscious of evil in others." Alice Haywood (*From Want to Wealth; or, The Working Girl's Triumph*) is "as innocent and pure-minded as an infant, and as modest as a wild-flower." Her very face "tells that she is as pure as a snowdrop." The same author, Caroline Hart, bestows on Elsie Brandon her dense innocence; she is "too innocent and modest to realize how when she walked on the street, men devoured her with their eyes, and turned to watch her." In behalf of Lil, the dancing girl, Caroline Hart leaves no page of the dictionary unturned. There are the usual similes, "pure as a saint," "pure as an angel," "pure white lily," and in addition two gems that are probably unique, "pure as a child's dream of heaven," and "stainless as an altar cloth"! Lil's dancing manager is convinced, and tells her, "If you were any less pure than one of the ice floes from a northern pass, then they might find some fault." The hero "loved to think of her as pure. He wanted her to remain a sweet and tender memory to him surrounded with the halo of chastity." "God!" he muses, "it is women like her that make you glad your mother and your wife must be of the same sex! It is little pure things like that that make you sorry God himself is not one of them. It would be so much easier to trust him."

This clamorous insistence on what might better be taken for granted sounds like an inferiority complex of Victorianism. The "lady" doth protest too much; she is pushing for a status in society which society is not disposed to grant. In society one must still have delicacy, a frail flower which does not flourish in shop or mill. So says *Chambers's Journal* in April, 1856.

Where women, in the labours or callings they undertake, are obliged to give up privacy, it is felt that the delicacy so highly appreciated in the female character is likely to suffer. A lower rating, with all that it implies is inevitable.

So says also the American, E. P. Roe, seventeen years later.

Have you no part in sustaining that public sentiment which turns the cold shoulder of society toward the woman who works? . . . What does the "best society," in the world's estimation, say to the daughters of these same families? "Keep your little hands white, my dears, as long as you can, because as soon as the traces of toil are seen on them you become a working-woman, and our daughters can't associate with you, and our sons can't think of you, that is for wives. No other than little white hands can enter our heaven."

So multitudes struggle to keep their hands white, though thereby the risk that their souls will become stained and black increases daily. A host of fair girls find their way every year to darker stains than ever labor left, because they know how coldly society will ignore them the moment they enlist in the army of honest workers.

"Darker stains than ever labor left." Whenever society turns from the contemplation of its own luminaries it sees these blots against the ranks of labor. Is there any record of women earning their living that is not darkened with them? The Cook who began the unforgettable tale on the road to Canterbury broke off with his blunt characterization of a

> *wyf that heeld for countenance*
> *A shoppe, and swyved for hir sustenance.*

"and of this Cokes Tale maked Chaucer ne more." So it was in the novel of the eighteenth century, and so it is still five hundred years after Chaucer. The villain challenges the reputation of Nellie, the beautiful cloak model: "She is beautiful, you say, and yet earns an honest living?" Mr. Harrison, who with one foot in the grave insults Elsie Brandon, is also cynical; he was "simply unable to comprehend a working girl fighting so hard for her honor when her dishonor would be so profitable." Even the hero rationalizes his mock-marriage with Elsie on the ground that he is really protecting her because a girl who is beautiful and poor "cannot go long unruined in this world." The hero in *Only a Working Girl* resents an aspersion on the heroine's reputation: "You talk like others of the world in which you move. Do you not know that a woman may work with her hands and yet have a soul like snow?" He ought to know; he has tried and failed. The greater the likelihood the more insistent the protest. Lil, the dancing girl, exercises a profession then considered extra-hazardous to chastity, and we have seen the lengths to which the author goes to assure us, not once but ten times, that Lil's is unblemished. Obviously this is an inferiority complex; obviously, too, it is something more. We have seen the value of innocence in the marriage market, for itself and as a connotation of youth. If it is of value as a dowry, it is like money, and like money in inferior novels, where there is little there cannot be too little, and where there is much there cannot be too much. Either money or innocence, it would seem, must be mountain high and dazzlingly bright to attract the dull eye of the reader for whom these novels are written. The author, if he knows his trade, lays on innocence with a trowel, and makes it as dense as Elsie Brandon's.

The lure of innocence and ignorance is particularly strong in a bourgeois era of marriages postponed because of economic "necessity," times when parents demand evidence that their daughters' suitors can maintain them in ease and security. In such times, young men seek the society of girls they respect and admire for gratification of mind and spirit, and turn to the prostitute to satisfy the needs of the body. The two needs are kept separate by impassable barriers and emphasized by significant contrasts. One feels this in Mrs. Gaskell's description of the attraction which Ruth had for young Bellingham (*Ruth*, 1853).

There was, perhaps, something bewitching in the union of the grace and loveliness of womanhood with the *naiveté, simplicity,* and innocence of an intelligent child. There was a spell in the shyness, which made her avoid and shun all admiring approaches to acquaintance. It would be an exquisite delight to attract and tame her wildness, just as he had often allured and tamed timid fawns in his mother's park.

Fifty-five years later in Edward Booth's *The Post-Girl,* the desirable shade of ignorance is definitely green.

Do you think man is such a poor judge that he does not know the merits of green fruits, or so witless that he does not know the dangers of the ripe? Keep [he admonishes women] your thoughts and bodies green, like oranges for shipment, for indeed you are perishable fruit.

This comes in 1908, very close to a century after Jane Austen had giggled over the then current phrase about a woman's reputation being no less brittle than beautiful. What price innocence?

Whatever its price it is all their own. Of the working-girl heroines of the second half of the nineteenth century, seventy per cent have no mothers to guide them. Even those who are not orphans are, most of them, unfortunate; their mothers are cripples or invalids, demanding the energy of care and nursing, unable to act as chaperons. It is the practice of the greater as well as of the lesser novelists. Charlotte Brontë's heroines and Laura Jean Libbey's are orphans. So are those of Thackeray, Reade and Gissing; so are those of Grant Allen and of Geraldine Fleming. *No Mother to Guide Her* was the title of a melodrama that was still on the stage in the early twentieth century. It might have been the title of almost any novel in English, and of most of the plays. The experienced novel reader must answer unhesitantly as did the Pirates of Penzance to the Major General: "Have you ever known what it is to be an orphan?" "Often." In fact the quality of being an orphan is so universally a part of the quality of being a heroine that one can scarcely discuss it, for it does not establish a type apart from the others. It is a literary fashion which it is easy to rationalize in a general way. The heroine must have and hold the sympathy of the reader; the orphan conventionally commands the sympathy of all; the heroine who is an orphan from the beginning gets the conventional sympathy of the reader at the outset, and has only to hold it from then on. To the working-girl heroine it is particularly useful. Her need is for pity; whom shall we pity more than the poor orphan? In her relations with the villain, her virtue is all her own if he fails, the fault is all his if he succeeds. In her struggle against difficulties in whatever path she follows to success, the strength is all her own with which she overcomes her obstacles. The device increases the contrast between her situation at the beginning and at the end of the tale.

In the melodramatic working-girl novels, the appeal to pity is gushingly sentimental. Caroline Hart in *From Want to Wealth* devotes a chapter to the situation of Alice Haywood under the caption "A Waif on the Stream of Life," and quotes,

> *Near a whole city full*
> *Home she had none.*

When willful Gaynell (of the Passaic cotton mills) is in dire distress, Laura Jean Libbey asks, "Had God forsaken her? Could her angel mother whom she had never known look down upon the misery and persecution of her orphan child without appealing at the great white Throne for mercy and protection for her poor little Gay?" A girl friend reminds pretty madcap Dorothy Glenn, "the jolliest girl in the book-bindery,"

> Remember you have no one to warn you. You are an orphan in this great cold world, and—and you are so young that you don't know life, and cannot realize that every young man who smiles into your eyes and says flattering things is *not* in love. When you have no relative to confide in, you ought to have a girl friend older than yourself.

And when Estelle Everett (the prettiest typewriter in New York) tells the hero that she does not know who her parents are or even whether they are alive, the author (Julia Edwards) tells the reader that "the knowledge that she was alone in the world made him feel unutterably tender toward her."

Naturally, where pity is aroused for the motherless waif, admiration for her courage is sure to follow, but many authors use the no-mother-to-guide-her device primarily to rouse admiration without regard to pity. They picture vividly her efforts to survive in "this great cold world," and as often as not to help a crippled sister or brother to survive also. The rebuffs, the trials and temptations she must endure all test her metal and prove to the reader that she is worthy. Though some authors do not try to invoke pity, none but Grant Allen deliberately rejects it. After wading through swamps of pity the reader is quite refreshed when Lois Cayley says:

> I am told I ought to have been terribly alarmed at the straits in which I found myself—a girl of twenty-one, alone in the world, and only twopence short of penniless, without a friend to protect, a relation to counsel her. But, as a matter of fact, I must admit I was not in the least alarmed. Nature had endowed me . . . with plenty of high spirits . . .

It is just here that she tells us of having "large dark eyes with a bit of a twinkle in them" and the ability to guide a bicycle—she has a college education to guide her.

Most often if the heroine falls or is tempted the fact that she had no mother to guide her is offered in extenuation of whatever fault there be. When Ruth Hilton succumbs to her lover, Mrs. Gaskell speaks directly to the reader, "Remember how young and innocent and motherless she was!" Carmen Deane (*Only a Working Girl*) believes the falsehoods of the rake; "There was no one to warn Carmen Deane. She had no mother, no father. Both had died long ago, and now Carmen was only one factory girl out of many." Laura Jean Libbey devotes a whole chapter to the extenuation of Lotta Marlowe's credulity under the imperative caption, JUDGE HER NOT HARSHLY —REMEMBER SHE WAS SCARCELY MORE THAN A CHILD—THIS HAPLESS YOUNG GIRL THROWN ON

THE WORLD'S WICKED MERCY. The passengers on the train where the temptation takes place look on indifferently.

They did not trouble themselves to whisper words of warning into her young ears; they saw that she was very youthful, scarcely more than a child; they did not know that she had had no mother since early infancy to teach her right from wrong, or to beware of chance acquaintances—or that a man's handsome smiling face could hide a villain's heart—or that snares were laid for the innocent and guileless.

And again,

Think not hardly of her, dear reader; think how young she was, with no one to guard or guide her, and to fall in love with a young and handsome man seemed quite a natural thing to do.

But appearances are deceptive. It does not do to classify as orphans all who appear to be so in the first chapter. Little Orphant Annie may turn out to be the Princess Anne after all, with a perfectly good King and Queen to own her, except that they carelessly lost her in her infancy. Some five per cent of our working-girl heroines of the nineteenth century attain their high and true levels by this Cinderella turn of fortune. In this class are Estelle Everett, the pretty typewriter, Nellie, the beautiful cloak model, Pretty Rose Hall, Willful Gaynell, Pretty Madcap Dorothy, and the Pretty Factory Girl of Newark. Eric St. Ross uses the device in *Only a Mill Girl,* Caroline Hart in *From Want to Wealth.* As a *deus ex machina* it is apt to have too much of the machine. Kate O'Fulford's lover must bend his pride: "I thought of you as a mill girl, and one with whom it was impossible to mate," but overpowered by her beauty, charm, bravery, unselfish friendship, even her education, he offers her his hand and his heart. But she has pride also: "I shall never become your wife unless I am cordially welcomed by every member of your family." Here is a deadlock, but it does not last long, for the author obligingly discovers for Kate her long-lost mother, none other, indeed, than the sister of her lover's father. Since she is his cousin, Kate is "just as good as" her lover. Sometimes another relative serves the purpose. Agnes Renier, as we have seen, finds a rich aristocratic grandfather in France. So does Dorothy Glenn (of the book-bindery). Gay Esterbrook enjoys all the immunities of orphanage, then in turn all the advantages of wealthy parentage by adoption.

The Cinderella romances run very uniformly true to type in ending with Prince Charming and a happy prospect of life with him. Only a small per cent, perhaps four or five, of the working-girl novels have any other ending. There are three other endings, death, voluntary celibacy, and loss of virginity without marriage, any one of which spells tragedy which is no province of the kingdom where Cinderella dwells. George Gissing's Thyrza (1887), Mrs. Gaskell's Ruth (1853), and perhaps Grant Allen's Herminia Barton (1893) are in the realm of tragedy. Between the two kingdoms is Juliet Appleton, Grant Allen's heroine in *The Typewriter Girl*, 1896. She is a Girton girl, an orphan and penniless. She does not ask for pity, nor yet for sympathy; but jokes about "adapting herself to her environment in order to win out in the struggle of the fittest," and goes out and gets herself a job. She and her employer fall in love. Then Juliet learns that he has been engaged to "a sweet little thing" for five years, and now wishes to break the engagement. She knows the character of the girl, and steps aside that the unfit may survive. Instead of going into a decline, she gets another job. The story ends with her remark, "I am still a typewriter girl—at another office."

This finale fixes the position of Juliet Appleton between two worlds. If she had come forty years earlier, she would have had to go into a decline and die as a result of the sacrifice. If she had come forty years later she might have been in a position to eat her cake and have it too. By 1935 the tired business man has found out what makes him tired, and looks to the office as relaxation from the strenuosities of "home," as the "realtors" call two rooms and a garage. Let two magazine writers of that year explain the situation. One writes on *Getting along with Women,* and tells us that he grew up

in the midst of an immediate family of women comprising mother, sisters, an aunt, and a cousin, without another man or man-child in it besides myself. I learned about women from my sisters and my cousins and my aunts. Then fate pitchforked me into a world of women; in newspaper agencies, movie studios, theatrical offices, it has been my fortune over a period of 20-odd years not only to work with women but of late years to supervise and direct their steps. Indeed, as I look back upon it, I can see that I have been occupying all my life a very advanced outpost in the country of the Amazons.

Is business a world of women? The other writer amplifies the idea.

Let no man deceive himself. The great American office is more completely a female bailiwick than the great American home . . . with the disappearance of the upper-class Victorian home, the male was no longer master in his own dining room and dreadful in his own den . . . He was, on the contrary, the more or less equal mate of a more or less unpredictable woman. And he resented it . . . And finding himself unable to re-create the lost paradise in his home, he set about recreating it in his office. What he wanted in the office was not the office mistress described by American short-story writers. His very pretty and very clever and very expensive wife was already mistress enough and to spare. What he wanted in the office was something as much like the vanished wife of his father's generation as could be arranged—someone to balance his check-book, buy his railroad tickets, take his daughter to the dentist, listen to his side of the story, give him a courageous look when things were blackest, and generally know all, understand all.

Claudette Colbert enacted this on the screen in *She Married Her Boss.* Faith Baldwin put it in the novel, *Office Wife.* This is what the working girl comes to if she steadfastly refuses guilty splendor. Is it the same old story, be good and you will be happy? The difference between *Cinderella* and *Office Wife* is the difference between the dream of romance and the vision of actuality of the business world. *Virtue Rewarded* and *She Married Her Boss* may seem to come to much the same thing in the import of the titles, but in phrasing the two titles measure the distance between the age of elegance and the age of slang, and in significance the two works measure two centuries of the progress of the poor working girl, from insignificance to influence.

CHAPTER X

NEW GIRLS FOR OLD

Oh she rises with the lark,
And she scorches in the park,
Until she's done a hundred miles, or thereabout.
Her shoe is number nine,
And her foot's as big as mine;
And I don't think that's the kind of girl I care about.

In 1832 Sir Walter Scott died; in 1837 Victoria came to the throne of England. By all literary calendars the first date closes the Romantic Period; the second opens the Victorian Era. No one seems to mind the five-year interim that is neither one period nor the other; it passes as a mere pause in neutral in the process of shifting gears. It is easy to see it as a time of transition. It included the last work of Charles Lamb and the first work of Thackeray, late work of Wordsworth, Southey and Coleridge, and early work of Tennyson, Browning and Dickens. It is the time of the Reform Bill, the Emancipation of Slaves Act, the beginning of the High Church Movement. All these serve to mark the time for the literary historian as conveniently as if they had really been made for his purpose.

The novel of the former age seems to culminate, or at least to find itself in the novels of Jane Austen and those of Scott. These two know precisely what they want to do, what they are doing, and how to do it. Richardson knew what he wanted to do, but he did not know how to do it so as to avoid being called a "garrulous and pottering expositor" by a critic who could not or would not understand him. Fielding saw his material steadily and saw it whole, but he was nervous about his literary

Journal des Demoiselles.

1845

NICE VICTORIAN GIRLS

Passive and proper, docile and decorous, sober and sedate

foundling. He was sure enough that he was the father, but he was by no means sure which muse on Parnassus was the mother—or was he boasting of his conquests? Before Jane Austen nobody knew just what the novel was; after Scott nobody cared. Charlotte Palmer did not know; "It Is and It Is Not a Novel," take the responsibility yourself. Mrs. Opie wasn't sure she had written a novel; she only knew the tale was moral. In the nineteenth century the novelists left it to the critics. By then the novel had forgotten its ancestry, and whether it issued from the servants' quarters or worse, it stood on its own feet, did not look backward, nor try to trace a pedigree back to Parnassus.

Socially, too, Jane Austen and Scott denote the completion of a phase. Pride and Prejudice have ceased to recriminate, have kissed, and agreed to live happily forever after (on ten thousand pounds a year). Darcy sees that Mrs. Bennet's plebeian manners are not a whit worse than the aristocratic ones of his aunt, Lady Catherine. Elizabeth sees that Darcy's self-esteem is the same thing as the self-respect which she flings in Lady Catherine's face. Kind hearts may be more or less than coronets, but that is beside the point; the important thing is that there is room for both in the right little tight little island, and each may serve a useful purpose. So they married and settled down. Everybody hoped they wouldn't quarrel. The children were all Victorians.

Scott too expressed this social compromise a century after Steele set to work to bring it about, and a century before Mr. Chesterton named it Victorian. A quotation from Scott's introduction to Bage's novels cited in Chapter VIII contains his strictures on Fielding and Smollett, phrased with Victorian suavity, indicating that he does not consider profligacy gentlemanly. Completely Victorian is his comment on Bage's extension of the aristocratic license to gallantry to include "females," and on women's influence in society and female chastity as "the corner-stone on which civil society rests." The "Victorian" compromise, too, Scott expresses very clearly in his urbane remarks on Bage's revolutionary antipathy to aristocracy and idealization of the lower classes. He smiles indulgently at Bage's nervous radicalism. "Men of rank in the present day are too indifferent, and too indolent, to indulge any of the stormy passions, and irregular, but vehement desires which create the petty tyrant." The lower classes do not afford "exclusively that rich fruit of virtue and generosity, which Mr. Bage's writings would teach us to expect." "Those who weigh equally will be disposed to think that the state of society most favorable to virtue, will be found amongst those who neither want nor abound." Again in his strictures on Bage's "man as he should be," Hermsprong, Scott points out that the author proposes as "the ideal perfection of humanity a man who is guided to goodness by reason." This Scott calls an "error" because there never was such a man. Bage made the proper distinction between man as he is and man as he should be, and needs not Scott to point out to him that there never was such a man; Scott does not refute Bage by showing it. He merely makes a comment which is of the essence of Victorianism. It is the comment which the Victorian makes on the romantic, that Matthew Arnold made on Shelley, "beautiful but ineffectual angel, beating in the void his luminous wings in vain." If there is anything wrong with Shelley, it is that he flies too high to do any good to anybody. "The romantics," says the critic, "sought to go up to dwell with the Vision on the Mount; the Victorians sought to bring the Vision down to dwell with men." The distinction is sound, and it marks Scott as Victorian. Can anything be more Victorian than Scott's exposition of the value of female chastity? Surely nothing more clearly expresses the social compromise which Mr. Chesterton calls Victorian than Scott's rebuke of Bage's revolutionary doctrine. Scott was a gentleman in the Victorian sense of the word, and he made himself a gentleman in the older sense by acquiring title and landed estate. Is not the compromise between the classes complete when a gentleman in every sense the word held can declare for the middle class in such terms as Scott uses: "the state of society most favourable to virtue will be found amongst those who neither want nor abound"?

The compromise was not merely social and political, it involved all ideals, from people's chosen patterns for their appearance, the silhouette, to religion and ideals of happiness. Byron's ideal of happiness was the aristocratic all-or-nothing pattern. So was Napoleon's. Wordsworth suggested to Napoleon a more modest standard.

> *Wisdom doth live with children round her knees:*
> *Books, leisure, perfect freedom . . .*

Byron shrieked profane derision:

> *There's something in a stupid ass:*
> *And something in a heavy dunce;*
> *But never since I went to school*
> *I saw or heard so damned a fool*
> *As William Wordsworth is for once.*

What has wisdom to do with happiness? Merely to suggest, as Scott to Bage, as Arnold to Shelley, that it is unattainable in this world, that a lower ideal, content, is quite possible, that too high ideals are fallacies. In art, the all-or-nothing-no-compromise school produces stark tragedy or iridescent dreams. The Victorian-compromise school trying to bring the dream within human reach and to get the values of tragedy without pain ("a cheerful Thanatopsis") reduces art to melodrama and sentimentality. By formula these are what we should expect in art which is of Victorian time rather than of all time, and on examination these are what we find.

Dickens and Thackeray are justly called the great Victorian novelists, their work dates in Victoria's reign, and it has the qualities we name for the Queen. But if the work for which we know them best is truly Victorian, neither the Queen nor the dates had anything to do with it, for both novelists drew it from the former age. The case for Dickens rests on the dozen or so of titles that fall in the two decades, 1834-1857, between *Sketches by Boz* and *Little Dorrit;* the four or five others, be they what they may, are not in line with the Micawbers and Pecksniffs that made Dickens famous. The heroines of these novels have already passed across our stage (in Chapter VI) as modulations of the Lass with the Delicate Air, the brood of Ann Radcliffe. Of such heroines, be they of Radcliffe, Dickens or anyone else, the greatest common denominator is passivity. The cardinal item of their code is that which Shaw exploded the moment the Good Queen (who proposed to Prince Albert) was dead, namely that no female of delicacy, no true woman, no nice girl, took any forward steps in the process of her own courtship. The works of fashion using this model exaggerate the feature and show a heroine who takes no forward steps in any process, indeed, no steps whatever in any direction. The greater artists drew their lines with more of exactitude and discrimination. Jane Austen shows us the feature without exaggeration. Elizabeth Bennet is not, indeed, a Cleopatra, but still less is she a Griselda. Against her background of circumstance she stands out clearly in the colors of self-determinism. In such scenes as that of Darcy's first proposal and the famous one with Lady Catherine, she rises to complete command of the situation, as she does ever when the situation seems to her to call for it. No one who does and can act with such energy and effect can be called passive. When Elizabeth refrains from action, it is through wisdom, not through weakness; a wisdom, too, beyond her years. Often one of the last lessons we learn from life is that direct action seldom serves. We feel the wisdom of Elizabeth's course when all shapes to her wish. Is it by chance, or because she is what she is and does what she does? Of course there is chance in it; the book would not be human if there were not, but no chance could help her if she did not trim her sails to it. What would have been her chance of success if she had rushed out to rope Bingley for her sister or Darcy for herself? That is the way Lydia went to work, and it took an effort of greater power than Elizabeth knew to salvage Lydia from the consequences. Elizabeth has "honor, anger, valor, fire," but seems to find them quite as useful in reserve as in display. It is this refusal of Jane Austen to go to extremes in either direction that brings her to her supreme achievement. The best of heroines before her time, Clarissa Harlowe, Sophia Western, Emilia Gauntlet, are fine upstanding girls of whom any age might be proud, but their main attraction is that of their sex; they are men's women, created to express the charm that women have for men. They do not exhibit what Jane Austen seems to give us for the first time, the best of womanhood, as endearing to women as to men, shining through any and all colors of fashion and undimmed by the changes of time. It matters not what school of manners trains her, whether sensibility, delicacy, prudery, repression, freedom, self-expression, or sex experimentation, the result is much the same. If she is endowed at the outset with intelligence, balance, poise, humor, sensitiveness, imagination, sympathy, health, healthy-mindedness, pride, bravery, modesty, endurance, as so many heroic women are in life who fortunately for themselves never gain fame for the heroic rôles they play, then it matters not whether circumstances overwhelm her or not, hers is the victory. Perhaps these terms are too high-sounding for Elizabeth Bennet. She does not play a tragic rôle. But if her part were cast in *Richard Feverel* it would be that of Lucy Desborough. Meredith shows this figure at its best. Dickens was not up to it. Scott and Thackeray show it, but not until Jane Austen had shown it to them. Trollope has it more often than any other.

Scott's Amy Robsart is a good example because hasty readers

of the twentieth century think of her (as many do also of Elizabeth Bennet) as passive and sentimental. One of them says of her, "Amy was of the passive, extremely sheltered type who knew only to obey her husband. Her habit of weeping coupled with her fainting spells certainly mark her as a typical lady of her age." Here is a total impression obviously without attention to details, for Amy does not faint at all, and never weeps without good cause. Does her white skin pass her for a blonde? She cannot qualify, for her eyes are hazel and her hair dark. She loves her husband devotedly, and submits reluctantly to his demands so long as he is successful in concealing from her their import. When she finds them subversive of her honor and his, she rejects them, tears his letter and stamps it under foot, issues her orders imperiously as becomes a countess, and wishes she were a man for five minutes to deal with Varney as he deserves. In the presence of the Queen she submits to her husband's dishonorable plan only to save his life. One or two of Scott's heroines are pale and passive; Mary Avenel is one, but such figures are not typical of him. For the most part he gives us vigorous human girls with solid figures, active minds and active bodies. So does Thackeray, though readers who do not get beyond *Vanity Fair* will not discover it if they remain content to generalize from Amelia Sedley. Thackeray does not love Amelia Sedley. He does love Ethel Newcome, though some of the young men and women in the novel do not, because she has too much downright honesty and vigor of mind and tongue in the expression of it. Both Scott and Thackeray place these figures in times before Victoria, and as works of art they are timeless. Thackeray's friend and contemporary, Trollope, has heroines no less real, no less beautiful, no less permanent, and he dates them as of his own time and dresses them in the clothes and manners of the genuinely Victorian era. Of the era as a whole he gives us the most authentic picture we have, in terms of a gallery of heroines that for quantity and quality is unrivalled in the annals of fiction. These are the girls of the older years that we relinquish for the new woman. It is worth our while to scrutinize their portraits.

Trollope is first and foremost a realist. He seeks no illusion but that of actuality. His sense of fact does not allow him to make his heroine an angel, an impossible pattern of perfection, and then provide another woman as a scapegoat to bear the necessary burden of sin. He does not keep good girl and bad girl sealed, labelled and unmixable. Of course his heroines are good girls, just as good as anybody could ask, but no better. They are close enough to the average so that we accept them whole-heartedly as of our own kind, and just enough above the average to set a reasonably good example. Each and every one of them is what Trollope would call a "lady," by which he seems to mean a woman of intelligence, refinement and right-feeling who is above the working class by birth and breeding. Trollope does not show a working-class heroine, though one or two of them appear as governesses. Take them for all in all, they are as fine a lot of young women as one could wish to see. They have "honor, anger, valor, fire." They are thoroughly womanly, and have imperfections that make them entirely human.

Lucy Robarts, the heroine of *Framley Parsonage,* is a favorite no less with Trollope himself than with his readers. In his *Autobiography* he says of her, "I think myself that Lucy Robarts is perhaps the most natural English girl I ever drew." The brush-work of this portrait is worth examining. In describing her appearance it is noteworthy that he presents first what might be called her defects.

She was smaller than either of her three sisters, to all of whom had been acceded the praise of being fine women. . . "Dear, dear!" had been said of her, "poor Lucy is not like a Robarts at all . . . Only think what Blanche was at her age. But she has fine eyes for all that; and they do say that she is the cleverest of them all." And that, too, is so true a description of her that I do not feel that I can add much to it. She was not like Blanche; for Blanche had a fine neck, and a noble bust . . . a true goddess, that is, as far as the eye went . . . Lucy had no neck at all worth speaking of,—no neck, I mean, that ever produced eloquence; she was brown, too, and had addicted herself in no wise, as undoubtedly she should have done, to larder utility. In regard to the neck and colour, poor girl, she could not help herself; but in that other respect she must be held as having wasted her opportunities. But then, what eyes she had! . . . They flashed upon you, not always softly; indeed not often softly if you were a stranger to her; but whether softly or savagely, with a brilliancy that dazzled you as you looked at them. And who shall say of what colour they were? Green, probably, for most eyes are green—green or grey, if green be thought uncomely for an eye colour. But it was not their colour, but their fire, which struck one with such surprise.

Lucy Robarts was thoroughly a brunette. Sometimes the dark tint of her cheek was exquisitely rich and lovely, and the fringes of her eyes were long and soft, and her small teeth which one so seldom saw were white as pearls, and her hair, though short, was beautifully soft—by no means black, but yet of so dark a shade of brown."

He goes on to speak again of her teeth, visible "only now and again, when in some sudden burst of wonder she would sit for a moment with her lips apart," then goes back to the comment that she "was the cleverest of them all . . . The people of Exeter had expressed such an opinion, and had been quite just in doing so . . . Lucy Robarts was blessed with an intelligence keener than that of her brothers and sisters."

Here we see a device of Trollope's so often used that one is tempted to call it a formula except that it is never obtrusive or annoying. First he shows us the least attractive items of her appearance—"Poor Lucy; think what Blanche was at her age"— no neck to speak of—green eyes." Then having firmly impressed us with the fact that she is quite commonplace, he is safe in glorifying her a little without making us feel that he is romancing, so he gives us her glorious eyes, the "exquisitely rich and lovely" tint of her cheek, her fine lashes and rich soft hair—and then she was clever, but her cleverness is nothing like a terrifying familiarity with Greek, Hebrew and differential calculus.

If to be passive is to be Victorian, Lucy Robarts cannot qualify; better take her as evidence that passivity is not so Victorian as we may have thought. One of her prudent advisers suggests that she might have been more guarded than to have cared for Lord Lufton before he declared himself.

"Guarded!" [she exclaimed] "Yes, that's it; that's just the word. But it's he that should have been guarded. He should have had a fire-guard hung before him, or a love-guard if you will. Guarded! Was I not guarded till you all would drag me out? . . . Why is Lady Lufton to have it all her own way? Why am I to be sacrificed to her? I did not want to know Lady Lufton, or anyone belonging to her."

When the time comes we learn that Lady Lufton is not to have it all her own way. A few chapters later she sends Lucy a rather peremptory note asking her to go to Framley Court for an interview. Lucy's reception of the note is a nice touch. Her sister suggests that Lucy had better reply to the note, "but Lucy marched off, hardly answering this proposition. 'What's the use of such a deal of ceremony?' she said. 'I know she's at home; and if she is not, I shall only lose ten minutes in going.'" Lady Lufton has set the stage for the interview. She greets Lucy without rising from her chair.

"My son," continued her Ladyship, "has spoken to me on the subject of—I think I understand, Miss Robarts, that there has been no engagement between you and him?"

"None whatever," said Lucy, "He made me an offer, and I refused him." This she said very sharply;—more so, undoubtedly, than circumstances required; and with a brusqueness that was injudicious as well as uncourteous.

Lucy holds command of the situation by questioning Lady Lufton.

"Am I right in presuming that he has spoken to you on the subject?"

"Yes, he has.". . ."And may I ask what he has told you?". . . Lady Lufton began to reflect that the young lady was taking too much of the initiative in this conversation . . . [but she takes a long breath and tries to begin the lecture she had prepared]. "Wait half a moment, Lady Lufton," says Lucy, and in a brief, pointed paragraph tells Lady Lufton exactly what she has done, and why she did it, ending with the frank admission, "I loved him from the first. I was foolish enough to think I could know him and not love him." "I saw all that going on," said Lady Lufton, with a certain assumption of wisdom about her; "and took steps which I hoped would have put a stop to it in time." "Everybody saw it. It was a matter of course," said Lucy, destroying her Ladyship's wisdom at a blow . . . "But my dear Miss Robarts," began Lady Lufton . . . "I beg your pardon, Lady Lufton [said Lucy]; I shall have done directly and then will hear you."

and the next time she pauses, Lady Lufton is reduced to a helpless interrogative "Well?" Then, when after four more paragraphs Lucy comes to an end, Lady Lufton's prepared speech has evaporated, and her feeling toward Lucy has changed so far to respect that she is almost ready to give up her objections to her as a future wife for her son.

Grace Crawley's interview with Archdeacon Grantly in *The Last Chronicle of Barset* is as different from this as she and the Archdeacon are from Lucy and Lady Lufton, but like it in the way Grace stands firm on her self-respect and the integrity of her position. To similar effect is the interview of Lucy Morris with Lady Fawn in *The Eustace Diamonds*. These girls are not passive; neither are the others of Trollope: Mary Thorne, Lady Glencora Palliser, Lily Dale, Mary Wortle, Rachel Ray, Florence Burton. They are not aggressive, but one cannot abuse them with impunity. Here is the authentic Victorian heroine, nothing extenuate, naught set down in sentiment. It is the work of an artist drawing from the living model, seeking to put the feeling of reality into his work. As works of art, these heroines are useful to check against the fashion models.

Such a model is *Trevelyan,* which comes in the landmark year, 1837. It is dripping with sentiment, and, in spite of the fact that its action takes place between the Egyptian campaign of 1801 and the Battle of Corunna in 1809, its sentiment is that of the dawn of the Victorian era. It was the sentiment over which Praed's ballroom belle wept, and the "talented man" laughed at her, "for sentiment's quite out of fashion." *Trevelyan* is a novel without a heroine. If you had a "really nice" girl here, there would be no story, but Theresa is not quite nice. She is an illegitimate daughter and a foreigner, something like the wicked romantic lady of the anti-Roussellians of the generation before, only not bad enough to put ideas into the heads of young persons. Her function is not so much to endure sorrows as to provide them, notably for the new Colonel Trevelyan, afterward General Trevelyan and Lord Launceton. She has a bit of aristocratic gaiety, and the feeling toward it of the aristocratic author, Lady Caroline Scott, is not very different from that of the daughters of Calvin. We have it from Trevelyan's point of view. Think of coming on your secret sorrow after five years and finding her looking like this!

She was dressed in the fashion of Revolutionary France, a costume which, from the total separation of the countries for the last five years, had been little seen, or at least was not then generally adopted in England. Her back and shoulders, of most dazzling beauty, were naked nearly to the belt, and the lines of her graceful figure were scarcely concealed by the statue-like drapery which hung over it, and which appeared to be secured around her merely by the girdle that enclosed her waist. Long dark glossy ringlets hanging down on each side of her cheeks and throat, at the moment entirely hid her features; but the general contour of her head, rivalling the beauty of a Grecian bust, gave full promise of perfection in the averted face. Trevelyan beheld all this with mixed feelings of admiration and disgust [until he perceived that it was Theresa, then] At once every pulse of his frame ceased to beat, and his senses became confused—he wildly looked again. . . .

At five-and-twenty, Theresa was still more beautiful than at eighteen; her figure, the principal charm of which had before consisted in the slim airiness of youth, was now beautifully rounded into a woman's form; her complexion was still more brilliant, her eyes more sparkling. But Trevelyan withdrew his from their glance with a sort of mental shudder, for they had in them an expression which turned his very heart sick, although he could not—would not —have described it;—they told him of scenes to which they had probably been witness, and which appeared to have left upon them a stamp of their lawlessness! [He overhears scraps of conversation] which told him that *that* love for which he had sacrificed his own existence was gone!—and all he heard and saw *would* tell him (although his blood curdled at the obtruding suspicion) that Theresa was no longer the pure, spotless being she had once been.

Theresa, then, is not nice enough, but Augusta is a bit too nice. She had "dry formal notions of duty which ever converted pleasures into toils," "habitual placidity of temper," "a most unbending adherence to her own opinion." When Trevelyan's father died and he succeeded to the title, Augusta felt no emotion, her "calm disposition was a stranger to all such useless, self-inflicted sufferings." When visitors came to

offer due condolence and congratulations to the new Lord and Lady Launceton, Augusta received them all with proper courtesy, and returned all their visits at the proper time and in the proper order . . . She continued also in the same exemplary manner to fulfill all her duties to her poorer neighbors, lecturing her schoolmistress, ordering the children's hair to be cut and their faces washed, and doing that in the same manner, and with precisely the same feelings, with which she dispensed food to the hungry and clothes to the naked. . . . Augusta was not of a communicative disposition, and admitted no one into her confidence when she could possibly help doing so . . . Trevelyan was soon aware that all attempts at similarity of sentiment between him and his wife were vain.

Here the social compromise shows as a negative in its application to the two women; we see what they are not to be, and the picture is reversed; the bourgeois faults show in the peeress, and the aristocratic faults in the illegitimate daughter of an unknown Italian woman, though on her father's side Theresa's blood may be as good as Augusta's. The compromise seems to be so completely accepted in the lady author's mind that neither Lord Herbert Leslie nor any of his family raise any objection to Theresa on the grounds of illegitimacy or of the obscurity of her mother. It is necessary to have her illegitimate, and it is necessary to have her married in order to develop the sorrows of Trevelyan. In these lie the sentimentality of the book. If it is sensibility it is not liquid sorrow; the tears fall on the pages of the book rather than flow from them.

The sentimental figures of the first decade of Victoria are those we saw in Tennyson's early poems and Heath's *Book of Beauty;* the Lass with the Delicate Air is still going strong. She is not confined to England. Frederika Bremer produced Scandinavian examples which were popular in translation. W. A. Alcott, the American, wrote a manual for turning her out synthetically, *The Young Woman's Guide to Excellence,* 1840, which is in the line of descent from Steele's *Ladies Library,* Mrs. Chapone's letters, and many other such. From Alcott we learn that we must not so much as mention physical exercise.

I must omit of course, in a work like this, intended for young women, the mention of any motion more rapid than walking. Running, to those who have passed into their teens, would be unfashionable; and who could endure the charge of disregarding the fashions? Who could risk the danger of being regarded as a romp?

There are other things, too, that we must not mention. Anatomically we get no nearer to a young woman's sexual characteristics than "that portion of the general system which gives to woman her peculiar prerogative, as well as her distinctive character."

In 1846 the heroine still has the delicate air, is helpless in business affairs and shudders at bourgeois bluntness of manners. An

author who professes to be an old man, but is really Mrs. Anna
Caldwell Marsh at the age of fifty, portrays Emilia Wyndham.
Her sorrows are too long drawn out to be set forth here in
detail. She was young, beautiful, happy, courted by an aristocratic Adonis of a Lieutenant Colonel, but her father was a
spendthrift and a fool, and her world crashed about her. Suddenly she found herself in the house with her mother a corpse,
her father a paralytic, and bailiff's officers in possession. What
can the poor girl do? Her cruel uncle forces her into marriage
with her father's solicitor, Mr. Danby, faithfully adoring, but
brusque, a bit suspicious and jealous, and such manners! Such
a mother! But the compromise works. She learns to love her
husband and to help him in his business. Again Pride and
Prejudice wed and mingle, and we know again that the children will be Victorians.

If this is sentimentality there is in it by definition much of insincerity. If Victorian art is moral before it is anything else, it
is sentimental, insincere, and in so far as it is insincere it is not
art. But it is easier to perceive insincerity when we look back at
former times than when we look about us. We can look back at
the change of manners from the Cavalier style of the Restoration
to the Puritan style of a century later and see no more than a shift
of emphasis from one insincerity to another. In Steele's time we
see the outward daintiness of a Watteau gown over the rank
odor of the unwashed skin. A century later we see the outward
austerity of sexual purity over the unchangeable urge of human
appetites. Manners are fashions of meeting situations. In so
far as they are standardized they seem necessarily to involve more
or less hypocrisy, for they are insincere in so far as they conceal
real feelings, and that is as often as not their only real service.
They are sincere if they live long enough to shape real feelings
through habit, or if the wish behind them to put people at their
ease is sincere. Is the Victorian code any less sincere than any
other?

We may think of the revolutionary-romantic period as an upheaval of feeling that broke the smooth surface of society, and the Victorian code as the repression of the disturbance and the restoration and reinforcement of the surface. Its general principle seems to be the standard of appearances; "save the surface and you save all." Its principal items are observance and conformity to the mores, to itself. Persons who are "so nice" are "just like everybody else." In all things there is deference to precedent. Like Freedom, the code itself "slowly broadens down from precedent to precedent,"—or should we say, narrows down? In this it is like the constitution; itself is the unwritten constitution of society. In the word "slowly" we may find much of its value— to restrain the forces that would push us rashly toward change until values are more safely tested. In "precedent" we may see its evolution. From times of religious strife comes its pious principle, "fear God," its adherence to the Church of England and its putting of dissenters outside the pale of fashion. From war and threat of revolution comes the second item, "hate the French," its doctrine of the permanence of the established order and economic security. Revolutionaries, romantics and atheists are criminals, and, worse, unfashionable. From the courtly-chivalric code of feudalism come some items of the attitude toward women. They must be guided and guarded. Tennyson Victorianizes the old code. The young man must

> *Love one damsel only, cleave to her,*
> *And worship her through years of noble deeds*
> *Until he win her.*

Further color the code takes from the Church Fathers. Woman is inferior intellectually and weaker physically, easily smirched; she must see no evil, hear no evil, speak no evil, know no evil; she must not know that evil exists. All sex is evil; it must be concealed. To be sure, she must experience it if she is to bear children. Let it be done in the dark, for procreation only, never spoken of. The man, who knows about these things, must pretend in the presence of women he respects that he knows nothing, and go to women he does not respect for any sort of gratification incompatible with such deference, such, for example, as his body needs during years of noble deeds when he has no comfort from his chosen damsel save her smile on his aspiration.

This is the code of manners through which the Victorian damsel smiles. In Trollope's Barsetshire she is a real woman. In Heath's *Book of Beauty*, in *Trevelyan*, in *Emilia Wyndham*, she is an image in a fashion-plate. With all her delicacy she is a fairly hardy perennial; she has not changed a tint in fifty years when we meet her in the first years of Victoria. In the first decade of the nineteenth century she must not go to walk before breakfast lest she sit down to the table with the "appetite of a ploughboy and the complexion of a milkmaid." In the fifth decade she must not, after she is old enough to need a brassière, indulge "in any form of motion more rapid than walking," for fear of betraying somewhere below her neck some "portion of the general system which gives to woman her peculiar prerogative, as well as her distinctive character." If she does not grow old it must be because she never was young. But in the next fifty years she grows young and a bit gay, though in other respects she is still mainly Victorian. Lois Cayley "pilots" a bicycle, Carmen Deane is skating when the hero sees her as we saw her in the last chapter. Gay Esterbrook is a "little hoydenish madcap." Perhaps she derives from William Black's *Madcap Violet*, 1877, and Mrs. Hungerford's *The Hoyden*, 1894. Whatever these heroines may have lacked or had above the neck, they had something below it that would propel them faster than a walk, and something clearly more specific than a "portion of the general system." The old girl cannot afford to be called a romp, the new girl announces herself on the title page as a madcap and a hoyden. The social ferment that gives us new girls for old is a process of such complexity as to defy complete analysis, but it makes an interesting study.

Mary Wollstonecraft may be said to have begun it when, in 1792, in her *Vindication of the Rights of Woman,* she sailed over the entrenched positions of her opponents, dropped high explosives, and mapped enough territory to keep her followers busy for a century and a half. She made direct hits on the Lass with the Delicate Air, the prude, the innocence-ignorance theory, on Rousseau, on Dr. Fordyce; she mopped up a lot of liquid sorrow; she advocated athletics; she heralded emancipation. Some of these detonations reverberated in other chapters; others are pertinent here.

She proposes at the outset to dismiss "those pretty feminine phrases which the men condescendingly use to soften our slavish dependence," and to despise "that weak elegancy of mind, exquisite sensibility, and sweet docility of manners, supposed to be the characteristics of the weaker vessel." She wishes, she says, "to show that elegance is inferior to virtue, that the first object of laudable ambition is to obtain a character as a human being, regardless of the distinction of sex; and that secondary views should be brought to this simple touchstone." This, she says, is a rough sketch of the entire plan. We may infer that the delicate air is a pattern and practice of real life, that it exists outside the novel, and that it seems to the earnest critic of manners and ethics a symptom of a fundamental malady of society. She sees it and sensibility as

a kind of sickly delicacy that turns away from simple unadorned truth; and a deluge of false sentiments, and overstretched feelings, stifling the natural emotions of the heart, render the domestic pleasures insipid, that ought to sweeten the exercise of those severe duties, which educate a rational and immortal being for a nobler field of action.

She has known in life a character familiar in the novel.

I once knew a weak woman of fashion, who was more than commonly proud of her delicacy and sensibility. She thought a distinguishing taste and puny appetite the height of all human perfection, and acted accordingly. I have seen this weak sophisticated being neglect all the duties of life, yet recline with self-complaceny on a sofa, and boast of her want of appetite as a proof of delicacy that extended to, or, perhaps, arose from her exquisite sensibility: for it is difficult to render intelligible such ridiculous jargon. Yet, at the moment, I have seen her insult a worthy old gentlewoman, whom unexpected misfortunes had made dependent on her ostentatious bounty, and who, in better days, had claims on her gratitude. Is it possible that a human creature should have become such a weak and depraved being, if, like the Sybarites, dissolved in luxury, everything like virtue had not been worn away, or never impressed by precept, a poor substitute, it is true, for cultivation of mind, though it serves as a fence against vice?

In the Age of Reason woman is confined to the exercise of feeling.

It would be an endless task to trace the variety of meannesses, cares, sorrows, into which women are plunged by the prevailing opinion, that they were created rather to feel than to reason, and that all the power they obtain, must be obtained by their charms and weakness . . . And, made by this amiable weakness entirely dependent, excepting what they gain by illicit sway, on man, not only for protection, but advice, is it surprising that, neglecting the duties that reason alone points out, and shrinking from trials calculated to strengthen their minds, they only exert themselves to give their defects a graceful covering, which may serve to heighten their charms in the eye of the voluptuary, though it sink them below the scale of moral excellence?

The use of reason, fresh air, and sufficient exercise would go far to correct the abuses.

I am fully persuaded, that we should hear of none of these infantine airs, if girls were allowed to take sufficient exercise and not confined in close rooms till their muscles are relaxed and their powers of digestion destroyed. To carry the remark still further, if fear in girls, instead of being cherished, perhaps, created, was treated in the same manner as cowardice in boys, we should quickly see women with more dignified aspects. It is true, they could not then with equal propriety be termed the sweet flowers that smile in the walk of man;

but they would be more respectable members of society, and discharge the important duties of life by the light of their own reason.

The scorn is withering with which she refutes various fallacies which she finds in Rousseau's *Émile,* that woman should be weak and passive because she has less bodily strength than man, that she was formed to please and to be subject to man, that it is her duty to render herself agreeable to him, that she has nothing but her beauty and her subtlety to recommend her to him, that she must obey her husband absolutely, that her ignorance keeps her chaste. Mary Wollstonecraft denies flatly the major premise of this argument, that woman was formed only to please and to be subject to man, and in the name of reason defies the charge of heresy; "were an angel from heaven to tell me that Moses's beautiful, poetical cosmogony, and the account of the fall of man, were literally true, I could not believe what my reason told me was derogatory to the character of the Supreme Being." God is not responsible, then, it is society, with Rousseau its spokesman, that represents so flatteringly this degraded state of women, no less pernicious to society itself than to its victims. She urges upon all women to subordinate every duty to that of improving their minds. She does not believe that female morons can guard the priceless pearl of chastity by the density of their ignorance and the protection of heaven. She warns women against the belief that ignorance is protection; in fact it is quite the opposite. She jeers at clerical invocations to heaven to protect innocence. The idea that women have no sexual appetites is a pernicious fiction.

. . . to prolong that ardour [of unsatisfied passion] it is indelicate, not to say immodest, for women to feign an unnatural coldness of constitution. Women as well as men ought to have the common appetites and passions of their nature, they are only brutal when unchecked by reason; but the obligation to check them is the duty of mankind, not a sexual duty.

She calls upon her sisters to believe that reason is more than downcast eyes, and intelligence than rosy blushes. Her call to women is essentially the same as Swift's call to men: "I wish to see women neither heroines nor brutes; but reasonable creatures." And in calling on them to make themselves so, she sounds her prelude to emancipation, "It is not empire—but equality, that they should contend for."

The time had come, it would seem, to be off with the old girl and to get on to something new. Mary Wollstonecraft spoke the word, and it went forth to the ends of the world, but if the world had been listening it might have heard premonitory sounds earlier. There was Mary Astell, for example, who spoke just a hundred years earlier; reason was large part of her faith, education part of her scheme for the salvation of women. Education, too, in something more solid than the meretricious arts of husband-getting was in these earlier plans, that suggested in the *Gentleman's Magazine* of 1739, for example, and in *Millennium Hall* in 1764. If academic subjects are part of the scheme, they have a hint of them also; among the courses for business and industrial training they put French, geography and music. Rousseau spoke for a change in the education of women, and even before his word reached England, Sarah Fielding had spoken to similar effect. But Rousseau's suggestions did not please the puritans. He would educate women to gratify men rather than to ensnare them. Much of the clamor for and against Rousseau in England had to do with his *Émile* and his ideas on the education of women. Perhaps there was more against him than for him, but there was a noise, and the old ideas came under fire. Mrs. Barbauld, Maria Edgeworth and Hannah More were on the side of sober sense, education for a life of married usefulness and happiness rather than in the science of getting a man. They were contemporaries of Mary Wollstonecraft; they might have read the *Vindication of the Rights of Woman* before they wrote their contributions. For them, no doubt, Mary Wollstonecraft was too revolutionary, as she was for Mrs. Opie, whose *Adeline Mowbray* is a voice raised in opposition. Maria Edgeworth was as strongly against Rousseau, as was Mary Wollstone-craft, but she was also against the revolutionary female; she might conceivably have had Mary Wollstonecraft in mind when she drew Harriet Freke. Mrs. Inchbald is in step with Mary Wollstonecraft, or even a step or two ahead. Her *Simple Story* pointed out in 1791 that the trouble with the old model was her education. The heroine, Miss Milner, is too frivolous for her high-minded husband to do anything with her. That is the thesis of Part I. In Part II, her daughter, Matilda, is better educated, and has the better fortune her author thinks she deserves. By the time the reader has gone through the tale

he has beheld the pernicious effects of an *improper education* in the destiny which attended the unthinking Miss Milner. On the opposite side, what may not be hoped from that school of prudence, though of adversity, in which Matilda was bred?

Holcroft at the same time, and Bage a little later, suggested some of the specifications of the new model. Their suggestions had little effect, however, except to call forth such strictures as those of Scott, for the heroines they put together were blue-prints from the drafting room; they soon faded. The artist must find his model in life, and it took half a century, perhaps a whole century, for life to develop any such types. On real life the influence seems to have been Mary Wollstonecraft. She brought the heat to a focus and fired the train.

In the field of education of women, her footsteps seem easier to follow in the United States than in England. In the American oxygen of freedom the revolutionary spark blazed quickly. The rights of women in education were almost abreast of the rights of men in politics, and if Tom Paine is the father of the one, Mary Wollstonecraft is the mother of the other. Historians of education tell us that it was on the tide of her influence that women came into their educational rights in the new United States. The beginnings were small, but they came early. By

1800 New England was dotted with academies that would admit girls for part of the year or part of the day. Bradford Academy, Massachusetts, 1803, is one that began with girls on part time, but before long began to specialize in the education of girls, and by 1836 dealt with them only. It gave them, too, a solid curriculum of philosophy and such sciences as chemistry, astronomy, geology and botany; there was logic also, and rhetoric, and metaphysics. This is a substantial bill of fare if it was well digested, on the face of it seemingly more like that of a college for men than an academy for girls. Probably Harvard College had at the time less of science and more of ancient languages. Others of later foundation than Bradford were earlier in devoting themselves exclusively to women: Hartford Female Seminary, 1823, Abbott Academy, Andover, Massachusetts, 1829, South Hadley Female Seminary (Mount Holyoke), 1836. All these appear to be in advance of anything of the sort in England. The first conspicuous date there is 1848, the founding of Queen's College. The date is conspicuous also in the United States as marking the Woman's Rights Convention. In England at the same time the suffrage movement had not got beyond a stray handbill or two. In 1833 Oberlin opened its doors to men and women impartially, and in 1835 the first American normal school for women opened in Lexington, Massachusetts. The following decade laid wide-spreading foundations on which the structure rose rapidly after 1870. In 1864 in opening Vassar College, Matthew Vassar said to the Trustees, "There is not in our country—there is not in the world so far as is known,—a single fully endowed institution for the education of women." Was he boasting of his endowment? Meanwhile women were seeking professional training as ministering angels. They made their way into established medical schools for men against stubborn opposition, and where the opposition was insurmountable, established medical schools for themselves; in 1864 a magazine for women notes three such in the United States. If all this is what Mary Wollstonecraft wanted, and if the realization of it was due to her influence, she would have little to complain of in the progress of the century after the publication of the *Vindication of the Rights of Woman*. All this education has not changed human nature, but it has changed fashions, fashions of thought in groups of women large enough to be reckoned with. It has not solved all problems, perhaps not many yet, but it has given a great many women who were capable of profiting by it happier lives and higher interests and completer expression than they could find in the development of perfection in housekeeping. Probably the first appearance of this in the novel is in Grant Allen's *Typewriter Girl,* in which it seems to be the heroine's college training that enables her to see herself and her troubles in a sane perspective in which she does not see them too seriously. In 1814 Madame D'Arblay's heroine in *The Wanderer* has no such emancipation of mind.

In freedom of the body the century beginning with Victoria saw similar progress, but it was more in increasing clamor of protest than in actual relief of pressure on the body. The dress which Theresa demonstrated in *Trevelyan* was free enough, but it was in 1837 a mere memory of thirty-five years ago, a passing fashion from France, out of fashion when France became the enemy in the great European involvement of the Napoleonic wars. In the great European involvement of a century later, France was an ally, and a hundred years after *Trevelyan,* at least in 1935, such a dress as Theresa wore would be quite acceptable for a similar occasion. Obviously she wore no stays. There were corsets which those who needed them might wear with the chemise-like dresses of the revolutionary styles, but those who did not need them were ostentatious in dispensing with them, and Theresa was one of them. These corsets resembled the dress-reform waists of the last quarter of the nineteenth century, and there is no record that any were cut to wear with backless dresses. For a brief period English women were as free from the imprisonment of stays as their inhibitions and their figures would allow. Political events do influence fashions, but the fact that these styles in England lasted hardly longer than the brief Peace of Amiens may not be significant. Then it was, however, that fashions swung sharply back to the wasp waist and the armor of chastity. It may have been this taste of freedom, or it may have been Mary Wollstonecraft that set the ferment to working, but it is in her own time we can see the first bubble rise. Thomas Jefferson Hogg records it in his *Life of Shelley*. One can only guess the date; 1812 or 1813 perhaps. Shelley "stopt suddenly at the door of a house in a fashionable street" telling Hogg, "It is here we dine."

. . . the door was thrown wide open, and a strange spectacle presented itself. There were five naked figures in the passage advancing rapidly to meet us. The first was a boy of twelve years, the last a little girl of five; the other three children, the two eldest of them being girls, were of intermediate ages between the two extremes. As soon as they saw me, they uttered a piercing cry, turned round, and ran wildly up stairs, screaming aloud.

The children, it seemed, expected Shelley alone; Hogg learned about it later. They were allowed to "nakedize" as a privilege on a theory of "philosophic nakedness." It was Benjamin Franklin's idea, air baths early in the morning in their rooms for adults, more freedom for children. Hogg is not in sympathy, and wishes to make a good story; "there was to be soon a return to nature, it was believed." Neither is he in sympathy with dress reform, an anecdote of which follows the anecdote of nudity.

There have always been, off and on, a considerable number of people doing the stays movement. This part of female apparel had many enemies at that period; stays, it may be easily believed, found no favour with the advocates of nakedness. I heard much from them of the sin and danger of wearing stays, and I listened patiently to many a fierce, angry diatribe against them. I was once taken to a

lecture on stays, to be delivered by a first-rate, scientific blue . . .
The audience was pretty numerous, and, with the sole exception of
myself, consisted exclusively of females . . . Bundles of stays were
handed to her; these she successively applied to the plaster casts, and
demonstrated how grievously they offended against every principle of
anatomical science; launching forth into an animated invective against
busks, which, whether they were of wood, of whalebone, or of steel,
found no quarter. She then exhibited pictures of crooked shoulders,
distorted spines, contracted chests, and manifold deformities, painful
to behold. She assured us, that all these calamities, and many others,
were occasioned solely by the pernicious pressure of stays . . . she
assured us, as if from revelation, that a benevolent Providence never
intended the fairest of his creatures . . . to commit their captivating
persons to devilish engines of torture and destruction.

If there were "always" people "doing the stays movement," they
have left no easily traceable records. Here and there was a child
of nature or a Lucy bride who knew not the pressure of stays
on the sides of nature till she encountered them as an evil of
civilization; we had glimpses of some, Sarah Fielding's Ophelia
was one, in Chapter V. Men have inveighed against corsets,
and men have insisted that women wear them; Churchmen have
denounced them from the pulpit, physicians have frowned on
them, but where is the "stays movement"? If there was one, it
may have begun with adherents of Rousseau, who expressed
the idea in *Émile.*

I cannot but think that this abuse, pushed in England to an inconceivable point, will cause in the end the degeneration of the race,
and I maintain that the effect which one thus obtains is in bad taste.
It is not agreeable to see a woman cut in two like a wasp . . . this
defect would be very unpleasing to the eye in the naked figure; why
should it be a beauty under the dress?

Such expressions are easy to find, but not until this anecdote of
Hogg's does a woman come in sight actively campaigning, lecturing, seeking to gain converts, and it is hard to find another
till fifty or sixty years later.

We have had, also, an athletic heroine or two—Mary Raymond, for example, the victim of prejudice, and Catherine Morland, if Miss Austen will allow us to call her a heroine. But if you do such things you may be called a romp, and what could be less desirable? Even in the land of William A. Alcott, however, we can find early beginnings of better things. In 1825 an American teacher is said to have introduced some form of physical culture into a girls' school. Before that men students were no better off. A reminiscence of the Reverend Dr. Cazneau Palfrey tells of the introduction of gymnastic exercises into Harvard College in his Senior year, 1826. At the instance of Dr. Follen, gymnastic apparatus were placed in an unoccupied dining hall and on the Delta where Memorial Hall was built later, for the use of students who wished to exercise. One of the students who used them was William A. Stearns of the class of '26, who in November, 1854, was inaugurated President of Amherst College. In his inaugural address he expressed the wish to introduce into the educational plan "regular drills in gymnastic and calisthenic exercises." The result was Barrett Gymnasium, 1860, which sixty years later, still standing though long since outgrown, was called by local tradition the first college gymnasium in the United States. The exercises for girls would seem to have been quite ladylike; no danger of becoming a romp. One set described for ladies in 1832 suggests bending the knees gently, and rising on the toes. In 1856, Catharine Beecher published her *Physiology and Calisthenic Exercises*. From it we may learn that to acquire "a round and perfectly formed hand and arm . . . one of the most attractive points of womanly beauty," practise this:

Place the elbows on the hips and hold them there. Swing the lower arms in a circle . . . Swing them first outward, and then inward, till twelve are counted each way.

The costumes illustrated for such exercises are decorous. Skirts are long, and under them are pantalettes showing in some drawings, in others long bloomers gathered at the ankles. If these young ladies do not wear stays, they have remarkable natural waists. Miss Beecher insisted that to get the maximum effect from her system of exercises, dress design must be radically changed in three particulars: there must be less clothing about the hips than fashion then called for; nothing must hang from the waist, all weight to hang from the shoulders; the upper part of the body must be as warmly clad as the lower. To this end she herself designed a new undergarment, an early dress reform affair, perhaps the first "combination" uniting waist and petticoat to hang from the shoulders.

This was not far from the time when bloomers were named for the redoubtable Amelia. Under the name "Turkish trousers" they had been known and used since Lady Mary Wortley Montagu brought them from the Orient and wore them, mostly in private, in London, along with the turban which had so much vogue. Mrs. Bloomer did not design the costume, Mrs. Elizabeth Smith Miller is responsible for it. It was a knee-length tunic without belt worn over full Turkish trousers gathered at the ankle. It substituted an elliptical silhouette for the hourglass shape then in fashion, but it was capable of grace and beauty of interpretation on Watteau lines. Mrs. Bloomer, however, could not interpret it to her public—it was she who wore it, and from her it is named. Others wore it, and did their best, but the public would not have it. Probably those who urged it were "advanced," "strong-minded," not graceful or winning; they won nothing but abuse, and they complained of it. Fourteen of them signed a complaint which *The Home Journal* printed in 1854.

We have been for years oppressed, and many of us have had our health seriously injured by the unhealthy and uncomfortable forms of dress, adopted by the women of our country from fashions made by foreign modistes.

Some months since, being convinced that, like our fathers, we had "the inalienable right to life, liberty, and pursuit of happiness," we changed our dress for one short, light, and easy,—which was named by the common voice, from one who wore it, the "Bloomer dress". . . But the result of our wearing it has been . . . a uniform system of insult and outrage. Ladies of irreproachable character, walking in the streets of New-York accompanied by their husbands and brothers, have been hissed and hooted and most insulting words addressed to them.

We wish now to understand whether we have a civil and political right to wear a healthy and decent dress . . . or whether the New-York public is a mob by majority.

This gets scant sympathy from the editor:

Without advocating the Bloomer dress which (pantaloons and all) is needlessly unbecoming, we may venture to express the opinion that a cloth gaiter protecting the ankle, and a bad-weather dress short enough to escape the mud, would be neither conspicuous nor inelegant . . . Pure principles first, and cleanliness and health, before all other things else in woman, are what men look and pray for, in all whose charm they wish to strengthen and perpetuate.

The implications here are clear, that anything conspicuous is not in accord with pure principles, and that the first wish of a lady is to be the answer to a gentleman's prayer. You must conform to fashion and to the patterns set by the novels. Frederika Bremer's sister Charlotte says that their mother "had a detestation of strong, stout, tall women," that she "read vast quantities of novels, and I suspect that the hope of one day beholding in her daughters delicate, zephyr-like heroines of romance, was constantly haunting her imagination." Frederika's heroines are of the rococo pattern of delicacy and strength. The same pattern is in William Carleton's *The Black Prophet,* 1847. In Horatio Smith's *Adam Brown,* 1843, Matilda, a pretender to gentility, betrays the falsity of her pretensions by hoydenish behavior, but the same author in 1830, in *The New Forest,* pronounces in favor of a damsel who is dressed so that she can go faster than a walk; perhaps fashions in hoydens changed between the two dates.

Here and there a fashion note suggested hygienic possibilities still within the bounds of fashion. One of 1840 describes an arrangement of bands and gathers which "will make your dress appear sufficiently bouffant and form a proper contrast to the waist, thereby sparing the necessity and agony as well as the injury of tight-lacing." After Catharine Beecher, the next glimpse we have of the combination is in Godey's *Lady's Book* for 1858, where the "Nonpareil Garment," chemise and drawers cut together, is recommended to "Ladies travelling, to those giving out their wash. . . ." The next is in *La Vie Parisienne* for 1865, where the word appears under a sketch intended to be piquant of a model wearing a garment combining waist and drawers. She wears stays and chemise under it, and it is not intended to relieve weights and pressures. In fiction we get our earliest glimpse of it in Louisa May Alcott's *Eight Cousins,* 1874. Rose's doctor uncle refuses to let the twelve-year old girl wear a corset; he hangs her frocks from her shoulders, banishes petticoats, and clothes her fundamentally in a long-legged, long-sleeved woolen undergarment which "for want of a better name I shall use an Indian word and call pajamas." Louisa Alcott, it seems, did not see *La Vie Parisienne.* At about the same time the stays movement (it really was a movement by then) begins its work on the fainting heroine. Charles Reade, who is as often a propagandist as he is an artist, has it in *A Simpleton,* 1873. Reade dramatizes all the arguments against tight lacing, and assures us in his preface that he has every item documented. The heroine has all the ills that tight lacing can bequeath her; her lover is a physician who tries to save her and nearly loses her by his indelicate solicitude for her health. The "Cut my lace, Charmian," situation takes on a hygienic aspect.

Her father screamed for help in dismay. In ran Harriet [Charmian], saw, and screamed, but did not lose her head; . . . whipped a pair of scissors off the table, and cut the young lady's stay-laces directly. Then there was a burst of imprisoned beauty; a deep, deep sigh of relief came from a bosom that would have done honor to Diana; and the scene soon concluded with fits of harmless weeping, renewed at intervals.

The women of these times went into the water, but it seems unlikely that they could have done much swimming. An American observer described an English bathing costume of 1872 which she makes us see as an arrangement of heavy bags which could not be worse if it had been deliberately designed to be as grotesque as possible and to hold the maximum amount of water. Of what the Frenchwomen wore we have an excellently realistic vision in Randolph Caldecott's sketches of Trouville done for *The Graphic* in 1879. It is a tunic with trousers that look very much like the drawers of the period. The text accompanying the drawings confirms the suspicion that the women bathers did not swim. They indulge in "a romp in the shallow waves," and do not always "dip enough to drip." An "adventurous wade to the farthest post" is "the morning's chief amusement." A fashion plate of 1870 shows an American "bathing costume" which is truly a costume—anything but a swimming-suit. It includes a hat which is something between a derby and a shrapnel helmet, a "sacque" or "basque" with pert little tails, that would not fit over anything less than an armor-plate corset, a tunic, issuing from under the basque, to a little above the knee, Turkish trousers to just below the calf, and sandals of which the crossed ribbons come boot-high. This is surely an early example of "spectator sports" wear, and indicates that Amelia Bloomer had some influence on fashions. The bathing suit with the long bloomers and tunic changed between 1880 and 1890 into the type well known then and later by the shortening of the bloomers to the knee. But so long as they were bloomers they were bags of water, and girls could not do much swimming in them. None the less girls were learning to swim, sometimes in sur-

1869

THE NEW ATHLETIC HEROINE

reptitious nudity or borrowing of their brothers' one-piece suits, comically striped, sometimes in formal lessons from a "professor of the art."

Skating came into fashion in the sixties and seventies, a vogue imported from the court of the Empress Eugenie. Costumes for it showed the Bloomer influence, at least in the United States. Here is one from *Godey's* for 1864:

Skating is now so universally recognized as an institution among ladies, as well as among gentlemen, that not a little taste and ingenuity are exercised in getting up costumes, which will be at the same time warm, convenient, and picturesque. To be sure, most ladies content themselves with drawing up their soft woollen and merino dresses over gaily striped and ornamented underskirts, but not a few invent, or have invented for them charming skating costumes, especially adapted to the requirements of this graceful and healthful exercise, and also pretty and graceful enough to suit the most exacting taste.

The most suitable and admired of these costumes are made in French flannel, and consist of a Garibaldi, Turkish pants and short skirt, which leaves the limbs free for exercise . . . We have seen a costume of cuir colored flannel ornamented with bands of red leather. The pants should be pretty wide, and drawn with an elastic band. Where it is not convenient to procure a costume, an ordinary walking dress, drawn up over the Balmoral skirt with one of Madame Demorest's excellent elevators, of which we gave our readers a description last month, answers just the same purpose. The only advantage of the regular costume is that there is less weight to carry, and it is certainly more effective. A long skirt is, of course, worn over a skating dress in going to and from the place of rendezvous.

A fashion plate of 1869 shows gentlemen skating in overcoats and top hats, ladies in heavily draped skirts and tightly laced waists—the ice is merely a background and provider of display attitudes. For "parlor gymnastics" the costume was no lighter than for skating.

One very tasteful dress was of Russian gray Empress cloth . . . trimmed with leaf-green velvet; the depth of velvet at the bottom of the skirt was about eight inches . . . The body was a plaited Garibaldi, with deep yoke pointed in front and extending to the waist, finished with cut velvet, and braided to agree with the skirt . . . Wide Turkish pants of the same completes the dress.

As a fashionable silhouette the pattern of ultra-spheral delicacy had gone. In *Emilia Wyndham,* Emilia has a fairly full figure even in her teens, and the not-quite-nice girl who barely escapes the inevitable penalty of Goldsmith's law is small, slender, dark, a madcap sprite, perhaps a supposedly Gallic type, become unfashionable during the wars against France, superseded by the type supposed to be typically British, large, poised and blonde. Wood engraving begins to show them in book illustrations, and in the best period of that art Millais and Tenniel drew them and the Dalziell brothers engraved them. They stalk through the novels of Trollope and George Eliot in the pages of *Harper's Magazine.* In the woodcuts they are rather sombre figures; in hand-colored fashion plates they are more cheerful. In the fifties the silhouette was almost cone-shaped when an outside garment concealed any accent on the waist. At its best, as we see it in Winterhalter's paintings or a canvas like Monet's *Dans le Parc,* it has an effect of floating lightness; in the fashion notes of the time the word is "bouffant." In the sixties we begin to pick it up in the family photograph album. The figures here, and in the wood engravings, look strong and capable, but not active or athletic. Some of Renoir's paintings show this figure in the nude; Courbet shows it, and Feuerbach. What has become of the sylph? Probably she did not avoid the camera; she must have worn more clothes. In the last decade of the eighteenth century she wore a transparent dress with a maillot under it. In the third decade of the twentieth century she wore a knee-length dress with filmy shorts under it. In the third quarter of the nineteenth century she wore all the weight she could stagger under.

The restoration in France saw prompt reaction against freedom. A fashion drawing of the time shows Mlle. Busc and
M. Corset dancing airily with tightly laced waists. With the
return of the corset came drawers. Women did not wear them
even with farthingales in the eighteenth century; we have visual
evidence of the fact in various "suppressed plates," collectors'
items of engraving. But when dresses became transparent the
maillot seemed necessary. Little girls began to wear trousers
at the same time as their brothers and fathers, when knee-
breeches went out at the time of the Battle of Waterloo. This
was part of the movement in England to dress children as children rather than as miniature adults, which shows in the work
of the painters of the time, groups and single portraits of children by Romney, Raeburn and others. In them we see boys
wearing loose trousers barely to the ankle, and girls also with
the addition of a loose dress hanging straight from the shoulders.
Later there were times, probably when girls wore longer skirts,
when the pantalettes were mere ruffled cuffs intended to show at
the bottom, held by tapes above the knees. Older sisters wore
them, or girls kept on wearing them, in the thirties, and in the
forties, as skirts spread outward, women, perhaps the same girls
grown up, wore them, no doubt to save modesty in the tipping
of the stiffened bell-like skirts. When the skirts tipped, one
saw edging, tucks and ruffles below the knee; if the tip was
still more perilous, there was the tail of the chemise sticking
out through the placket of the *pantalon*. A fashion note in
the spring of 1864 told the secret of the Empress's spreading
skirt.

It is frequently a matter of curiosity to know how the Empress con-
trives always to appear with such well-setting skirts, for her Majesty
has *never* worn a cage, she only wears muslin petticoats which are
gored to a point and trimmed with well-starched flounces; these are
much deeper at the back than at the front. This is a costly contrivance,
and is not suitable for those who take much walking exercise.

Here is a fashion like so many others, a badge of aristocracy, a boast of extravagance, a vaunt of inactivity. Admittedly these numerous petticoats, gauzy though they may have been, flounces, starch and all, weighed more than butterflies' wings on a waist laced down to sixteen inches. The crinoline, the substitute for the petticoats, was heavy too; it was originally a horsehair fabric, afterward a cage of hoops. There is in 1863 a satirical portrait of Miss Impulsia Gushington, who, having lost her dress, appears in a hoop skirt which seems to be made of wooden barrel hoops, but we know that in the United States they were made of light wire. In the later seventies the spread of skirts narrowed front and sides, but continued extended in the rear by "crinolettes" or bustles. In this time illustrations begin to be conspicuous in advertising, one of the earliest of which shows Miss Alcott's "pajama" garment now called a "union suit," cut and sewed from red or white flannel, with pocket-like gores for the breasts. Over this a woman would wear corset and chemise, long cotton stockings, drawers, two or three cotton petticoats and perhaps another of taffeta or silk, bustle, and heavily draped dress. Skirts were lined, most of them stiffened and weighted with substantial interlinings. The "best black silk" that "would stand alone" must have been like the Wife of Bath's head-kerchiefs, "I dorste seyen they weyeden ten pound."

Did it weigh on the spirit as well as on the body? In England Victoria's mourning for Albert was heavy and long drawn out. In the United States certainly this is the saddest period in the history of clothes. The black silk dresses were decorated like hearses with funereal cords and tassels. Men wore funereal stovepipe effects in trousers and hats, of which nobody saw the joke until they were cast in bronze as statues of heroes. Machines were beginning to make both clothes and furniture—to make them ugly, not to make them liveable; the only merit of either was that it served to wear out the other. In England where are the laughers of the first twenty years of Victoria's reign? The giggles of Barham and Theodore Hook were dying down. Dickens laughed, but not at anything serious; we can hardly take him seriously today. Marryat was light-hearted at times, savage at others, but he does not make himself heard down the corridor of the years. Neither does Douglas Jerrold. Edward Lear laughed, but not at anything in particular; he rightly disclaimed any significance in his mirth. *Punch* began in 1842, but it was not funny till later. Tom Hood made famous puns, and wrote *The Bridge of Sighs,* known today as a faded flower of sentimentality. Even if we grant all these, they are outnumbered five to one by the portentous solemnity of the great guns of the time. Small wonder if the bravest faltered at the prospect of a withering "We are not amused," from the throne! Is it going too far to say, then, that Thackeray had the joke to himself till Meredith released the Comic Spirit, which turned its oblique light on the solemn age and trilled silvery laughter?

England had its current of laughter in the eighteenth century, but one listens in vain for anything of the sort in the American colonies or the new republic. Piety and wit could not live together. The puritan clouds disperse for a moment of pale sunshine in some of Washington Irving's work, but that was soon over, the merest lucid interval in the long procession of dark years. The sky was perhaps a little lighter in the second quarter of the nineteenth century, but pompous solemnity is the note, and one longs for a brisk assault of laughter to disperse it. The South did its best to preserve in life the tradition of "merry" England, and made an all too respectable showing of the gentlemanly vices. In literature, and one suspects in life, its sense of duty toward such observances was somewhat puritanic, a dutiful preservation of mother country tradition such as colonists always show. It is hard to see anything but solemnity in American literature before the Civil War.

If Puritan and Cavalier, the throw-off from the Revolution in England, brought their quarrel with them to the American settlements, they were for long too well occupied to fight it out. In New England, the middle-class Puritans were very busy trying to hammer a living out of a granite wilderness. In the South, the gentlemen were almost as busy trying to find someone to do their work for them. They could not enslave the natives, and their first colonies dwindled and starved for lack of workers. Perhaps, too, Dutch, Quakers and others in the middle colonies served as insulators. The American Revolution drew hostile elements together in a common cause against a common enemy, and thereafter, so long as they could keep themselves diverted by twisting the lion's tail, they didn't quarrel very much, but the time came when hating the British ceased to be a career in itself. Then perhaps for the first time we may imagine the Puritans lifting their eyes and looking about them. To the southward they beheld the gentlemen living and behaving like gentlemen, gay (by puritan standards), at ease, rich by the toil of other hands than their own. This will never do! Something must be wrong. Slavery must be wrong. To be sure, the Bible does not say so, but it makes people idle, rich, happy. Of course our little allegory does not shadow forth the whole story of the Civil War, but it does attempt to point to one thread in its "crimson web." Many a quarrel was then fought to a bloody truce; one of them surely was that of Cavalier and Roundhead, adjourned three thousand miles in space and two hundred years in time. And somehow as its tragic thunders died down we found that we had learned to laugh. Before the Civil War there was solemnity, and after it there was Mark Twain. Was it Lincoln who brought us to a state of civilization completely beyond the scope of all Washington's greatness? Lincoln was a tragic figure, acquainted with grief; he listened to the "stern daughter of the voice of God," and his greatness was that he could laugh as he listened.

Did literature listen as he laughed? Washington and Lincoln are the American patterns of the gentleman. Washington had a coat of arms; Lincoln was a rail-splitter. If the man of the people taught his nation to shake off the pious solemnity which the man of lineage had imposed on it, the social compromise has caught itself by the tail.

In the history of heroines, the dawn of the new light and the new lightness gleamed first in England. The master who fixed the portrait of the old heroine in the days of her passing began his work at the same time as did the immortal hand and eye that framed the symmetry of the new heroine. The old master was Anthony Trollope; the herald of the new light was George Meredith. The first of Trollope's novels that lives is *The Warden,* 1855, presenting Eleanor Harding. The first of Meredith's fiction is *The Shaving of Shagpat,* 1856, introducing a new spirit, for a time invisible and unknown, ultimately transforming. There are no words for it but Meredith's own. In *The Egoist,* Colonel de Craye thinks of Clara Middleton, "she had not uttered words; she had shed meanings." Harry Richmond says, "I followed my father's meaning as the shadow of a bird follows it in sunlight." Meredith sheds meanings. He flashes in the bright air, and we follow with our feet on the ground, making the best speed we may. The critic undertakes *The Shaving of Shagpat* as he does *Midsummer Night's Dream* in the face of Bottom's devastating warning, "Man is but an ass if he go about to expound this dream." *The Shaving of Shagpat* is a dream. It is swift and intricate as the flight of a swallow. If we plod breathlessly after its shadow we may trace a pattern. A simple-minded youth sees his task simply, and undertakes it in terms of direct action. A woman shows him the infinite intricacy of the affair, and guides him through its mazes which he could never have followed but for her. This bears about as much relation to *The Shaving of Shagpat* as a diagram of the path of the shadow on the ground would bear to the bird itself and its breathless flash through the bright ether. The tale is superb in imagery and sweep, gorgeous in color beyond all comment of criticism to convey. There is nothing to compare with it since Beckford's *Vathek*, which is after all a poor second, for *Shagpat* far outdistances it in scope and speed because it is winged with humor. It is brilliant and airy as the Comic Spirit; its speed is that of light, the oblique light. There is no way to know it but to read it; read it and remember that Meredith was a poet before he wrote it. One of the poems that came before it was the *Ballad of Fair Ladies in Revolt,* only a few years after *The Princess* in time but half a century beyond it in spirit. For more than half the history of their move towards freedom, Meredith held up before women higher ideals for them than they ever had for themselves. If they had read him and understood him they might long ago have canonized him and raised their battle-cry, "St. George for Women!" *The Shaving of Shagpat* has in it the informing essence of Meredith's work that follows it; it is poetry, and it idealizes the feminine spirit. It is more than idealization, it is heightened perception; it is a ray beyond the X-ray that reveals the soul and its potentialities, that should reveal them to women and to men.

In so far as *The Shaving of Shagpat* is genuinely a landmark in the history of Pamela's daughters, it is no less in the history of English fiction. There is not in the novel any earlier dramatization of the idea that man might not find his way to high achievement and greatness without the woman to point it out to him. A hint of it perhaps there is in Scott, when he shows the help and guidance that such heroines as Diana Vernon and Catherine Seyton afford their respective heroes. We may if we like read it here and there in myth and folk-lore. Ariadne gave to Theseus the clue to the labyrinth. There are a few of the fairy tales in which the Princess lays aside her ladylike inactivity of mind and body to help the hero through the noble deeds that shall win her, but more usually the feminine wisdom that helps him comes from an old woman, and may be taken to represent experience rather than intuition. It is rather the Ariadne myth that Meredith has illuminated to high significance if the reader can see it. But of course the complacent Sir Willoughby Patternes of his time did not see it.

Beginning not long after *The Shaving of Shagpat,* a change comes over the spirit of the heroine of the minor novel, a change of fashion from the pattern known as Victorian. It is as if someone speaking with authority said "Let there be lightness." The wine has gone flat; let us have something with fresh bubbles. Meredith, indeed, implied it, but no one heeded him; he had few readers in his day, and none too many in any day, for he writes not for the sluggish mind. He was the morning star which none hailed as the harbinger of the rising sun. He can hardly be held responsible for the departure, but he signals it. From his day through to the end of the century we see the attempt to put synthetic effervescence into the insipid heroine. Heroines are introduced with such tags as "beautiful but wilful," "beautiful but slangy," "beautiful but a tomboy," "beautiful but clever," "beautiful but petulant," with such persistent parallelism of phrase that one is inclined to think of the time as the era of "beautiful but . . ." This is a definite stage in the development of the heroine, a stage which heroes went through earlier. Before Tom Jones, all heroes were perfect except for the tragic flaw in the tragic hero, and the anti-hero of the picaresque romance. Fielding showed a hero with faults which even today readers find it hard to forgive or condone. Not till a hundred years later does any novelist raise in regard to a heroine the leading question "Can You Forgive Her?" and even then, as in Trollope's novel of that title, we apply it to the merest peccadillos. The first stage is that in which all heroines of romance are perfect, and women who are bad are horrid and have picaresque novels all to themselves. This is the age of Pamela and Moll Flanders. Next the erring sisters are admitted to the same building as the perfect ladies, but have a wing to themselves with impermeable walls. The perfect heroine is in the main novel and the picara in the interpolated tale,—"The Memoirs of a Lady of Quality," "Miss Matthews Relates her History." Even so early as Fielding, however, the separation is not water-tight; in *Amelia* Miss Matthews plays more part than merely to relate her story. The third stage is that of the double heroine, the perfect and insipid Amelia and the spicy Becky, the one "beautiful" and the other "but." The fourth stage combines the beautiful and the but in the one heroine, whose beauty is set off by the quality thought of as a blemish, as by a mole or a patch. The fifth stage might be called "beautiful and . . ." or beauty plus, in which the vivacious qualities are put forward as additions rather than as subtractions. The sixth stage—or is it still the fifth?—comes in the twentieth century, in which the heroine (still beautiful) does all that Tom Jones does and we regard her in about the same light.

It is true that we can make "beautiful buts" out of heroines before 1860, but we must do it ourselves, the authors do not attach the label. In 1806 Lady Morgan created Glorvina, the Wild Irish Girl of the spheral delicacy. We might call her beautiful but wild except that she is not wild; she is a violet by a mossy stone which not even a botanist could distinguish from the garden variety. No artist who can depict a beautiful girl can make her other than beautiful but, for if she is human she is not perfect. Marianne in *Sense and Sensibility* is beautiful but possessed of "an irritable refinement of the mind" which made her attach too much importance to the "delicacies of strong sensibility and the graces of polished manner." Note the adroitness with which Jane Austen turns the prime virtue of the heroine of the day into a fault, making a "beautiful but" out of what would have been to any of her fellow novelists a "beautiful and." Three years later, 1814, we have Mrs. Brunton's Ellen Percy in *Discipline*, beautiful but proud and self-

important. Discipline teaches her the Christian virtue of humil-
ity. In 1818 we have Catherine Morland (*Northanger Abbey*)
who is first a tomboy; at fourteen she plays cricket and baseball,
rides horseback and runs round the country, doubtless in the
trousers and tunic costume which Romney and Raeburn depicted on girls of that age. Then she changed her ways of
living and set out consciously to become a heroine. She was not
born a heroine, and did not succeed in achieving the status.
Others there are who have some of the traits of beautiful but,
without fully qualifying, such as the revolutionary heroines of
Bage, Holcroft and their kind. The revolutionary novel dies
down in the work of Horatio Smith, who gives us robust, healthy
girls, Helen in *Reuben Apsley* and Hetty in *Walter Colyton*
(1827 and 1830). There are, however, no buts about them;
their qualities are not presented as blemishes, they win on their
merits. Theresa in *Trevelyan* would have been an example if
Lady Scott had approved of her and made her a heroine. As
she stands she is more in the nature of a bad example, "Maidens
of England, take caution by she."

The revolutionary ferment continued to work mildly in the
novel, and may have developed elements in the soil which
brought out some of the coloring of the new heroine. The
Byronic hero came into the novel through Byron's friend
Trelawny, whose hero in *The Adventures of a Younger Son,*
1834, may be in part Trelawny himself, but is surely more
than half Byron. His mate of soul and body is a child of nature,
a Haidee, who is orientally soft and languorous in love, but all
steel, fire and gunpowder in heroic crises. She appears by the
hero's side at the most perilous climax of every wildly dangerous exploit. She will coolly hand him a spare gun in the very
jaws of a charging lion, dive fathoms deep to cut him free from
fatal entanglements under water, cover his body with hers amid
flying bullets on the parapet of his besieged fort. She, however, is a perfect heroine; no one ever holds these exploits

against her as unladylike. More civilized are the mates of the later toned-down Byronic heroes, the soldierly ones of Charles Lever, and the equally hard-riding ones of Frank Smedley. Lever's heroines are apt to be more or less athletic, good horse-women at any rate, spirited, vivacious, sometimes a bit witty but not disconcertingly so. Frank Smedley's are mere dummies for rescue, and as brides they are wax figures for the display of satin and tulle. More civilized still, and still to much the same effect, is Laura Smyly in Marmion Savage's *Bachelor of the Albany,* who, coming when she does, in 1847, gives us a momentary pre-view of the new model of the later decades.

The Smyly girls were up to anything—girls of the world—no nonsense about them, extremely amusing, and easily amused, the very girls for country-houses, buxom, handsome, frolicksome, mettlesome girls; they rode, walked, danced, sang, and were both capital talkers and capital listeners . . .

[Laura Smyly was almost thirty; she] was uncommonly lively and entertaining, with as good a knack at a nickname as any lady in England. It was no wonder she had not been married, for she was too poor for some men, and too clever for others; besides, she was not the sort of girl to fancy a briefless barrister, or elope with an aide-de-camp. Mrs. Spread used to say she had a great deal of the character of Beatrice—a shrewd tongue, with a good understanding and a warm heart. [The same speaker mentions her later as] the girl who carries her heart in her mind, and would love you after your own fashion, with remarkably sound and well-regulated understanding.

And when the hero proposes to her, he offers her, not his hand and his heart, but his hand and his understanding. The qualities here add spice; the time had not come, however, when they could be made popular without the apologetic "but."

Not even Trollope could do it. The fact is that if we scan his pages for signs of the times, what we read is not so much that it was time for a new model heroine as that the girl of the day had the needful spice if we choose to interpret her realistically. His first portrait, Eleanor Harding in *The Warden,* is too distressingly ladylike for young readers of 1935. In *Barchester Towers,* 1857, she is the charming young widow, Eleanor Bold, who dealt Mr. Slope "a box on the ear with such right good will, that it sounded among the trees like a miniature thunder-clap." We might, then, be justified in saying that in the pages of Trollope himself the new heroine comes out of the old chrysalis with an audible pop. Eleanor is beautiful, yes, but

it is to be feared that every well-bred reader of these pages will lay down the book with disgust, feeling that, after all, the heroine is unworthy of sympathy. She is a hoyden, one will say. At any rate she is not a lady, another will exclaim. I have suspected her all through, a third will declare; she has no idea of the dignity of a matron; or of the peculiar propriety which her position demands . . . She cannot altogether be defended; and yet it may be averred that she is not a hoyden, not given to romping, nor prone to boxing. It were to be wished devoutly that she had not struck Mr. Slope in the face. In doing so she derogated from her dignity and committed herself. Had she been educated in Belgravia, had she been brought up by any sterner mentor than that fond father, had she lived longer under the rule of a husband, she might perhaps have saved herself from this great fault. As it was, the provocation was too much for her, the temptation to instant resentment of the insult too strong. She was too keen in the feeling of independence, a feeling dangerous for a young woman, but one in which her position peculiarly tempted her to indulge. . . . But, nevertheless, she should not have raised her hand against the man. Ladies' hands, so soft, so sweet, so delicious to the touch, so graceful to the eye, so gracious in their gentle doings, were not made to belabour men's faces. The moment the deed was done Eleanor felt that she had sinned against all propriety, and would have given little worlds to recall the blow.

Here we have an explicit, full-length declaration of the exact meaning of "but." It is worth extended quotation and careful scrutiny if one wishes to mark the exact line where Trollope stands between the old and the new, with his eyes turned back toward the old. A more conspicuous example of the same thing is one which it is not so easy to concentrate into a paragraph. It is the figure of Lady Glencora Palliser dramatized through several novels as it is built up through trying experiences in *Can You Forgive Her?*, *Phineas Finn*, and others between 1864 and 1876. With her beauty and nobility of character, Lady Glencora has several buts. She is active, faulty, generous, highspirited, clever, witty, audacious, unconventional. As one of the three figures on which he stakes his hope of literary immortality, Trollope devotes many words to her in his autobiography.

She has . . . beneath the thin stratum of her follies a basis of good principle, which enabled her to live down the conviction of the original wrong which was done her, and taught her to endeavour to do her duty in the position to which she was called. She had received a great wrong;—having been made when a little more than a child to marry a man for whom she cared nothing;—when, however, though she was little more than a child, her love had been given elsewhere. . . . She is by no means a perfect lady; but if she be not all over a woman, then am I not able to describe a woman . . . I do not know that she was at all points a lady, but had fate so willed it she would have been a thorough gentleman.

Here again we have an exact survey of the dividing line between the old and the new. Lady Glencora ran counter to the conventions of the time; a clergyman attacked her for it in a letter to Trollope, and Trollope defended her at the same time that he subscribes to the conventions of the time. He moves forward, and looks lovingly back.

We have a glimpse in *Barchester Towers* of the spirit of the time as one sees it who looks back. Mr. Plomacy suggests to Miss Thorne that the ladies will want to take part in her revival of medieval sports.

"Can't they look on as their great-grandmothers did before them?" said Miss Thorne.
"It seems to me that the ladies ain't contented with looking now-a-days. Whatever the men do they'll do . . ."

Miss Thorne made no reply. She felt that she had no good ground on which to defend her sex of the present generation from the sarcasm of Mr. Plomacy. She had once declared in one of her warmer moments, "that now-a-days the gentlemen were all women and the ladies all men." She could not alter the debased character of the age.

Lady Glencora is a bit inclined to pull wires; her husband has to teach her not to interfere in politics. But she is not inclined to a career; if she might pull the wires she would remain behind a screen. Others of her time were beautiful but ambitious, beautiful but strong-minded, to an extent that makes the marriage-*vs.*-career novel seem to stem from the stock of beautiful but. The prospect of a career comes into the novel first, perhaps, on the American scene. J. G. Holland's *Miss Gilbert's Career,* 1860, displays it in the title and bids for priority in the class. Miss Gilbert is beautiful, she has a feminine heart, but (Holland implies the but, he does not express it) she is self-willed, self-confident, she has a masculine head. She echoes the words of the impassioned Countess of Leicester, "I wish to God I were a man!" The combination ought to serve her well in the career she chooses, that of a novelist. So it does; she is successful, but success is dust and ashes to the taste. The experience teaches her the true feminine rôle; her self-confidence is humbled, she is glad to bow to the will of the man who becomes her husband. After all, beans is beans still to Cinderella, she has not yet become Jack, magician of the beanstalk. We might have learned this earlier from poetry, *The Princess,* 1847, in which Tennyson playfully sketches a college of beautiful but intellectuals, rejecting marriage for the cause. Love pops in like a mouse into a sewing circle, and the establishment breaks up in arpeggios of silvery shrieks and butterfly flights. This was a year before the founding of Queen's College.

Blackmore's Clara Vaughn, 1864, was beautiful but petulant and obstinate. Mrs. Annie Edwards's *Archie Lovell* is "the story of a pretty young hoyden whose audacity is only equalled by her innocence." The same author drew a "bohemian" heroine later in *Ought We to Visit Her?* Cigarette in Ouida's *Under Two Flags* is a bohemian, beautiful but vivacious. "She was passionate, impetuous, she was vain, she was wayward, she was as fierce as a little velvet leopard." In Augusta A. Evans's *Vashti,* 1869, Salome Owen is beautiful but wilful and Vashti is beautiful but frozen; she does not believe in God. Margaret Hungerford's Molly Bawn is beautiful but petulant and frivolous; she breaks conventions through innocence. Her Airy Fairy Lilian, 1879, is beautiful but slangy, also frivolous but rather smart than innocent. Justin McCarthy's Dear Lady Disdain is beautiful but boyish to the extent that she dislikes sentimentality and is averse to love-making. Others show in such titles as *Vixen* (Mary E. Braddon, 1879), *Madcap Violet* (William Black, 1877), *The Beautiful Wretch* (William Black), *The Hoyden* (Mrs. Hungerford).

In the 80's, we find that qualities which twenty years before had been faults which would bar a heroine from gentility have become virtues; beautiful but is slipping over into beautiful and. We can see the change working in the decade of the seventies. In its early years comes Lenore Herrick (Rhoda Broughton, *Good Bye, Sweetheart*). She is beautiful of course, but we need note only two details of her face: "her nose, though not in the least rétroussé, belongs rather to the family of upward than that of downward tending noses." Her eyes are large, "though not with the owlified largeness of a 'Book of Beauty.'" Here is the first appearance of a new style of nose for an active heroine, unless Tennyson can claim priority in the same year, 1872, for Lynette, beloved of Gareth. Lynette was not fast, but she rode a fast horse, and until she was worshipped by a few noble deeds was rather scornful, petulant and wilful, though after she was married she became a veritable Griselda. Her nose was "tip-tilted like the petal of a flower." Perhaps Tennyson is repudiating his earlier Claribels and Lilians as Rhoda Broughton repudiates Heath's *Book of Beauty*. But Lenore does not repudiate all earlier patterns; she carries the reader's mind back as far as Clarissa, who was originally delicate, but had cultivated an air of health. So Lenore; "when I was little I was very, very ill—I'm not over-strong now, though you would not think it to look at me . . ." Paul expresses proper incredulity as he looks at "the girl's full womanly figure, at the plump though slender dimpled hand . . . at the round, cream-white column of her proud throat." Thus the charm of physical delicacy is suggested by a negative, whereas the bloom of health is the present reality. Negative, too, is the suggestion of the livelier faults.

"I am not a flirt."
"No?" (more interrogatively than assertively).
"Nor fast."
"No-o," (rather slowly and doubtfully).
"I am *not* fast," she repeats stoutly; "how can I be? I do not hunt; I do not drink hock and seltzer for breakfast; I do not smoke."
"Good Heavens! I should hope not!"

She is not really nice; she says she will try, but she does not seem to relish the epithet.

"I shall spend all my days and all my nights in trying to be a really nice girl by the time you come back. A really nice girl.—I have been called a tall girl, and an odious girl, and a sharp girl, and now and then a deuced handsome girl; but never to my recollection in all my life, have I been called a nice girl."

In the beginning she is too up-to-date for the hero, but she wins her way with him. "Girl of the Period!" he exclaims, "from all such good Lord deliver us!" If he calls on God to put asunder what He hath joined after the end of the book, we do not hear of it, and she may stand for us as the girl of the period. Of the same period is Nina Kostalergi, an Irish heroine of Charles Lever's. She is very beautiful. "Kearny never came into the room where she was without being struck by the elegance of her demeanour." But once when he came into the room, Nina "was busily engaged in pinning up the skirt of her dress in a . . . fashion which . . . displayed more of a marvellously pretty instep and ankle than he thought strictly warranted." None the less, "people began to say, 'See how admirably M. Kostalergi has brought up that girl! how nicely mannered she is, how lady-like, how well-bred . . .'" Perhaps they did not know that coffee in the drawing-room was only half a success so long as the gentlemen sat over their wine; and as for the daily cigarette Nina smoked with it, Kate, in her simplicity, believed it was only done as a sort of protest at being deserted by those unnatural protectors who preferred poteen to ladies.

Bertha M. Clay throughout the decade can forgive mixed and assorted faults to heroines who look like mixed and assorted Greek goddesses. We meet them in such novels as *Love Works Wonders, Repented at Leisure, A Dark Marriage Morn, Thorns and Orange Blossoms*. Pauline Darrell has the "graceful lines, the beautiful curves, the grand free grace of the world-renowned Diana of the Louvre; there was the same arched, graceful neck, the same royal symmetry, the same harmony of outline." But there is also a "superb bust of Juno," and one could "almost fancy that its head had been modeled from hers." Pauline has a proud spirit, which her trials humble to atonement. Ethel Gordon early "gave promise of a magnificent womanhood," and there is mention of "ancient Greeks" and their Venus. "There was no flaw in her beauty," yet, lest it should not be perfect without imperfection, "she did not possess the cold, perfectly regular beauty of a woman without a fault. There was pride, and, perhaps, some little degree of temper in the bright eyes, just as there was something of independence and hauteur in the curved lips." Her father warns her, "I want you to correct this pride in yourself; to learn submission to wise and gentle guidance, so that a woman's greatest ornament, a meek and gentle spirit, may be yours . . . Submissiveness and gentleness, Ethel,

form a woman's diadem." Here is lip service to the older code
along with bowing at the altar of the new. Violet Beaton
(*Thorns and Orange Blossoms*) marks the line as between one
generation and another. She has a "delicate style of loveliness,"
yet she is distasteful to the aristocratic ladies of her lover's
aristocratic family.

The ladies of his family had always affected to be, if they were
not actually, delicate and fragile; they considered health and strength
rather as vulgar attributes. Violet, on the contrary, rejoiced in superb
health, in a magnificent constitution; she did not even know what the
words "languor" and "fatigue" meant as applied to herself, and consequently she had a capacity for enjoyment that seemed marvellous
to him. When they were in Switzerland, she could climb the highest
mountains quite as well as he could, she could walk as far, she could
endure as much fatigue—yet she was refined, and as far from being
masculine or strong-minded as it was possible to be. There was no
fairer picture than that of this beautiful girl—health glowing in her
face, her eyes sparkling, her lips crimson.

Here we may see how far we have come on one line of advance
since the mid-eighteenth century. Clarissa had delicacy and
health, but she rated no such adjectives as "superb health,"
"magnificent constitution," nor could she have climbed the highest mountains; she would have languished at the very sight of
them. It is to this eighteenth-century ideal that the generation
before Violet Beaton cling; the next generation is for the athletic
ideal, the model with the Diana legs and the Juno bust. The
line here falls between the third and the last quarters of the
nineteenth century. But athletic as she is, Violet must still
wear the demeanor of the modest flower—not masculine nor
strong-minded—never, never! Her "sin" is that she leaves her
husband; her discipline is the long hard road she must travel
to get back to him and assume the attitude of submission. We may
read here an item of the Victorian code, which Victoria weighted
with all her royal influence; when you leave your husband, you
pass into oblivion.

"I was wondering whether in any circumstances whatever a wife ought to leave her husband."

"Certainly not," was the stern reply. "No matter whether she be in the right or in the wrong, the world shows its estimate of such women by ignoring them. I should say that a woman in fear of her life might be justified in leaving her husband, but even in that case I do not quite approve of it. I think this, that let the man be as bad as he may, his wife should have patience with him, and try to make him better."

Lady Lovel is another who "was simply perfect—nothing could have added to the superb beauty of her figure." And again the Greek statue; "the famous Venus herself was equalled." But she is a proud beauty; she breaks hearts to feed her vanity. She breaks one too many, and must suffer for it. The experience leaves a mark of imperfection on her perfect beauty; " 'You have something that looks like a wrinkle on your forehead.' Lady Lovel sprang from her chair in alarm." Are a dozen broken hearts worth a wrinkle on a perfect forehead?

In the next decade, 1880–1890, we still have heroines who are beautiful with apology or subtraction, but the apologies are more often for mental than for physical vigor. In 1883 Edgar Fawcett shows in *An Ambitious Woman* one who is beautiful but ambitious. We might even say of Meredith's Diana Merion that she is beautiful but intellectual, for in the society of her time the vigor of her mind amounts to a tragic flaw. But in the same year it seems that it was not so grievous a fault to be strong-minded as it was a decade earlier, for the word in a title does not damn the book. William A. Hammond gives us *A Strong-Minded Woman*, 1885, in which Theodora Moultrie is beautiful but intellectual. For physical vigor there are few apologies; it calls rather for praise. At least one author shows us in 1880 a girl who can swim, but he represents her as of Napoleon's time. It is Blackmore's Mary Annerley, who rides horseback unaccompanied, for she is a farmer's daughter. "With the multitudinous tingle of youth" she runs barefoot along the

beach; "she could swim pretty well from her frequent bathing"; she is expert at climbing the rocks of the cliff. Frankfort
Moore's *I Forbid the Banns,* 1883, indicates that there was still
some demand for physical delicacy, but it is only a hint. Bertha
Lancaster "was tall and beautifully shaped . . . as she walked,
the strong breeze blowing from the sea forced her garments
against her body and held them there until every delicate curve
was suggested." With this hint of delicacy we must have vigor,
the symbol of which, as before, is the Greek statue, here the
Winged Victory, which the author clearly intends to suggest.
But if these Greek statue heroines were presentably dressed in
their time, they had no such bodies as their authors would present to our mind's eye. The corsets, and even the dress-reform
waists of the 80's, compressed the diaphragm and the waist and
emphasized the breasts and the abdomen. If sculptors and
painters then had used for their nude studies models with the
fashion figure of the day, their work would show the pregnant or abdominal silhouette of the fifteenth and sixteenth
centuries, typical of the work of Lucas Cranach, with a con-
cave curve from under the breast to the overprominent abdomen.
There are photographs from life of nude models of the 80's
which show just that. Even when the artist's pattern was not
Greek, the figure would not fit fashionable clothes. In 1883
Mercié received a medal for his Venus, a plump young woman
verging on embonpoint, with rather short body and short
legs, whose abundant breasts and hips would fill the corset of
that date, but whose diaphragm and waist would burst it or
suffer ruin if she tried to wear it. The taste for the Greek figure
in these novels suggests romance; it is not what anyone would
see if the girl of the period took off her clothes.

It is in the seventies and eighties that these Greek goddesses
haunt the imagination of the novelists and the imagery of the
novels. It is the time of the pseudo-classical draperies of the
aesthetic movement, of Walter Pater's *Marius the Epicurean,*

of Lew Wallace's *Ben Hur,* of the "Grecian bend," and with the "Psyche knot" it carried on into the early nineties. Its influence was that of the tale of Troy revivified by Schliemann's spectacular discovery of its site and of the golden tombs of Mycenae. It was the time, too, when the Victory of Samothrace, the "Winged Victory," discovered in 1863, was set in its conspicuous position in the Louvre. Like the discovery of the tomb of Tutankhamen in the twentieth century, this blaze of splendor from forgotten kings fired the popular imagination, and not only lent theme, tone and color to all the arts of the time, but blended with the fashions. Both discoveries were aptly in accord with the fashions of the day; one may believe that if they had been transposed in time—if the Egyptian discovery had come in 1880 and the Greek one in 1920—neither would have had so much influence. In the 1920's the slender, lightly swathed Egyptian silhouette and the square cut of the hair fell easily in line with prevailing modes. The 1880's saw delicacy in the lines of the Winged Victory. Women were experimenting with athletics, but had not gone far, and thought of the athletic woman as one with a strong, heavy figure. The 1920's connects athletic achievement with a type of figure which fifty years earlier would have been considered one of fragile delicacy, and considers the Winged Victory indecently fat. The contrast appears clearly in G. B. Stern's *A Deputy Was King,* 1926.

Val had reasons just now for being peculiarly sensitive about her appearance. She responded to suggestion.—Gradually she avoided sight of herself in the mirror; gradually she avoided sight of Loraine running, Loraine climbing like a cat, Loraine slippery and boneless, leaping down from walls with hardly a jar in her contact with the ground, or slinking from bough to bough in the tree-tops. Val wondered if Stephen Greenways had ever looked from Loraine to her, and used the word—no, she could not use it herself . . . it was such an uncomfortable little monosyllable, like a germ in the air. Even the Winged Victory might not have carried herself so superbly if a tourist had once murmured in her hearing: "Fat"—and passed on.

Delicacy in 1880 was the modelling of a heavy body plus infinite prudery of mind. Forty-five years later it dwelt in a "boneless" body with the muscles of a panther and a mind with no inhibitions except such as would suppress modesty. In the advertising of the 1920's nothing is considered indecent but obesity. Writers and artists exhaust their ingenuity in the effort to tell women about garments for heavy figures without suggesting fat, but they seek no euphemisms or indirections of word or illustration in demonstrating devices for occasions which most women of the eighties would have died rather than mention even to one another. Fashions will go back to the dawn of history to find the very newest thing, but not unless it finds there what it happens to fancy.

Whatever delicacy there was in the modelling of Bertha Lancaster's body, that of her mind belongs to a new girl, unknown to Heath's *Book of Beauty*. Julian Charlton tells her at their first meeting that she has gone straight to his heart. "The girl did not look down to her plate with a blush as she would have done had she lived fifty years earlier. She turned her eyes full on his face"—and asked him to pass the marmalade. She is well in advance of her time; she does not "believe in" marriage, and tries to get its benefits without incurring its penalties. Others who do not go so far still contrast with the old types of delicacy. Rider Haggard's Jess rides like a man on her African farm. Hammond's strong-minded woman, Theodora Moultrie, is no less strong of body than of mind.

There was no physical weakness about Theodora. She could eat a good piece of beefsteak for her breakfast, with the accessories of bread and butter and a cup of coffee; besides doing justice to her other meals; and then she walked four miles every day. Rain or shine, snow or sleet, hot or cold, no matter what the weather, she walked four miles. [Her sister Lalage] was more robust and powerful, and of greater powers of endurance. While Theodora would walk her four miles a day and feel that it was as much as was good for her, Lalage would think nothing of three times the distance, and be as fresh when it was finished as when she began . . . every movement had the grace and accentuation which only well-developed muscles can give.

Burke's idea of feminine delicacy seems to be out of the picture. Susan Ferrier was looking slantwise at it in 1824 when she showed Lord Rossville forbidding in the name of Burke Miss St. Claire to walk before breakfast and come in with the appetite of a ploughboy and the complexion of a milkmaid. But with twelve miles and a beefsteak spheral delicacy has vanished beyond the spheres!

Only in a general way can we correlate the progress of this new ideal of physical vigor for women with the progress of the "stays movement," of emancipation, of athletics for women. What would Moore's hint of the Winged Victory mean to a reader of 1883 who realistically imaged the silhouette of the day? If Bertha Lancaster was dressed as other women of that time, she was "hearsed in complete steel" or whalebone from the upper curve of her breast to the lower curve of her abdomen. Could any wind give the modelling of the front of her torso in delicate curves? She wore many petticoats and a heavy draped skirt. A novel of the twentieth century, *The Perennial Bachelor,* by Anne Parrish, 1925, looking back to about this time, sees there a Winged Victory, and then, when she and other girls are undressing in the boathouse tells us to the last garment what they wore. First we see them

Getting out of their tight dresses, their shoes and stockings, stepping from circle after circle of petticoats, calling "Don't look!" to each other, as they took off corset covers, drawers, corsets shaped like hourglasses, chemises, and longribbed shirts, getting into their blue flannel bathing suits . . .

Then, a little later, "The wind kindled Maggie's cheeks, strained back her thin, dark blue dress until she was a flying victory." This, too, when she was dressed for church, wearing no less and probably more than the day before. Could the most indiscreet wind do more than indicate that she had two legs? It

could not be delicate, but it might be slightly indelicate. None
the less, a study of the silhouette of this period and its evolution
from the bell-shaped one which preceded it suggests that something of the Winged Victory was consciously or unconsciously
behind its development, some aspiration toward speed and lift
shaped its lines. If the spreading silhouette of the fifties had
flexibility enough to yield to the wind so that fullness of front
and sides could be made to stream backward, a figure wearing
it in the face of a gale might show some such lines as the
silhouette of the middle eighties. Both seem founded on rather
heavy figures to the extent of large breasts, hips and buttocks,
yet there is something of motion in both; the one floats, the other
goes forward. Neither is at its best in sitting poses. That of the
fifties is an all-around silhouette; that of the eighties is definitely a profile. We may interpret these fashions as an attempt
to put into the dress a lightness, a speed, which would not have
been quite the thing in the bodies of the wearers. The change
from the one to the other began in the middle seventies and
was complete by the middle eighties. These are the years of the
trend we have been following in the novel toward more bodily
activity on the part of the heroine.

Among these girls, most of those who take exercise still keep
to forms used in earlier periods, horseback riding and walking.
These may be more or less strenuous, from a walk round the
grounds or a canter round the park to mountain-climbing, cliff-
scaling, and riding to hounds neck and neck with the men.
Lenore Herrick said she was not fast, she did not hunt, but
some of Trollope's heroines hunt, though only the fastest go
fast. Skating came into some vogue in the seventies, but we see
little of it in the novel; Blackmore's Alice Lorraine speaks of
it in 1875 as an aspiration. Tennis came out of its ancient court
and appeared on the lawn in the middle seventies, and women
played lawn tennis from the beginning, but not until 1898 does
Grant Allen mention one of his heroines (in *The Incidental*

Bishop) as of the "lawn tennis type." Only one heroine can swim; probably she acquired the skill by "bathing" naked in secluded coves or at night as does Rose Salterne in Kingsley's *Westward Ho!* That came out in 1855, and Rose is not the only one of Kingsley's heroines of whom he gives us a glimpse in the nude; but others are more discreet than the pious Canon, and we see no more heroines learning to swim in that fashion till the early nineties; though we should note Judd's Margaret who did so in the seclusion of the American backwoods long before Kingsley—Margaret lived in the early days of the Republic, and Judd wrote of her in 1845. Bicycles for men came on the market in the late seventies; we see pictures of them in early illustrated advertising about 1879. Three or four years later women's magazines tell their readers about tricycling for women, but women did not take extensively to it. The best of the tricycles were cumbersome machines that made heavy going on the comparatively rough roads of that time. On wheels the men had much the advantage.

So they did also in tennis. People who were "doing the stays movement"—by this time going strong—were interested. Mrs. E. M. King, Honorary Secretary of the Rational Dress Society, wrote in 1882 an article for the Monthly Gazette of the Bicycle Touring Club. She notes that "the opinions of English society are changing quickly and surely as to what women may or may not do." This she finds especially observable in sports; there is hardly an athletic game but women may take part in it with men if they please. She cites a tennis match in which an expert player, none other than Major Wingfield, who introduced lawn tennis to the British public, had difficulty in beating a woman player, and gallantly acknowledged that he could not have done so if her clothing had not weighed more than his. The test showed that her clothes weighed ten pounds and his weighed only four and a half. Probably her clothes were a street costume and his were specially light. In an American women's magazine of 1883 we read in an article on "Dress for the Mountains" that

> An alpine climbing dress exhibited by a lady at the exhibition of the Rational Dress Association in London, as worn by herself in all mountain excursions, consists of brown serge, the short skirt arranged with tabs, buttons and elastic so that it can be shortened at will. Narrow trousers fastened on a circular band, plaited blouse bodice with belt, stocking suspenders from the waist. The whole weight of the dress, underwear included, four pounds nine ounces.
>
> For mountain climbing and wear, the drawers, which is all that Lady Harberton's "divided skirt" amounts to, might very well be substituted for an underskirt, and made of the same material as the dress.

In the adjoining column an article on "How to Dress for Lawn Tennis" says nothing of the weight of the costume except to remark that "a lawn tennis dress should be simple, and cool, and light weight." A comparison of weights made in August, 1928, showed a man's street costume, coat, waistcoat, oxford shoes with rubber soles, including everything he carried in his pockets, weighed ten pounds, and a woman's costume complete weighed two and a half pounds. The man's shoes with thick crêpe rubber soles weighed two and three-quarters pounds. If they were playing tennis both costumes would weigh less, but still his shoes would outweigh her entire costume by an even wider margin. The dress reformer of the eighties sees a similar handicap in cycling. Tricycling, she says, offers to women, "something to vary the dull monotony of their lives, the daily monotonous walk, the perpetual sauntering along the same streets, gazing vacantly into the same shop windows." Tricycling would be an improvement, but it is hampered by long skirts. She mentions the divided skirt, and prophesies that the future of the tricycle depends on the advent of a more rational costume.

In the United States there was in the first half of the nineteenth century a good deal of experimentation with costumes and clothes patterns, most of which was in the direction of reform. It went on in groups that usually combined religious and social and community experiments of the kind that flourished most in the third and fourth decades of the century. Many of these for one reason or another designed and adopted a distinctive costume. In the Old World, religious orders have done this time out of mind, and more often than not the costume of the order was indicative of reform, looking toward simplicity, symbolic of ritual poverty, adapted to the work of the order. In the New World the process was much the same. The costume of the Quakers distinguished them from others and expressed their principles of modesty and simplicity, their protest against vanities and vexations of spirit. The Shakers, beginning in colonial times, brought together the ideas of religious principles, industrial community life, and a special distinctive costume. Many communities involved women working with the men in the factories of industrial groups, or in the fields. In some of these the uniforms seem to have been much like the suit named for Mrs. Bloomer, either tunic or waist and short skirt over Turkish or other loose trousers. In this era were born the dress reformers of a generation later, Elizabeth Stuart Phelps Ward, Annie Jenness Miller, Abba G. Woolson. Through lectures and books they promulgated their system during the seventies and eighties. They were rational, but not extreme. The "union suit" was the foundation—in those days it was complete from neck to wrists and ankles—corded waist with few or no bones, and in some systems something like the envelope chemise, the names of which, "chemilette," "chemiloon," indicate that it stood for a combination of chemise and drawers or chemise and corset cover. The reform looked toward ease, freedom and simplicity. Not many women went over completely to these reforms, but they benefited some of the women some of the time, and in one direction at least they led to something. The reform in children's costume in England in the time of the French Revolution had lasting effects, but it had its ups and downs.

Fashion plates through the nineteenth century show children's fashions following those of their elders closely enough to indicate that the idea of dressing children like miniature adults never completely dies, and children, little girls in particular, look at times very uncomfortable. Even in the nineteenth century, little girls, even baby girls, were laced to form their figures. Corded waists appear in illustrated advertising in the late seventies alongside of the armor-plate corsets, and all through the eighties and nineties. In the eighties young girls often wore them instead of corsets; in the nineties it was the usual thing for girls to wear them until they were grown up enough to graduate to stiff corsets. Some of them never did graduate. These girls and their daughters effected the emancipation of the twentieth century.

Viscountess Harberton sponsored the divided skirt, and venturesome women began to ride horseback astride. In 1882 she wrote a letter to the editor of *Knowledge* attributing prevalent consumption among women to tight lacing. Other correspondents tried to refute her, and a little later she wrote again in rebuttal, "We have not yet fully come to the end of the evil to the community of this system of 'waists.'" Her mention of printed matter indicates that the stays movement was well before the public. "How many people," she asks, "realize the fact that 28 to 30 inches would be the size of the waist of a healthy woman of medium height when left to nature?" Fifty years later the question would be, who does not know it? and the answer, only those who do not see the tabloids and the movie magazines. But in 1883 tennis had not gone far on its progress toward shirt and shorts for women. The article on "How to Dress for Lawn Tennis" decries the "spectator sports" idea in terms of a girl

surrounded by her ribbons and ruffles which she is mortally afraid of disturbing. This is absurd and idiotic. In a game, a girl who is worth anything will endeavor to hold her own and ask no favor. In the field she is on equal terms, and she will endeavor to maintain this position and arrange her dress to be as little of an obstacle as possible.

But in the description of the costume we find little that looks like bodily freedom. "Sleeves should be set high" to "facilitate freedom in the use of the arms." "Low-cut shoes are best." All else has to do with the appearance of the outer dress. From another item of the same year we learn about "summer gauze underwear," and that "there have been great improvements made in the 'whole' suits or combination underwear since their first introduction, and they are now so soft, so graded in texture, and smooth and delightful to the touch, as to be a positive luxury." These as described are not knit garments, but lightweight knit undergarments were then on the market. An article on "Hygienic Dresses" of 1883 mentions a tennis dress with shoulder straps which may or may not have supported weight. Another is draped with a Scotch maud or plaid which can be detached and worn for protection; "as a light and slightly walking dress this is said to have no equal." Another is "adapted to modern use of classic Greek principles," probably by contriving it to exhibit a sixteen-inch waist. The mention of some of the colors and fabrics, however, "terra-cotta plush" for example, suggests the aesthetic movement of those days, that which Gilbert satirized in *Patience*. This movement induced some women for a time to wear loose robes, and in the department of the magazine devoted to humor there is a more or less satirical drawing in which the aesthetic young ladies are somewhat less tightly laced than the fashionable ones. Some lines of these aesthetic dresses lingered in the tea-gowns of the early nineties. With all the noise about athletics, the Lass with the Delicate Air is still walking the earth in a sixteen-inch waist. Perhaps even in fiction she has gone out only to slip in by the back way. George Gissing confers the delicate air on his working-girl heroine, Thyrza, in 1887, when higher up the social scale heroines walk twelve miles and breakfast on beefsteak.

We have a portrait of the strong mind that is nourished on the beefsteaks.

Theodora, while not courting political advancement for her sex, was a strenuous advocate for greatly enlarged courses of study for women and an elevation to an intellectual stage above that which they then occupied . . . [She became proficient in comparative anatomy and had] dissected every kind of an animal from man to insects. She held advanced views relative to the development hypothesis, and had conducted a series of experiments in evolution which had led to the most astonishing results . . . But notwithstanding this decided intellectual bias, Theodora was deficient in none of the mental characteristics of a true woman. The emotional part of her being was well developed. . . . She had always contended that a woman could, when actuated by high and ennobling motives, attend the dissecting-room and study human anatomy without losing any of the freshness of bloom of her womanly nature . . .

Here is an implied background of prejudice; Meredith in the same year, 1885, exhibits more of it in *Diana of the Crossways*. He shows the code of the upper middle class "boasting an aristocracy of morals, and eminently persuasive of public opinion, if not commanding . . . held to represent the austerity of the country . . . at present a relaxed austerity . . . not quite on the level of their pretensions . . . socially absorbing, very powerful to brand a woman's character, whatever her rank might be; having innumerable agencies and avenues for that high purpose, to say nothing of the printing-press." This is the legislative body that still in this time is keeping Goldsmith's law in force. It is the panel from which juries are drawn to render verdicts under the "unwritten law" of a man's right to take life in defense of his property rights in his wife. Throughout Victoria's reign, novels which challenge any item of this code are exceptions. One such appeared as early as 1883, F. Frankfort Moore's *I Forbid the Banns,* the heroine of which, Bertha Lancaster, we glimpsed as the Winged Victory. She refuses on principle to marry her lover.

"I do think that you fail to see that for us to go to the church and to ask the priest to join us in what is indeed a holy bond would be equivalent to an acknowledgement that God had not joined us in that holy bond, the moment we loved one another."

"My God! Bertha, do you mean to say that we should live together as man and wife without going through any ceremony?" cried Charlton.

"Ceremony?" said she after a pause during which her face was suffused with a lovely blush. "Ceremony? O Julian, I am ashamed of you!". . . He really could not bring himself to ask her to think of their children. Even the plainest speaking must have its limit. . . .

"I will not do you this wrong, Bertha," said he . . .

She shook her head and smiled. "I forbid the banns," she whispered.

Here is the challenge, but the lone challenger does not win, does not even hold out to the death against the serried ranks of society. She admits her error and surrenders. A dozen years later we have a heroine whose courage and whose convictions hold out to an end that is very bitter. This is Grant Allen's *Woman Who Did*. Like Bertha Lancaster she refuses marriage on principle, lives with her lover, has her child, and endures all the insults society can put upon her. The bitter end comes when her daughter turns out to be a prude and repudiates her. From this she has no refuge but suicide. It was an uncompromising challenge, heard round the world on the great circle of the British dominions; it echoed bravely, but the walls did not fall. Another as brave but less ringing came in the following year from Topeka, Kansas; today we may read it by title only, a waif in a dealer's catalogue, without learning whether it was a novel or a treatise. It is *My Century Plant,* by Lois Waisbrooker, catalogued under "Sex Revolution," described as "a startling book, claiming that a woman has a right to dispose of her person without the sanction of law or priest."

Sarah Grand (Mrs. Haldane McFall) challenged too. She did not know exactly what she wanted, but she knew what she didn't want. She didn't want any men around. In *Ideala,*

1888, *The Heavenly Twins,* 1893, *The Beth Book,* 1897, she delivers a tirade which increases in vehemence and diffuseness till the reader feels sure the condition is pathological, androphobia; she froths at the mouth whenever a man comes on the scene. *Ideala* is an early sketch of the new woman; we know that she is new because she knows that everything old is wrong. In *The Heavenly Twins* it all comes out. It is expounded in terms of three cases of marriage. Evadne learns the truth (which the author does not dare specify) about her husband just after the wedding, as she is about to leave the house on her wedding trip. She escapes from him at the station. After much negotiation which gives opportunity for much exposition of the author's views, she rather weakly agrees to live in the same house with him to save appearances. He lives up to the agreement, and they get on very well until she gets interested in the public side of the movement for more freedom for women. Again she yields and agrees not to disgrace her husband's name by going on the platform. The result of the suppression of her normal activities is a nervous disorder bordering on insanity with homicidal mania. Her husband dies just in time to save her by making way for her to marry her physician, an elderly, sympathetic, intelligent man. Childbearing goes far to make her normal, but she nearly commits suicide once or twice to save her children from a heritage of unspecified evil. Angelica, the better half of the Heavenly Twins, picks out a kindly gentleman twenty years her senior; "Marry me," said Angelica, stamping her foot at him. "Marry me, *and let me do as I like.*" He obliges her to the very letter of her modest request. Disguised as her twin brother, she carries on an emotional and artistic friendship with a tenor singer of romantic background, a sexless sort of intrigue, which ends when he discovers her sex. He has been worshipping her from a distance in her own person, not knowing she was married, but her behavior seems to destroy his ideal. After this Angelica learns to love her husband, and becomes a normal woman. Edith Beale, romantically in love with a beautiful blond Captain, marries him and his inherited taint of blood, dies raving, and leaves a diseased child. This is the fate from which Evadne was saved by an eleventh-hour warning. The author nourishes a standing quarrel with men, but a rational human being in trousers may win faint approval if he is nearly sexless. She draws four in this book, only one of whom begets children. "The Tenor" after he has pulled Angelica out of the water, takes off her outside garments, a boy's suit of boating flannels, without discovering her sex. *The Beth Book* spreads the tale thin and evaporates in clouds of vague resentment. We learn little from it that we have not learned before, except how heroines learn to swim. Beth undresses on the beach and goes in boy-fashion. All this vaporing is lost motion as directed toward progress.

The pneumatic tire accomplished altogether more than did Sarah Grand to make men and women into people rather than merely aristocrat and plebeian, tyrant and slave. During the Civil War, England had favored the aristocrats. After the war, the real and would-be aristocrats cultivated Anglomania, and the plebeians cultivated Anglophobia. That was the time when Mrs. Astor could invite four hundred people to her ball on the assumption that there were four hundred people in society and not four hundred and one, and her assumption made it so. It raised in the plebeians an irritation which made "the four hundred" famous as a phrase. The retort from the other party took the form of conduct which could not have been better calculated to increase the irritation, the simian eccentricities of Harry Lehr at Newport, and the reports, accepted by the proletariat as gospel, of the dissolute conduct of the Prince of Wales. There were indications that the Social Compromise was not so generally acceptable as it had been. It passed the crisis, however, to live more or less prosperously for several decades. Many causes contributed to its recovery, but none more conspicuously than the pneumatic tire. Up to then the precarious perch of the bicycle was no place for a nervous man, or for any woman but a show girl. By 1890 the safety models had made bicycles popular; by 1895 pneumatic tires had made them universal. The more people were on the road, the less the social distinctions in manners, morals, customs and costumes. When the shopgirl and the debutante, the clerk and the clubman, were on wheels, there was less distinction than when the one was on foot or in the street-car and the other in coupé, dogcart or tally-ho. At the same time appeared the first "horseless carriages," and it was the pneumatic tire rather than the gas-engine that made them ultimately successful. Steam road-carriages were coeval with the first bicycles or velocipedes. For want of balloon tires and shock-absorbers they developed tracks and became railroads. Steam models were successful along with the early internal combustion models, and would be so again were our supply of gasoline to run low. It was the pneumatic tire that made power-driven carriages successful on the road. Society took to them to show that they could afford them; wage-earners took to them whether they could afford them or not.

The bicycle brought its experiments with fashions which looked toward freedom however they may have felt. There were "short" skirts, to the shoe-tops, bloomers (worn usually with skirts, sometimes without), high-laced boots with high heels, low shoes with low heels, and the athletic girdle corsets. Of these there is a mere glimpse much earlier; in 1863 *La Vie Parisienne* illustrated it under the name of *Cienture Regente* or *corset bijou,* something very much like the girdles of the nineties, with the same prophecy, that women would never go back to the old "cuirasse." There is no evidence that at that time they ever left it. But they took definitely to the girdle in the nineteen hundreds, and it, together with the first beginnings of elastic corsets, put the "cuirasse" out of business in a few years. These girdles were mainly "straight front." Women who wore them strictly learned a posture which looks strangely distorted in the nude as we see it in the figure Falguière modelled closely to the life from the dancer Cléo de Mérode. The shirt-waist threw an unbroken curve over it from neck to waist, making a full-bosomed, low-breasted silhouette which called for ruffles or pads under it for flat-chested girls. On the bicycle, the girdle demanded a strict position. If a girl bent to her work in a sandy rut or on an up slope its long front steel stabbed her between the breasts and excoriated her below the navel. But it left the shoulders free, and worn loosely was less enveloping than the corded waists which were originally designed to take the place of armor. In the novel we see in retrospect a girl's graduation from waists to girdles in Ruth Suckow's *Odyssey of a Nice Girl,* 1926, and in Una Hunt's *Young in the Nineties,* 1927, though in the novels of the nineties underclothes were kept out of sight. In these books also we see the reaction toward lighter clothing on the part of women who were forced as girls to wear prickly flannels and starched drawers, heavy waterproofs and winter coats, rubbers and galoshes. Golf came in with Anglomania, a rich man's sport, a by-word and a scoffing with the proletariat, making styles of clothes that looked athletic. But it did not help a girl's swing to hang a five-pound cape around her shoulders. Bicycles and golf, however, reduced the number of petticoats from half a dozen to one and accustomed the eye to shorter skirts, and "The Rainy Daisies" went far to gain sanction for short skirts in wet weather.

Perhaps the nineties do not look gay as we peer critically over our shoulders, but the weight of repression was lifting. Speed on the railroads reached "a mile a minute" and was rising. Speed on the highways reached fifteen miles an hour, sometimes. Colors of dress-goods would seem dull to an observer of forty years later; even summer colors were light rather than brilliant. Of course dyes have improved, but even so, a girl in the nineties did not dare to seem to invite attention. "Red an' yeller, catch a feller!" There were attempts to brighten life by applied ornamentation that seem grotesque. There was the Empire bathtub and the Grecian vase water closet, only one degree better than the Venus with the clock in her belly. But the Grecian vase had a vigorous siphon action, and the Empire bathtub stood on its own claw feet with no black walnut fence round it to harbor cockroaches. They were set with bright unboxed pipes and tiles and enamel. Open plumbing was on its way in life, and heading towards literature. The bathroom was evolving as stage scenery. The chaperon was fading to the extent that in fiction girls may travel alone (anyway, in pairs), seemingly without fear lest the young men should do them some harm. They went to Europe; they went round the world; impossible to guess how they did it, for they were still tied to the Saratoga trunk, the huge carrying-case of mountains of starched ruffles. But the wardrobe trunk was in sight; in this decade it appears in advertising addressed to men. And while "Bachelor Maid" fiction was making a fuss over "nice" girls who claimed the freedom of apartment life, articles of the early eighties on "How We Live in New York" make it clear that business women had been doing it for ten years before its possibilities dawned on Mrs. Burton Harrison.

The gaiety of the nineties, however it looks in retrospect, was "quite unlike the life of our dear Queen." Strachey tells us so:

From the social movements of her times Victoria was . . . remote. Towards the smallest no less than towards the greatest changes she remained inflexible. During her youth and middle age smoking had been forbidden in polite society, and so long as she lived she would not withdraw her anathema against it . . . In 1870, her eyes having fallen upon the report of a meeting in favor of Women's Suffrage, she wrote to Mr. Martin in royal rage—"The Queen is most anxious to enlist everyone who can speak or write to join in checking this mad, wicked folly of 'Woman's Rights,' with all its attendant horrors, on which her poor feeble sex is bent, forgetting every sense of womanly feeling and propriety. Lady —— ought to get a *good whipping.*

The stirring was that of a youth movement, and the Queen's long life was drawing to a close. The life of "Victorianism" was longer than hers; was it too drawing to a close? Did it end with the death of the Queen, or is it something we have always with us? It conquered before she was born; is it still victorious after her death?

CHAPTER XI

VICTORIA, WHERE IS THY VICTORY?

'Ave you 'eard of the Widow at Windsor?
KIPLING.

A thousand claims to reverence closed
In her as Mother, Wife, and Queen.
TENNYSON.

QUEEN VICTORIA died on January 22nd, 1901. What she left behind her, Strachey aptly symbolizes:

There should be no changes and no losses! Nothing should ever move —neither the past nor the present—and she herself least of all! And so the tenacious woman, hoarding her valuables, decreed their immortality with all the resolution of her soul.

She gave orders that nothing should be thrown away—and nothing was. There, in drawer after drawer, in wardrobe after wardrobe, reposed the dresses of seventy years. But not only the dresses—the furs and mantles and subsidiary frills and the muffs and the parasols and the bonnets—all were ranged in chronological order, dated and complete . . . Mementos of the past surrounded her in serried accumulations. . . . The dead in every shape—in miniatures, in porcelain, in enormous life-sized oil paintings—were perpetually about her . . . Every single article in the Queen's possession was photographed from several points of view. These photographs . . . were placed in a series of albums, richly bound . . . The fate of every object which had undergone this process was irrevocably sealed. The whole multitude, once and for all, took up its steadfast station. And Victoria, with a gigantic volume or two of the endless catalogue always beside her, . . . could feel . . . that the transitoriness of this world had been arrested by the amplitude of her might.

It was a futile dream of stability, instinctive, scarcely articulate, a blind reaction against mutability and death. When a dog died she fixed its effigy. "Sharp, in silver gilt, dominated the dinner table; Boy and Boz lay together among unfading flowers in bronze." The dog was stabilized in its gilt image, the image was fixed in a photograph, the photograph bound in an album, the whole series fixed in Victoria's mind.

If this was her victory over mutability, it was more transitory than any of the transitoriness she may have conquered. The dream passed with her passing. The young heirs had been whispering round her deathbed. They wasted little time over the trappings of woe, but began promptly and vigorously to turn out the outmoded wardrobe, the futile gestures of permanence, gold statues of departed friends, silver-gilt dogs and horses which they saw as neither useful nor ornamental, and all the ancestral dust and cobwebs. Faster and faster they worked. By 1920 they were crashing the old taboos out of the windows as fast as they could drag them into daylight. Champions of the old order, dead or alive, had no restraining power. They could only shriek and hold up their hands in horror, or turn in their graves five hundred revolutions to the minute without generating any power for righteousness. The children of chaos unheedingly carried on their destructive work. Their dearest delight was to view themselves with increasing alarm. With every jump toward the everlasting bonfire they giggled, "My! just watch our dust! Where do we go from here? What are we coming to? O Calvin, where is thy sting? O Victoria, where is thy victory?"

To survivors of the old order the change was breathlessly sudden, abruptly indecent, even fundamentally devastating. Did "these young people" know what they were about? The death of the Queen or the turn of the century might well signalize a change of fashion, but why should it bring about a revolution in manners, nay more, in ethics? One there was who saw more than others, a far-sighted historian whose term of life began

AS IT WAS.

THE PRESENT FREE AND EASY STYLE.

IS THIS THE STYLE OF THE FUTURE?

VICTORIA REVOLVES IN HER GRAVE

with Victoria's reign. Henry Adams perceived that the era ended was not a fashion period of about the extent of his life, or even his life plus the eighteenth century, but the breaking of a phase of human thought continuous since the beginning of history. Speaking of "the motion of thought" before 1900, he says, "one could watch its curve for five thousand years," during which it varied once or twice in speed and curved once or twice in direction, "but all these changes had never altered the continuity. Only in 1900 the continuity snapped." We call the date 1900, but we may place it where we will within a decade.

Vaguely conscious of the cataclysm, the world sometimes dated it from 1893, by the Roentgen rays, or from 1898, by the Curies' radium; but in 1904, Arthur Balfour announced on the part of British science that the human race without exception had lived and died in a world of illusion until the last year of the century. The date was convenient, and convenience was truth.

"The human race without exception"—Adam and Eve then were early Victorians, and God, who made them in his image, was their only known predecessor. God created order out of chaos. Science informed Henry Adams between 1893 and 1904 that "order was an accidental relation obnoxious to nature." God is order, and order exists nowhere but in the wishes of man. God created Adam, and science revealed to us several millenniums later that man created God. The cycle runs from Adam to Adams.

To the reader educated in the time when the name of Victoria was a byword and a scoffing, Adams's phrases for the whole trend of human thought seem to describe nothing but Victorianism. He points to the time "when God was a father and nature a mother, and all was for the best in a scientific universe." Even the term "universe" is part of the dream; "the child born in 1900 would . . . be born into a new world which would not be a unity but a multiple," a world which he terms "the new multiverse."

As history unveiled itself in the new order, man's mind had behaved like a young pearl oyster, secreting its universe to suit its conditions until it had built up a shell of *nacre* that embodied all its notions of the perfect. Man knew it was true because he had made it, and he loved it for the same reason."

So also with the woman:

She did not think of her universe as a raft to which the limpets stuck for life in the surge of a supersensual chaos; she conceived herself and her family as the centre and flower of an ordered universe which she knew to be unity because she had made it after the image of her own fecundity; and this creation of hers was surrounded by beauties and perfections which she knew to be real because she herself had imagined them . . . Neither man nor woman ever wanted to quit this Eden of their own invention.

All this is essentially Victorianism, but Victorianism is only a local and temporal phase of the dream, the wishful vision of law and order in the universe and in human life. If we look back down the five thousand years we may see society and religion dreaming and reacting blindly in their sleep, striking stupidly at prodders who would awaken them. Their word was that of the sluggard, "You have waked me too soon, I must slumber again." The history of these centuries would be that of the attempts of society to deal with those who "try not to know what is truth lest they falsify their facts," who will not falsify their facts to accord with society's truths. The Victorian era, beginning with the eighteenth century, is like a half-waking time of the dream, when reason beginning to reassert itself at once sees and accepts the irrationality of the illusion. Tennyson got pretty well aroused by the death of Hallam in 1833, but by 1850 he had through a sheer act of faith turned over and gone to sleep again. Browning succeeded in keeping his eyes shut, and dreamed only that God was in his heaven and all right with the world. Matthew Arnold in a sort of nightmare saw chaos as truth:

the world, which seems
To lie before us like a land of dreams,
So various, so beautiful, so new,
Hath really neither joy, nor love, nor light,
Nor certitude, nor peace, nor help for pain;
And we are here as on a darkling plain
Swept with confused alarms of struggle and flight,
Where ignorant armies clash by night.

But he could not break the current of five thousand years. Neither could Thomas Hardy, who discovered that God, if any, was beneath the contempt of man, and took it very seriously. Robert Louis Stevenson laughed and continued to walk with God. Samuel Butler discovered what Shakespeare knew, that parents and children did not love each other by "nature," and what Fielding knew, that virtue and vice were relative rather than antithetical, and something again that the Greeks had a word for, "Pleasure, after all, is a safer guide than either right or duty." But he remained a mere prophet until a lesser prophet, Bernard Shaw, honored him in his own country. Victorians had proclaimed in all ages that God was infinite, but when science confronted them with his infinity as fact, they lost their God and fell into panic. The disturbance in the discovery was that the perfection of their universe was the very proof that God didn't make it. Science closed the doors on the old vistas of mirage, the old lights went out, and there was panic in the dark. But in the dark the scenes changed; the lights came up on other vistas; panic subsided, dissolved in laughter, diffused itself in other forms of motion, heat or light. Many there were who awakened only enough to turn off the alarm-clock and set it back to medieval concepts of the social order, or forward to other mirages as unrealized or as unrealizable as ever.

Few there were who were conscious of what had happened. *The Education of Henry Adams* was published in 1918. Adams finished writing it in 1907, and up to that time did not learn what the education of a child born in 1900 could be. What could it be but a short view of chaos against a background of infinity? God created the universe, and the universe came to an end with Victoria and the nineteenth century. The new multiverse had as yet no history. For a time people behaved like the barber when the Mississippi steamboat blew up, who "stood with one toe projecting over space, still stirring his lather and saying not a word." Then the invisible and intangible chaos began to pattern the surface behavior of the new generation.

In the first decade of the twentieth century, college students born before the proclamation of chaos could worry over the questions posed in *In Memoriam:* "Shall man . . . who trusted God . . . be blown about the desert dust, Or sealed within the iron hills?" The following generation, confronted with an abrupt "There is no God," from Schopenhauer or Thomas Hardy, coolly retorted, "So what?" From war and other risks of high power, high pressure and high speed, they seemed to have learned that we die tomorrow and are likely to stay dead for some time. They learned to take the gates of civilization as they took those of war. "Gangway!" was the word. Soldiers and nurses had learned farewell to arms. Soldiers who learned all about wine by drinking sparkling Volnay for champagne learned all about women in "the terrible Battle of Paris." At least they learned army prophylaxis, and the soldierly approach to a woman, an abrupt demand after five minutes' acquaintance, "Say, let's get out of here." A "straight-up proposition," take it or leave it. And as often as not she took it, took a chance, or the act was one of simple faith in antiseptic or contraceptive which she carried in her compact or in her purse. The voice of Freud spoke from the mountain top out of a cloud, and what they heard him say was, "You are naught but sex. Be yourself. This is the first and only commandment." As they heard, so they understood and obeyed. Let a woman of thirty writing in a magazine article of a girl of fifteen recall what all who were alive at that time remember well. Her words may reveal glimpses of the "education" of a child born after 1900. The Jean of the discussion is a successfully sketched type of character of the period. She writes a note to her boy friend. "I've had a bath . . . all ready for bed . . . wouldn't you like to see me!"

"Read it!"

I read it.

"M-m," I said doubtfully. "But—do you really think you ought to ask Clive if he'd like to see you when you're all ready for bed, darling?"

The blue eyes widened in honest astonishment.

"But why not, Mary? Don't I look nice?"

"You look adorable, and it's all right," I laughed, abandoning the point. To myself I was thinking, "How much franker and more honest children are today than they were fifteen years ago . . ."

Mary chats with Jean's mother, who reassures her.

". . . These kids are children, romping and playing together. Oh, Jean does have a lot of gay little love affairs on hand all the time, of course, but she's an absolute infant about them. There's a new boy every week, quite normally, and she runs straight to me with it . . . There's never any real love-making. All this talk about necking— well, it just isn't true, that's all."

We are, Mary reflects, well rid of the old taboo on nudity:

Jean . . . had dropped off all her clothes and had walked back and forth across the room showing her very lovely young body with as much unconcern as my five-year-old does; a thing which would have been utterly impossible for me at her age . . . What nonsense, I reflected amusedly. How much more sensible Jean and her friends were. "It is really a wonderful generation," I told myself.

But another letter reveals the devastating truth. Jean writes to Clive:

But darling, it spoils everything to have you worrying to death all the time about something happening. Nothing's going to happen, ole angel. Now tell me, how could it? . . . be just a little careful and then forget all about it. We'll go out in the car Friday nite, won't we? I'll get mine if your dad won't let you use his.

It leaves Mary aghast and groping.

I wonder—you understand, I'm merely groping for a little light—if here in this youth-ridden country of ours (for surely no land ever made such a cult of youth and so worshiped it as America) we haven't all grown a little afraid of our children. . . . "Don't act like a parent, mother," Jean says reproachfully if my friend occasionally ventures a prohibition.

Discipline and restraint are out of the question, and experts offer only generalizations.

Sex experience before marriage is no tragedy, they say; and so noted a philosopher as Bertrand Russell goes further and says it is desirable.

But the matter is too personal.

They might out-argue me; they probably could. But the trouble is that after all this is said, I'm still sick—sick—with the knowledge that it is Jean—*Jean!*—to whom all this is happening. Girls in general —it's all right to have theories about them. But *Jean!* And every girl is special to somebody.

And where does it get Jean? The reward of virtue is just what it was in Pamela's day, "The average boy of today is no less insistent than his father was in demanding an immaculate girl for his wife," so at least Mary believes. Virtue is not winning in manner; virtuous girls are "sulky or shy . . . afflicted with a painful sense of social inferiority" in contrast with the social ease of "gay, sweet, lovely Jean who at fifteen is passing from one pair of arms to another." And there is no cuirass to protect chastity.

A brassière which is only the narrowest flimsiest strip of lace, not even covering the budding, firm young breasts; step-ins quite loose and short; stockings which she has usually rolled about her slim ankles; a dress of thin silk. And that is all . . . I have seen her many a time start out dressed like this in a car with a fifteen- or sixteen-year-old boy . . . In thirty minutes they may be . . . as alone together as any married couple in their bedroom . . . When I was a girl . . . the way we dressed rendered an impulsive embrace impossible.

The old armor, then, was a protection in so far as it made the act deliberate. Shall we go back to it?

"Well, what do you want?" asks someone. "Corsets and three layers of clothes again? Abolition of the movies? The old-fashioned, unathletic girl?" Of course I don't. I suppose what I want is a miracle. I want to keep freer clothes and movies, and girls who are vigorous and independent. But I also want to keep the *jeune fille*. I want to be my child's friend, but I want to be her parent too.

The article is worth extended notice, not because it is outstanding, but because it is typical. Anyone who lived in the time with a memory old enough to register details can fill out the sketch. Aunt Tabitha never got used to the smoking and swearing. We tried not to shock her with what we knew about cocktails, pocket flasks, bathtub gin, kissing, petting and necking. She may have seen the bathing suits on the public beaches grow small by degrees and beautifully less—was it she who complained that they were nothing more than "three postage stamps"?—but we tried to keep her from knowing how frequently they were altogether omitted. We know now if we didn't at the time what went on in high schools, from casual experiments to organized practice of nudity and sexuality. Occasional scandals revealed that it went on in colleges and universities. Science gathered data on sex practices of men and women in all walks of life. Sociologists, physicians, psychiatrists, anthropologists and others have analyzed and interpreted them. They come forth documented with "case histories" in abundance which corroborate the writer of the magazine article and go far to convict the novelists of prudery. We may read in these documents a decision which erases Goldsmith's law from the statute books. By the test of fact it becomes a mere fable of what will get you if you don't watch out. It appears that sixty per cent of women in all ranks of society have sexual experience before or without marriage. We have no statistics of the number who felt constrained to die, but we may safely guess that however many have felt so, few have perished. So we saw

> *The sticks break, the stones crumble,*
> *The eternal altars tilt and tumble,*
> *Sanctions and tales dislimn like mist*

and nothing on which anyone could stand unshaken except his own "pinpoint of the truth" if he was lucky enough to have anything of the sort. There was no conceivable attitude toward it all that was not represented, but none represented widely enough or authoritatively enough to be called the attitude of society.

In this time of confusion the novelists played their parts. The prophets sounded the overture. Joyce's *Ulysses* was the first note of chaos in literature almost before people were aware of its approach in life. James Huneker's *Painted Veils* comes in the first year of the experimental decade. Journalistic novelists, too many to enumerate, behaved like newsreel camera-men when something unexpected breaks suddenly. As soon as they could shift their ground and adjust their focus, shutters clicked and reels whirled to turn out pictures of new types of girls in action as heroines. In *Painted Veils* the curtain rises on the bathroom, and the heroine is discovered at her bath and in a mood of self-inspection to which we are freely admitted. It is noteworthy that Esther Brandès as we see her has practiced no depilation whatever, and that Huneker dares a degree of realism which painters and sculptors had only just begun to show. Perhaps it was the Spaniard, Zuloaga, following the example of his compatriot, Goya, who set the modern example. His *Celestina*, 1913, *Nude Woman and Parrot*, 1913, *Nude Woman with Red Carnation*, 1915, show the pubic hair in no way compromised as shadow. But it is hard to determine priority, so many others were doing the same sort of thing at not far from the same time, Zorn, Greiner, Klinger, Modigliani, Matisse, and many others. Zuloaga's paintings were exhibited in the United States in 1917–18, and if anyone was either shocked or surprised at his breaking of the age-old tradition, we heard nothing of it. Perhaps it is easier to show this realism as beauty to the eye than it is to make it so with words, for novelists and poets are rare who attempt it. Robinson Jeffers does it; she has red hair and the white skin that goes with it:

> *He saw that vision once more.*
> *The form and whiteness, the little gay colored flower of the*
> *pubic hair.*

Startling was the suddenness with which the conventions of yesterday seemed to have dropped into the oblivion of forgotten things. Parents may have remembered, but the child born since 1900 never learned that the chariest maid was prodigal enough if she unmasked her beauty to the moon, had never known the time when every heroine must be as virginal as Virginie, who would rather drown than strip to swim ashore. The new model will undress in a mixed company with about the same amount of urging as it took her predecessors to sit down to the piano, and about the same self-consciousness.

" . . . we want a real nautch dance in the altogether." She glanced about hesitantly. "Don't be old-fashioned," murmured Armand. "I thought you had come clear of your repressions.". . . Isn't she superb?" whispered Owen in Ray's ear; "Where would you have found an American girl ten years ago with such courage?"

The self-consciousness here, on the part of the onlookers no less than of the naked dancer, is the idea that they have got rid of things they call "repressions," something outside the skin which can be shed like, and with, clothes. One of the wisest of our psychologists, Dr. M. Esther Harding, thinks that these things lie deeper, near to the centre of a woman's being, that they are a core of "instinct," deeply buried habit and feeling, accumulated with the evolution of race and sex. Such things we cannot shed with our clothes. In her very illuminating book, *The Way of All Women,* she tells us,

Ordinarily the woman releases herself from the restraints of her modesty through an animus opinion, telling herself: "It is absurd to feel this way. Men do not feel so. Why then should I be hampered by so silly a prejudice?" Through this argument she divides herself into two distinct parts. She becomes over-frank and outspoken, acting on her rationalized opinion, but this apparent frankness is achieved by repressing her real feeling, which means that she reserves the real essense of the matter . . . The woman says, "The prudery of the Victorian age is stuffy and ridiculous. Let us be frank and get rid of all this hyper-modesty." But her very instinct is to be modest . . . a woman's revealing of herself is a matter of feeling rapport, it is not at all a matter of reason or logic. So when through her animus, a woman assumes a pose of frankness in these matters, it necessarily follows that she must repress her deeper feeling, as well as her sexuality and act as though sexuality did not exist.

This analysis may help us to understand the daughters of the new multiverse—but not of Pamela!—who cast off their virginity as an outmoded garment of Victorianism, a self-conscious gesture of rationalization. Some do; about sixty per cent of them, and heroines at that. The novelists show us how they do it. One could fill out a racy chapter on how they fall. We have climbed to dizzy heights, clear up on the mantelpiece, gone through the looking-glass, and see the Victorian code queerly in reverse. The importance of not being a prude is to keep your psyche from being a nest of nasty complexes. If you are a virgin, it must be because you are a prude; you can't be anything worse—unless it is "Victorian." Dorothy is an artist:

"I'm slowly being dunned into it," she remarked with a wry smile; "my friends all exclaim, 'What, you're still a virgin? How terrible! How can you expect to do good work? How can you expect to know

LIFE?' They make me feel as though I were doing something disgraceful. Gosh, Ray, I don't attach any sentimental value to my virginity, but I haven't the faintest idea what desire is! Certainly I've never felt it for any man. Must I go through with it just because the books and magazines have made sex the latest fad? I've never been a slave to styles before; I don't see why I have to begin now. Do you?"

Louise comes in with her eyes dancing:

"Oh, Ping, I've done it! . . . I know what happens after they lock the door and put four little dots. . . ." She laid her hand on his and pressed it excitedly. "I knew I wasn't just talking! I knew I'd have the courage to go through with it! Ping darling, it thrills me to think I had the strength to make the break! I'm proud of myself! . . . I've slept with a man!"

When Charles stops the car in the right place, Anne tells him what she expects of him:

"I've been thinking of losing my virginity."
A torrent of emotions overwhelmed her. She had done it. It was time, she thought grimly. She had kissed men, petted them, let them fondle her body intimately, and always, always, kept on the side of technical chastity. Sometimes she had hated herself for it. Had she proposed to him too boldly, too subtly, too hastily? And why him? A boy she had met at a dance a few weeks before . . . His voice came from a distance calmly. "And you've made up your mind?"
"No."
"Then—I'll do it for you."

In these passages the act is a self-conscious following of the new code. Viña Delmar's Dot Haley is not self-conscious, nor is her code new:

Dot felt his hand on her knee. It was indecent. She could not discourage it without shaking off his kiss, and the kiss was very sweet . . . She did not try to stop him and discovered almost immediately that that was a mistake . . .
"Dot, answer me."
She said what was on her mind. "I'd be a bad girl."

"No, you wouldn't. A bad girl is something different. You'd never let anybody else touch you, would you?". . .

"Do you mean that you're going to let me?"

"I guess so, Eddie." Pause. "Yes, I'm going to let you."

Two weeks later, Dot discovers that a friend of hers has been in sexual relations with a man for a year or more.

"I ain't shocked, only I didn't think you would."

"That's no compliment," said Sue, gravely. "A girl is a damn fool who holds back . . . Gee, Dot, you don't know yourself how you get loving. There's damn little a fellow don't know about you before you say yes. You'll let him get so far it ain't decent anyhow, and then you stop him. And what for? So that you can tell your girl friends how scared you was on your wedding night."

What price mystery? What price innocence? Remember if you can the Victorian heroine sitting in her room while the author tries to tell us that she is in love without knowing it:

Sweet, tender creature! and yet thou art ignorant of all this. Thou art ignorant of the very name of those bewitching feelings that are stealing away thy soul.

Thus do the novelists dramatize the statistics and the studies of the scientists. There is at least one of the sixty per cent who recognizes herself as a unit in a statistical table.

"Sixty thousand illegitimate births a year comes to about a hundred and sixty-four a day, or seven an hour, or one every eight minutes and twenty seconds. Statistics are very consoling. They take away the uniqueness of one's discomforts. Every year—you see, I've had nothing to do for days except to study statistics—out of one hundred and fifty-nine unmarried females of child-bearing age, one gives birth to an illegitimate child. This year it so happened that the lot fell to me."

This tale, *An Unmarried Father,* by Floyd Dell, 1927, is a through-the-looking-glass reverse of the picture of the irresponsible artist leaving the woman with an illegitimate child

to "pay." Here the irresponsible artist is the woman who takes
the love contact lightly, refuses the man's offer of marriage, rebels
against the enforced penalties of maternity, and leaves the man
with the child on his hands to bring up in the face of the conventions of society. Here is suggested a right of women unknown
to Mary Wollstonecraft. Two other rights of women denied by
the ancient wrongs are the right to love without parenthood and
the right to motherhood without marriage. Both these claims
come forward in fiction of the nineties; in the experimental
decade they become insistent. In 1920, Sir Harry Johnston,
looking backward at the suffrage movement in *Mrs. Warren's
Daughter,* sees the claim to motherhood without a husband as
part of it.

If a woman likes to go through all the misery of pregnancy and the
pangs of delivery on her own account and without being legally
tied up with a man, why can't she? Beryl, at any rate, is quite un-
ashamed, and says she shall have as many children as her earnings
support . . . that it will be great fun choosing their sires—more
variety in their types— Is *she* the New Woman, I wonder?

In Webb Waldron's *The Road to the World,* 1922, she may even
claim the right to sexual experience without love:

"I wonder whether you could understand a woman who would
choose to give herself without love?"
"Yes," he said slowly.
"Then will you take me tonight—just for the joy of it?"

The Bachelor Girl comes out in a new edition. Joan is
working her way through college, and much of the time it is all
work and no college. She has a perfect figure—this time the
Greek goddess is the Venus of Cyrene; her measurements match
it exactly. Impecunious sculptors and painters employ her as a
model, but she is not in the big money, magazine covers and
underwear advertisements, because her legs are not dispro-
portionately long. She lives in Greenwich Village in a sort of

club, all men but herself, and she is one of them, in and out of the shower-bath with them, even sharing a bed with one when beds are scarce and no harm done. Her lover is in Philadelphia on a job which he would lose if they marry, but they snatch precious week-ends when they can; they have registered at country hotels and auto-camps as man and wife. She has a friend who has a cottage on Long Island, where Joan and Dick may now and then take refuge. Sometimes the owner and her husband are there, and all four share the cottage and the private beach in primitive nudity. All the boys in the house in the city respect her relationship with Dick, though at least one is desperately in love with her. What novel is this? It isn't a novel; it is a transcript from life: a bachelor girl of 1929. If you prefer it in fiction you may find it in a British setting in Storm Jameson's *The Happy Highways,* 1924, a study of the period of ferment just before the war, in London. Margaret lives with a group of students in London, but the reader does not see beyond the living-room of their quarters; we do not know whether doors of bedrooms and bathroom were open or shut. She is engaged to a man named Keith, and has been in sexual relations with him. All the boys in the quarters fall in love with her, and she with one of them, Joy. He finds it hard to understand why Margaret doesn't break with Keith and take him. She tries to explain.

"Don't think I shan't regret . . . I shall want you. I shall want to die . . . I can bear those things . . . But I couldn't bear the other kind of regret. The sense of betrayal and weakness. A light woman, taking one love and then another. The idea offends me as an ugly picture might. It's nothing to do with the moral rubbish. It's just that I feel able to bear the one misery but not the other. Ah, you don't understand. I don't understand. I only feel . . .

". . . In your thoughts haven't you been just what you say you cannot be? It's the spirit that matters. You're exalting the body above the spirit."

She stumbled over her words. "No—it is not so . . . It does matter that the body is withheld. It matters everything. Body is personality as much as spirit. And I can control my body. A wanton spirit is harder to control, but it needn't mean a wanton body—"

She broke off with a short distressed laugh. "What is the use of talking ethics, Joy? This has nothing to do with ethics. It is a matter of feeling. What I feel another may not—and feeling is the guide . . . I do what I must . . ."

Feeling is the guide, the girl's feeling for her own integrity. Let a girl do what she will, if she respects herself we are called upon to respect her. The author dramatizes this, and appends a note of explanation.

It is, after all, not so easy to slough off the puritan reverence for words that can make our bowels turn to water at the mere flourish of phrases about chastity and license. And yet it must be done, if we are ever to be free men again in a commonwealth of real things. If an enforced chastity is no chastity at all, neither is a spineless indulgence of every stray desire to be swollen by the title of license. License, after all, implies an exercise of the will.

No doubt of the coming change. And since the world cannot be pushed back either to a joyous paganism, or to a joyless purity fostered and shaped by the cat o' nine tails, it must even go on its way.

Where does the way lead? . . .

I think it almost certain that in the immediate future, feeling will be taken more and more for a guide in the conflicts that arise between wish and tradition. The arbitrary inhibitions no longer have a secure hold on minds. On those minds, I mean, that are not partakers in the divine infallibility. Common men like ourselves go looking within to our own half-realized desires for understanding and assurance.

So much emerges from the chaos. Personal integrity and individual feeling take, or are to take, the place of external authority and guidance, and arbitrary inhibitions. There is a glance toward a new world of feeling to take the place of the old "order." Storm Jameson wrote the lines in 1924 as of a dozen years earlier. A dozen years later a psychologist, Dr. Harding again, makes a similar suggestion.

. . . we are passing to-day through a distinct phase of culture like those which affected men so profoundly in the past.

One cause of this phase is the weakness and lack of the specifically feminine values, inevitable while women were exclusively occupied with men; the outcome promises an increased solidarity among women, resulting in an entirely new development of those values which have to do with feeling and relationship. This change in women, according to the historical precedent, should also modify and revivify the relations of men and women to each other.

The eighteenth century called for the man of feeling. The multiverse looks forward to an era of the woman of feeling. The whole novel of sensibility, written by "ladies," was a pale and ineffectual dream of such a world. "Feeling a guide in the conflict between wish and tradition" looks somewhat like Fielding's demand on our sympathy in behalf of Tom Jones a hundred and seventy-five years before *The Happy Highways*. During all that time heroines are held steady by external authority and inhibitions, but we see the image begin to waver in 1905. Lily Bart in Edith Wharton's *House of Mirth* has neither inhibitions enough nor integrity enough to see her through. The result is deterioration of character ending in suicide. Her sins seem mild enough in retrospect. Society condemns her because she smokes a little, takes a drink now and then, and is seen leaving the apartment of a bachelor friend with whom she has had a harmless cup of tea. Twenty years later she might have smoked cigars, lapped gin out of the bathtub, and lived with three or four of her adorers at once without forfeiting her status as a heroine.

By such signs it seemed that Victoria's victory either never was or had suffered sudden reverse. There was no word for it but reversal, no image, as people saw it then, but "through the looking-glass." They saw no orderly process in it of evolution; it was mutation. Since they could not see farther back than five thousand years, they could find nothing in the records of human experience acceptable as precedent. It is hard to find anyone, unless it be Henry Adams, who really saw it coming. Those who in the last decade or two of Victoria had viewed the signs of the times with alarm seemed to their younger contemporaries merely those who always see the progressive decline of formal manners as degeneration. Those who in the time of chaos said, "I told you so," if they were wise, seemed merely wise after the event. With no better wisdom than theirs, we may look back over the first two decades of the century for the signs we might have read if we had known what to look for.

The most obvious of these is the war. A majority of those who saw the experimental decade as hell broken loose thought that the war blew it and everything else wide open. Truly it is enough to account for almost anything, for so much that it seems futile to suggest a reckoning; we can only mention a few major items that bear on the discussion. The results of the great general emotional strain on all who lived through it, whether at the front or as far behind it as may be, were incalculable. Those at the front communicated the tomorrow-we-die feeling to all the rest, and the feeling dictated the behavior, the lifting of all inhibitions. There was no virtue but that of power, no doctrine but that of force. There were the new concepts of speed. Force to the uttermost meant money to the uttermost, and we learned to reckon it in terms of light-years as we have had to do ever since, first as profits, later as indebtedness. There was the relationship between those who fought the war and those who brought it about. In the midst of the catastrophe and for a decade after it the older heads spoke to the younger ones in a spirit of *mea culpa*. "We have made this mess of our lives, of civilization, of the world," they said. "We do not see the way out. If we could get you out of it—ourselves too, but especially you— we would give our lives to do it, but we cannot. We hand the job over to you." For a dozen or fifteen years the younger ears heard only these words from the older lips. "What we have done is all wrong." "I'll say it is," was the ready reply, "stand aside. Leave it to us." The elders never expected youth to take them so literally; indeed, they never realized that youth had done so. When youth turned its back on all that age had taught it, youth knew but age did not that the about-face was conscious, and was the last gesture of obedience to a direct command. "What we have done was all wrong," said age. "Then the opposite must be right," said youth. After that, age might have recognized the retorts that came to its remonstrances: "Don't talk like a parent," "Father, the world into which you have thrown me doesn't care a tinker's damn what you or anyone of your age thinks about anything," or, more colloquially and less articulately, "Oh, yeah?" "Shut up!" "Go to hell!" These were not to be dismissed as explosions of temper or gratings of rasped nerves; they were to be reckoned with as expressions of motivating policy and belief. The patter of the time indicated a formulated policy. Louise announces triumphantly that she has "slept with a man," and Ray calls her a "cheap prostitute." Louise explains her principles:

"I wasn't interested in the physical aspects; it was achieving my liberty, my freedom, that was so magnificent! I've cut away from the past with a clean knife. Now I'm able to fit in with the new and modern life! You can't know what that means for a woman . . . all the nicest girls are doing it these days. The double standard is gone; women are taking their love where they find it, just as men always have. Don't you see, that's what makes us their equals; that's what our emancipation means. We've been victims of ignorance and oppression too long; now we're going to be free, independent. We're going to help recreate the world! . . . Our grandmothers held hands before marriage, our mothers kissed, and we sleep with our men. That's the evolution of freedom. . . . [It is noble] in the same way our pioneer grandmothers were noble . . . they were pioneering for the freedom of a new continent. We are pioneering for the freedom of a new moral code."

Such was the process, and perhaps about the extent, to which the war reversed the picture. It took one generation through

the looking-glass, and left the other standing in its tracks looking at an alien and strangely reversed world.

The war which seemed to so many to have caused the change
was more probably only a conspicuous explosion in the chaos.
Continuity snapped like a gas-main in an earthquake; fire and
explosion were inevitable. Other manifestations were less spectacular. Drifts toward change we have seen in other chapters,
moving, some slower, some vaguely, some directly, toward
the brink. Not all Victoria's influence in her latter days could
stop men from smoking, nor women, nor exercise the slightest
restraint on the suffrage movement. Her obsequies were royal
in funereal solemnity. As soon as they were over, Bernard
Shaw set off a giant cracker, *Man and Superman,* which blew
the dearest fiction of the Victorian code higher than a tin can,
and everybody cheered and laughed. Mr. Kipling gave us
popular idioms for the new-fashioned doctrine, and we talked
of the deadliness of the female of the human species in comparison with the male, and of *vamps* and *vamping.* He had already
spread in widest commonalty the irreverence of Tommy Atkins,
given a good bit of swagger to the mucker pose, and raised
vulgarity a level or two above its source. In this he was ably
seconded by Albert Chevalier and his coster songs. Slumming
parties made interesting discoveries in cheap dance halls of the
behavior of working-class couples who had nowhere else to
conduct the preliminaries, or finals, of courtship, and brought
new manners into ballroom and drawing-room at first as matters of supercilious hilarity—"Look, they do it like this!" So
we began to hear of the "bunny hug" and, what is more,

> *Everybody's doing it!*
> *Doing what?*
> *Turkey trot!*

With the casting off of mourning garments for the Queen
(the coronation of Edward VII was in August, 1902) chaos began to come to the surface in the form of a queer confusion in

fashions for women. Fashion makers whose wills had long prevailed found their voices were without authority. There was a time of hesitation, of experimentation, until there emerged a new authority, not queen nor empress, nor yet vaguely "Paris," but the new woman herself. It is safe to say that this is the first time in the economic history of fashion when woman took matters out of the hands of the dealers, and tried to decide for herself. Up to then dealers in fashion goods had naught to do but to decide what they wanted to sell and tell women that it was the fashion, to feed the goose what they pleased and to collect the golden eggs. When she broke loose, the goose with characteristic indirection kept her eye on freedom and walked away from it, as if the longest way round was the shortest way home, as no doubt it was. She confined her diaphragm, her waist, her abdomen, her hips, and boasted of the freedom of her shoulders, breast and legs; the umbrella drawers of 1902 were to much the same effect as scanties and slip of 1935. She pinned on huge picture hats that lifted her scalp with every breath of wind, or weighted and extinguished herself with pounds of peachbasket hat, and brought about the revolt of the bare-headed movement. She tied her legs together with a hobble skirt, and experimented with reactionary trousers, divided skirts and slit skirts. The language of fashion was that of Babel. There were shirt-waist silhouettes that were all breast to the waist, Directoire silhouettes that were all waist to the breast, princess silhouettes sheathed from breast to thigh, and flaring below, peg-top silhouettes, straight-line silhouettes, mannishly tailored silhouettes, pouter-pigeon silhouettes, and who could say that one was more the vogue than another. There were sheath-like corsets, long and "topless" as the towers of Ilium. There were corsets brief as the soul of wit behind with points high and low in front, and there were corded waists with a dozen buttons down the front and half as many on each side as points of attachment. There were circular drawers like a short divided skirt; there were knit drawers that flared, one garment for two; there were knickerbocker drawers, gathered at the knee, offered at once to valetudinarians to keep the thighs warm and to hardy athletes as making for low visibility in high action. As this garment comes into favor for daily dress it goes out of favor for the bathing dress. The "swimming suit" makes its début in a pattern offered by a women's magazine in 1907. Bathing suits were then in two pieces, either a combination waist and bloomers with a skirt to button on, or a combination waist and skirt with bloomers to wear underneath. The swimming suit is a combination waist and drawers open at the knee in one piece without skirt. It was made to swim in, not to hold water in bags gathered at the knees. Probably, too, it was worn without stockings. If so, it began a campaign against stockings on the bathing beaches which was settled after about twenty years with a victory for bare legs and a whole new field of business for the safety razor trade. The swimming suit was made of flannel, the waist cut rather full and pleated lest when wet it should model the breasts too specifically. When the movies began to show bathing beauties, and Sunday supplements featured Channel swimmers and beach posers, knit bathing suits became general. At first they avoided too intimate revelations, were rather baggy over the chest and long in the skirt, but the legs were tights that held no water to speak of. By degrees the skirt became vestigial and disappeared, and the wearer learned that if her nipples were nearly as obvious as the nose on her face they were quite as harmless.

At close range all this showed nothing but confusion, but seen in perspective it shows evolution toward freedom. The experimental silhouettes were those of youth. Skirts that cleared the ground had definitely emerged from the welter of fashion by 1910. It was a real freedom they brought, too, for a woman walking on the street had for the first time in a generation or more two hands to use for whatever she needed them for instead of merely the one she wasn't using to hold up her skirts. For those who were "young in the nineties," holding up the skirts was an immemorial gesture of womanhood, and high-school girls looked forward to it, longing to be as old as their mothers. In their middle years the youth movement took these girls back to skirts of high-school length first, later to that of the primary school. Almost the first reversal of the through-the-looking-glass change was the shift from age to youth in the silhouette. Under Victoria, girls dressed like their mothers. Under Edward, mothers dressed like their daughters. Under George, grandmothers dressed like twelve-year-olds. It is true that some of the indications of the time might seem to point to heavy figures. There were times of "willowy" figures which made sales for ruffles, "bosom forms," hip-pads, even for bustles, but for one who needed additions to attain the figure of fashion there would be ten who needed subtractions. For nearly all the silhouettes that jostle one another in the fashions of this time, Directoire, princess, and all the others, called for the rococo figure of youth, delicacy and vigor, the deep chest, round high breasts, taper waist, round but youthful hip and thigh, and long legs. A woman who had not such a figure might struggle with the fashions as best she could; a girl who had it might wear what she pleased. By 1921 she might even wear no corset, for the silhouette, whether princess or peg-top, tended to un-corseted effects, which seems to mean anything intended to look as if the breasts were free. The corset, in spite of multiple lac-ings and auxiliary devices to bring unruly figures within the lines of fashion, was evolving toward the vanishing point. Manufacturers of boned corsets did not see the trend; they wondered vaguely how soon fashion would turn in their favor, or whether they had better turn to elastic goods. Not till 1919–20 did they feel so alarmed as to resort to imperatives in their advertising: "Uncorseted? Emphatically, no! Never did the frocks of fashion demand such careful corseting!" This at a time when so many women were learning that for them frocks formal or informal demanded no corsets. Here was another new freedom, though they did not know what it meant. Still another was that of neck and arms, for as dresses shortened in the skirt, they shortened at neck and sleeves. A generation has grown up that knows not the choker collar, the stock, or other constrictive swathing of the neck, and the history of depilatories and deodorants is the history of freedom of arms and shoulders. If there were any in this time of wavering fashions who saw the lines of evolution, they did not make their voices heard, and the silhouette of adolescence when it came in 1925 was almost universally considered a mutation, a freak. Before the war we did not know where we were going, but we were on our way to what the later critic calls "this youth-ridden country of ours," the cult of youth which we worshipped. Look first upon the picture of Victoria as she was in her later years, then upon that of the twelve-year-old silhouette of 1925, and see the same reversal of Victorianism in terms of women's clothes that ran parallel to it in morals and manners.

Perhaps science had more to do with all this than merely to sound its unheeded signal of the dissolution of continuity. Applied science may also have had an indirect influence. By the time short skirts arrived, they looked more like a declaration of bodily freedom than a move toward sanitation. In the times when women swept the streets with long skirts, they did not know so much about germs as they did when they began to hold up their dresses, but that is not the whole story. The long train was an affectation of superiority, a costume that suggested no existence outside the drawing-room and the carriage. Holding up the dress for walking was a gesture of democracy, of athletic vigor, of independence. And as skirts grew shorter streets grew cleaner. Tobacco chewing and spitting yielded to smoking, but it was not till the cigarette put all other forms of tobacco into minorities that sidewalks were noticeably freer from filth. With bicycles and rubber tires, city pavements improved to the almost complete elimination of mud, real mud, that would pull off your rubbers. Storm sewers carried off "mud-puddles" and lessened the danger of splashing. Alleys that were once lined and paved with garbage, dead cats and manure were cleaned up in the nineties, and horse manure was sedulously gathered from the streets. Next the horse began to fade out of the picture, and the pavements were sterilized a thousand times a day with carbon monoxide. We were relieved of the risks incurred from flies and English sparrows (until the sparrows learned to pick fresh-roasted insects from the radiators of parked cars) and took on a fresh lot from automobile fatalities. By then women had ceased to take any risks from sweeping the streets with their skirts; if they did so, they would collect less of dust than of oil stains. The universality of the automobile taught us just what the hat means to us, both men and women; to what extent it is a useful article of apparel and to what extent it is merely a concession to formal manners. The automobile enables women in increasing numbers to dress for no more of out-of-doors than from door to curb and from curb to door. This led to various oddities and incongruities. With body clothed as lightly as that of a marathon runner, a woman would wear shoes that would cripple any man so that he could not walk a block, a step. Again, when the woman who walks must dress like the woman who rides, she must have Russian boots to protect silk stockings from the weather. That did not last long; to buy Russian boots to walk in classes one permanently as a pedestrian; one cannot pose in them as someone temporarily deprived of the use of the car. In general, it would seem that the influence of the automobile on costume was to lighten it more definitely than ever did the carriage.

It was not, then, the war that shortened skirts; they were short, according to the standards of the day, before that. The war taught women to discard them altogether. Women in uniform wore skirts short enough to clear most of the mud they were likely to encounter as far behind the lines as they were supposed to be. At home, women workers who took the places of the men who were at the front promptly took to overalls. After it was over, or sooner, women found that surplus uniform breeches with the conspicuous flare from belt to knee were cut to the feminine rather than to the masculine figure. The war brought other new freedoms and extensions. It demonstrated that business and industry could use more women than any but agitators had been willing to believe, and placed them with more or less permanence in many occupations new to them. It helped them to win the suffrage in England, and, if it was their movement, prohibition in the United States. Its general lifting of inhibitions gave impetus to new forms of intimate dancing. The tango became conspicuous about 1914, and the next ten years saw all the armor of chastity discarded for the intimacies of the dance floor. It is impossible to determine how much all this added to the sum total of gaiety, to the restoration of laughter. Laughter of a sort became fashionable, but more often than not it seems as synthetic as the gin that produced it. The novel reflects a cult of not taking anything seriously, but it denies itself by taking itself with imperative seriousness; its anti-sentimentalism shows merely as a fashion or color of sentimentalism, an affectation of being hard-boiled at a time when profound emotions were near the surface and must be concealed at any cost. It is this which led, perhaps, to a new type of sophisticated sentimentality that revived the old melodrama to present it as farce, and evolved the new variety, the "comedy-melodrama," which is just as sentimental as the old, but professes to laugh at itself as it goes along.

Some of the changes which ushered in the new era were conspicuous. Light, power and communication ran in swift currents everywhere till no homestead, however far from city or neighbor, was ever again isolated or remote. Movies came out of the nickelodeons into the real theatres and began to charge real prices. Horseless carriages turned into automobiles, became trustworthy (or at least reasonably steady performers) and fool-proof (that is, anybody could drive them). At the first hints of electric communication without wires people shook their heads; there must be a limit somewhere. Other changes, perhaps even more significant, attracted less general attention. Nietzsche had been dead a dozen years before a few students in the United States began to hear his voice; later there were more who read to learn what had driven the Germans mad. Krafft-Ebing's *Psychopathia Sexualis* came out in English, except for crucial passages which were in Latin for the benefit of "the learned professions," to whom it was addressed. But others got hold of it, and dusted their Latin lexicons to dig out terms and facts that later were matters of common conversation in mixed companies. The facts were there, and the expositor was a psychiatrist, but when Freud and Havelock Ellis came along they made him look old-fashioned in his use of Latin for a fig leaf, and the clear image of the moralist always looking over the shoulder of the scientist. Brill presented Freud, and Havelock Ellis presented himself, and we changed all that. No more the fig-leaf Latin; everything came out in terms as plain as language could supply. The courts floundered in trying to distinguish obscenity from science, and bootleggers of forbidden books profited by the free advertising which the perplexities of the courts gave them. Still there were plenty of women who did not know what it was all about, girls who experienced suicidal fear lest a man's kiss had made them pregnant, a state of ignorance (or innocence) as abysmal as that of the most primitive savage. For them if they chose to accept it came enlightenment in the form of books bringing the fullest possible exposition of the technique of sexual practice. These the public encouraged with one hand and suppressed with the other, as in universities and colleges where they were under lock and key in the library and openly on the counter in the students' co-operative store.

The anonymous critic of the magazine article quoted above speaks of the youth movement as distinctively American, "surely no land has ever made such a cult of youth and so worshipped it." If fashions in clothes are the index figure of the movement, it would seem to have been a gift, for better or for worse, from the United States to the world. One historian of fashion, Dr. Nystrom, shows convincing evidence to that effect. In his invaluable *Economics of Fashion,* he has a chapter on "Fashions Originating in America" in which he shows the importance of American changes in the comfortable but ugly British sports clothes.

Whereas the English produced sports clothes that were practical and comfortable, for the most part the English gave little attention to making these clothes artistic. In America there has been a constant development for more than twenty years to make them more beautiful. There has also been a trend to make sports clothes suitable for use in "spectator sports" and for all sorts of daytime functions and occasions. So there has come into existence in America such styles of sports clothing as jumpers, dresses, ensembles, sports dresses, sports hats, and so on, not only comfortable and practical in the extreme, but of artistic appearance as well. American sports clothes style has set the fashion for the world. Paris creators have been slow in following this lead, and even as late as 1920 there were several well-known style houses which had not yet recognized sports apparel for women.

The list of "items of style wear which either are now or have been powerful in fashion and which originated in America" is too long to quote entire and too significant to neglect. It includes the jumper, the middy blouse, women's athletic underwear, women's gymnasium and athletic clothing, knit underwear, union suits, silk and muslin underwear cut to simplest lines, fine knit underwear in colors, the corsetless figure, boyish silhouettes, "Boyshform" brassières ("a typical American creation"), the combination girdle and hose supporters, various types of sweaters and other knit goods, the tendency toward shorter skirts, simplified bathing suits, the beach complexion fads, rubber heels for shoes, rubber-soled shoes, galoshes worn with flapping sides, health shoes, Helen Wills eye-shades, pajamas for women, hosiery in light and nude shades, bobbed hair. Dr. Nystrom presents the list as "tentative and incomplete," and says that many of these items reached Paris and issued forth from there with French labels. The list is almost in itself an index of the youth movement, springing mainly from the United States, and carrying the eye back to its earliest recognizable symptoms two or three decades before its culmination.

Nowhere so well as in the United States could the movement in its germinal stages have been so well heated and watered. Distinctively American are the two institutions which England and the Continent are slow in adopting, the American bathroom and the American house temperature. Of course English people were notorious for their daily baths at a time when in the United States the ceremony was in its primitive stages of the wooden tub in the kitchen on Saturday night. The Englishman was a hero, too, who took his daily tub in a large cold room with nothing more heartening than an open fire which sent all but one half of one per cent of its heat up the chimney. But he did not have to heat the water himself, or carry it or the tub, or fill the tub and empty it; he was the feudal lord of many servants. The American bathroom evolved in a democracy with no servant class; it came about just because there was no servant class. What an American would call an ordinary bathroom is a triumphant, almost miraculous achievement to so recent a novelist as Arnold Bennett. It is comparatively new on its native heath; its history hardly extends over two generations, and we have not totally lost the old tradition. Water and gas companies tell us that even with gas to heat the water the peak load for bathing comes on Saturday night. It is not surprising that bathrooms should multiply more slowly on the Continent than in the American backwoods (if any such there be). Any farmer who can get water to run through a pipe can buy the equipment of a modern bathroom from his mail-order catalogue and install it easily in a board shanty, but ancient stone palaces are resistant to plumber's tools. It is harder yet to pierce Romanesque foundations twelve to twenty feet thick for heater flues.

In the United States, the generation that was "young in the nineties" grew up with adequately equipped and heated bathrooms. The habit of using them was doubtless fostered by athletics. Many a boy and many a girl brought up on the Saturday night tradition acquired the daily bath habit in a college gymnasium and brought it home along with the athletic habit. Many a girl at home from college on vacation would begin the day with a bath for an eye-opener, take another after tennis, another after swimming to get the salt off her skin, and one before going to bed to insure sleep. For such a program anything more than brassie and shorts under the dress is too much, and for a house adequately heated according to American standards, the scanty costume is enough.

There were times before adequate heating when women wore scanty clothing; Mrs. Trollope drew a vivid picture, and her illustrator drew another, in 1832, but even on her own showing they wore more clothes, except perhaps for the feet, than any girl wore in any weather in 1932. The brassie-shorts-dress costume was not possible when houses were heated with open fires and stoves. It was not possible when horsecars had no protection from cold but a mess of slushy straw in the aisle, or when flimsy wooden railroad cars were never warm enough from the coal stove boxed in one corner until they smashed up and caught fire from the scattered coals. Even coal furnaces and steam-heat will hardly do. One is tempted to say that such dressing was made possible by new processes of welding which could be taken into the field to make continuous steel pipes

for oil and natural gas. Acetylene welding surely made its contribution to the feeling of freedom, youth and well-being that
goes with light clothing. Can anyone feel "bundled up" without
feeling either old or sick?

In the years between the death of Victoria and the outbreak
of the war, then, the critical historian may see in retrospect
what people seemed unconscious of at the time, currents drawing society toward the vortex of the youth movement which came
in the decade between 1920 and 1930. In the earlier time we can
see when we look back to hunt for them, many back eddies
that were essentially reversals of Victorian ideals, reversals which
as the forces grew more tumultuous seemed to swing the whole
ship round and send her stern foremost. Then she swung
sharply again, ostensibly toward her old course. Surface currents send straws scurrying in all directions at once; the straws
tell us which way the wind is blowing then and there, but we
must lift our eyes to the clouds to gauge the drifts that make the
weather. In the time of confusion there were straws that blew
back quite as briskly as any that blew forward or to right or
left. Was orthodox faith scoring a great victory or merely prop-
ping its sagging walls when it put the science teacher on trial,
and celebrated a triumph by making the scene of the action into
a "university" to teach the doctrine of the infallibility of the
Bible? Was Victorianism victorious on the eve of its reversal
when it wrote into the Constitution of the United States an
amendment which would have made the worker of the Miracle
of Cana a candidate for the Federal penitentiary? In spite of
all the need for knowledge which the new freedom brought
them, most girls in the United States were left to learn about
sex by any chance. The majority of mothers taught them nothing essential, and most school and even college courses that
ostensibly included such knowledge were better calculated to
preserve ignorance than to arm against danger. Perhaps this is
all of a piece with the fundamentalist war against science.

There were critics in the decade of turmoil who told society that with all its reversals, with all of its boasted speed, it did not advance beyond Victorianism because it still tried to escape conditions it did not like by shutting its eyes to them, by trying to believe they were out of existence when they were out of mind, instead of learning as many of them as possible in order to harmonize our actions with such of them as we cannot alter.

Was it the puritanism of the former age that the youth movement took arms against, by opposing to end it? Victorianism was in some respects less puritanic than were its opponents. Ben Jonson named his type puritan Zeal-of-the-Land-Busy; his characteristics are intolerance, the zeal of the propagandist, and all the bad manners that go with these. His conscience directs him not only to teach his neighbor to be good, but to begin each lesson with a slap in the face; less than that is dereliction of duty. This is the spirit in which post-war youth loved to insult its Victorian grandparents. "Anyone who likes Tennyson is a cad," wrote an undergraduate of that period in an examination paper. Tennyson's offense was that he was a puritan because he did not call a spade a steam-shovel before the steam-shovel was invented. So was Thackeray because he did not show us every motion of Becky Sharp's experience with Lord Steyne. So was George Eliot because though she was emancipated in her own mind she went to church in order not to offend her father. So was Browning because he calls the motive power of humankind "love" rather than "sex." So was Robert Louis Stevenson because he put his radical firecracker under one chair and another of sleeping orthodoxy, winked at us, and walked away without lighting the fuse. "Victorian cads! prudes! puritans!" shrieked the twentieth-century no-compromiser, and slapped their faces. Was it the cool aristocracy of their manners that enraged their critics? That was what irked the puritans of Cromwell's time. They had their bitter experiences in the seventeenth century, accepted Steele's compromise in the eighteenth century, came out with a serviceable suit of good manners in the nineteenth century, and were cursed for them in the twentieth century.

Even in the Jubilee Year of King George V, which brings these studies to their close, Tennyson has not ceased to be a cad. Tolerance, that is, is no virtue; contrariwise, it is the first of the deadly sins. "Haven't I always been tolerant?" wails the heroine of a screen drama of that year (1935)? "Damn your tolerance!" says the hero, who for reasons of his own (not those of the plot) will "class angle" everything. "Tolerance will never get us anywhere!" And so we see what is the matter with Tennyson; he will always be a cad, or whatever they choose to call him, to young reformers who do not wish to see freedom "slowly broaden down," but are trying to make it suddenly blow up. Intolerance is just as characteristically a puritan quality as bad manners and the necessity for taking serious things seriously.

During the experimental decade some who stood on the sidelines saw their world with its back turned toward Victorianism, and tried to make out which way its face was turned, whether toward the style of the worker or that of the idle rich. The code of any class that aspires to a higher class apes the code of the class to which its practitioners aspire. Was (or is) the "mucker pose," the "pride to know no spur of pride," like that which followed the French Revolution, fashion aping the working class, which was then the ruling class? Or was the new freedom in sex morality and speech a turn toward the courtly-chivalric code as it stood before the Reformation darkened chivalry with the Hebraic shadow? If so we might read much of the hullaballoo of casting the old taboos overboard as the effort to shake off habits formed by five hundred years of Bible reading ending with the death of Victoria, which either by effect or by coincidence marks the time when we decided that the Bible was a bore. When fundamentalism and orthodoxy were strong enough to write our noble experiment into the Constitution, the critics on the sidelines wondered how long they would retain their hold if they could not hold the rising generation to Bible-reading. It was a time when in theory everybody was rich, and the Bible harps on the virtues of poverty. It was the time when the promised land was imaged in terms of two cars in every garage and two chickens in every pot, time to forget about the camel and the needle's eye—that kingdom was for the poor and the poor in spirit. We had the early example of the Church itself, which had to soft-pedal the virtue of poverty and keep the Bible in unreadable languages when it began to get rich. Let the bankers preach thrift as they would, people knew that they did it as the Church did of old, because they needed the money; people showed no indication in that time of after-the-war prosperity of being willing to standardize their scale at Poor Richard's level. When knighthood was in flower, two of the things that made aristocratic manners what they were were wealth and education. When "prosperity" was in flower, all wore silk stockings and rode in closed cars and went to the universities. Wealth and education were theoretically speaking widespread to the verge of universality; whatever the facts, newspapers and politicians did their best to make the American people believe it of themselves. Accordingly they prided themselves on turning their backs on as many of the middle-class virtues as their middle-class background would allow them to reject. But a five-hundred-year-old habit is not easy to cast off. Perhaps the "mucker pose" represents its inhibitions. Perhaps it is more fun to believe we are gentlemen posing as muckers than to know that we are muckers pretending to be gentlemen.

James Truslow Adams's apt term, "the mucker pose," means, of course, that we are not muckers; at least not those of us who are posing. Neither, so long as we are posing, are we ladies and gentlemen. Years ago there was a so-called distinction between the Yale man and the Harvard man which might point the moral. Just graduated and looking for a job, the Yale man, so it was said, "came into the office as if he owned it, and the Harvard man as if he didn't care who owned it." It bears the hall mark of the old series, but the metal is sound. If the Harvard man really didn't care, he was a gentleman. If he only looked as if he didn't care, he was a first-class imitation. The true aristocrat really "doesn't care a tinker's damn." Neither broadcasted wealth nor broadcasted education have ever given Americans enough of this feeling to go round. Americans who truly have it come by it otherwise. For the most part, too, whatever appearance we cultivate, we seek it and preserve it with a nervous meticulousness that is anything but careless, that is essentially middle-class. American women travelling abroad are said to be distinguished by the brilliant perfection of their appearance and manner which they present to the inspection of the older societies of Europe. This is as far toward aristocratic manners as our new freedom has taken us, to be careful of the perfection of our carelessness.

In 1929 the stock market broke, and the youth movement tried to go into reverse without slackening speed, which resulted in queer noises. "Victorian," which in 1928 was a term of such black opprobrium that you had to smile when you said it, in 1930 became the catchword of the latest fashion. Skirts that would have shocked Aunt Tabitha were called "long," though Aunt Tabitha wouldn't have known them the way they hung with nothing under them. Black walnut pieces became antiques; they were rummaged out of places of banishment, servants' bedrooms and secondhand shops (which became "Antique Shoppes"), and a piece or two along with a dish of wax fruit and some crystal lustres made a drawing room "Victorian," though again Aunt Tabitha would not feel at home in it. The doctrine of thrift went into reverse. In 1928 bankers preached thrift while people spent profligately on credit profits that existed on paper. A few years later people went round the cash and carry stores counting their pennies while the bankers barked themselves hoarse trying to teach us that the only possible salvation was to spend money faster than you could earn it. Thrift was no longer a Christian virtue nor a theological virtue; it was nothing but a crime. The "rights of women" went into reverse. Women began to go clinging vine. Having obtained nearly all the rights they had clamored for since the days of Mary Wollstonecraft, they began to look back with nostalgia toward the age of privilege. They pulled down the spacious house of Victorianism, and before they cleared away for a new building they seemed to begin a disconsolate hunt for love among the ruins. As for those who still turned their hearts toward

> *folly, noise and sin!*
> *Shut them in,*
> *With their triumphs and their glories and the rest!*
> *Love is best.*

To weaklings who looked back, the frying-pan from which they had leaped looked cosier than the fire in which they found themselves. "What price sturdy self-respect?" At first they asked the question in jest and did not stay for an answer. Toni, in G. B. Stern's *A Deputy Was King,* 1926, is the head of a prosperous business which she has built herself.

"Val," she suddenly burst out, "it's the biggest fallacy going, this splendor of independence and work we hear so much about. Haven't you been told over and over again how lucky you are to be born into an age where girls are given a chance to earn money and be on their own? Well—we've had time to try it! What's the verdict? What do you think about it?"

"Oh! I'd like to be kept," said Val, frankly. "I'm with you all the time. Kept in idleness . . . What does that remind me of?—A little western flower . . . 'Before, milk-white, now purple with love's wound, and maidens call it—kept-in-idleness.' And in a really opulent and vulgar way, for choice. A large, luscious villa on the Riviera;

cars; furs; money no object; presents every day. One never gets
enough presents . . ."

"One never gets any at all," Toni amplified the complaint.

They recall the valuable presents which grandfathers and uncles
gave to "the Charming Ladies" of the former age.

"And they *accepted* these valuable gifts?" Val was shocked. "Well,
well, well—how much more fortunate are we, with our sturdy self-
respect rather than gaudy trinkets!—Yes, I think decidedly one ought
to be kept, and do as little as possible for it. Long live the parasite!
You just coo a bit, and then somebody or other gives you a cheque,
and you've done nothing to earn it."

"Earning!" Toni groaned; "sweat of one's brow. Sturdy self-
respect, indeed! What'll you sell your sturdy self-respect for, Val?
One thousand pounds a year? Five thousand pounds?"

"No! Damn it! Let's do it well while we are about it. Twenty
thousand pounds a year!—And all in payment for nothing but simply
so beautifully being!"

If anyone had heard this startling conversation, from two representatives of an enlightened and progressive age, the artist, famous enough
in her own line, and the cool, responsible, successful business woman,
he might have found it hard to realize that both knew they were
talking nonsense . . . as much an outlet as, twenty or thirty years
ago, rebellious discussion had been an outlet, declarations of "the
right to lead one's own life."

They seem to have had it on their minds just then. The
anthropologist was telling them that the woman who managed
husband, baby and camp was merely fulfilling a normal life,
and that she was not to be pitied; pity rather the woman who
has nothing more worth while than the movies, a Pekingese and
a box of chocolates. Toni, in *A Deputy Was King,* juggled
with business, husband and children, one up and another down,
but pretty successfully on the whole. In the same year, 1926,
Storm Jameson dramatized them as *Three Kingdoms.* The
heroine of this novel has a masculine name, Laurence Ford,
and a boyish silhouette, but she is woman enough to have a

husband (kingdom number 1) and a son (kingdom number 2), and, when her husband is at the front during the war, she builds up an important business (kingdom number 3). These three she manages with Napoleonic strategy; she nearly loses this one, that one, the other, but carries her performance through, as the blurb assures us, "trials, successes, failures, and glorious rebirth." It is the idealized behavior-pattern of the boyish silhouette of 1926. It is the reversal of the marry-in-the-last-chapter-and-live-happy-ever-after type of novel. It is the reversal of the behavior of the heroine who falls in love in the first chapter and marries in the last. It is the reversal of the Cinderella plot, which, as appears in Chapter IX, never found out that it had been reversed, but kept on repeating itself placidly in the novel and on the screen through the decade (as it had through the centuries) of folly, noise and sin. Cinderella spoke for the weaker sisters, the "kept-in-idleness" school: "Folly, noise and sin don't get you anywhere." Folly? well, perhaps not where Goldsmith said; no farther perhaps than the mourners' bench, the rows of weeping girls in the waiting-rooms of the women doctors, girls who had found out by experiment that being a little bit careful and then forgetting all about it wasn't always enough. One might almost trace the cycle from the age of elegance through the age of innocence and the age of insouciance by way of the familiar quotations. The age of elegance threatened the death penalty. In the age of innocence Kingsley was not so severe: "Be good, sweet maid, and let who will be clever." The age of insouciance said, "If you can't be good, be careful." The next stage, 1930, was a reaction, but not so far back as the age of innocence; it said, "Be good, sweet maid, and let who will be careful." It was in 1930 that Havelock Ellis spoke again to tell "Why We Have Taboos." If no one heard him it was because all who needed to know had found out by experiment.

With the end of the experimental decade the experimenters changed their styles. Do we need a psychiatrist to correlate the new silhouette with the new psychology? Dr. Harding does it for the present with a wary eye to the future.

The early professional women affected . . . a somewhat masculinized dress and manner, as well as certain masculine characteristics, which were not assumed but which really expressed a psychological fact, namely, that in these women there was developing an attitude of mind which had formerly been considered to belong typically and exclusively to men . . . The recent lengthening of hair and softening of styles of dress may perhaps presage a return to a more feminine form of psychology. As I write, this phase of development may be passing and another already preparing to take its place.

The novel was prompt to exhibit this model, *The Premeditated Virgin*, by Nalbro Bartley, 1931. Mary Ann Plowden is

A flapper out to debunk tradition without suffering personal casualties. She is of the post-war generation whose parents, slightly mad from too much freedom—or not enough—have discarded any sane sense of values. No nearer their as yet unnamed goal, they furnish their daughter a monumental example of what to avoid. She of the "new silhouette" wants to charm the world even as her mother shocked and her grandmother unintelligently accepted it. To her, virginity is a matter of efficiency rather than morality. The era of short skirts and long drinks being over, the premeditated virgin of the thoughtful thirties is prepared to be a victim of self-experimentation instead of repeating her mother's mistakes. The premeditated virgin is keen about tomorrow rather than thrilled with today. And tomorrow's possibilities, translated into frank teacup confidences, simmer down to how to get and keep a husband who is a little above par. Suspicion be hanged!

Mrs. Bartley focusses the new silhouette as sharply as she can:

[Mary Ann's] wide-awake blue eyes were strangely suggestive of both spring flowers and speakeasies. Fern brown hair was wound in stiff rosettes behind each ear and parted sedately in front. Her eyebrows were thin, sophisticated arches but her only make-up was a splash of crimson accentuating the dimpled chin. Her clothes suggested the day of three-flounce petticoats and Delsarte gestures—a delicately peplumed frock of rosebud print—print, mind you, neither silk nor slimpsy satin. It had a high waist and a circular skirt. (Mary Ann wore a circular petticoat too . . .) Her stockings were modest, yet alluring white lisle, the proper background for flat-heeled patent leather pumps. Her one ornament was an old-fashioned locket on a braided gold chain . . . There was a faint odor of violets about Mary Ann. [To a girl of another type] Mary Ann symbolized today's formidable rival . . . these strange half childlike, half witchwise girls who knit stockings as well as they mixed cocktails, who danced minuets—but at roadhouses, who are likely to have several children but very possibly several husbands . . . She might have been a ghost ancestor come to read a lecture on modernity. Not exactly an ancestor with that vampirish shaping of eyebrows, the quaint but come-hither spot of crimson beside the chin dimple, the studied coiffure and clothes. Rather a clever actress playing the rôle of a rustic lass. No, neither an ancestor nor an actress—enter, the new silhouette!

Mary Ann has two lovers, Seth, an aviator, brilliant and interesting, and Brady, old-fashioned, uninteresting, a "good provider." She wants Seth, and he wants her, but he will not marry, and she will not accept him on any other terms. She is willing to marry him for a time, then get a divorce and settle down with Brady; "I'll marry you any time you say—for just a week, or even a day," she announced unexpectedly. . . . "A bargain offer, isn't it?" whispered Seth. "No, I won't cheat . . . I won't accept it." At last, however, he does accept.

"You are marrying me for always," he said, "and then forever". . . The game was hers, she told herself with naïve triumph, won more by charm than Lady Luck, more by sportsmanship than sophistication, more by common sense than yellow hair or youth. Best of all, Seth had wanted her to win it.

With the story completed from Pamela to Mary Ann Plowden, we may see it temptingly rounded to full circle, from the premeditated virgin of 1740 to the premeditated virgin of 1931, and we might well leave the two to take their bow under a descending curtain. The figure of the full circle is tempting from its very symmetry, but it would write us down a round zero as the sum total of human progress, leave us open to a charge of futility after chapter on chapter of discussion. There are times enough when human progress looks to one who does not seek to accelerate it like the going ahead of an ant moving endlessly round and round the rim of a flower-pot. But if we look attentively at Pamela and Mary Ann Plowden as we have them side by side, we perceive that the differences between them are more significant than the resemblances, and that the orbit of progress is not the circle but the epicycloid, the path through the air of the fly on the carriage-wheel. The fly goes in circles, but if the place he has left is any less desirable than that toward which the carriage moves, his motion, however repetitious, may be called progress. Pamela and Mary Ann Plowden are both premeditated virgins, but they wear their premeditation with a difference, and we may gauge the difference as a measure of progress. Pamela's choice was a narrow one; she was held pretty helpless by the society of her time. In her game against fate her scope is restricted, her moves are sharply limited. She wins not only because she moves shrewdly but because luck is with her. Hers is a sort of poker game in which all the skill and intelligence she can bring to bear are, when the game is legitimately played, subordinate to luck. Mary Ann Plowden plays a different game, one in which skill, intelligence, knowledge, wisdom, may have much more scope. Intelligence and human feeling come as the cards are dealt; Pamela had these. Mary Ann Plowden has also resources of accumulated experience unknown to Pamela. Her game is more like chess. Is there any situation, any move of offense or defense, not provided for in the manuals? Is there any element of feminine charm that has not been isolated in the laboratory and made available to her who has money or energy to command it? Is there any twist of masculine psychology that has not been traced and charted? Mary Ann need not be helpless if she has the intelligence to acquire knowledge and apply it to experience.

On the past she may depend for facts, but not for truth; that she must seek for herself. Of that the continuity snapped nearly a generation before she was born. In the clamor of the new chaos the most nearly dominant note is that of self-sufficiency. Pamela leaned on her parents, on authority, on the social order, on God. Clarissa was somewhat more independent; she said that if she satisfied her conscience she could rest without the approval of society. This means merely that to her the voice of society was not the voice of God. Left without the approval of society she looked to God; without hope in this world she dwelt in her hope for the next world. Mary Ann Plowden definitely rejects her mother, who has lost her universe and found nothing in the multiverse to uphold her. Mary Ann does not lean on authority, or social order or on God. She does not seek a verdict from society. She does not pray, or "invoke the protection of Heaven" for herself or for her virginity. For any protection that she must have she invokes her own brain and summons her own powers. She "stands unshook" upon such truth as she can find, and she finds it in herself. No system, so the message runs, will do anything for you. Salvation in the midst of chaos is an individual matter. It is in yourself, and is to be attained only by exercise of the will. This is explicit in the passages quoted above from *The Happy Highways*. It appears explicitly and implicitly in other novels which like *The Three Kingdoms* are advertised with news of the "glorious rebirth" of the heroine. Mary Ann Plowden, then, premeditated virgin though she is, is not a repetition of Pamela, nor yet a ghost of Pamela come to read a lecture on modernity. She is the new silhouette of body and spirit. The child of chaos has accepted the multiverse.

> *. . . And so my sonnet ends,*
> *With, thank ye, thank ye, honest friends,*
> *For all your loves to Pamela.*

IF ANYONE SHOULD ASK

[In order to avoid formal footnotes, wherever possible the author and title of the work quoted have been given in the text. Below are cited only the references to those passages for which this procedure was not convenient.]

CHAPTER I, PAMELA

The account of the popularity of *Pamela* on p. 4 is based on that of Mrs. Anna Laetitia Barbauld given in her introductory essay on Richardson in Volume I of her edition of *British Novelists,* London, 1820, 50 volumes, and on that of Austin Dobson in his *Samuel Richardson* (London: Macmillan & Co., 1902), pp. 30–32. The comments of Pope and of Mr. Lucas on p. 5 are found in the essay of Mrs. Barbauld. Dr. Johnson's opinion is from Boswell, *Life of Johnson* (ed. Murray, London, 1835), I, 235. Those of Dr. Watts and of Mrs. Barbauld on p. 6 are also from her essay. Charlotte Palmer's opinion of *Clarissa* quoted on p. 7 is from her *It Is, and It Is Not a Novel* (2 Vols., London: Hookham and Carpenter, 1792), I, 181. The testimony of Defoe referred to on page 12 is found in his *The Compleat English Gentleman* "Containing Usefull Observations on the General Neglect of the Education of English Gentlemen with the Reasons and Remedies The Apparent Difference between a Well Born and a Well Bred Gentleman Instruccions how Gentlemen may Recover the Deficiency of their Latin, and be Men of Learning tho' without the Pedantry of Schoolds." (Written about 1728–29; ed. Karl D. Bulbring, London: David Nutt, 1890.)

CHAPTER II, WHAT COULD THE POOR GIRL DO?

The statement about gentility on page 23 is from Georgiana Hill, *The Women in English Life from Mediaeval to Modern Times* (London: R. Bentley & Sons, 1896), II, 45. The quotation from Addison on the same page is taken from the 323rd *Spectator.* On p. 25 the pronouncements of the clergyman, a Mr. Sprint of Sherbourn, Dorsetshire, are taken from his sermon printed under the title: "The Bride-woman's Counsellor, Being a Sermon Preach'd at a Wedding, May the Eleventh, 1699," as quoted in Myra Reynolds, *The Learned Lady in England, 1650–1760* (New York: E. P. Dutton & Co., 1919), p. 147. Defoe's observations cited on pp. 25–26 are from his *The Complete English Tradesman* (2 Vols., Oxford: Printed by D. A. Talboys for Thomas Tegg, 1841), I, 216–220, except the note about domestic service which is from his "The Behaviour of Servants in England." The letter quoted on pp. 29–30 is from *Letters and Works of Lady Mary Wortley Montagu* (ed. Wharncliffe, London: Bickers & Son, 1861), II, 225. Cited on p. 30 is Steele's comment from the 199th *Tatler,* and on p. 31 are Defoe's statement from his *Tradesman,* I, 113, and Dr. Johnson's dictum from Boswell, *Life,* IV, 219. The facts concerning women driven to prostitution in the 18th century given on p. 32 were gathered from E. Beresford Chancellor, *The Lives of the Rakes* (6 Vols., London: P. Allan & Co., 1924–25), particularly the third volume, *The Life of Colonel Charteris and The Duke of Wharton;* from Hogarth's "The Harlot's Progress"; and from accounts in the *Gentleman's Magazine.* The quotation about Dorothy Petty and the facts about Joan Dant on p. 35 are taken from Alice Clark, *Working Life of Women in the 17th Century* (London: G. Routledge & Sons, Ltd., 1919), p. 33. Miss Clark quotes from "The Case of Dorothy Petty in Relation to the Union Society, at the White Lyon by Temple Bar, whereof she is Director," 1710 (British Museum). The phrase about the quill and the broomstick on p. 97 is from E. W. Blashfield, *Portraits and Backgrounds* (New York: C. Scribner's Sons, 1917), p. 184. The facts about Elizabeth Elstob mentioned on p. 38 can be found in A. Kippis, *Biographica Britannica,* Vol. V (1178–1793); George H. Rose, *New General Biographical Dictionary,* 1858; Myra Reynolds, *The Learned Lady in England,* pp. 169–185. The title of Mrs. Cellier's plan referred to on p. 39 is "A Scheme for the foundation of a Royal Hospital, and Raising a Revenue of Five or Six Thousand Pounds a Year, by and for the Maintenance of a Corporation of Skilful Midwives, & such Foundlings, or exposed Children, as shall be admitted therein: As it was proposed and Addressed to his Majesty, King James II by Mrs. Elizabeth Cellier in the Month, June, 1687" and can be found in the Harleian Miscellany, V, 142–147. The stories of Katherine Daffy, Joanna Stephens, Mrs. Mapp and their activities, mentioned on pp. 39–40 are recorded respectively in John Ashton, *Social Life in the Reign of Queen Anne* (London: Chatto & Windus, 1883), p. 315; in the *Gentleman's Magazine*, VIII, 21, 275, 548–550, 606; IX, 49, 159, 298–299, 315; X, 185; and in the same magazine, VI, 422, 482, 484, 487, 747; VII, 616.

CHAPTER III, THE IMPORTANCE OF BEING A PRUDE

The quotation at the head of the chapter is a nursery rhyme from Mother Goose. The Mona Milton referred to on p. 48 is a character in James Huneker's *Painted Veils* (New York: Boni & Liveright, 1920). The statement on p. 50 of the 18th century concept of woman as virtue surrounded by wickedness is supported by abundant evidence from the *Tatler* and *Spectator* papers, from the *Lives of the Rakes,* and from the *Gentleman's Magazine;* see also pages 286–289 of Chapter VIII. Mrs. Barbauld's comment cited on p. 51 is also from her Essay on Richardson, mentioned above. The excerpt from Nathan Drake on p. 62 is from his *Essays, Biographical, Critical, Historical* (London: Printed by C. Whittingham for John Sharpe, 1805), I, 48. The quotation of Steele on p. 64 is from the 126th *Tatler.* The excerpt from Thackeray's *Vanity Fair* on p. 66 is the beginning paragraph of Chapter LXIV, called "A Vagabond Chapter." The observations of Greville given on pp. 67–68 are from P. W. Wilson, *The Greville Diary* (New York: Doubleday, Page & Co., 1927), II, 115, 131, 206, 207. The quotation from Malory on p. 84 is from "The Book of Sir Launcelot du Lake" of his *Morte D'Arthur. Lady Chatterley's Lover,* mentioned on p. 84, is of course by D. H. Lawrence and appeared in 1930. The picture of Serena in *The Faerie Queene* referred to on p. 85 is in Book VI, Canto VIII, stanzas 38 to 43, and that of Philoclea in the *Arcadia* is in Part II. The phrase quoted on p. 87 "gentlemen born, aye, and have been any time these four hours" is from Shakespeare's *The Winter's Tale,* Act V, scene ii. The title of Jeremy Collier's work referred to on p. 87 is "A Short View of the Profaneness and Immorality of the English Stage," 1698. Chaucer's remark on p. 89 about Emelye is from his *Knight's Tale,* line 2286. The extract quoted on p. 94 is from Ruth Suckow, *The Bonney Family* (New York: Alfred A. Knopf, Inc., 1928), p. 186, and the quotation at the close of the chapter is from the 126th *Tatler.*

CHAPTER IV, LIQUID SORROW

The Sir Philip mentioned on p. 99 in connection with Fanny Burney's account of Sophy Streatfield is Sir Philip Jennings Clerke, a M.P. for Totnes and, according to Boswell, a highly picturesque personage. A choice addition to the phrases of liquid sorrow found on pp. 100–102 is the following taken from *Vancenza; or, The Dangers of Credulity,* 1792: "the pearly drop of sorrow that hung upon the down-cast eye, spangling its fringed lid with the gem of sensibility." The explanation of the context of the quotation from *Beowulf* on p. 103 is given on p. 105. The phrase "man of sorrows, acquainted with grief" is from the Bible, Isa. 53:3. The observation on p. 107 of Horace Walpole is taken from his Preface to the Second Edition of his *Castle of Otranto,* 1764. Sterne's comment on p. 114 about his father is found in a short sketch of his own life written by the author shortly before his death, and is quoted in Percy Fitzgerald, *The Life of Laurence Sterne* (London: Chatto & Windus, 1906), p. 12. Another example of humanitarian sensibility besides the one cited on p. 119 is one very reminiscent of Sterne from the anonymous *Wanley Penson: or, the Melancholy Man,* 1791, in which the hero exclaims: "No! not in his most wanton moments would Penson wittingly wound a worm." The lines of Wordsworth quoted on p. 123 are from his lyric, "Three years she grew in sun and shower." George Eliot's epigrammatic definition cited on p. 126 is from her *Felix Holt,* Chapter XXVII. The date of Keats' letter to Benjamin Bailey which is quoted from on p. 136 is November 22, 1817.

CHAPTER V, CUT MY LACE, CHARMIAN

The quotation on p. 142 from Malory is found in "The Book of Elaine" of his *Morte D'Arthur.* The epigram of Sarah Fielding quoted on p. 153 is from her *David Simple,* I, p. 57. The quotation from Chaucer's Legend of Lucretia on p. 153 is, of course, taken from his *The Legend of Good Women.* The story of Le Bone Florence of Rome mentioned on p. 153 may be found in Joseph Ritson, *Ancient English Metrical Romances* (Edinburgh: E. & G. Goldsmid, 1885) III, 46 ff. So famous is Sophia Western (pp. 154–156) that it seems hardly necessary to specify that she is the heroine of Fielding's *The*

History of Tom Jones, a Foundling, 1749. The date of the second edition of Holcroft's translation of *Caroline of Lichtfield* discussed on p. 160 is 1786. We refer on p. 163 to the plates of Thomas Rowlandson (1756–1827), famous artist and caricaturist of the period. The quaint use of punctuation marks by Lord Timothy Dexter referred to on p. 166 is observable in his *A Pickle for the Knowing Ones; or Plain Truths in a Homespun Dress,* 1838, to the second edition of which he added the following note: "fouder Mister printer the Nowing ones complane of my book the fust edition had no stops I put in A Nuf here and thay may peper and salt it as they plese," and followed the note with row after row of varied and assorted marks of punctuation for a solid half-page. The story of this picturesque personage of Newburyport, Massachusetts, who styled himself "First in the East, first in the West, and the Greatest Philosopher in the Western World" is told by J. P. Marquand in his *Lord Timothy Dexter* (New York: Minton, Balch & Company, 1925). The line "cover her face; mine eyes dazzle; she died young" is from Webster's *The Duchess of Malfi,* Act IV, scene ii, l. 274, and also quoted on p. 168 is the phrase "eloquent, just and mighty" which is from the famous description of death by Sir Walter Raleigh in the section "Of the Falls of Empires" in his *Historie of the World.*

CHAPTER VI, THE LASS WITH THE DELICATE AIR

The book of Prof. Dr. C. H. Stratz referred to on p. 175 is *Die Schönheit des weiblichen Körpers* (Stuttgart: Ferdinand Enke, 1920) and the photograph mentioned is opposite p. 306. Swift's views, cited on p. 183, on the weaknesses of the aristocracy are found in his *Gulliver's Travels,* Part IV, "A Voyage to the Country of the Houyhnhnms," Chapter VI. Pope's famous line, quoted on p. 182, is from his *Moral Essays,* Epistle ii, l. 43. The quotation from Steele on p. 183 is from the 24th *Tatler.* On p. 188 the accounts of depilation are all taken from Alfred Franklin, *La Vie Privée d'Autrefois* (23 vols., Paris: E. Plon, Nourrit et Cie, 1887–1901), I, App., 9–11. The German commentator referred to on p. 191 is Curt Moreck and his remark is in his *Das weibliche Schönheits-Ideal im Wandel der Zeiten,* 1925, p. 142. Gregory the Great's comment on the Angles, quoted on p. 194, is recorded in Bede's *Ecclesiastical History of the*

English People. Maggie Tulliver, mentioned on p. 195, is the heroine of George Eliot's *Mill on the Floss,* 1860. The stanza of Winthrop Mackworth Praed, quoted on p. 212, is from his poem, "The Talented Man."

CHAPTER VII, AUNT TABITHA

The extract on p. 220 from *The Ladies' Calling* is given as quoted in Myra Reynolds, *The Learned Lady in England,* pp. 316–317. The quotations on p. 221 are from Edward Young's *The Merchant; An Ode on British Trade and Navigation.* The explanation of the old negro woman quoted on the same page is from Agnes Repplier's article "The American Spinster" in the *Century Magazine,* July, 1913. The quotations from Malory on p. 222 are found in his *Morte D'Arthur,* Book IV, Chapter XVIII. On p. 225 the extract from Mary Astell's plan is given as quoted in Florence Smith, *Mary Astell* (New York: Columbia University Press, 1916), p. 52. Steele's beautiful compliment to Lady Elizabeth Hastings, on p. 226, is found in the 49th *Tatler* and his discussion of Mary Astell's plan in the 32nd and 63rd. Defoe's opinions quoted on p. 228 are from William Lee, *Life and Works of Defoe* (London: J. C. Hutten, 1896), III, 127–130, 325. George Wheeler's plan referred to on p. 239 is entitled "A Plan of a Protestant Monastery" and was printed in 1698. It is very similar to the plan of Mary Astell discussed on p. 225. Scott's compliment to Jane Austen, quoted on p. 243, is recorded in his diary under the date of March 14, 1826 (J. G. Lockhart's *Life of Scott,* VIII, 42). The quotation on p. 250 from William A. Alcott is from his *The Young Woman's Guide to Excellence,* and the discussion of women's work is from an article, "The Employments of Women," *Chambers's Edinburgh Journal,* XX (Aug. 13, 1853), 156. The extracts on p. 251 are from an article "Woman's Work," *Chambers's Journal of Popular Literature, Science and Arts,* XXV (April 26, 1856), 257, and from "The Employments of Women" in *The North British Review,* XXVI (February, 1857), 291 ff. The article referred to on p. 253 is in the *Dublin University Magazine,* LVI (December, 1860), 702–717, and the one quoted on p. 253 is Frances Power Cobbe's "What Shall We Do With Our Old Maids," *Fraser's Magazine,* LXVI (November, 1862), 594; the one on p. 254 is entitled "On Old Maids," *Blackwood's*

Edinburgh Magazine, CXII (July, 1872), 94. William Hosea Ballou's *The Bachelor Girl*, referred to on p. 256, appeared in 1890, and publishers' catalogues ever since have reflected the popularity of the phrase. Some of the titles listed by them are: *The Bachelor Girl in London, Bachelor Maid & Her Brother, Bachelor Girl in Burma, Bachelor Betty, The Bachelor Girls and Their Adventures in Search of Independence, Reveries of a Bachelor Girl.*

CHAPTER VIII, SOME DO

An illuminating example of the application of the Goldsmith law discussed on p. 268 is provided by Hannah More in her *Strictures on the Modern System of Female Education,* 1799, in which she tells women to "Pity the wretched woman you dare not countenance; and bless Him who has 'made you to differ.' If unhappily she be your relation or friend, anxiously watch for the period when she shall be deserted by her betrayer; and see if, by your Christian offices, she can be snatched from a perpetuity of vice. But if, through the Divine blessing on your patient endeavours, she should ever be awakened to remorse, be not anxious to restore the forlorn penitent to that society against whose laws she has so grievously offended; . . . To restore a criminal to public society, is perhaps to tempt her to repeat her crime, or to deaden her repentance for having committed it." The title of Robert Henryson's poem mentioned on p. 270 is *Testament of Cresseid* in which Criseyde becomes a leper and a beggar. Jane Austen's treatment of Mr. Villar's dictum referred to on p. 284 is quoted on p. 316. The story of the young girl described on p. 286 is from the *Gentleman's Magazine* for May, 1740. The phrase quoted on p. 295, "the villain gets his flogging at the gangway," is from Kipling's famous poem lamenting the passing of the three-volume novel, "The Three-Decker."

CHAPTER IX, SOME DON'T

The quotation on p. 332, "We shipped as able bastards till the wicked nurse confessed," is also from "The Three-Decker." The facts concerning women and the agrarian revolution given on p. 337 are from Ivy Pinchbeck, *Women Workers and Industrial Revolution, 1750–*

1850 (London: G. Routledge & Sons, Ltd., 1930). The quotation on p. 328 is from Frederick's song to the daughters of "the very model of a modern major general" in Act I of Gilbert and Sullivan's *Pirates of Penzance*. Charlotte Brontë's characters listed on p. 341 are the heroines of *Jane Eyre, Villette,* and *The Professor,* respectively. Unfortunately, space does not permit us to give many titles, or even in full the title pages of the dime novels listed on p. 347, but two of the choicest ones are Laura Jean Libbey's *Willful Gaynell, or The Little Beauty of the Passaic Cotton Mills,* a romantic story of the life and love of a lovely working girl (1890), and *Pretty Madcap Dorothy, or, How She Won a Lover,* a romance of the jolliest girl in the book-bindery, and a magnificent love story of the life of a beautiful, willful New York working girl. The authors of all the novels listed on p. 347, except *Nellie the Beautiful Cloak Model,* 1906, are given somewhere in the chapter. *Nellie* is a novelized version by Grace Miller White of Owen Davis' melodrama and motion picture of the same title. *For Gold or Soul* mentioned on p. 348 was written by Lurana Sheldon in 1900, and *Love at the Loom,* 1895, referred to on p. 357 is by Geraldine Fleming. The quotation on p. 359 is from *What Can She Do?,* 1873, by E. P. Roe. On p. 366 the quotation from the anonymous article "Getting Along with Women" is from *Harper's Magazine,* CLXXI, 614–623 (October, 1935), and the other extract is from the article "Women in Business" in *Fortune,* Vol. XII, No. 2 (August, 1935), p. 50.

CHAPTER X, NEW GIRLS FOR OLD

The comment of Matthew Arnold quoted on p. 370 is from the close of his essay on Shelley in his *Essays on Criticism, Second Series* (London: Macmillan & Co., 1888), p. 252. Wordsworth's lines on p. 371 are from his sonnet of 1801, "I grieved for Buonaparté." Of the women characters of Trollope named on p. 378, Mary Thorne is the heroine of *Dr. Thorne,* 1858; Lady Glencora Palliser appears as a main figure in *Can You Forgive Her?,* 1864, *Phineas Finn,* 1869, *Phineas Redux,* 1874, and *The Prime Minister,* 1876; Lily Dale is the heroine of *The Small House at Allington,* 1864; Mary Wortle of *Dr. Wortle's School,* 1881; Rachel Ray of *Rachel Ray,* 1863; and Florence Burton of *The Claverings,* 1867. The phrase "slowly broadens down from precedent to precedent" quoted on p. 383 is from Tennyson's poem beginning, "You ask me why, tho' ill at ease," and the three lines of poetry, slightly paraphrased, are quoted from his *Idylls of the King,* "Guinevere," ll. 472–475. William A. Alcott is responsible for the roundabout phrase, quoted on p. 384: "portion of the general system which gives to woman her peculiar prerogative, as well as her distinctive character." The magazine referred to on p. 390 is *Godey's Lady's Book,* LXVIII (January, 1864), 93, and the three colleges noted are The Female Medical College of Philadelphia, The New England Female Medical College for Women, and the New York Medical College for Women. For a picture of the general fashion of Theresa's dress, discussed on p. 391 and described on p. 379, see the illustration opposite p. 164. The quotations from *The Home Journal* on pp. 395–396 are from N. Parker Willis' *The Rag-Bag,* 1855. Charlotte Bremer's observation on p. 396 is from her *Life, Letters and Works of Frederika Bremer* (New York: R. Worthington, 1880), p. 5. The description of the English bathing costume on p. 398 is found in *Demorest's Monthly Magazine,* 1872, p. 567. The quotations about fashions on p. 399 and p. 401 are from *Godey's Lady's Book* for February, 1864, January, 1864, and May, 1864, respectively. The phrase "stern daughter of the voice of God" on p. 404 is from Wordsworth's poem, "Ode to Duty." The line "Maidens of England, take caution by she," quoted on p. 409, is from the "Moral" of Thackeray's ballad, "The Willow-Tree," and is followed by

> Let love and suicide
> Never tempt you aside,
> And always remember to take the door-key.

Of Bertha M. Clay's "mixed and assorted Greek goddesses" discussed on pp. 416–417, Pauline Darrell is heroine of *Love Works Wonders,* 1877; Ethel Gordon of *Repented at Leisure;* Violet Beaton of *Thorns and Orange Blossoms;* and Lady Lovel of *A Dark Marriage Morn.* The article of Mrs. E. M. King referred to on pp. 424–425 was reprinted in *Knowledge,* Vol. II, No. 36, p. 95 (July 7, 1882). The description of a "Dress for the Mountains" quoted on p. 425 and the article "How to Dress for Lawn Tennis" on p. 425 and p. 427 are taken from *Demorest's Monthly Magazine,* 1883, p. 658. The controversy about tight lacing noted on p. 427 is recorded in *Knowledge,* II, No. 36, p. 59 (July, 1882) and pp. 267, 299 (September, 1882). The article on "Hygienic Dresses" mentioned on p. 428 is in *Demorest's Monthly Magazine,* 1883, p. 661. The quotation on p. 435 is from Lytton Strachey, *Queen Victoria* (New York: Harcourt, Brace and Company, 1931), p. 409.

CHAPTER XI, VICTORIA, WHERE IS THY VICTORY?

The line from Kipling at the head of the chapter is from "The Widow at Windsor," *Barrack-Room Ballads* (New York: The Macmillan Company, 1893), p. 179. Those from Tennyson are from "To the Queen," dated 1851 in his *Works* (Macmillan, 1893). The quotation from Strachey is also from his *Queen Victoria,* pp. 399 ff. The three quotations on pp. 439–440 are from Henry Brooks Adams, *The Education of Henry Adams* (Boston: Houghton Mifflin Company, 1918), pp. 457–459. The lines quoted on p. 441 are so familiar that it seems hardly necessary to specify that they are the closing lines of Matthew Arnold's "Dover Beach." The sentence about pleasure on the same page we quote from Samuel Butler's *The Way of All Flesh* (2nd ed., London: A. C. Fifield, 1908), p. 85. The barber on the Mississippi steamboat is a figure of Mark Twain's from *Life on the Mississippi,* Chapter XX. The phrases from *In Memoriam* cited on p. 442 are from strophe LVI. The magazine article extensively quoted on pp. 443–445 appeared anonymously under the title, "Help!— Parents or Pals—How Are Mothers to Safeguard Their Schoolgirl Daughters?", in *Liberty,* February 27, 1932. The quotation on p. 446 is the "Moral" of Stevenson's fable, "Something in It" (*Fables,* Scribners, 1902, p. 56). It ends,

> Sanctions and tales dislimn like mist
> About the amazed evangelist.
> He stands unshook from age to youth
> Upon one pin-point of the truth.

The lines on p. 447 from Robinson Jeffers are from his *Give Your Heart to the Hawks* (New York: Random House, Inc., 1933). The quotations on p. 447 and on pp. 448–449 and on p. 456 about Dorothy and Louise are from Irving Stone, *Pageant of Youth* (New York: Alfred H. King, 1933). The facts concerning modern woman's attitude toward virginity given on p. 448 are taken from *Sex Life of the Unmarried Adult,* edited by Ira S. Wile (New York: The Vanguard Press, 1934), pp. 33, 34, 238. The extract about Anne and Charles on p. 449 is from Philip Wylie, *Heavy Laden* (New York: Alfred A. Knopf, 1928), and the quotation from Viña Delmar is from her *Bad Girl* (New York: Harcourt, Brace and Company, 1928). The quotation from Dr. Harding on p. 454 is from her *The Way of All Women* (New York: Longmans, Green and Co., 1935). Mrs. Trollope's description of American clothes referred to on p. 467 is found in her *The Domestic Manners of the Americans.* The lines of Browning quoted on p. 473 are from his poem "Love Among the Ruins." Kingsley's oft-quoted line given on p. 475 is, of course, the first of his

> Be good, sweet maid, and let who will be clever.
> Do noble deeds, not dream them all day long,
> And thus make life, death, and the vast forever
> One grand sweet song.

The article of Havelock Ellis mentioned on p. 475 appeared in *The Mentor,* January, 1930, and the observations of Dr. Harding on p. 476 are again from her *The Way of All Women.* The quotation closing the book is, as is the quotation at the beginning, from Pamela's *Verses On My Going Away* in Letter XXXI, Vol. I of Richardson's *Pamela.*

INDEX

Adam Brown, 396

Adams, Henry, on snapping of the continuity of human thought, 439–440, 441, 455

Adams, James Truslow, 471

Addison, Joseph, satirizes idleness of women, 23; affectations of defects, 182

Adeline Mowbray, 388

Advantages of Education, The, 57, 311; quoted: 57–58, 312–313

Adventures of a Younger Son, The, 409

Adventures of Count de Vinevil, The, 107, 108, 277; quoted: 90–91, 152, 178, 278–279

Adventures of Emmera, The, 125, 183, 296; quoted: 92, 93, 117–119, 120, 184, 295

Aeneid, 157

Aguilar, Grace, 50

Alcott, Louisa May, 397, 402

Alcott, William A., 250, 381, 394

Allen, Grant, 355, 361, 363, 365, 391, 424, 430

Allerton, Mark, 339

Ambitious Woman, An, 356, 418

Amelia, 115, 116, 291, 408

Anciennes Poésies Françoises, 188

Ann Vickers, 339, 340

Anna St. Ives, 126

Anne, Queen of England, 226

Antony and Cleopatra, 140; quoted: 138–139, 168, 170

Apollonius and Sylla, 330, 331

Arabian Nights, The, 142, 189

Arcadia, 85, 107, 147, 156, 330; quoted: 148–149

Archie Lovell, 413

Aristocracy, sensibility and fainting are traits of, in romance, 12, 13, 106–108, 143, 147; has no prudery, 15; has leisure, 23; relation to money, 45, 114; gaiety of, 62; Restoration noblemen not genuinely of, 86–87; Collier's attack on freedom of, 87; seeks to avoid resemblance to lower classes, 104; familiarity with classical literature a mark of, 106; possesses the delicate air, 182; "doesn't care a tinker's damn," 472

Aristophanes, echoed by Steele, 57, 64

Arne, Thomas, 169

Arnold, Matthew, opinion of Shelley, 370, 371; reaction to his age, 440–441

Art, prevalence in 18th century for adolescent models, 6, 7, 73; French *gravures galantes,* 74; contrast between 16th- and 18th-century erotic, 74; effect of Christianity on, 102; debased by sentimentality, 112; silhouette of 18th century in French painting, 158, 175, 176; history of realistic depiction of nudity in, 185–191, 446–447; depiction of sloping shoulders in, 192; relation to life of, 193; depiction of angels as blondes in Italian, 194; all-or-nothing *versus* Victorian-compromise school in, 371; characteristics of Victorian, 382; depiction of 19th-century silhouette in, 400, 419; portraits of children in, 401; Greek fashion in, 419–420; Egyptian fashion in, 420

Astell, Mary, plan for women's education, 225, 229, 230, 234, 251, 254, 388

Athletics, beginnings of physical culture, 394; heroines who indulge in, 394, 410, 417; swimming of women, 398–399, 424; skating, 399, 423;

Date Due